Yizkor (Memorial) Book of Lyubcha and Delyatichi

Memorial to Two Jewish Communities

Edited by Ann Belinsky

Translation of *Lubtch ve-Delatitch; Sefer Zikaron*

Original Book Edited by:

K. Hilel, Haifa, Israel

Original Book Published in Israel, 1971 by the

Organization of the Former Residents of Lubtch-Delatitch in Israel

Published by JewishGen

An Affiliate of the Museum of Jewish Heritage - A Living Memorial to the Holocaust
New York

Yizkor (Memorial) Book of Lyubcha and Delyatichi
Translation of *Lubtch ve-Delatitch; Sefer Zikaron*

Copyright © 2014 by JewishGen, Inc.
All rights reserved.
First Printing: February 2014, Adar Rishon 5774
Second Printing: September 2019, Elul 5779

Translation Project Coordinator and Editor: Ann Belinsky
Layout: Howard Morris
Cover Design: Gerald Simon
Publicity: Sandra Hirschhorn
Indexing: Marjorie Geiser

This book may not be reproduced, in whole or in part, including illustrations in any form (beyond that copying permitted by Sections 107 and 108 of the U.S. Copyright Law and except by reviewers for public press), without written permission from the publisher.

Published by JewishGen, Inc.
An Affiliate of the Museum of Jewish Heritage
A Living Memorial to the Holocaust
36 Battery Place, New York, NY 10280

"JewishGen, Inc. is not responsible for inaccuracies or omissions in the original work and makes no representations regarding the accuracy of this translation. Digital images of the original book's contents can be seen online at the New York Public Library Web site."

The mission of the JewishGen organization is to produce a translation of the original work and we cannot verify the accuracy of statements or alter facts cited.

Printed in the United States of America by Lightning Source, Inc.

Library of Congress Control Number (LCCN): 2013922520
ISBN: 978-1-939561-14-5 (hard cover: 458 pages, alk. paper)

Front Cover Photograph: Image from the original Yizkor book - Children at the Lubtch Tarbut School
Back Cover Photographs: THEN AND NOW - The Castle of Lubtch, The Nieman River, Memorial Stone for the destroyed communities, with former residents

JewishGen and the Yizkor Books in Print Project

This book has been published by the **Yizkor Books in Print Project,** as part of the **Yizkor Book Project** of **JewishGen, Inc.**

JewishGen, Inc. is a non-profit organization founded in 1987 as a resource for Jewish genealogy. Its website [www.jewishgen.org] serves as an international clearinghouse and resource center to assist individuals who are researching the history of their Jewish families and the places where they lived. JewishGen provides databases, facilitates discussion groups, and coordinates projects relating to Jewish genealogy and the history of the Jewish people. In 2003, JewishGen became an affiliate of the **Museum of Jewish Heritage - A Living Memorial to the Holocaust** in New York.

The **JewishGen Yizkor Book Project** was organized to make more widely known the existence of Yizkor (Memorial) Books written by survivors and former residents of various Jewish communities throughout the world. Later, volunteers connected to the different destroyed communities began cooperating to have these books translated from the original language—usually Hebrew or Yiddish—into English, thus enabling a wider audience to have access to the valuable information contained within them. As each chapter of these books was translated, it was posted on the JewishGen website and made available to the general public.

The **Yizkor Books in Print Project** began in 2011 as an initiative to print and publish Yizkor Books that had been fully translated, so that hard copies would be available for purchase by the descendants of these communities and also by scholars, universities, synagogues, libraries, and museums.

These Yizkor books have been produced almost entirely through the volunteer effort of researchers from around the world, assisted by donations from private individuals. The books are printed and sold at near cost, so as to make them as affordable as possible. Our goal is to make this important genre of Jewish literature and history available in English in book form, so that people can have the personal histories of their ancestral towns on their bookshelves for themselves and for their children and grandchildren.

A list of all published translated Yizkor Books can be found at:
http://www.jewishgen.org/Yizkor/ybip.html

Lance Ackerfeld, Yizkor Book Project Manager

Joel Alpert, Yizkor Book in Print Project Coordinator

This book is presented by the
Yizkor Books in Print Project
Project Coordinator: Joel Alpert

Part of the
Yizkor Books Project of JewishGen, Inc.
Project Manager: Lance Ackerfeld

These books have been produced solely through volunteer effort of individuals from around the world. The books are printed and sold at near cost, so as to make them as affordable as possible.

Our goal is to make this history and important genre of Jewish literature available in English in book form so that people can have the near-personal histories of their ancestral towns on their bookshelves for themselves and for their children and grandchildren.

Any donations to the Yizkor Books Project are appreciated.

Please send donations to:
Yizkor Book Project
JewishGen
36 Battery Place
New York, NY 10280

JewishGen, Inc. is an affiliate of the
Museum of Jewish Heritage
A Living Memorial to the Holocaust

Lyubcha and Delyatichi Yizkor Book

Title Page of the Original Yizkor Book

לובץ' ודלטיץ'
ספר זכרון

העורך: ק. הלל

הוצאת אדגון יוצאי לובץ' ודלטיץ' בישראל
תשל"א – 1971

Translation of the title page of the Original Book

LUBTCH-DELATITCH

IN MEMORY OF THE JEWISH COMMUNITY

Edited by

K. HILEL

Printed in Israel 1971

(Typeset: "Sefroni" - Phone 524767, Haifa
HaMadpis Hechadash Printers - Haifa)

Dedication

The translation of this memorial book is dedicated to the Jewish communities of Lubtch and Delatitch and the surrounding areas, which were annihilated during World War II.

"Only guard yourself and guard your soul carefully, lest you forget the things your eyes saw and lest these things depart your heart all the days of your life. And you shall make them known to your children and to your children's children" (Deuteronomy 4:9)

Comments by the Translation Project Coordinator Ann Belinsky

It is my pleasure to present below the completely translated Lubtch-Delatitch Yizkor Book.

I was very moved to translate the following text by Yaakov Zacharavitch (Pages 355-356) "Words at the Memorial Service for the Martyrs of Lubtch and Delatitch":

> "From year to year there remain fewer and fewer of the remnants of our town, and who knows if our children will keep alive the memory of the towns and their families that they never knew, but have only heard about.
>
> There is a prayer in our hearts that this book - the headstone that will be raised in memory of the two communities - will be used as a source for study and learning, about the stories of the Jews of the town, and that our children and grandchildren will remember, through reading it, all our dear ones, who were burned on the stake and died martyrs deaths."

I hope that this book will be read by as many descendants as possible of the townspeople from Lubtch and Delatitch and that by the translation appearing below, we have indeed kept alive the memory of our towns and families.

Map of Belarus (2014) showing location of Lyubcha and Delyatichi

Lyubcha, Belarus is at 53°45' Latitude / 26°04' East Longitude

Delyatichi, Belarus is at 53°47' Latitude / 25°59' East Longitude

Delyatichi and Lyubcha are located 65 miles to the west of Minsk

Delyatichi is 4 miles to the North and West of Lyubcha

Geopolitical Associations During Recent Times

Delatitch	Town	District	Province	Country
Before WWI (c. 1900):	Delyatyche	Novogrudok	Minsk	Russian Empire
Between the wars (c. 1930):	Delatycze	Nowogródek	Nowogródek	Poland
After WWII (c. 1950):	Delyatichi			Soviet Union
Today (c. 2000):	Dzialacičy			

Lubtch	Town	District	Province	Country
Before WWI (c. 1900):	Lyubcha	Novogrudok	Minsk	Russian Empire
Between the wars (c. 1930):	Lubcz	Nowogródek	Nowogródek	Poland
After WWII (c. 1950):	Lyubcha			Soviet Union
Today (c. 2000):	Lyubcha			Belarus

Names of the towns:

Throughout the book, names the two towns have been transliterated as **Lubtch** and **Delatitch, as they appear on the original title page in English** "Lubtch-Delatitch. In memory of the Jewish community".

The towns are known in other languages as:

Lyubcha [Russian], Lubcza [Polish], Lubtsh [Yiddish], Lubča [Belorussian], Lubcz, Lubec, Lubecz, Lubch, Lubtse, Lyubch, Lubtch, Lubtz, Ljubcha

Delyatichi [Russian], Delatycze [Polish], Delatitch [Yiddish], Dzialacičy [Belorussian], Delyatyche, Dzjaljacicy

Acknowledgements for the Publication of the English translation

This work was started by the original coordinator, **Ofer Cohen**, who had a special interest in Delatitch, and who transliterated the Lists of Martyrs of Lubtch and Delatitch appearing at the end of the book. He also prepared information about Delatitch for the Belarus newsletter, and it appears in the Appendix (Pages 404 and following).

Allen Katz originally brought attention to my personal family that many of our ancestors lived in Lubtch and indeed started a success story of tracing a whole group of new relatives. He was instrumental in introducing us to the Yizkor book and also translated the chapter on Page 250.

Following this, my sister **Shirley Horwitz** translated two articles by and about our relatives (Pages 199, 267), and I translated a third one (Page 130).

The project of translating the whole book started when I heard a lecture by **Harvey Spitzer** about The Origins of Yiddish. I turned to him to ask if he would translate the Yiddish chapters of the book and he willingly and enthusiastically took up the challenge, and translated them all. In addition, I gratefully acknowledge the proficient translations by Harvey of Hebrew chapters concerning Rabbis and religious institutions. At the same time I started to translate all the other Hebrew chapters. All chapters in Hebrew were sent to Harvey for final editing and polishing, and his professional approach has enhanced the quality of the final translations in both languages. Without his devoted and constant help, this Yizkor Book translation could not have been completed.

I especially thank **Lance Ackerfield**, Yizkor Book Project Manager, and his dedicated team for putting the original translation online in the JewishGen Yizkor Books website.

I especially thank **Joel Alpert**, Yizkor Book in Print Project Coordinator, for his guidance and patience with me during preparation of the book text for publication.

Ann Belinsky, Translation Project Coordinator

A Short History of Lubtch and Delatitch

This memorial book is dedicated to the Jews who lived in the towns of Lubtch and Delatitch - two small towns on the Neiman River in present-day Belarus. Both towns were rebuilt on their ruins in the first years after World War I. Delatitch, the smaller town, was in fact, joined to the Lubtch community, and used their religious services. Most of the chapters relate to the town of Lubtch but the life of the inhabitants would have been very similar.

Lubtch - a town in the district of Minsk, on the Neiman River, is located 6 miles from Novogrudek. The first reference to Jewish settlement is from the 17th century. By 1897 there were 2463 Jews living in the town (73% of the population). Delatitch was about 3 miles away. They were remote towns, in an area of poverty-stricken villages.

In the 19th and early 20th century the Jewish population was involved in wholesale commerce in trade such as flax; others were craftsmen: tailors, shoemakers, carpenters, painters and rope makers. Some owned shops in the towns, while others peddled their wares in the surrounding villages. The Neiman River flowing by the towns served for transportation of rafts loaded with logs from the forests. The Jews were the main suppliers of food and clothing to the rafters and lumberjacks. There was meager farming and no industry.

During the First World War, inhabitants of the towns were expelled and fled to other places including South Africa and the USA.

After the First World War, when the Jews returned to the Lubtch, a network of *chederim* developed, where children were taught the Talmud, Hebrew language and a few secular studies. Under Polish rule in the 1920's, the *chederim* were abolished and the *Tarbut* school was established. The language of teaching was Hebrew and the youth received a general basic education. Many well-known Rabbis were born in Lubtch and led the congregations faithfully, or moved to the larger towns. The synagogue area was always bustling with worshippers on Shabbat and Holy Days. In Lubtch there were a number of institutions for mutual help, among them *Linat Hatzedek* (Overnight Charity), and the *Chevra Kadisha* (Burial Society).The cultural life in the town developed, with a library, a drama circle, and an orchestra. The fire brigade was organized.

Four Zionist organizations were active in the town: *HeChalutz*; *Poalei Tzion*; *HaShomer Hatza'ir* and *Beitar* and the young people were educated towards the fulfillment of their dream to go on *aliya* to *Eretz-Israel*. This became the solution for many of the youth who were unemployed and whose families were impoverished following the economic crisis affecting Poland in 1932-1935.

With the outbreak of World War II on September 1, 1939, and the invasion of the Red Army, many youth were drawn to the idyllic life painted by the Soviet leaders.

On April 1, 1940, Lubtch became the administrative and political center of the region. Offices and bureaus sprung up and hundreds of people found employment. In September 1940, of the 2,115 people living in Lubtch, approximately 1,500 were Jews. In general, the Jews of Lubtch breathed more freely, economically speaking, and anti-Semitism lessened. A new Jewish generation was growing up which believed that the new regime opened wider horizons.

However, on June 22, 1941 the Germans attacked the USSR. The Soviet people and their families began fleeing towards Minsk. The Jews were terrified of the approaching enemy. The Germans captured 51 men who were taken out of the town and shot. This was followed by a decree for all Jews to move into the Lubtch ghetto. The entire Jewish community was squeezed into 27-30 houses. Every couple of days the Germans would come with the police and take out 40-50 people to "work", and they would disappear. On August 7, 1942 (24th *Av* 5702), the Germans carried out a mass slaughter. Five hundred people from the Lubtch ghetto were taken to Vorobievitch and herded into a nearby barn which was then set on fire. Those who managed to save themselves from the flames were shot while escaping. Thousands of Jews were killed that day including men, women and children from Lubtch, Delatitch, Neyshtot (Niegnievitch), Karelitch (Korelitz), Ivenietz, Zhetel, Derevna, Zholodok, Novoyelnia and Novogrudek.

Only a few managed to escape and join the partisans in the nearby forests. At the end of 1943, the German forces attempted to completely liquidate the partisan movement in western White Russia, without much success. The Russians retaliated and the partisans cut off the roads taken by the retreating Germans, sowing death and destruction among them. At the beginning of January 1944, the Red Army liberated the area.

The partisans and those who had succeeded in hiding were once again "free" people. Some returned for a short time to their hometowns, but did not wish to remain. Destruction was widespread. The Jewish communities were obliterated, and not a trace remained of the once flourishing and spiritually rich Jewish life. The survivors set out on the difficult paths of emigration to the USA, Canada and other countries, including clandestine immigration to Palestine.

This book details the history of Lubtch and Delatitch, with personal accounts of the lives of the people who dwelt there, until the catastrophe which overwhelmed and annihilated almost all. Fate determined that some individuals should survive to relate the terrible story of pain and torment, to engrave the "Remember!" in the life of our people - to remember and never forget.

Additional Notes by the Coordinator

The Translations:

In these translations, we attempted to keep consistency in spelling of names. Ending of words were either transliterated as "itz" or "itch", depending of the Hebrew or Yiddish spelling. However, we acknowledge that the two endings are interchangeable, and should be treated as such for genealogical research. Indeed the family of Allen Katz in Israel spells and pronounces their name "Yankelevitch" whereas the same family in South Africa spells their name "Jankelowitz". In honour and respect to the South Africans, who both sponsored the publication of the Yizkor book and also contributed to it, we have used both transliterations according to the geographical addresses of the contributors.

In this context I add some comments about the authors:

The editor writes his name of the editor on the title page is given as K Hilel. However, there are also chapters signed as H.K. or Hilel Kroshnitz. All relate to the same person. The Preface on page 3 does not have any given author, but Ofer Cohen gave them as K. Hilel, probably from personal knowledge

Several chapters are signed Ch.Y. These relate to the author Chaim Yankelevitch. Several chapters are signed G.Y. These relate to the author Gershon Jankelowitz.

Translation of Yiddish/Hebrew words:

Within the texts, the translators have also included words which are acceptable in their original language, such as *Yeshiva, Bet Midrash, Kolel, Melamed* etc. The English definitions/translations of these and other words are usually given in square brackets [ ] in the texts.

"Gabbay" and "Shamash"

The roles of "*gabbay*" and "*shamash*" can be interchangeable and have several meanings.

In Judaism, the term "*beadle*" ("*shamash*" in Hebrew, or "*sexton*") is sometimes used for the *gabbai*, the caretaker or "man of all work," in a synagogue (Wikipedia).

Harvey Spitzer writes with respect to the *gabbay*:

'The *gabbay* has several functions. One is as treasurer of the synagogue and collector of dues (Alcalay and Oxford dictionaries) and another is to be in charge of the maintenance of the shul if there is no official *shamash*. They therefore serve as sextons. The Encyclopedia Judaica adds that a *gabbai* "performs the services of a beadle (sexton) in many congregations where work is plentiful". They also (and very importantly) distribute the honors of *aliyot* and reading the *Haftara*, etc. In England, a *gabbay* is often called a "warden".'

Lists of Residents of Lubtch and Delatitch in Israel:

<u>Pages 358-360</u>: The editor and author K. Hilel (Hilel Kroshnitz) does not appear here, although it seems fairly certain that he was a resident of Lubtch (see e.g. page 15).

<u>Pages 358-360 and 362:</u> These lists of people living and who have died in Israel, are, naturally, updated only to the date of publication of the Yizkor book (1971).

<u>Pages 338-351</u>: Benyamin Kivovitch (photo p. 351], the nephew of Yisrael Slonimsky, made *aliyah* from the USSR in December 1973, together with his wife, son and daughter.

Notes by Ofer Cohen for the List of Martyrs of Lubtch and Delatitch (Pages 375-377):

1. Note that in the table of contents of the Yizkor book of Lubtch and Delatitch: most of the articles – over 60%– are in Hebrew. All the rest are in Yiddish. There are no articles in English.
2. Regarding the list of Holocaust victims from these two towns:
2.1 The list mentions anonymously and collectively "the Jews from the tiny village Nagnivich and other villages".
2.2 Many names were unknown to the editors of the list. Hence, they only mentioned the victim as "husband", "wife", "child," and so on. I have followed their convention. The blank entries mean that the original did not have any information-- for instance, because the victim was a widow at the time of the pogrom.
2.3 Some of the names will appear in different transliterated forms. This is because the names in the book may appear in Yiddish or Hebrew spelling, some as nicknames, and some may even have spelling mistakes. In all the cases we have made as accurate a transliteration as possible.
2.4 In few places the names were not separated, so the family relationships could not be understood. In these cases I made the following assumptions:
2.4.1 If the first name is male – this is the husband. If the 2nd name is also of a male – I assumed there was no wife.
2.4.2 If the first name is feminine – this is the female head of household, who was a widow.
2.4.3 The rest of the names were of the children.
2.5 Transliteration rules: I wrote the names as they are pronounced in Yiddish. I followed the text in the book even if is appeared to be incorrect.
2.5.1 The Hebrew letter "Heit" (the 8th letter – as in Khayim) is transliterated here as "kh".
2.5.2 The Hebrew letter "Kaf" (the 11th letter – as in "Yocheved") is transliterated here as "ch".
2.5.3 CH is used also in its English sound, such as in Churchill.
2.5.4 Z is used as a transliteration of the 7th letter.
2.5.5 TZ is being used as in the name "Yitzkhak".

Glossary

Admor - Rabbi. A Jewish spiritual leader or rabbi, especially of a Hasidic sect. It is an acronym for "**Ad**onainu, **M**orainu, Ve**R**abbeinu," a phrase meaning "Our Master, Our Teacher, and Our Rebbe." This is an honorific title.
Aguda -society
Agudat Yisrael - ultra-orthodox party, anti-Zionist organization
Aliyah - Ascent = Immigration to Israel
Beitar Brith Yosef Trumpeldor - The Revisionist youth organization
Beth-Midrash - A Synagogue for praying and studying the Torah, study room
Chassid (*pl* = **chassidim**) - pious, devout ones
Cheder (*pl* = **chaderim**) - elementary schools
chazan cantor
Chevra Kaddisha - Burial Society
Chug - club
Chuppah - wedding canopy
Dybbuk - spirit of a dead person
Eretz-Israel - The Land of Israel - name given to Israel before 1948
Gabbay - dues collector, sexton, beadle
Gaon - Honorable Sage
Gemara - part of the **Talmud**
Gizbar - treasurer
Gmina - Local Council
Goyim - gentiles
Gra - the Gaon from Vilna
Hachshara - training, training farm
Haftarah - excerpt from the Prophets read in the Synagogue
Halacha - Legal part of Jewish traditional literature
Hashomer HaTza'ir - Young Guard youth movement
Hechalutz - Pioneers youth movement
Hechalutz Haklali General Pioneer youth movement
Hechalutz HaTzair Young Pioneer youth movement
Hora - traditional circle dance
Kabbalah - Jewish mysticism
Kaddish - Liturgical doxology said by the mourner
Kapai - Palestine Workers Fund
Karabelnikas - peddlers
Kasher/kosher - suitable for use (usually refers to food according to Jewish dietary laws)
Keren Hayesod – United Israel Appeal- literally "The Foundation Fund" is the central fundraising organization for Israel, established at the World Zionist Conference in London on July 7–24, 1920, and officially declared on December 24, 1920. The resolution called on "the whole Jewish people", Zionists and non-Zionists alike to contribute toward building of the Land of Israel through the Keren Hayesod
Keren Kayemeth Le'Yisrael (KKL) - **The Jewish National Fund**. Its goals were buying land, planting groves and other reclamation works in Eretz-Yisrael
Kibbutz Hakhsharah -Training Kibbutz for the pioneers before their aliyah to Eretz Yisrael
Kleinbahn - small train
Klezmer - Jewish folk musicians and their music

Kloiz/klois - synagogue, small prayer room
Knesset - Israeli parliament
Kolel - Yeshiva for married men
L'chaim - To Life! (a toast)
Maariv - daily evening prayer
Maggid - traditional East European Jewish religious itinerant preacher, skilled as a narrator of Torah and religious stories
Maskil - an adherent of the European Jewish "Enlightenment" movement between the 1770s and 1880s, which sought to reeducate Jews so that they could fit into modern society
Matsah (*pl* = **Matsoth**) - Unleavened bread for Passover
Melamed (*pl* = **melamdim**] - teachers
Mikve - ritual bathhouse or ritual bath
Mincha - daily afternoon prayer
Minyan - prayer quorum
Mishnah - (*pl* = **Mishnayot**) - Collection of Oral Laws compiled by Rabbi Yehudah haNasi, which forms the basis of the Talmud
Mizrachi - religious Zionist movement
Musar - Ethics Movement
Mussaf - Additional Sabbath or Festival prayers
Osadnikes - Veterans of the Polish Army sent by the Polish government to settle in White Russian territory, the **Kresy** (current Western Belarus and western Ukraine)and given incentives to "Polishize" the territory. The territory was ceded to Poland by the Polish-Soviet Riga Peace Treaty of 1921 and occupied by the Soviet Union in 1939.
Poalei Zion (Workers of Zion) - Socialist workers party
Rosh-Chodesh - the beginning of every Hebrew month
Shacharit - daily morning prayer
Shamash - synagogue beadle
Shlichut - overseas service
Shofar - a musical instrument made of a ram horn, used for Jewish religious purposes
Shtetl - village,
Shtetlach - small towns
Shema Yisrael - Title of a central prayer in morning and evening services. It is traditional for Jews to say the Shema as their last words
Shul - synagogue
Shulhoif - the backyard of the Synagogue
Shulkhan Arukh (The prepared table) - authoritative code of Jewish laws, written by Yoseph Caro (1488-1575)
Tahara - ritual cleansing of the dead person
Tallit - prayer shawl
Talmud - a central text of Rabbinic Judaism, with 2 components (Mishnah and Gemara)
Talmud Torah - Religious school for young pupils
Tarbut - Culture. It is also the name of a chain of Jewish schools throughout Poland
Tefillin - phyllacteries
Tisha B'Av - Fast of the ninth of Av, a day commemorating the tragedies that have befallen the Jewish people

Torah - Learning, teaching, the first five books of the Bible, rabbinical commentaries on them
Vorek - meadow
Yahrzeit - anniversary of a relative's death
Yekopo - assistance organization
Yeshivah (*pl* = **Yeshivot**) - rabbinic seminary, Talmudic college
Yiddishkeit - Judaism
Zaddik - righteous man

Months in Hebrew calendar:
Nissan, Iyyar, Sivan, Tammuz, Av (or Menachem Av), Elul, Tishri, Heshvan, Kislev, Tevet, Shvat, Adar

Jewish Festivals:
Rosh Hashana - New Year
Yom Kippur - Day of Atonement
Passover - commemoration of the liberation of the Israelites over 3,300 years ago from slavery in ancient Egypt
Lag B'Omer - a minor festival between Passover and Shavuot
Shavuot - commemorates the giving of the Torah on Mt. Sinai
Sukkot - Festival of Tabernacles
Shmini Atzeret - Eighth Day of Assembly
Chanukkah - Festival of Lights

Family Notes

Table of Contents

Title	Author	Page
The Map of Lubtch		1
Map of North-East Poland (1939)		2
Preface* [H]	K., Hilel	3
Preface [Y]	K., Hilel	3
Chronicles of the town of Lubtch [H]	B.M.S.	4
Documents relating to Jewish settlement in Lubtch [Y]	Kahn, P.	5
Lubtch under Polish Rule [H]	Yankelevitch, Chaim	8
There once was a Jewish village called Lubtch [Y]	Kroshnitz, Hilel	15
Chronicles of the Jewish community in Lubtch [H]	Shmulovitch, Hillel	29
A Jewish town named Delyatichi (Delatitich) [H]	Cohen, Dov	33
My hometown [H]	Eshed (Asherovsky), Frumka	36
From "HaMelitz", August 25th, 1898 [H]	Bonimovitch Chalpak, Yitzchak	42
A wise son-in-law… [Y]	Jankelowitz, Gershon	42
The Hebrew school in Lubtch [H]	Dichter, Yitzchak	43
The "Chorev" school in Lubtch [Y]	"Dos Wort" 618, 636, Vilna 1937, 1938	56
A "periodical" in Lubtch (reported by M. Tsinovitch) [H]	"Hatzfira"#18 (1894)	58
After the event… [Y]	Hilel Krosnitz	59
Rabbis of the Lubtch community [H]	Tzinovitch, Moshe	60
Reb Itchele's curse [Y]	Shlimovitch, Yitzchak	78
That's how we lived… [Y]	Jankelowitz, Gershon	78
For the general good… [Y]	Leibovitch, Shalom	82
The 1915 fire in Lubtch [Y]	Shlimovitch, Yitzchak	82
A Comedy [Y]		86
Small Towns of Houses and Trenches [Y]	Kaganovitch, Moshe	86
A Red-Headed Bride… [Y]	Yankelevitch, Chaim	88
"As is" [Y]	Kroshnitz, Hillel	89
The Hidden Light of the Jewish Mother in Lubtch [H]	Dichter, Chana	89
My Dear Mother [Y]	Manger, Itzik	94
I Remember My Village Delyatichi (Delatitch) [Y]	Brenner, Mina	95
No One Leaving and No One Coming [Y]	Kroshnitz, Hillel	103
Lubtch Until the First World War [H]	Sampson, E.	104
The Pastoral Picture has Vanished and is No More [H]	Vilner-Bruk, Chaya	110
The Castle in Lubtch [H]	Perkofchik, L.	113
Frosty Weather in the Summer [H]	Eliav, E.	115
The Branch of "HaShomer Hatza'ir" in Lubtch [H]	Shmulovitch, Hillel	118
Wealth Passes On, One Must Remain a "Mentch…" [Y]	Jankelowitz, Gershon	125
The Dream Has Remained… [Y]	Kroshnitz (Faivishevitch), Mina	126
Youth Movements in Lubtch [H]	Simchoni (Movshovitch), Chemda	130
The Mathematicians… [Y]	Jankelowitz, Gershon	134
The Trial [H]	Shimshoni, T.	134
Episodes from the Town [H]	Sampson, Eliyahu	137
The Request is Heard… [Y]	Yankelevitch, Chaim	139
Only the Memories are Left… [H]	Avrahami, Sara	140
Educational and Cultural Institutions in Lubtch [H]	Boldo, Chanan	142
Wealth… [Y]	Jankelowitz, Gershon	146
Memories of My Town [H]	Engel, Rachel	148
A Wedding [Y]	Yankelevitch, Chaim	150
A letter from the Mendele Library, Lubtch [H]		152
Remembrances [Y]	Balott, Rose (Reiche- Bayla)	155
The National Spirit of the Jews of Lubtch [H]	Shavit-Faivoshevitch, Avraham	156

Title	Author	Page
Real Horseradish [Y]	Yankelevitch, Chaim	159
Lubtch on the Neiman [H]	Kabak, Dov	159
Lubtch Foods [Y]	K., Hilel	164
"Lubtch Pigs" [Y]	H.K.	168
Days of Activity and Hope [H]	Sonenzon, Chaim	169
The Connection of the Family of President of Israel, Yitzchak Ben Tzvi, to Lubtch [H]	Alef (collated by), A.	171
An Incident About an Informing Report [Y]	Leibovitch, Shalom	174
The Righteous Rabbi R' Shmuel Bakshter [H]	Tsinovitch, Moshe	174
Minikes, Chanan Yaakov [Y]	Jaffe, Mordechai	179
The Actor Matityahu (Matus) Kowalsky [Y]	Tzinovitch, Moshe	181
Expulsion From and Rebuilding of Lubtch [Y]	Shulman (Shlimovitch), Nachum	183
Mutual Support in Lubtch [H]	Tzur, Mina	188
Cultural Life in Lubtch [H]	Levanon, Elka	189
The Town is Engraved in My Heart [H]	Spotnitzky, Baruch	190
Days of Joy and Sorrow [Y]	Kagan-Sirlis, Chana	192
R' Shmuel Meizel and His Family [H]	Tzinovitch, Moshe	195
Lubtch in the 1930's [H]	Yankelevitch, Elka	199
The Amateur Club [H]	Shimshoni, T.	201
My Town Delyatichi (Delatitch) [H]	Shmukler, Avigdor	203
Remember and Do Not Forget! [H]	Degani (Litchitzsky), Yona	206
Two Religious Undertakings in Lubtch [Y]	Rabinovitch, Shalom	209
A Remark Regarding the Abovementioned Correspondent's Report [Y]	Tzinovitch, Moshe	210
Activity of the Branch of the "Board of Yeshivot" in Lubtch [Y]	Rabinovitch, Shalom	211
Rabbis Born in Lubtch [H]	Tsinovitch, Moshe	212
Rabbi R' Chaim Krasilov z"l [And three other Rabbis] [H]	Hacohen Eliav, Avraham	222
No More Wars... [Y]	Yankelevitch, Chaim	227
Chaim Bruk, May The Lord Avenge His Blood! [Y]	Shalit, Moshe	228
The "Chevra Kaddisha" in Lubtch [H]	Shimshoni, T.	229
Remember! [H]	Shragai, Yehoshua	231
The Memory of My Town is Kept Safe in My Heart [H]	Solominsky, Chaya	234
The Gaon Rabbi Eliyahu-Chaim Meizel, Head of Court of Lodz and His Relationship to Lubtch [H]	Tsinovitch, Moshe	237
Between Two World Wars [H]	Bruk, Avraham	240
A Chazan (Cantor) in the Town [H]	Shimshoni, T.	245
Farewell to the Town [H]	Kivelevitch, Shmuel-Yaakov	246
Yehoshua Levinson, Bible Scholar [H]	Tzinovitch, Moshe	248
Alter Yosselevitch [H]	Tzinovitch, Moshe	249
A Panoramic Gem [H]	Kalmanovitch, Meyerim (Meir)	250
The History of the Town (From the Encyclopedia Judaica) [H]		251
My Town (A Poem) [H]	Yankelevitch, Chaim	252
(Poem) [H]	Amitai (Faivoshevitch), Ayala	255
Memories [H]	Degani, Yona	257
My Sister Itka, of Blessed Memory [H]	Levanon, Elka	259
To the Memory of My Family [H]	Solominsky, Chaya	260
My Father, Avraham-Aharon, of Blessed Memory [Y]	Berkovitch, Eliyahu	261
Memories from My Father's House [H]	Sivitsky, Aryeh	262
Only Letters Remain... [H]	Sonenzon, Chaim	264
My Grandmother Chaya [H]	Nashkes, Puah	265
My Rebbe, Rabbi Chaim [Y]	Shlimovitch, Yitzchak	266
Tuvya the Sexton [Y]	Shulman (Shlimovitch) Nachum	267
My Grandmother Rivka [H]	Simchoni (Movshovitch), Chemda	267

Lyubcha and Delyatichi Yizkor Book

Title	Author	Page
My Father Eliezer, of Blessed Memory [H]	Aharonovsky, Danny	268
Their Memory Will Remain Forever in My Heart [H]	Pintel (Pines), Freda	272
An Eternal Light for My Family [Y]	Aronovsky, Shmuel Binyamin- Chaim	273
In Memory of My Brother Avraham, May His Blood be Avenged! [H]	Kalmanovitch, Golda	275
Max Shmulevitch, of Blessed Memory [H]	Degani, Yona	276
The Holocaust and the Heroism		278
I Won't Forgive! (Poem) [Y]	Berliner, Yitzchak	280
One of the Family... [H]	Yankelevitch, Natan	281
I Was in the Ghetto [Y]	Yankelevitch, Yisrael- Gershon (Yisrol)	285
I Revenged our Innocent Blood [Y]	Yanson, Velveke	292
Scrolls from The Flame [H]**	Slonimsky, Yisrael	304
In the Lubtch Ghetto [Y]	Solomiansky, Shifra	317
Rosh Hashana in the Forest [Y]	Yankelevitch, Yisrael	323
A Partisan in his Late Years [Y]	Leibovitch, Shalom	325
Under the Nazis in France [Y]	Zablotzky, Risha	332
(untitled) [Y]	Meyerson-Kowalsky, Lyuba	337
Little Pages from the Flame... [Y]	Slonimsky, Yisrael	338
(Poem) [H]	Yankelevitch, Chaim	352
Words spoken by Nachum Shlimovitch at the memorial service for the Martyrs of Lubtch and Delatitich [Y]	Shlimovitch, Nachum	353
Words at the Memorial Service for the Martyrs of Lubtch and Delatitich [H]	Zacharavitch, Yaacov	355
Former Lubtch and Delatitch Residents Now Living in Israel [H]		358
List of Jews from Lubtch and Delatitch who came to Israel, and Who Have Since Died [H]		362
Martyrs of Lubtch – List of Lubtcha Jews who were killed in the Holocaust [H]		363
Martyrs of Dclatitch – List of Delatitch (Delyatichi) Jews who were killed in the Holocaust [H]		375
Photographs		378
Epilogue [H]		399
Table of Contents of the Original Yizkor Book		400

Appendix of Material not in the Original Yizkor Book — 404

Delyatichi between the Two World Wars	Ofer Cohen	404
The Map of Delyatichi		408
Photographs from Ofer Cohen		410

Notes:

[H] - Written in Hebrew, [Y] - Written in Yiddish

* This is the same article as that written in Yiddish on Page 8
** This is the same article as that written in Yiddish on Page 338, but with different photographs

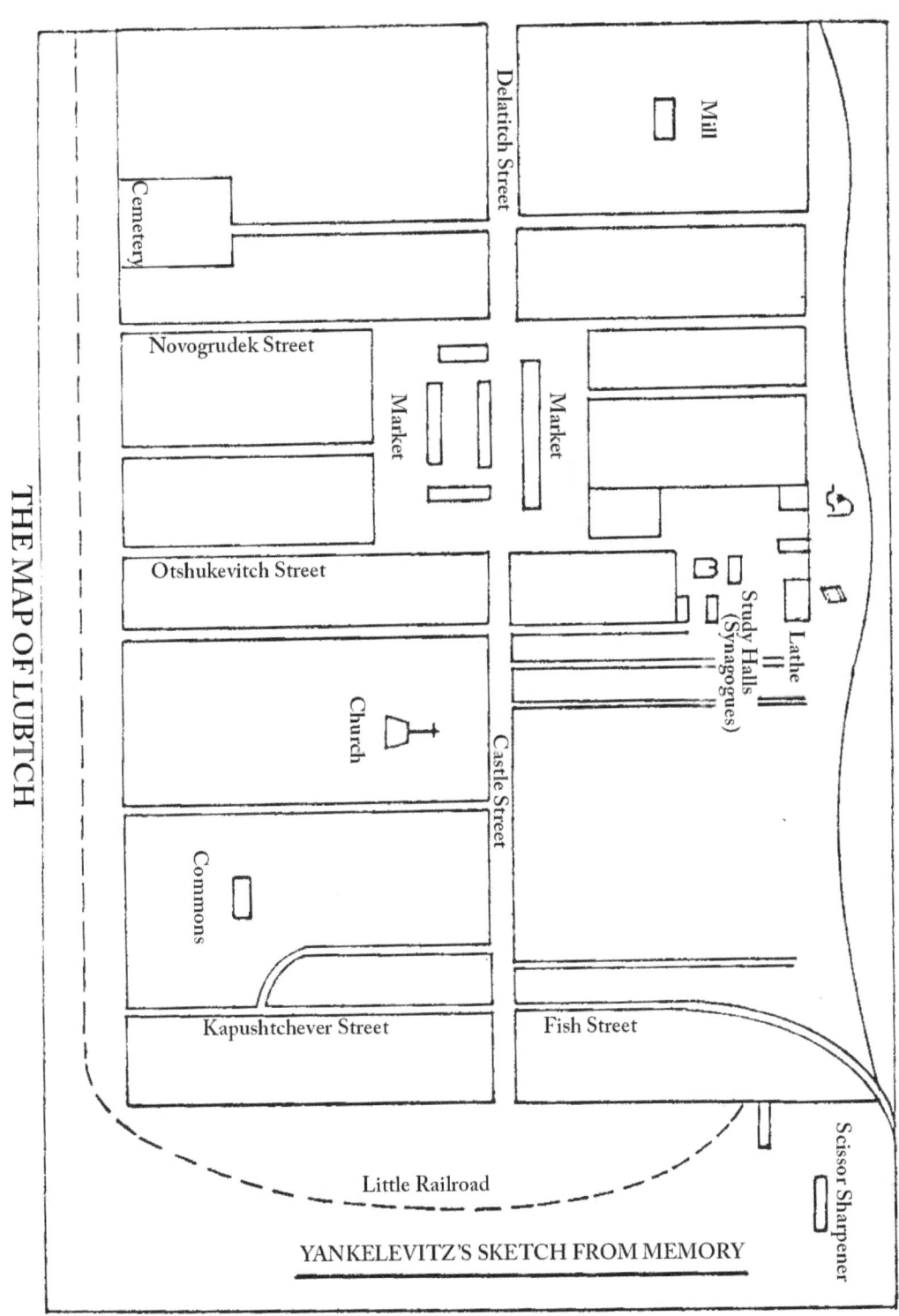

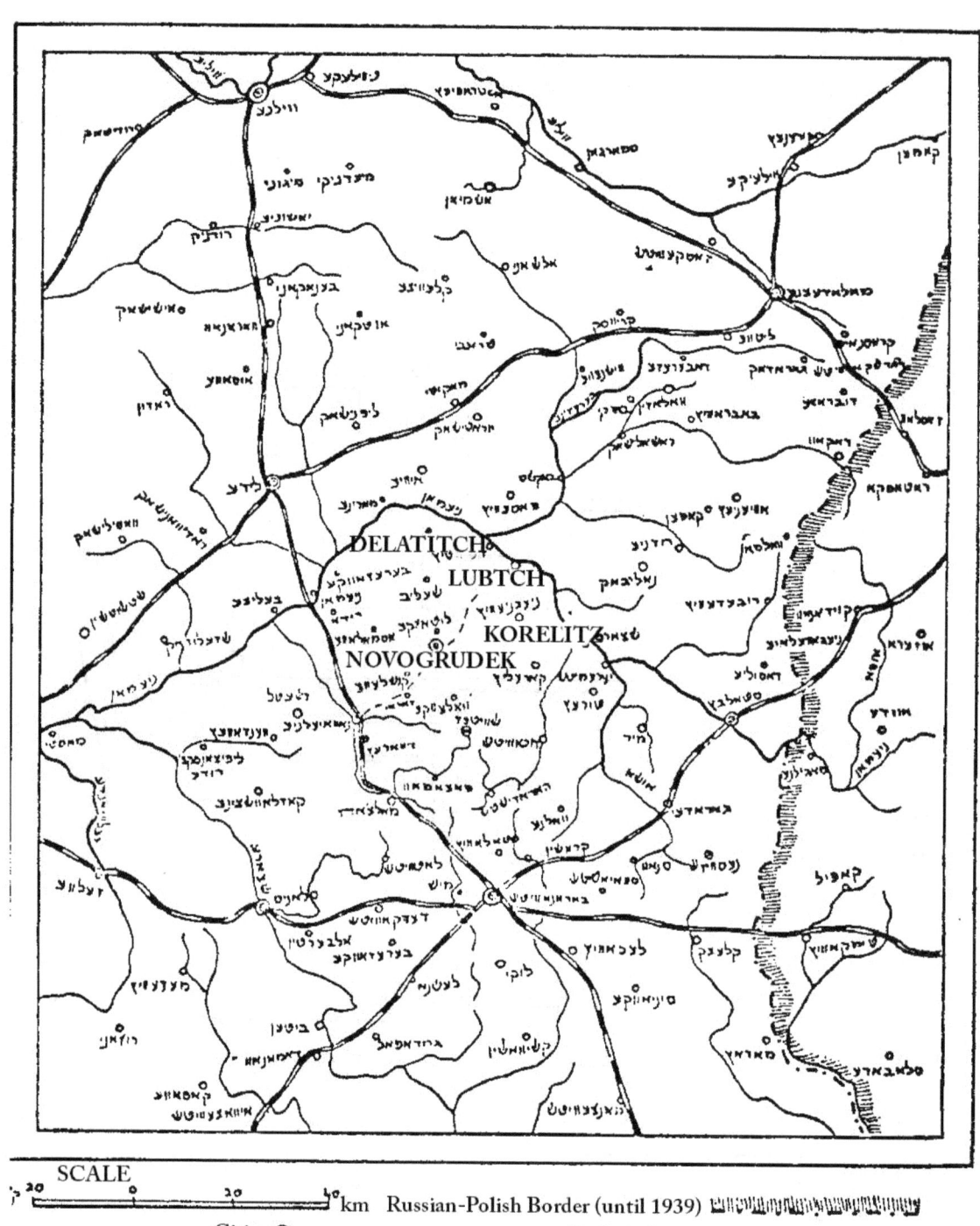

MAP OF NORTHEAST POLAND (1939)

[Page 7 - Hebrew] [Page 8 - Yiddish]

Preface

K. Hilel

Translated from the Yiddish by Harvey Spitzer

The task of Holocaust literature is not only to relate but mainly to remember, remind and not let the world and future generations forget what the Germans with their faithful collaborators – Poles, Ukrainians, White Russians, Latvians, Lithuanians and other murderous peoples- did to our closest relatives: parents, brothers, sisters, grandfathers and grandmothers, aunts and uncles - all those with whom are life was bound up through the holy bond of family, relationships and national ties.

To remember for generations those whose lives were cut off, not to let forget and never to forgive their murderers, to educate the young generations in that spirit, to instill in them a feeling of honor for their ancestors, to hate the Exile and love all the more the independence we have established, our national pride- the State of Israel.

It is for this very reason that we are putting out this book, a small link in the golden chain of past Jewish life, without which the future can have neither meaning nor content.

Just as the sea is reflected in a drop of water, so Jewish life in Eastern Europe is reflected in the memories, stories, descriptions, and personal experiences and accounts of the simple country people, about their Jewish homes, cities, villages, and communities of which nothing remains but destruction and mountains of ashes.

With a feeling of piety and reverence for our past, we present this book to the few survivors of Lubtch and Delatitch and to the members of our young generation as well, who will continue to forge new links in the golden chain of Jewish existence and creativity.

Let us hope that this book will fulfill its mission. Amen!

[Pages 9-10]
Chronicles of the Town of Lubtch

B.M.S.

Translated by B.M.S from the article in Polish in the "Povshchena Encyclopedia," Warsaw 1864, pages 312-313.

Translated from the Hebrew by Ann Belinsky

Lubtch - a town in the region of Novogrudek, district of Minsk, on the Neiman River, is located 6 miles from Novogrudek. The settlement is very old. According to the Lithuanian historical archives, the student of Yatek Odrubondzh, Hoyt, the blessed priest from Krakow, also a Dominican priest, who was serving as a priest in Lithuania during the pagan period at the time of Mandog, received a friendly reception in Lubtch from Agadzhai Kian, a well known immigrant from Kiev. There he founded the Catholic Church and the Dominican Mission (Spiritual Memoires, Vol. 3, page 24). Nerbet, however, assumes that the first Bishops' cathedra in Lubtch was established in the time of Mandog, a matter that does not match the facts or all the critical sources. (Vol. 4, additions, page 10). These works prove that Lubtch was an ancient town.

Until the 15th century, the town belonged to the estate of the Grand Duke, until Alexander Yaglontchik presented it as a gift in 1499 to his secretary Fedek Karpetovitz. In 1528, the town was transferred - by purchase – to Albrecht Gestold, the Vivida of Vilna, and in 1547, it was passed to the ownership of Yan Kishka, the great knight of Lithuania, who was a well known sympathizer of "Aryanism" in Lithuania. In 1592, he founded a printing office for non-catholic religious books in Lubtch. His first printer was Pyuter Balstos Kamita. He was followed by his son, Yan Kamita, and the third one was Yan Langa Havnagli. The printing office, which was at first only dissident, and then was definitely Aryan, ceased operating in 1655 because of the wars and plague. The printed works were printed in Polish and Latin, and more than 10-15 of the well known books are rare.

King Zygmund III, according to Kishka's wishes, who was already the commander of the Vilna Fortress, on the basis of the rights of 1590, gave Lubtch rights of Magdaborg: a special symbol, fixed fair days etc. The owner of the town built a castle from stones on the banks of the River Neiman, a thing which glorified the impression of the town, which looked fortified and prosperous. This prosperity continued for several decades. In 1606, the town Lubtch was given as a present to the Radizivil family. In accordance with the request of one of the Radizivils, - Yanush –, in 1644 King Vladislav IV gave Lubtch Magdaborg rights, and fixed market and fair days. But during the reign of Yan Kazimizisch, because of the war ravages, Lubtch remained destroyed and unpopulated. Lubtch sank into economic distress, from which it did not recover. The castle of Kishka was abandoned and ruined, the Magdaborg Rights were cancelled, and from the two fairs, there remained only one fair per year, the horse fair on Saint Eliash Day.

Today the town is poor, despite its very comfortable geographical position at a commercial and industrial junction. The Jewish population is involved in wholesale commerce, some are craftsmen: tailors, shoemakers, carpenters and rope makers. There is also a small lacquer factory, managed by Jews. In the town there are 179 households, of which 75 belong to Christians, and the rest to traditional Jews. The Christians are mainly involved in agriculture and a few in weaving. This industry has the capacity to develop as they know here how to make cloth called "*chamishimiot*", which is better than the Dutch materials, despite the fact that it is handmade in primitive workshops, and they don't have any spindles. Until now only farmers provided them with threads as sharecroppers or taxpayers. The local weavers are dependent on the palaces and the farmers who bring the threads for sale.

[Pages 11-15]
Documents Relating to Jewish Settlement in Lubtch

Published in YIVO "Bletter", Vol. III, May 1932

by P. Kahn

Translated from the Yiddish by Harvey Spitzer

In the historical chronicles, Lubtch is mentioned as far back as the middle of the 13th century. In 1574, the village was in the possession of the Polish magnate (Wielki Kreitshi Litewski) Jan Kishke, widely known for his wealth and as a free thinker, and who was openly an adherent of Arianism.[1]

In 1592, this same Kishke set up a printing press in Lubtch in which anti-Catholic works were printed in Polish and Latin, and which today are very rare and valuable. In 1606, Lubtch was given as a gift to the Radziwills who, at the end of the 18th century, gave the village - as a possession for generations - to the rich and influential magnates, the Sapieha family.

Jews lived in Lubtch from earliest times, but nothing is known of the actual beginning of Jewish settlement in that village *(shtetl)*.

Among the material from the so-called "Radziwill Commission"[2] in Vilna, I came across an act[3] which pertains to the Jewish community of Lubtch in the 17th century. This is an original document of privileges which Kazshimiezsh

Jan Sapieha[4] granted in 1690 to Avraham Hashkevitsh, a farmer and the most influential member of the Jewish community in Lubtch.

At that time there was another great fire in the village in which the synagogue and adjacent buildings including the bathhouse and cemetery were completely burned down. In order to receive permission from Sapieha, who was the owner of the village, to rebuild the synagogue, the aforementioned court-farmer, Avraham Hashkevitsh, turned to him with a request. The farmer took advantage of this appropriate moment and asked Sapieha to grant the Jews rights and freedoms which Jewish communities enjoyed at that time in the Greater Principality of Lithuania.[5]

Avraham Hashkevitch won these rights, and in the privileges of January 30, 1690 which Sapieha granted in Vilna (Vilnius) we read:

"Each and everyone, who will now and in the future have to know about this, people of all ranks, religious and secular, citizens of the city of my inheritance, Lubtch: Today and in later times, I hereby announce through this act of worldly privileges granted to the community of Jews in Lubtch that, taking into account the great destruction which God allowed to happen in the city through a fire, during which the synagogue belonging to the Jews was burned down to the ground with all the buildings and since, on account of that misfortune, the Lubtch farmer, Avraham Hashkevitch, humbly turned to me, in the name of the entire community, with a request to build a new synagogue and also to confirm other freedoms such as those enjoyed by other communities in the Greater Principality of Lithuania. Therefore, I was inclined with kindness to grant this request and, considering his faithful service, I have permitted the aforementioned Avraham Hashkevitsh and the other Jews who live here now to bring in Jews from elsewhere in order to expand the settlement of the city, to live and build a (wooden) or brick synagogue with all necessary buildings and an arched synagogue for women, everything according to their own desire as well as a *mikve* (ritual bathhouse) and a women's bathhouse, and to set up the gravestones on the previous places without any costs and obligations for these places. Only for places where they themselves live, will they be obligated to pay a tax into my coffers according to inventory and not having other obligations, they are free to give apartments to soldiers (and) except when I myself am in the city, they (the soldiers) can have lodging (in Jewish homes) but without any food provisions.

As for legal decisions, the Jews must come to the court in Lubtch and stand before the administrator of justice with free rights to appeal his decisions to me or to my commissars (ministers). Trials must not take place on Jewish holidays, market and fair days. I also guarantee that, according to long established custom, they may be free to own breweries and malt houses and to sell all kinds of strong beverages without any interference on the part of the farmers for whom they must bring the proper payment. They may take up any kind of trade for their own use without any hindrance from anyone.... They may also have assurance to engage in business and to bring in – whether by land or by water - whatever merchandise they want and also to own stores in the city and to sell, after bringing into the payment offices what is owed to the government treasury. These freedoms which have been accorded to them by the privileges act must not be tampered with by me or by my successors and we must keep them for all time.

Promulgating this act of privileges, I hereby affix my signature below with my seal. Issued in Vilna, this 30th of January, 1690.

Kazshimiezsh Sapieha, Head of Greater Principality of Lithuania

This Charter of Privileges is written on parchment measuring 35.5 x 43 cm. Two round seals and special sheaths of the Radziwill and Sapieha families hang on a silk cord. On the margin of the parchment there is an addendum from a later period which indicates that on August 3, 1797, Avraham ben Heshel and Yitchak ben Hirsh in the name of the Lubtch community delivered the original of the act of privileges in order to enter them into the acts of the Novogrudek district.

After the above mentioned fire, Lubtch was apparently quickly built up and the Jewish community increased. At the board of assembly of the main communities of the states of Lithuania[6] which took place in Indor (Amdor, Grodno district) and which dealt with the imposition of a poll tax on the separate communities, amounting to 60,000 Polish guilder for all the Jews in Lithuania, it was determined to levy a tax in the amount of 800 guilder for Lubtch and neighboring villages. The board of assembly for the Lithuanian communities in Mir, autumn 1751, levied a poll tax of 510 Polish guilder on the Lubtch community.

Footnotes

1. Arianism is a heretical system in Christianity which arose at the beginning of the 4th century. The Bishop of Alexandria, Arius, (d. 336) taught that God the son is not the same as God the father. This was opposed to the accepted dogma of the Christian faith. Those who came under the influence of Arianism showed themselves to be more tolerant of non-Christians in general and of Jews in particular. Arianism once had numerous adherents among the Polish nobility.
2. The "Radziwill Commission" was created by a decree of Czar Alexander I and its task was to put order into the entangled inheritance affairs of Dominic Radziwill, who fell in battle, fighting on Napoleon's side. The Commission existed from 1816- 1838. The abundant material of the Radziwill Commission, some 2,000 fascicles, can be found in the Government Archives in Vilnius (Vilna).
3. Government Archives in Vilnius, collections of the Radziwill Commission, vol. 41, 13/306.
4. Kazshimiezsh Jan Sapieha was one of the greatest magnates in Lithuania and held very high positions in the Greater Principality of Lithuania. He was finance minister, senator and "*voyevoda*" from Polotsk and later from Vilna and was also leader of Lithuania. He died in Grodno in 1720.
5. Sigmund I, King of Poland and of Greater Principality of Lithuania, confirmed the Brisk privileges as a general act of privileges for all Jews in Lithuania.
6. See "*Pinkas Hamedina*" and "*Pinkas Va'ad Hakehilot Harashiot b' Medinat Litta*" (Published by S. Dubnow).

Brought for printing: **Moshe Tzinovitch**

[Page 16]

"3rd of May" celebrations by the "Gmina" (Local Council) Building

[Pages 17-24]

Lubtch Under Polish Rule

by Chaim Yankelevitch

Translated from the Hebrew by Ann Belinsky

The origin of the name "Lubtch" is unknown, and even the history of the town is unknown, - who founded and established it, and when Jews settled there, because it was so small. The Neiman was used as a source for identification and pride, the address was "Lubtch on the Neiman".

One kilometer north of Lubtch, dipped in a sea of green, was the Vinova Estate, lazily warming in the sun and surrounded by small forests. The place was attractive for pleasant walks on Shabbat and Holy Days, a hiding place for loving couples, and for a meeting place for the youth. On the 3rd of May - the national festival of Poland – and on *Lag B'Omer*, it served as a meeting place and starting point for processions.

Chaim Yankelevitch

From here originates the stream – that begins as a sort of small lake – which flows into the Neiman. The Jews would place barrels of cucumbers for pickling in this lake, before the winter, and before the lake froze. When the warm rays of the sun melted the snow in spring, the barrels would be pulled out. These cucumbers and their taste had great fame, and whoever had not pickled cucumbers by himself would run to buy the cucumbers together with their juice ("*russel*").

On the left hand side of the path Hanan Boldo's mechanical flour mill stood imposingly. The mill was an innovation in the area, because most of the mills were operated by the many rivers in this region. The farmers would bring the yield of their yellowing fields – wheat and cereals - to Boldo's mill.

A little past the flour mill came the first street of Lubtch, named after the very small town of Delatitch, which was situated 5 kilometers north of Lubtch, and joined by strong neighborly ties.

This was a fairly long road inhabited mainly by Christians, who incited their dogs against the Jewish children who happened to be there alone, and sometimes they also assailed the inhabitants with loud shouts. The Jewish youth would gather in groups in order to cross this street, carrying "arms" in their pockets for defense – slingshots and stones.

East of Lubtch were the villages of Kapotscheva and Kopitchik. The Christian inhabitants of these villages were farmers and pet-breeders and made their living selling their produce to the Jews.

South of Lubtch was the large village Itchokevitch. On the south side of the town was the exit to the regional city of Novogrudek, which was located at a distance of 20 kilometres from Lubtch, and from there to the whole world.

The town was connected to Novogrudek for administrative purposes. There was lively commerce between the town and Novogrudek, so therefore it was necessary to set up transport between Lubtch and the regional city.

My grandfather told me that in his time, when he wanted to go to Novogrudek, he would get up with the first watch, before dawn, take his *tallit* and *tefillin*, and with a stick in his hand, arrive in Novogrudek in time to pray with the first *minyan*.

A common way of getting to Novogrudek was by horse and cart. Whoever had a horse and cart would travel this way. There were citizens for whom this was their livelihood, bringing passengers and goods to and from Novogrudek. The main part of the way was done by riding on the cart, but when they got to the hill by the village of Korvitch, the driver would politely ask the travelers to get off the cart, because the heavy weight was too much for the horse to pull, and the travelers would have to reach the crest by foot.

Modern means of travel also connected Lubtch to Novogrudek; there was a small train, "*kleinbahn*", in which people traveled comfortably and even could doze off during the trip. Whoever was lucky enough to find a place by the window would sit there and not move lest someone else would grab it...

A number of years before the Holocaust began, a bus also connected the town to Novogrudek. Although it was more expensive, it was more comfortable, more frequent, and the journey took less time.

The mail reached the town by train, newspapers came by train and bus; and rumors from the big world came with every person entering Lubtch.

In the North, the town was bordered by the Neiman. It originates on the Russian-Polish border, in the area of the town of Stolpatchi.

The Neiman – A beautiful large river, carrying its cool, good-tasting waters from a distance with the sound of merry ripples. Many edible fish swam in its waters. As if to beautify the river, its banks were decorated with grassy meadows, and to the north of its banks, ancient forests proudly raised their tree tops.

The Neiman was an endless source of entertainment and enjoyment. In the hot summers it was full of bathers, from the town and from other villages. The bathing was a pleasant enjoyable pastime, especially early in the morning when the river was flowing peacefully, caressed by the sun's rays and the water was extremely clear. In the hot summer evenings, one could see schools of fish in the clear waters - a heartening and comforting sight.

A view of the Neiman. In the distance: the castle and the church

Sailing on the river was another source of enjoyment. To start with, people would row upstream against the current, in order to return easily with the flowing current downstream. Often a number of boats were joined together, and then they would merrily return in a long string. And in this wonderful silence one would often hear sounds of music – some of the youth would bring musical instruments with them: mouth organs, the soft sounding mandolin which would make hearts tremble, and the wind instruments, and songs which would burst out of the throats of the rowers, with a great echo from all directions, carrying the songs infinite distances. These were work songs, love songs and songs of yearning and longing for Zion. It is no wonder that the Neiman was also a well-known and friendly "matchmaker" for young couples from the town.

The river is entwined among the memories of my childhood. Every spare moment we school children would run to it. We would run towards the up-current several kilometers upstream, and returned on pine-tree timbers which were destined to be exported.

A legend went around, that every year a human sacrifice would drown in the cruel river; and so children would refrain from swimming in the river until someone drowned. And as soon as someone drowned, we would run and swim there, despite the sadness on the loss of life.

In the spring and summer the river would overflow its banks and flood many districts; the area looked like a lake full of charm and splendor. The floods caused the farmers of the area much trouble and even complete isolation; the farmers that needed help lit fires, and the youth of the town would come in boats to their aid, bringing food for man and beast, to the isolated houses.

When winter arrived, the river froze over; through its thin ice covering you could see the depths below. The ice cover was used as a place for ice-skating and sledging, - thus also in the winter the river was a social meeting place.

In the center of the town was the marketplace. The place centralized all the areas of the livelihood and upkeep of the town: the grocery shops, building materials, grain shops, clothing etc. Every Tuesday there was a colorful market, and farmers from all the surrounding villages came to the place with their agricultural produce including meat and fruits and vegetables, as well as their homecrafts merchandise: coarse fabrics, carpets, embroidered tablecloths, wooden pots, wooden tubs etc. The market place hummed with the sounds of people, the bellowing of cattle and the crowing of poultry. The local Jews spent a lot of their time at the market, buying and selling and negotiating with the Gentiles in order to trade and buy produce.

The point of departure of the six streets of the town and its lanes was at the marketplace. Most of the houses of the town were one storey only, built from wood and their roofs covered with wooden tiles or straw.

In the center of the market stood the "Fire House" building, a large hall where the firefighting equipment was stored, and which was used at night-time for performances of the dramatic club, or for general meetings of the inhabitants.

Most of the families made a living from trade. Some owned shops in the town itself, others took their produce on horse-pulled wagons and peddled their wares to the villages and farmers in the environs; these peddlers were called "*karabelnikas*". Sometimes they received money in exchange for their merchandise; the main products they brought to the farmers were salted fish, salt, matches, soap, cheap fabrics, buttons, threads, needles etc. The wandering peddler received a warm welcome from the farmer and enjoyed generous hospitality, but despite this, the farmer knew how to haggle with him over the prices.

The area of Lubtch was known as a large supplier of flax, and many Jews traded in it. The farmers of the area grew flax for sale as well as for weaving linen cloth on home spindles and also for producing linseed oil for their needs.

The forests that the area was blessed with were an important source of livelihood; the cheap "wood" was used for home heating in the winter, and the better kinds of "wood" were used for building, while the choicest logs of "wood" were exported all over Poland, and even to Germany and other European countries.

An animal fair in Lubtch

Because of the swamps, it was difficult to take the trees out of the forest; they were usually cut down in the winter – when the water froze – and were taken out by sledge. In places where trees could be felled in the summer, they were transported to the far away areas by raft; many Jews traded in trees, and thus supplied the needs of the tree traders who came from the large cities; there were even a number of houses which were used as a small hotels for the wood traders that were visiting.

There were also craftsmen: tailors, painters, blacksmiths, sewers, bootmakers, carpenters, builders and others. The group of craftsmen was not organized, they worked unlimited hours and their income was distressfully low.

When there were disputes between Jews and gentiles, the matter was brought to the governmental court.

One of the most famous cases that took place between the Jews of Lubtch and farmers of the area had to do with the ownership of a parcel of grazing land by the Neiman. The land belonged to the Jews, who had a deed of purchase to prove it. But during the First World War it was lost somewhere. When this became known to the Gentiles, they served a claim for ownership of the land. After many court hearings and the efforts of the town leaders and many appeals, the community won the case and the plot of land was returned to its ownership. There was much rejoicing – the end to the court expenses, and now there was much grazing land for free, and this was especially important since almost every Jewish household kept a cow in the stall.

A misunderstanding between two Jews was brought before the rabbi of the town, and the matter was settled according to his decision.

The livelihood of the rabbi was dependent on his community, so the Jews limited themselves to buying yeast and Sabbath candles only from the rabbi. Sometimes the rabbi received gifts from home owners who came to him as litigants. This way the Rabbi of Lubtch could live honorably.

*

After the First World War, when the Jews who had been exiled from the town during the fighting returned, their first concern was to educate their children according to the ways of tradition of the People of Israel. A network of *chaderim* [elementary schools] developed, where the *melamdim* [teachers], who were experts in the smallest details of the Talmud, imparted knowledge to the pupils, and the paths of the Bible and its commentators were made clear to them. There were *melamdim* who also taught the Hebrew language and a few secular studies. Here is the place to mention R' Eliezer Kalmanovitch, who provided a deep explanation of Hebrew grammar.

When the Polish rule became consolidated, the township was ordered to build a modern school, according to the laws of the State. The *chaderim* were abolished and the *Tarbut* School was established, which was connected to the country-wide network of *Tarbut* Schools in Poland. Authorized teachers were sent to teach at the school and a headmaster with knowledge and experience came to administer the institution. The language of teaching was Hebrew, and the school was located in a large and spacious building that was built by the Jews of the town.

Within the walls of the institution, the youth received a general basic education. The teachers' primary goal was to give the pupils Torah with good manners, a nd above all, to instill in their hearts the Zionist idea and the yearning to live in Eretz-Israel.

In the evenings, young people who were organized into Zionist youth movements met in the school building. They were active and educated in these movements for the fulfillment of their dream to go on *aliya* to Eretz-Israel.

I remember the impressive ceremony which took place in the school in 1925 on the day the corner stone was laid for the construction of the Hebrew University on Mt. Scopus in Jerusalem. The teachers explained the deep significance of the occasion - surely the Jewish People is the People of the Book and from Zion will come Torah. In the Land of the Patriarchs, which is being built up, the foundation has been laid for imparting Torah. The people who were dispersed in seventy exiles, who had to struggle to enter universities, are now establishing a Hebrew university. After the ceremony we went around with the "blue box" to raise money for the "Jewish National Fund".

The school succeed in planting within us love of Eretz-Israel and for the new reality of the Land in the life of the Jewish People; the reality which laid the foundation for the establishment of the independent Jewish State.

[Pages 25-47]

There Was Once A Jewish Village Called Lubtch

by Hilel Kroshnitz

Translated from the Yiddish by Harvey Spitzer

*Dedicated to my father-in-law,
R' Yehoshua-Yaakov Ze'ev Feivishevitch, of blessed memory*

A Summer's Day In The Village

Five Jewish streets, a few lanes, a market place with houses and stores; another long street where the gentiles live, the Neiman River, which swaddles the synagogue yard- this constitutes the village.

To this we must add Jentchelski's mill at one end of the village, and the sawmill, on the shore of the Neiman River, rising above the houses with its tall, black chimney smoking all day long - at the other end of the village.

Castle Street occupies the seat of honor in the village. It is always dressed up and cleanly swept. The street boasts a lovely garden at the church as well as many-branched trees, beautiful homes and important owners- the pharmacist, Dr. Rabinovitch, Yisrael Saladucha, the wood merchant, and Chaim Bruk, the head of the community.

*

The night still struggles, unwilling to give up its place to the coming day. Darkness still lies over the village, but the morning star is shining and announces the arrival of a new day.

From the darkness emerges a figure - a broad shouldered, black wrinkled Jew, like a gypsy. A bag with food hangs dawn from his shoulders, a long whip clenched in his right hand. He has a deep, thick voice which pierces the quiet of the dawn. This is Moshe-Grunim, the village herdsman, who leads the village cows to graze in the meadows along the Neiman River. Moshe Grunim, a coarse, ignorant fellow, looks like a healthy country peasant. His voice is rough and firm. He speaks in chopped sentences. It is more like a roar than human speech.

Women half asleep rub their eyes, hurry out of bed, grab something to put on and run quickly to open the stable door to drive out the cows. The cows come together and the sound of their mooing, Moshe Grunim's roar and the crack of the whip is carried over the village.

The village has awakened:

Along the streets and lanes, a movement of people begins- men hurrying off to *shul* to catch the morning service with the first *minyan* to thank God for granting them another day of life.

An hour later, the rattle of wheels and horseshoes is heard echoing along the stony pavement. Traveling through the villages and hamlets are the itinerant peddlers - Jews who earn a livelihood buying flax, linseed, mushrooms, eggs, small hides, pig bristles and other agricultural products from the peasants. At the same time, they sell various kinds of merchandise to the peasants: soap, needles, matches, combs, mirrors and other "bargains". Others, however, buy torn clothes, bottles and old metal from the peasants. Most of the time, this is barter, wares for wares, from which both sides derive satisfaction. Butchers also go on horse and wagon through the villages buying calves, cows, and once even a sheep-the cheapest meat for the village pauper.

With a crack of the whips, the wagon drivers hasten their horses on. They are going to Novogrudek, the neighboring city in the district. Seated in the wagon are passengers clinging to their seats, still half asleep. Some of them are going to the district city to buy merchandise for their little stores and to bring it back later loaded on the same wagon. Others - it shouldn't happen to us - are traveling to see an important doctor or to a government office in the district city.

In the wagon next to Arl, a member of the strong and healthy Yedidovitch family, sits Rabbi Yossel, the grocer, enjoying a piece of sweet ginger cake. Seated next to him is Avraham-Chaim, the shoe store owner, who has been trying to draw Rabbi Yossel into a discussion about politics. Avraham-Chaim is an ardent Zionist, while Rabbi Yossel has become a passionate supporter of *Aguda* since Podolski, a scholar and *Aguda* activist, has been trying to find a good match for Rabbi Yossel's daughter. Rabbi Yossel does not let himself get drawn into any discussion. He calmly munches on the ginger cake and grumbles something to himself.

Seated in the wagon is also a young son-in-law, originally from Lubtch, who is now returning to Warsaw after a visit to the village. He is an ardent opponent of the *Aguda* and now has an opportunity to unleash his anger against *Aguda*. He gets involved in the discussion, gets excited and pours out his wrath on the "black clerics".

Arl, the wagon driver, keeps quiet, doesn't get involved in the discussion of such important passengers, but when their arguing gets too heated, he suddenly gives a crack with the whip and lets out a "giddyap!" in such a loud voice that the passengers tremble and become silent. Arl smiles, pleased that he succeeded in calming down the "hot heads". He takes out of his pocket a bunch of white kernels which he shares with the passengers as if to say: Eat, keep quiet and enjoy better the natural beauty around you.

In the village, the little stores and workshops are opening up. In the flax-granary, the flax is pressed by a machine which throws out four-cornered sacks ready to be sent off to Vilna, to the flax company which has a branch in the village. One can hear a rhythmical clip-clap from the granaries, the peasant girls stamping on the flax and cleaning it from the waste material.

Mitzkovski, the police officer, walks through the village like a ruler. He looks to see whether the houses are whitewashed, the pavement is swept and if the bread and cakes in the bakeries are kept under a glass cover. In Poland, everything must be clean and hygienic and if not, you have to pay a "*zlota*". This is often made cheaper by putting a smaller coin into the policeman's hand.

The village youth meet on the market place: Avraham Pertshik and his sister Sarah, Dovid Movshovitch, Kalmanovitch, Yoskeh Yedidovitch, the Kaplansky brothers, Palia Kapushtshevsky, the Lipchins, Motte Kivelevitch, and others. Most of the boys are tall, healthy and athletically built. The girls are well proportioned, charming and pretty. The young people mill about and have nothing to do. There is no work or livelihood, and there are no prospects for the future.

They stand in a small circle and just talk. They tell jokes and relate what those who emigrated to Palestine (Eretz Israel) write in their letters. Moshe Pikelni comes by with a bundle of newspapers. Everyone grabs a paper and talks about world politics. These are serious times, one event closely follows another, and the young people of Lubtch take a stand. Yoske Yedidovitch, a giant of a young man, a left-wing Zionist, thunders out against the Fascists. He assures everyone that if there is a war, socialism will triumph all over the world. And meanwhile, he has his eyes turned on a guest in his mother's small hotel which has been empty nearly a whole year.

Ovseyevitch, the tailor, comes out of his workshop - the work won't run away - and goes over to the circle of young people. He wants to know what they read about in the newspapers and gives his opinion. Yossel

Kapushtshevsky, a quiet, calm teenager who leans to the left politically, also comes over and listens quietly to the discussion. When everyone has been heard, he makes a null and void motion with his hand and interjects a short sentence:-- Our people will settle everything. The discussion is over for him and he hurries off to his workshop.

– Hey gang!, if you have a few cents in your pockets, let's go and play billiards, suggests Pertshik, and they leave and go over to Wilner in the restaurant to play billiards.

Moshe Levin's and Gershon Kapushtshevsky's sawmill is located in the vicinity of the old castle. All day long, a murmur is carried across the village from the machines which saw the logs that are driven down the river on rafts from the Nalibak district. This is the only place in the village where you can actually hear the living breath of work. Gentiles pull the logs out of the river, shout, curse their mother, and the pile of logs grows higher and higher. The athletically built Gershon Kapushtshevsky is all heated up by the work. He shouts, gives orders and doesn't let the non-Jews out of his sight as they drag the logs. His partner, Moshe Levin, is calm, polite, speaks pleasantly, measures the timber and records everything in a little book.

In the afternoons, the villagers go bathing and swimming in the Neiman River. The young people cross over the river on foot and run through the meadows on the other side. Some of them, however, rent a rowboat from Gentiles for a few cents and go for a ride down the river, singing songs on the river. And when night falls and the heavens are ablaze with stars and the shine of the full moon shines is reflected in the water, they imagine they are in Eretz Israel under its starry skies, and a song is carried over the Neiman: "How lovely are the nights in Canaan"!

When the sun sets, the small train arrives, huffing and puffing. Castle Street, which leads to the railway station, becomes crowded. Everyone is going to the train: some to meet a close relative or friend, some just out of curiosity and some who cannot wait till the next morning and want to pick up, right on the spot, a letter which is brought by train and which the postal clerk distributes a few minutes later, although it is already well after the official mail delivery hours.

The small train reminds the residents that their village is not separated from the world. There are cities and people, and if you want to, you can sit on the train early the next day and go directly to Novoyelnya and from there the way is open to Vilna and Warsaw.

– Supper is over. Sometimes supper consists of a dish of groats with milk and sometimes of a potato with its skin and a herring with a small glass of chicory, and sometimes of a piece of sausage with tea. And if the weather is nice, people sit on their porches and breathe in the fresh air and talk with their neighbors.

The young people are busy in the evenings. The "Mendele" library is open and they go there to exchange books. The theatre group, under the direction of

Alter Chemes (Shmulevitch) is putting on a new performance. In the *Hechalutz* chapter, a representative from the drama club has come just this very evening, and the people are going there to hear his talk. Late at night, when nearly everyone is asleep, loud singing is heard from the local chapter of *Hashomer Hatzair*. The stamping of feet while dancing the *hora* awakens and disturbs the older generation. They remember how they were once young and used to dance. They let out a sigh:- Oh, God, where have the former years gone?

*

The village has become quiet. Somewhere from a henhouse, a cricket chirps-chir, chir chir, its grating sound piercing the nocturnal tranquility. From the gentile pigsties, the oinking of pigs is carried through the village- oink, oink, oink. The Gentiles sleep soundly, the pigs in the pens give them rest. Jews sleep fitfully- they dream about making a living, providing a dowry for their daughters, paying their children's tuition and about good policemen who (don't) take bribes and about the gentiles with their pigs which have recently begun oinking at them very noisily like the Berlin swine: "Jew, Jew, Jew"!

Under Soviet Rule

On September 1, 1939, the radio broadcast the jolting report of the outbreak of the Second World War.

A few days went by and the war was only a remote idea in the minds of the villagers- it hadn't reached here yet. The newspapers stopped coming. The radio reports are confused. You can't get at the truth. The Germans are advancing, sowing death and destruction, and in our village people believe the Germans will be quickly defeated. It's a mere trifle that England and France are also fighting them! Meanwhile, life goes on as usual, almost without change.

Suddenly – confusion in the village! The police are running away in great panic without even trying to burn documents. The police officers, Frantzish- kevitch and Mitskovsky, reveal a secret that the Red Army is approaching. This report makes hearts quiver with happiness. We are simply overwhelmed with joy. The end of the war has come and mainly an end to the detested Polish anti-Semitic rule.

Several days go by and we still don't see anyone. The village is without leadership. People are eager to see their liberators, but apparently they are not hurrying to get here.

And look! Here they are! In all, a few uniformed men, in long gray cloaks, caps with red stripes, big boots, and their faces all smiles. We hug and kiss them. The young people can't keep away from them, thirstily swallowing down whatever they say. And they, those in uniform, can't stop telling about and describing the happy Soviet life. Eyes light up, the fantasy plays itself out, what a splendid time has come for everyone- and mainly, in fact, for the youth.

A meeting takes place in the big synagogue- Jews and Gentiles together. A representative of the new authority is talking - Dorosevitch, a former resident of the village, Vereskova. He calls for brotherhood between Jews and non Jews. He tells about the Soviet paradise and closes with a shout of Hurrah! for the "Father of the People" - Josef Vissarionovitch Stalin.

Hurrah! Hurrah!- an answer reverberates between the wall of the synagogue. The Torah scrolls in the Holy Ark wake up from their rest - Who is shouting like this in a sacred place? The window panes rattle and the carved cherubic angels over the Holy Ark seem to be getting smaller under so many painfully stinging Gentile glances.

My friend, the writer and educator, Zavel Reinovitch, a refugee in the village who is inclined to be cynical, calls to me: - You know why people are shouting "Hurrah" when Stalin's name is mentioned? - It's Hebrew- *Hu ra*! (He is bad).

For the time being, Soviet authority in the village ended with that meeting. Only Dorosevitch remained there, and everything was still going on as in the past under the old regime.

Meanwhile, the only change that took place was in the Tarbut School. As the use of Hebrew was strictly forbidden, classes were now taught in Yiddish. New teachers, mostly refugees, were hired and Zavel Reinovitch became the pedagogical director. Since there were no textbooks in Yiddish, the pupils studied from handwritten texts. The literature lessons with Zavel Reinovitch were hours of deep, soul stirring-deliberation. He led them through the noble examples of Yiddish literature - harnessed to grandfather's pony, laughed Shalom Aleichem's redemptive laugh, and when it came to Peretz's works, he taught them how the links of the good qualities in the golden chain of Yiddish were forged.

People were very happy that Yiddish was now granted equal status with other languages and enjoyed full government support. Who, then, could have imagined, in those first days, that in the new academic year 1940, a parents meeting would be called at which it was proposed to the parents to decide whether the school should stop teaching Yiddish and be turned into a Russian ten year school.

As things are done in the Soviet Union, where "the people alone decide their destiny", Poupko the shoemaker, an ignorant, loud mouthed Jew, was well prepared by the authorities, and he - the true "representative of the people"- stood up at the meeting and gave a speech, claiming that the people don't need a Yiddish school. "No! We parents want our children to learn only Russian!" The chairman then asked: "Who is opposed?" a question which smacks of threats and danger. Fingers were clenched in fists, but not one hand was raised against the proposal. And thus came about the end of the Yiddish (Jewish) middle school. The former Tarbut School began a new Russian metamorphosis.

Zavel Reinovitch left Lubtch. At out parting, he said with bitterness: "The end of Jewish schools is also the end of Jewish (Yiddish) national life".

On April 1, 1940, Lubtch rose to greatness. On that day it became the administrative and political center of the newly carved out Lubtch region, which took in an enormous area from the Naliboka district, including Tschars, Niegnievitch, Delatitch, Veroskova, Zenevitch, as far as the town of Lachovitch not far from the Neiman glass works.

Dozens of offices and bureaus sprung up in the village like mushrooms after a rain. First of all, there was the regional executive committee with all its departments: finance and taxation, education, health, communal economy, agriculture, statistics, planning and others. Departments of various governmental organizations were also opened such as *Zagotsherna*,(grains preparation), *Plodoovosht* (potato and vegetables preparation), *Zagotlion* (flax preparation) *Soyozpushnina*, *Potrev-soyoz* (cooperative trading) *Narkomzag* (government bank), *Lessplav*(milk production), *Melnitshni-Kombinat* (which united all the mills in the region, wood and electric combinations, sawmills, steel mills, and the electric power station), a court, militia, and a whole series of other bureaus and organizations.

To this we must add the bureau of the town council-*Mestetshkovi Sovet* with Yossel Kapushtshevsky as chairman, the so-called mayor or the village; two middle schools - Russian and White Russian, library, movie theater, hotel, hospital, ambulatoria, professional fire fighters organization with over two dozen salaried fire fighters- Jews and Gentiles; restaurant, food store, cold drinks and ice cream kiosk, department store (fancy goods, shoes, fabrics and perfumes) pharmacy, and a *Lessplov* store managed by the brothers, Paul and Meir Kapushtshevsky (who distributed merchandise to women refugees); buying center for small hides and pig bristles, store selling crude oil to peasants after supplying government products (grains, potatoes, flax, etc) - the former flax merchant, David Yedidovitch worked there; store selling books and musical instruments; bakery, bathhouse equipped with bathtubs and kept open all day long, small factory where they pickled mushrooms and produced wine from *grabinas* (the sour fruit of the grabina trees) managed by Shmuel Leibel Feivishevitch. There were also warehouses for grains, potatoes and vegetables, which the peasants were forced to supply to the government.

Hundreds of people were given employment in offices, enterprises, warehouses and stores-there was simply a shortage of workers. Anyone who knew a little Russian became an official. Peasants even came from surrounding towns to work in the village. Moshe Persky was the head bookkeeper at *Potrevsoyoz*, which did business in the entire region. About 15 or 16 Jewish teenage boys and girls worked in the same bureau. Yanes Itzkovitch was the head bookkeeper of the finances and taxation office.

The workshop owners, shoemakers and quilt makers, Jews and gentiles, were organized into a cooperative (*Artel*), which was swamped with work. The tailors did likewise. The chairman of both cooperatives was the quilt maker, Leova Levin.

Wagon drivers and some of the town vehicle drivers transported merchandise from the bases in the district city of Baranovitch, to which the region belonged. They also brought brandy from the Mir distillery and transported agricultural products to the train station at Novoyelnia.

According to official statistics from September 1940, 2,115 people lived in Lubtch, of whom approximately 1,500 were Jews, including 35 Jewish refugees from the Polish areas occupied by the Germans. Among the latter were writers, teachers, engineers, doctors, technicians and other specialists.

200 Soviet citizens still lived in the town. Among these were many Jews who worked in all the offices and organizations. Most of them worked in the Communist Party institutions, party regional committees, NKVD, party cabinet, *Voyenkomat,* [Military commissariat], *Osoaviachim, Komsomol* [Soviet Youth Organization], etc. It is worth mentioning here that the female secretary of the *Komsomol* - Katya- later remained with the Germans and distinguished herself with her sadism by torturing and murdering Jews. When the Germans were finally driven out, she was shot by the Russians.

In general, the Jews of Lubtch breathed more freely, economically speaking. They did not have any worries about finding jobs or making a living, and the anti-Semitism calmed down. As the Soviets had been in control for only a short time, there were still considerable reserves of merchandise remaining from Polish times and also as most of the peasants were not yet collectivized and supplied an abundance of agricultural products, the economic situation was, generally speaking, quite satisfactory, without any comparison to the difficult situation in the USSR itself. People were not bad off and were able to manage quite easily. Of course, with time, the reserves of merchandise would run out and the collectivized farmers would have little to sell in the city.

The former store owners and traders were sorely embittered, however. Their livelihood was cut off all at once. The larger stores were able to hold out for a few months until their entire stock was sold off. It was a long period of agony for Jewish business. Later the tax office imposed heavy taxes on them and took away their entire wealth. Some of the storekeepers worked on the black market while others who knew Russian managed to get government positions. But their anger was great and was expressed especially on the day the Soviet authorities fled the village. At that time a few former storeowners - with a fire of revenge in their eyes - swept the pavement in honor of the arriving German forces and laughed at the few Jews who were fleeing with the Soviets. May it not be to their disgrace! The poor things didn't know what was awaiting them.

In the one government store, one was able to freely buy bread (baked in tins so that it would be a bigger bargain) [*pripiak*], cans of real coffee which no one in the village used unless suffering from diarrhea, large bottles of "denaturate", which no one used either, "Fruktavi Tea", (a tea substitute made from dried leaves and waste products of fruits) and brandy. Day and night wagon drivers delivered full barrels of brandy, but it was all winy. The peasants no longer saved their money to buy dirt. They poured out their grief in "bitter drops".

From time to time they sold sugar, a cheaper kind of candy, cigarettes, soap and matches. But supplies and purchases were limited and you had to stand in line a whole day. Cold drinks were made with saccharin and people were able to get ice cream only when sugar was available.

In the second government store, you could always freely buy cheap perfumes, various and gaudy broaches, beaded necklaces and other items. From time to time, shoes, men's underwear, galoshes, socks and cheap items for women were brought in. In such cases, customers were already standing in line around midnight and it would often happen that after standing 10-12 hours on line, they got nothing. However, as mentioned earlier, people had not yet begun to feel shortages in goods, since they still had reserves from before and they were also able to buy "behind and around".

The garden surrounding the old castle was opened to the public. They made a park there - paved paths, put up benches, planted flowers, and young people would spend their time there until late at night, singing and looking for quiet, intimate little corners. In the uncompleted Polish warehouse for harvested crops next to the former Polish police station, a movie theater was opened which also served as place for people to meet.

The three study rooms and synagogues became produce warehouses where they gathered and stored the crops which the peasants had to supply and deliver to the government, but the churches were untouched. Every Sunday the Christians said their prayers there as before.

Jewish houses of over 100 square meters were confiscated. The owners had to leave their homes, and various bureaus and institutions set up quarters there. Houses from 80-100 sq.m. were nationalized. The difference consisted in the fact that the owners of the smaller dwellings remained in their homes but had to pay rent. They also had to take in neighbors, mainly newly arriving Soviet people and refugees.

The market place was moved to the former cattle market opposite the Gemina building. Stores were used for offices, warehouses and government shops. A plan was prepared - summer 1941 - to turn the former market place into a park and to set up a monument to Stalin in the middle.

In the village, there was also a radio connection which was installed in nearly all Soviet state communities. The radio broadcast news and folk songs over loudspeakers several times a day into the streets. Only a few people had the right to own a radio set. And in general hardly anyone had a radio set even in Polish times. For a few rubles, you could install a receiver in your home and in this way you had a home radio set, and the government authorities were warned of the "unsuitable" foreign propaganda. Rosenberg, an engineer and refugee from Lodz and his assistant, a technician, were in charge of the radio connection.

The "Mendele" library was closed in January, 1940. The books, which had been purchased by collecting money penny by penny over a course of so many years, were placed in a cellar which was sealed up with lead and there the books languished. In its stead, a new library was opened in Yosel Breinkes' former store. The new library contained 2,000 books, of which there were but 100 Jewish books from Soviet publishers. The librarian was Chaya Niegnievitsky.

All my requests regarding selecting books from the "Mendele" library which were considered legal in the USSR and putting them in the new library had gone unanswered.

All cultural undertakings in the village as well as meetings and assemblies were mixed, for Jews and Christians together. A Yiddish song or short talk was seldom heard. From time to time, the writer of these lines also had a "referat" in Yiddish on a literary theme which had to be squeezed into the "Sodom bed" of the Soviet "Freedom of the Word".

Every Sunday evening, dances were held mainly for young people. On these evenings, the separations between Jewish and Christian youth were thrown aside. A Jewish boy could flirt with a Christian girl and vice versa. Actually, this was only the beginning. The short time of Soviet rule was meanwhile the most important factor which managed somewhat to slow down a process of a more intimate drawing nearer of the young people of two worlds which, until then, had been completely separate. The first signs of such a drawing nearer called forth much worry and sorrow in Jewish homes and not one mother raised a finger "God forbid the moment should come"...

A new Jewish generation was growing up which believed that the new regime opened wider horizons and would give them the opportunity to study and attain something in life.

The youth had really blossomed. Young men and women were tall and good-looking. It was a pleasure to look at them. I especially remember Bruchke Gorodiski who, as a child, experienced the bitter taste of need in his mother's house, as she was a woman whose husband had disappeared before granting her a divorce. Bruchke grew up to be tall and handsome and also had unusual talents: he played the accordion and violin, sang and danced well, laughed happily and made everyone around him laugh. He worked in *Komsomol* and a great career was predicted for him.

We must note further that Lubtch was one of the smallest villages where none of the local Jewish population was arrested or sent away - not even the wealthiest Jews in the village. Who knows if it wouldn't have been better for them had fortune not favored them at that time?

*

On June 21, 1941, an evening of dance with an artistic program was held in the village. Afterwards, the young people strolled about the streets until late at night, singing and laughing loudly. No one had the slightest idea of what was going to happen a few hours later.

At 9:00 the next morning, June 22, the news was broadcast over the loudspeakers that the Germans had attacked the USSR. This was the way Hitler was paying back his partner - in the 1939 treaty - for the great economic and political help which he received from the Soviets against the free, democratic world.

The loudspeakers also broadcast Molotov's speech. People listened quietly and calmly. They had such faith in the strength of the Red Army that they even thought the USSR had begun the war and that Berlin would fall within a few days.

People could hardly sleep the first night of the war. All through the night airplanes, roaring overhead, were flying towards Minsk. Everyone was sure that these were our - Soviet - planes, flying back after bombing German positions.

In the morning, mobilized soldiers from the entire region began assembling in the park by the castle. They were arranged in groups and were waiting for the army representative to come and take them away.

At the same time, several Soviet party officials suddenly approached in a completely shot up tender. They had fled, in confusion, from the attacking German army.

There was a terrible panic. The Soviet people and their families began fleeing towards Minsk. The mobilized soldiers were instructed to go home and await further orders. The NKVD managed to burn some documents and also fled.

Terror befell the Jews - terror of the approaching enemy, but they didn't want to flee and save themselves. They were still hoping to find a way to survive the German Amalek.

We, however, decide to escape, quickly throw a few things on a wagon harnessed to a little horse, leave doors and windows open - free for the robbers, and seat the women and children on the wagon, all ready to set off on a distant and difficult journey.

Hennia Baksht, Moshe Levin's wife, dressed up in holiday attire, comes out of her house and calls to us:

"Where are you running? Why are you so afraid? Take my advice and stay home"!

Her mother-in-law, Frumeh Levin, lets out a sigh: "Oy. Woe to us"! and says: "God only knows who will be jealous of whom"!

The sun sets, painting the horizon red like a bloody lake. The houses are wrapped in a cover of dark blue. Lips fall upon the walls of the house and kiss the boards. Father's hand touches the "mezuzah", tears streaming down his face. His glance wanders over the houses of relatives and friends, etched in his heart, which is now oppressed as if squeezed in pliers. A pull on the reins, the wheels rattle over the pavement, the village behind us, sunk in the grayness of the twilight.

Dear village, our loving home, will we ever see you again? ...

On The Ruins Of Lubtch

A cold December day, 1945. Snow has not yet fallen, but the wintry cold bites the exposed parts of the body.

The village lies in ruins. Almost nothing remains of the Jewish street, only mounds of dirt like graves, and piles of bricks from ovens. Smoke-covered walls with torn down doors and windows are still standing from a number of houses. The wind weeps inside here with a sigh, the only lamenter of those who were once here and whose bones are today sown and scattered over gentile fields.

Today, however, the wind is not the only one bemoaning the lost community. Three more Jews have come to help it weep and wail.

Three Jews are standing there: the elderly father, his son and son-in-law. Three not very passionate Jews who have come back to the village, from the far and long, agonizing journey of the few remaining survivors. The dream they had for many years of staying alive to come back here, now lies all run out as they stand by this hill of earth which was once their home.

Father's eyes no longer cry; there are no more tears left in them, only grief and mourning. His lips mumble something, we can't hear what he's saying. Whether it's a *kaddish* [Liturgical doxology said by the mourner] for his mother - Rashe - whose 90 years were ended by a German bullet, a *kaddish* for his brothers and sisters, for his large, many-branched family of which no trace remains. And perhaps it is a quiet thanks to God, Master of the Universe, with a blessing for his son-in-law, who led him out of the burning hell just in time, saved him, his wife and children?

He suddenly bends down and looks for something in the little hill and pulls out a rusty door hinge. A fountain of tears gushes forth again and with these tears waters the last trace of his former home.

Three Jews from Lubtch walk through the streets. They're looking for traces of former Jewish homes. Here stood Chaim-Isser's house. Here was Moshke Berezinski's house, and right there was the spacious home of Chaim-Leib Levin, the rich manufacturer and store owner. Every mound of earth, every pile of bricks - another name which is etched in our memories. And right over there lived Dr. Rabinovitch, who married Yenta, the rabbi's educated daughter in the ghetto. Dr. Rabinovitch who, before his death, spit in impure German faces just as his father-in law, the rabbi, would do whenever a pig crossed in front of him on his way.

The street where the Gentiles live is intact. They were protected and warned by the oinking of the pigs. Today, the gentiles are the only proprietors in the village. They are already building new town-style cottages on Jewish places. The houses of the gentiles are filled with Jewish things. Even Jewish candlesticks decorate their homes - the only thing missing are Sabbath candles. Familiar Gentiles come over and wonder what we're doing there.

There are also Jews in the village- the elderly Shalom Leibovitch with his children. They were saved by joining up with the partisans. Shalom runs over to us and hugs and kisses us. There we were, two Jews standing in the middle of the former market place among the ruins, squeezing and kissing one another and weeping aloud, shoulders moving convulsively and lips trembling, unable to utter a single word.

At Shalom's house: a bottle of liquor on the table and a bite to eat with the drink. The last Jews of Lubtch are sitting around the table, drinking "*L'chaim!*" [To Life!]that they lived to meet again. Each "*L'chaim*" accompanied by a sigh, every drop of liquor salted with tears. Tongues chatter. We remember and remember events, happenings, episodes and names. Dozens of years of people's lives roll by and everything comes to the same- terrible end.

*

Three Jews are walking on a cold morning. They are making a pilgrimage to Vorovievitch, to the communal grave of the Jews from Lubtch. The cold wind drives them on, chasing and whipping them- Go faster, go faster! The Jews of Lubtch were driven along the same way, their heads and shoulders bloodily cut by whips and rubber poles - Faster! Faster!

Close by the right side of the Lubtch- Novogrudek road, not far from the town of Vorovievitch is the communal grave. A young peasant shows us the place. He tells us how the Jews were murdered there. He actually enjoys telling the story:

- Many, he says, fell into the pit while still alive and that's how they were buried. The Jewess, Sara (Sara Pertchik), a "beauty", was lightly wounded in her foot and asked us to save her. It was a pity to bury such a "beauty" alive! We could have played a game with such a "beauty", but the Germans ordered us to fill in the grave with soil as quickly as possible.

Photo of his tombstone: At the grave of Yehoshua-Yaakov Feivishevitch in Munich

Jews of Lubtch, control yourselves and don't choke that non-Jewish boy to death so that you defile that sacred place with his impure blood. Don't let your anger get the better of you! Old father, wipe away your bloody tears and don't let that non-Jewish boy have any joy from seeing you weep.

Three Jews bend down, take up handfuls of cold soil, warm it with their fingers- to transfer the heat of heart and soul to the soil- and put it to their lips, breathe their living Jewish breath on the soil and throw it back onto the communal grave - a greeting to the martyrs of Lubtch: Jews of Lubtch are still alive! They have outlived the Nazi Amelek - the Jewish People lives!

Another glance behind, a final look, forever - and our feet carry us further and further away from the defiled gentile earth and then - on the distant, agonizing way to the shores of the Jewish Homeland, which we have been dreaming about. Will we get there?...

Note: Our father, Yehoshua-Yaakov Feivishevitch, unfortunately, did not live to reach the shores of the Land of Israel. He passed away in Germany on 13 Adar 5707, Eve of Purim, 1947 and was buried in Munich.

[Pages 47-51]

Chronicles Of The Jewish Community In Lubtch

by Hilel Shmulovitch

Translated from the Hebrew by Ann Belinsky

Lubtch was a small town. To the north the Neiman flowed by, and behind it grew eternal, thick forests that spread over wide areas; in the west, downstream from Lubtch were the cities of Ivyeh and Lida; on the south-west side, at a distance of twenty-three kilometers was the city of Novogrudek, where the administrative institutions of the entire region were situated. Lubtch was connected to Novogrudek by trade and cultural connections.

A small train, remnant of the days of the First World War, connected Novogrudek to Lubtch. The railway station in "Castle Street" was used as a social meeting place for the inhabitants of the town who came there to meet the visitors; to receive mail and newspapers, and to carry on idle conversation about matters of supreme importance.

The Jewish community in Lubtch was resident on the lands of the aristocrat Peker, who was apparently close to the Tzar, and was one of his advisors for a month of the year. After his death, his wife married again to an aristocrat called Nabokov, who became owner of the estate.

Proof that there was a community in this place in the 17th century is found in the book of Dr Raphael Mahler "*Divrei Yemei Yisrael b'Dorot HaAhronim*" ("History of the Jews in the Last Generations" (3rd volume, 12th Chapter, Page 188).

Dr Mahler writes: Prior to the Chassidism movement founded by the Ba'al Shem Tov, there are also indications of a new behavior, either on the part of individuals or groups, who were called by the people of their generation "*chassidim*" (pious, devout ones). Regarding ascetic cabalists, the philosopher Shlomo Maimon writes in his memoirs: "One Shimon, from the town of Lubtch, tortured himself, wore sackcloth, and took upon himself "repentance of the Exile" and "repentance weighed in proportion to one's sin", and finally starved himself to death."

According to this evidence, the event occurred before the appearance of the "Ba'al Shem Tov", who was born in the year 1700 approximately, meaning that the community was already in existence in this area in the 17th century.

Another proof of the early presence of the community can be found in the "*Sefer Yechusin*" [Book of Lineages], which was written and edited by R' Tzvi Shimshi (Shimshelovitch), father of the President of Israel, Yitzchak Ben Tzvi.

In his book, R' Tzvi Shimshi describes his forefathers, from whom the whole family stemmed - "the couple Eliyahu Shimshelevitch and his wife Chana Feygah, who lived in Lubtch, between the years 5460- 5535, that is 1700-1775." This means that at the beginning of the 18th century, a community was active there.

Likewise, the Charter of Privileges also testifies to the existence of a Jewish community in the 17th century. These rights were given to the Jews of Lubtch on the 30th January 1690, by Jan Kazimirez Sapieha, the big "hetman" [chief, leader] of the Greater Principality of Lithuania, governor of Vilna and the district. We bring a translation of this charter in this book [Pages 11-15].

It may be that a community existed in the area before the 17th century, but we have no proof. However it is clear that the Jewish community lived in the area for hundreds of years - until it was destroyed and annihilated without leaving a single mark that would tell about its past.

The Livelihood and Occupations Of The Jews Of Lubtch

The town of Lubtch was blessed with fresh air and a wonderful view. The river flowed past it and forests surrounded it. And within this panoramic gem the Jewish community fought their daily war of existence.

The farming environment influenced the socio-economic situation of the Jews in the town, and the economic reality also had serious repercussions on the cultural activity of the community.

Jews of the place usually made their livelihood from trade and serving as middlemen with the Christian population in the villages. Although it was a farming area, the Jews themselves did not work on the land (except for a vegetable garden by the house for personal consumption), and not even industry developed there. The Jews earned their livelihood by very hard work and toil. Every tremor in the yields of the crops of the farmers in the area affected the economic situation that became worse and worse, because the anti-Semitic Polish government increased its interference and pressure in matters of trade, squeezed the Jews out and raised difficulties and restrictions on trade. From here one can understand that very rich people were absent in the town.

*

Close to the beginning of the Holocaust, the community included 320 households, who found their livelihood according to the division as follows:

Trade and Industry (51%)

Peddlers	58	Flour mill owners	4
Restaurants	7	Candy industry and vinegar	2
Hotels	3	Tree traders (foresters)	2
Making soda and ice-cream	1	Pharmacists (owning a pharmacy)	1
Horse dealers	9	Perfumeries	1
Leasers of orchards	2	General stores	24
Fish traders	1	Shoe stores	2
Flax and flaxseed traders	8	Grocery stores	8
Dairy owners and cheese industry	8	Material and textile stores	11
Sawmills and power station	2	Flour and grain stores	6

Craftsmen and professionals (37%)

Tailors	14	Butchers (owning butcher shops)	17
Seamstresses	4	Barbers (owning barbershops)	4
Boot-makers	11	Glaziers (selling glass)	2
Sewers	3	Metalworkers	1
Carpenters	6	Painters	2
Cap-makers	2	Photographers	1
Bakers	11	Wagon drivers	10
Blacksmiths	10	Watchmaker (selling also)	1
Tinsmiths	2	Electricians	1
Harness and saddle makers	4	Fishermen	2
Builders	2	Chimneysweeps	1
Rope-makers	3	Shepherds	1

Various (12%)

Doctors	2	Rabbis	1
Teachers	6	Ritual slaughterers	1
Clerks	7	Sextons	2
Community maintainers	1	Cantors	2
Undertakers	1	Various professionals	4
Ritual Bath Tenders	1	Yeshiva pupils	5

A total of 307 employed workers
Unemployed - 8
Widows making their living in whatever was available - 5

The population numbered approximately 1230 individuals on the eve of the Holocaust, as follows:

Heads of the Household	275	Of whom were widowers	17
Married women	295	Of whom were widows	37
Male children	340	Female children	320

In 208 households there were children, divided as follows:

Number of families	Number of children in the family	Total children
61	1	61
87	2	174
83	3	249
41	4	84
8	5	40
4	6	24
4	7	26
Total 268		660

[Pages 51-53]
A Jewish Town Named Delyatichi (Delatitch)

by Dov Cohen

Translated from the Hebrew by Ann Belinsky

In the First World War, I was still very young, but I remember the heavy artillery battle that took place between the German army and the Russian army. All the inhabitants of Lubtch were evacuated to the forest and we remained there all night; the next day, after the artillery barrage had been silenced, we returned to the town. We were "greeted" by the Germany army band, playing triumphal marches.

Since the Neiman river was now the Front, we were forced to leave the town again. The inhabitants were transferred first to a village by Silov, and when the battles intensified, the Germans transferred us further away to the town of Svilslotch - there we remained until the war was over. There I also began my classes at the *cheder* [elementary school].

Dov Cohen

We returned to a Delatitch which had been reduced to rubble and lay in ruins. The yard of our house was cut up by seven bunkers, but thanks to the help from the United States, we repaired our house and filled in the trenches in the yard. Our livelihood was ensured because we had opened a grocery store, where we later sold fabrics as well.

We began to organize community life in the town, we repaired the synagogue and built a bath-house. A branch of the *Keren Kayemet Leyisrael* [Jewish National Fund] was established, and my father, Yosef, of blessed memory, was the official agent of the Fund in the town and even organized various money raising drives.

My father was also the treasurer of the community income, which came from donations in the synagogue and from leasing the parcel of land by the banks of the Neiman to wood traders, who came for the summer months.

Delatitch was known as having good prayer leaders: my father - who had a pleasant voice, who read the Torah and blew the *shofar* [a musical instrument made of a ram horn, used for Jewish religious purposes] on Rosh Hashana and Yom Kippur. Avraham Gorodisky - with a bass voice - who prayed *shacharit*[daily morning prayer], and his brother Moshe who sang the *mussaf* [additional] prayers.

During the Ten Days of Penitence between Rosh Hashana and Yom Kippur, there was a lot of tension in the town, especially after the sermon of R' Yaakov Baksht, who expounded the law and preached every Yom Kippur.

At Simchat-Torah - there was much rejoicing in the town. Rabbi Beynish would dance with the Torah scroll in his arms, and everyone joined in enthusiastically; it was known that people who had heard a nice tune during the year kept it secret in order to sing it on Simchat Torah- as a surprise.

On the evening of Passover - the *matzot* [unleavened bread for Passover] were baked and it was a whole ritual. In our house, the house and oven were made kosher, and a large room was allocated for rolling the *matzot*. The utensils which were stored from year to year were taken out and the work began, from rolling and pricking the dough through to putting it straight into the hot oven. Every family baked much more than was needed in order to distribute it to the needy, and also part went to the Gentile customers who liked the *matzot* very much. My mother of blessed memory also gave *matzot* to poor, needy gentiles.

*

My father, R' Yosef Cohen of blessed memory, was the ritual slaughterer. To earn a living from "slaughtering" in the one town alone was difficult, but luckily, in the winter there was a lot of work, since the butchers from Vilna came to the area to buy calves, which they brought to Delatitch for slaughtering. In 1934 the police began to harass my father, sudden searches were made in our house and there were night time ambushes in order to catch father in the act of slaughtering. Finally he was caught, the calves brought for slaughter were confiscated, and my father had a court trial that cost a lot of money and caused the family much sorrow.

In 1934 I made *aliyah* [immigration] to Eretz-Israel, where I built my house, and married a girl from Rishon Letzion. My brother Aryeh made *aliyah* to Eretz-Israel in 1939, and set up his house and family in Kfar Saba.

My family was annihilated by the Nazis, who arrested all the Jews of Delatitch and sent them to the Lubtch ghetto, from there they were transferred a few months later to the Novogrudek ghetto. My three sisters managed to escape from the ghetto and reach the partisans, where they fought until they fell heroically.

[Pages 53-59]

My Hometown

by Frumka Eshed (Asherovsky)

Translated from the Hebrew by Ann Belinsky

The town was encircled by a very pleasant frame, vast fields on one side and the wide Neiman, on the other side. Behind the river were grazing meadows, and behind them - the villages. The third side - the "squire's" estate, and on the fourth side on the back of the hill surrounded by a huge garden, - was the palace of the well-known Nabokov family. At the foot of the hill was the river. Between the houses of the town and the Neiman, were the vegetable gardens of the Jews, inhabitants of the town.

In the middle of the town was the market place and in its center the shops were arranged in a square. This was the shopping center of the town. The market area was surrounded by houses, also in a square formation, from which the streets of the town led out, all leading from the market - to the fields, to the palace and to the close-by town - Delatitch. By the market was the "*Shulhoif*" [The backyard of the synagogue] - where there were three synagogues and a bath-house.

Frumka Eshed (Asherovsky)

Lubtch was a remote town, in an area of poverty-stricken villages. There was meager farming and no industry. The Neiman River hinted that there were distant locations where the people and places were well established and richer. The timber rafts floated on the Neiman, to the large centers, and added to the income of the town; the raft captains would stop at the town to stock up on food supplies for the continuation of the trip, and sometimes they needed clear markings on the raft: I and my brother would be busy at night time cutting out letters from thick white cardboard for the rafts.

In the winter days, when the river was covered by a thick layer of ice, it was used as a wide area for making trips and ice-skating. The towering palace was silent and locked most days of the year, only in the summer did its owners come, and added some interest for the Lubtch townspeople. However it is doubtful that they also added to the livelihood of the townspeople.

The town on its wooden structures (there were only two houses made of stone there, one was the home of the wealthiest man in the town), did not lie on the main transport routes and was not involved in commercial and social ties with other towns. In the autumn and winter especially, the few connections that did exist, were blocked. The town curled up then in mud, snow and frost and sank into the poverty-stricken daily life which continued sluggishly as if it were cut off from the world and had no connection to the goings-on in the big world.

The inhabitants of Lubtch were mainly Jews, and the gentiles - a few Belarussians and Russians, were mainly from the authorities, the priest, manager of the government shop *Hay'sh* and a few families that seemed well-off. On Sundays, gentiles from places outside of Lubtch would come to pray in the church, but during the week, the town had a Jewish character.

Trade was not abundant in the town. Only a few were well-to-do traders: traders of flax that was combed in the town itself, horse and cattle traders, fabrics traders - these made up the more well-off layer of society. The town was mainly based on practical work. The inhabitants were mostly craftsmen, and made their living also from the surrounding villages. There were taverns for the farmers. The vegetable gardens by the houses and the cows were of great help for existence. The townspeople also enjoyed the fish from the Neiman, which were sold cheaply.

My memories of the town of my childhood start from the beginning of the [20th] century. I was then very young, and two outstanding events have remained in my memory since then: the fires in the summer that regularly broke out in the town every year, and the muddy Novogrudek Street which led from the market, encircled the streets and had ditches on the side to drain the swamps. Once, when I was crossing the trench by a little bridge made of boards, I tripped and fell into the trench and almost drowned; by chance a girl from the market passed and saw something pink that was sticking out of the water and pulled me out.

These two phenomena, the fire and the swamps, bothered the inhabitants very much. The winter months were long and difficult, when the children were closed inside and locked up in the houses cramped with people, the windows were sealed, with no ventilation. With the beginning of the thaw, the children burst outside into the wide open space, but the streams of water and the deep mud in which the farmers' wagon left furrows were an obstacle to the springtime mischievousness of the children. When the summer came, the fear of fires would descend on the town. They always started at night-time, accompanied by the thunder of warning bells tolling from the Christian church, the trumpets of the firemen. The fear of the fires was etched deep in the heart of the children (although the fires never reached our home, and there was an assumption that the swamps in the streets were what had stopped the calamity). And the fear of the flames which consumed the houses without restraint has remained etched in my memory. More than once we sat at nights, on our packed bags, ready to flee, when the fires were raging in the neighboring streets. More than once children disappeared from fear during the fires, and were found after great efforts, even in the local cemetery.

The prevailing idea in the minds of the public was that the fires were a result of arson, as a way to get rich from the insurance; but as are the ways of Satan, there were no rich people in the town despite the many fires. The fires were so frequent that they were also used as a guide to the yearly calendar, to mark the dates of birth and other events: "that happened during the great fire"; or before or after it, etc. Another catastrophic event that would visit at the town was malaria, due to the swamp. The inhabitants were continually forced to swallow quinine.

Novice doctors came to the town, remained for a short time and left. People would say that every doctor left his mark behind - in the cemetery. In the case of the pox the doctor was careful not to enter the house, and passed on instructions from the outside, by the window. The instructions could be summarized as "Don't scratch your face" - and that was all, and "If the child cannot stop herself - bind her hands together". One doctor, Dr Shapira, remained in the town more than the other doctors, about ten years. He was a tall man, wide-faced, full of energy, devoted to his patients, but he too left for Vilna and became well-known there.

The birth rate among the Jews was high, but the death rate of babies was high too. In many families there were ten children, but usually several of them died. The children were the top priority of the parents. Much attention was paid to education; also orphans and children of poverty stricken families learnt at the *cheder* [elementary school] from the age of four. The girls were taught by special "*melamdim*" [elementary school teachers] who were thought to be inferior to other *melamdim* [for the boys]. For example, my *melamed* was a lumberjack by profession and became a *melamed* after a work accident. The girls' *melamdim* became teachers late in life, and the schoolroom was a room also used by the married son or daughter of the *melamed* for their trade.

The parents were interested that their children would study, and for this they sacrificed themselves, even the poorest of parents looked for a way to finance their sons' education. If they did well in Torah studies, they were sent to *yeshivot* [Talmudic colleges] in other towns, since there was no *Talmud-Torah* in the town and no *yeshiva*. Usually they learnt in the town until the age of fifteen or sixteen. The girls, as usual, were deprived of learning. Some learnt with private teachers to write a letter in Yiddish and addresses in Russian. Whoever did not continue in his studies would join his father's business, learnt a trade, or was unemployed. Some of the girls learnt sewing.

Until I left the town in 1907, there was no library, and no newspaper reached the town.

With the revolution in 1905, the revolutionary spirit penetrated the town too; young men and women gathered together, sang revolutionary songs, embroidered a red flag, wore embroidered Russian shirts, mainly colored bordeaux. There were extremists who made speeches in the synagogues in order to win over souls for their revolutionary ideology, to revolt against conventional ideas. "Brochures" appeared which were secretly passed from hand to hand, for fear of the authorities and also of the parents who were against the idea of the revolution.

The young men and women sang revolutionary songs at wedding ceremonies of young couples in order to demonstrate.

It was an important time of awakening in the town, the freeze was broken in the lives of the youth. Understandably, it aroused disagreements between fathers and sons, but the period was very short. Again the youth sank into their freeze, and the revolution - as if it had never occurred. It seemed that the town had become more impoverished and more remote than ever.; many youth left the town and wandered to the large cities - Minsk, Lodz, Warsaw, Vilna, (mainly to the cities where they had relatives), others went overseas.

The young people who went far, to the large cities, subconsciously took the image of their hometown with them, and being in a strange environment, were often overcome by longings for what they had left behind - their parent's house, the way of life of the small community, the weekdays and festive days, the vegetable garden behind the house, and the Neiman river. From a distance, the steady and compelling system of the town's social and ethical customs was painted in all its beauty. They themselves felt detached, far from their town, and had not yet been absorbed into the new society. In the foreign land, the wanderers knew not a few years of poverty, hard work, and often unbridled exploitation by their relatives, their "benefactors". But for the most part, they arrived at an economic base (most in business. I don't remember any who worked in foreign lands in crafts). They established factories and took care of their younger brothers and sisters who had remained "there". In this way Lubtch also contributed to the stream of Jewish emigration, especially to America and South Africa. Those whose travel expenses did not stretch far enough, emigrated to London and Paris. The parting from the family who remained in Europe was relatively easy, but from those who emigrated to America, leaving was difficult, a separation forever, - a separation accompanied by heartbreaking weeping.

*

How sad was the equipment that a girl aged 13 took with her when she left her hometown, when she left on her way towards her life's destiny. It was lightweight, all wrapped up in a colorful handkerchief, two or three blouses in the bundle, a Shabbat dress and one ruble in addition to the money for the long voyage - and the address of the uncle in the big city, on folded notes sewn into the pocket and into folds of the clothes. Her total education: she knew to read and write in Yiddish, Russian and a little arithmetic.

The town was far from the railroad, a distance of a day's wagon ride. The girl was amazed and frightened when the wagon-driver took her hand and led her to a strange creation on large iron wheels, a noisy, breathing creation, and said to her: "This is the train which goes to Warsaw, here is the ticket, look after yourself well."

In this manner the girl left the town, the same way as other young boys and girls before her, as also her two sisters had done before her and travelled over the seas, to America. She sat in the train and travelled to the unknown, but one thing she did know, and on that she had fought at home: there in the big city of Warsaw, she must fight for her future and succeed.

*

In 1934, when we were on *shlichut* [overseas service] on behalf of "*Hechalutz*" ["Pioneers" youth movement] in Poland, I returned to Lubtch, my hometown. This time we came there, Yaakov and I, not in a wagon, but in the "*mesilonit*" - a narrow railway. The small train chugged along slowly, breathing heavily, but nevertheless - advancing. Many of the town's inhabitants came to the station to meet the residents of Eretz-Israel who had arrived. I was excited, I remembered the young girl of thirteen with the little bundle in her hands, her limited education and her many hopes.

The town, it seemed, had not changed. The same marketplace, the same streets, the same houses, although most had been rebuilt after the fires, always looking old. And of course, the same wide Neiman river, flowing towards the horizon, to faraway places.

But even so, there were changes. The Hebrew school - small and modest, the pioneering youth movement which was active there, although it did not take the place over by storm, as had happened in other towns. However, several youth were already on *hachshara* [training farm before making *aliya*].

Lubtch was remote also after the war and the revolution; first it was Russian, then it became Polish, but it had always been, and remained Jewish. The daughter who came to visit her house took pity to the point of tears on the poverty and innocence of her town, and was very saddened to see it in its humiliation.

On the horizon - the clouds of fury of the Holocaust were threatening and the Jews there did not sense that they had to flee from the terrible storm.

My hometown was destroyed together with all the other Jewish communities in Europe. May these words be a memorial, a commemorative plaque to all that was and was totally destroyed.

The *HeChalutz* branch in Lubtch in 1933

[Page 60]

"Hamelitz", 7 Elul 5658 No.180 (Aug. 25, 1898)

by Yitzchak Bonimovitch Chalpak
Collated by M. Tzinovitch

Translated from the Hebrew by Harvey Spitzer

Lubtch (Minsk District) - The voice of the moaning of the victims of the fire in our town is heard on high. Infants and babies are lying on the streets, as there is no place to gather them up and shelter them. They were left naked and lacking everything, for within a short time the flames engulfed the whole town which became a pile of burning wood. Parents could not evacuate their children and no one was able to save any of their belongings, not even for the slightest relief, and were it not for the neighboring towns which offered us their food right after the fire, we would now have, God forbid, perished from hunger.

We are therefore announcing our grief publicly. Perhaps people will awaken to the loud sound of our distress and help us to whatever extent possible. To our great sorrow, the synagogues and study halls which were built as citadels were burned down, so that there is not even a place to pour out our prayers before the merciful God. The bathhouse, too, was burned down and we don't have the wherewithal to rebuild them.

May they take pity on the poor and destitute and help the souls of the impoverished. Those who show mercy will themselves be shown mercy and will be blessed with wealth in their homes.

[Page 60]

A wise son-in-law...
by Gershon Jankelowitz

Translated from the Yiddish by Harvey Spitzer

There was a Jew in our town whose name was Velfke Minkes. Velfke had five sons and three daughters. When the Russo-Japanese War broke out, Velfke's son-in-law went to America. He wasn't there was very long and came back to Lubtch.

When people asked him why he had come back, he answered:

---- Columbus discovered America. Let him stay there! I want to live in my small town, Lubtch.

[Page 61]

The Hebrew School in Lubtch
by Yitzchak Dichter, of blessed memory

Translated from the Hebrew by Ann Belinsky

"Who is like Thy people Israel, one nation on the earth?"

A "scattered and dispersed people" among the nations and countries, denied a normal state of life for thousands of years, yet knew how to organize its internal life (material and spiritual), to build institutions for mutual help, lofty spiritual institutions that have maintained the existence of the nation for generations.

Our nation apparently represents a unique case in history in that the nation lives in such difficult conditions while remaining loyal to itself and does not assimilate among the nations.

I shall write not about the leaders of the people or about the educated, but about the simple people - the tailors, shoemakers, small merchants and the workers - who put their shoulder to the task out of desire and awareness, who saved from their most essential needs (and there were those who really saved from their meager portion of bread) in order to help the Jewish institutions: the *Talmud Torah* (religious school), the *Yeshiva*, Jewish hospital and orphanage, etc.

Yitzchak Dichter

"Israel is no widower", i.e. Jewry has still some resources. Despite the fact that we were dependent on the kindnesses of the ruler - who usually was hostile towards us - a Jew has a benevolent and watchful eye and an outstretched arm to help. (Heroic stories will be told of Jews who gave their souls in order to come to the aid of a distant, failing brother, to offer help in time of trouble, etc.) These institutions were like a continuation of the independent life of which we were deprived. Here, in the tradition of generations, we continued to observe the commandment of supporting one's fellowman "so that he may live among you".

The Educational Institutions

The jewels in the crown of all the institutions that were built by the Jews in the Diaspora were the educational institutions. With its healthy sense, the nation felt that education of the young generation is the very soul and basis of the existence of the nation. A people that wants to maintain continuation of its existence must, first of all, see to educating the younger generation.

And, indeed, the people made sure that the new generation was educated. Without state permission, with no help from the government, they developed a wide chain of schools, from the *cheder* and *Talmud Torah* [elementary schools] for children, up to the *yeshivot* [rabbinic seminary] There was also a concern for the poor child lest he remain ignorant and illiterate, and if his parents could not afford to pay tuition, it was seen to it that he would learn in the *Talmud Torah*. Even when new winds began to blow in the world and in the Jewish community, the people did not change its ways or its learning, and "just as the lizard withdraws into its scales in order to protect itself from harm, so too the Jewish people withdraws completely within itself, deriving consolation, self courage, hope and security from the depths of its soul for the good days to follow, for the soon- to- come redemption."

The "Tarbut" School

In the period between the two World Wars, Hebrew schools called *"Tarbut"* [Culture] arose in the Diaspora. The Balfour Declaration at the end of the First World War gave a new impetus to the rebuilding of Eretz-Israel. The people saw in this Declaration the beginning of the Redemption with respect to the Messianic Age. And thus they saw a need to prepare tools for the revival of the nation and, first and foremost, the revival of the Hebrew language. In most cities and towns, modern Hebrew schools were established, where the language of instruction was Hebrew, except for the language of the country. The establishment of the schools and their maintenance was, as known, a state function of the first order. Much money was required for suitable buildings, a budget for paying salaries, heating, cleaning services, etc. Here, without any compulsion, the Jewish people filled this governmental function out of recognition of the importance of the matter.

I cannot count all the difficulties that confronted the parents and teachers committees. How does one go about setting up schools where the needs are many and the ability to do so is little? I do not know of a school that was closed for lack of budget, but I do know many teachers who received a salary for 8 months per year and less, and even so did not quit their job: the lofty ideal of national education for the young generation throbbed in the hearts of parents and teachers alike, urging them to make sacrifices and superhuman efforts. With their meager strength, the simple people succeeded in establishing and maintaining educational institutions from which came out the pioneers, the brave and the implementers. Much still remains to be told about Jews such as R' Chaim-Asher Osherowsky, who worked day and night to maintain the Hebrew School in Lubtch, and about parents who saved from their scanty bread and sent their children to the Hebrew School, when just across the street was the Polish school which took in all the children for free.

The Hebrew Schools of the Lubtch Community

The Hebrew School in this town assumed the national-educational role of the first degree. It absorbed all the children of the town and took them out of the gloomy *chederim*. Lubtch, in fact, was the only town in my time where there was no *cheder*.

Pupils of the Lubtch Public Primary School in 1925

The town's residents raised their hearts to this holy idea and sent their children to the Hebrew school exclusively. There were parents who were impoverished, yet they paid the tuition fees with honor. As was said above, all the children of the town, with no exception, learnt at the school, even the son of Mordechai-Baer, the beggar.

The parents committee tended to all the needs of the school. They wanted to give it the prestige of a school that pays its teachers a salary in order to invite the best teachers to teach there.

The aspiration to be innovative and modern attracted them, but they could not forgo religious studies and thus the method was "Hold on to this and don't withdraw your hand from that!" They invited graduates of teachers' seminars, but immediately stipulated they would also teach religious subjects. And they invited the honorable religious teacher in the town, Rabbi Yitchak Baksht, to teach *Gemara* (Talmud) in the sixth and seventh grades.

The standard of classes, as I assess it, was high. The teachers invested maximum effort, devotion and goodwill in teaching Hebrew. There were no suitable textbooks in Hebrew, however, so they translated from other languages, mainly from Polish. There were likewise no pedagogical journals or teaching aids. The teachers worked day and night to find suitable matter and translate it into Hebrew.

The School Library

Next to the school was a library with 1,000 books. It wasn't easy for us to accumulate enough money to erect the library. Persky, the teacher, was director of the library for many years. He did not offer his services for the sake of receiving a high salary and he worked with devotion and strictness.

The students exchanged books twice a week and the library was busy with children after school hours as well. It gladdened the heart to see them sharing the lists of books they had read, how they recommended to each other a good book. I loved to go to the school at these hours to listen to their ideas. I cannot forget these holy moments.

The Newspaper on the Wall

Every two weeks a newspaper appeared on the wall at the school. The newspaper played an educational-pedagogical role: to teach the child to read, to know what was going on in his environs, at school, in town and in the world and mainly in Eretz-Israel, and to develop expression in writing.

The newspaper was managed with responsibility, consistency and with much talent by the teacher, Yaakov Shmulovitz. The richest section was about the events in Eretz-Israel, which was the essence of our lives. Children always stood close and with fascination next to this section. It was possible to read in their eyes the happiness on every achievement in Israel and the deep sadness with every failure or tragedy.

Work of the *Keren-Kayemet* (Jewish National Fund) in the School

The work of the *Keren-Kayemet* in the school was directed with great enthusiasm, devotion and inspiration by the teacher, Chana Tzin-Dichter. The *Keren-Kayemet* served as a cornerstone for national education. The value of the land to the people and the ideas that the land would not be sold permanently found an echo of trust in the hearts of the pupils. Every new acquisition in Eretz-Israel was enthusiastically received and increased donations. In every class there was a JNF Corner and the Blue Box stood in its centre. Every good deed was marked by a donation: a good mark - a donation; finishing a book - a donation; an event in the child's life such as a birthday - a donation; bar-mitzvah - a donation; birth of a brother or sister - a donation, etc. I would like to tell you of a special event which indicates the spirit that beat in the children's hearts:

The editorial board of the *Tarbut* School newspaper:
Sitting from right to left: Golda Sonnenzon, Berel Solodocha, Shimon Yankelevitz, Esther Levin, Rachel Shlimonovitz, Yitzchak (Itsche) Faivoshevitz, Rita Aharonovski, Gittel Movshovitz.
Teachers standing: Alter Shmulovitch and Haim Persky

One of the pupils at the school was a boy named Hillel-Yaakov or, as he was called, Hillel-Yankel, the son of Mordechai Baer. He was a child without a mother, and his father was a beggar who would only return home twice a year, for Passover and the High Holy Days. Residents of the town looked after the child: as was customary in those days, the boy would eat "*yamim*" ("days") - every day at a different home. One of the women would look after him: where he would sleep and eat, making sure he was bathed and that his clothes washed and mended. The fact that he could never donate to the *Keren Kayemet* bothered the little boy, and when the children went up to give their donations one by one, Hillel-Yankel would remain sitting ashamed in his seat. The teacher, who felt his sorrow, offered him a loan of several *prutot* so that he could also donate, but Hillel-Yankel didn't agree. "What's the big deal?", he said. "It's your money". One Friday, Hillel-Yankel came to class with shining eyes. "I, too, have a contribution to the *Keren-Kayemet* today. I'm donating too." When the teacher asked him where he got the money from, he refused to disclose. During the last lesson, when the children went out to give their donations, the teacher invited him to be the first to go. With an uplifted head, he went out and donated all his property, 5 *grush*, and all the class applauded him, which delighted the child. Afterwards, the story came out: the woman at whose place he ate on Fridays was busy the same morning and had given him 5 *grush* to buy a bread roll. The boy, however, preferred to conquer his hunger and give a donation to the KK"L. The story of Hillel-Yankel and his donation reached the ears of the writer Tzvi Liberman from Nahalal, who was an emissary to Poland at that time, and he perpetuated the story in his book, "The Young Planter". We received two books from the author, and the teacher, Chana, gathered the children from several classes, including Hillel-Yankel, and read them the story. The child wept from pleasure.

The teacher would arrange parties at *Rosh-Chodesh* [the beginning of every Hebrew month] where information was passed about the income and activities of the *Keren Kayemet*. They would hear news about Eretz-Israel, sing songs, recite and dance. These parties conveyed to the children the atmosphere in Eretz-Israel, for which they worked to the best of their extent.

Children of the "Tarbut" School in 1929, next to the White Synagogue

Festivals and Celebrations at the School

Celebrations played a big part in the work of the school. Here we tried to discover the talents of the children in the area of the arts: in song, dance and theatre. The "*chug*" [club] was run by the teacher, Bonia Petochovsky, a modest, quiet, gentle and shy teacher. She would spend hours with the children at the school, after they had finished their studies. She always managed to find new talents. The fame of the school shows spread throughout the town and beyond. The parents of the children and the rest of the inhabitants came in throngs to the school shows. The show was the subject of conversation for a long time. The teacher instilled courage, made wings grow and planted ambitions of progress in the hearts of the children. All the teaching staff and the parents committee helped towards assuring the success of the show. There was much excitement in the school and in the homes as the time approached: they prepared scenery, sewed costumes, set up a stage, etc. As in all our work, we tried to put emphasis on an Eretz-Israel subject in all our celebrations. To this day, I remember the celebration on the subject of "Drying the Swamps in the Jezreel Valley". Before my eyes stand the special, original scenery that the teacher, Yaakov Shmulovitz, had prepared, and the costumes of frogs in the swamp.

On Polish national holidays, our school appeared together with the Polish school, and we were always better. The headmaster of the Polish school once asked me, "What is the reason that everything goes so well with you?" If only the headmaster knew how much work, and especially love and goodwill, the teacher invested in every performance, he would have understood the reason for the success.

The Clubhouse

We tried to find a place where the children could spend their leisure time in a cultural way. We decided to open a clubhouse by the school.

The teacher, Toni Tepper, was in charge of the clubhouse. She was diligent, responsible and well versed in handicrafts. The club was open three days a week and included a games room, a reading room, and a handicrafts room. In the games room there were various games such as drafts, chess, a ping-pong (table tennis) table, etc. In the reading room were books and children's newspapers. In the handicrafts room (mainly for girls) were various crafts. One cannot describe the happiness of the children coming to the clubhouse, which was an innovation in those days.

It was pleasant to come to the clubhouse in the evenings to observe and see how willingly and gladly the children played, worked and read there. We felt that we had removed the children from boredom to a life of creativity, and we saw the thanks and appreciation in their eyes.

The Influence of the School on the Life of the Jews in the Town

The school was the only ray of light in all the life in the town, and its influence was great in every area: in the cultural life, in the Zionistic activity, in the help that it gave to the youth movements, etc. Frequently, we would call for parents' and lecturers' meetings on various subjects. The assemblies usually took place on Friday (Sabbath) evenings and the school hall was always full.

The school also gave help to the Zionist movement and the Funds. The teacher, Persky, was for many years the representative of the *Keren Kayemet* in the town and made sure that a Blue-Box was present in every Jewish home. One of the teachers was in charge of the *Keren Hayesod* [The Foundation Fund] matters. He would sign up people with means to purchase certificates of the Fund, and when the time came for them to be paid, he tried to collect the money. In fact, he was always busy with this.

A lot of our time was devoted to the youth organizations. The teacher, Yaakov Shmulovitz, was most active in this sphere. We helped them with advice, guidance and especially with teaching the Hebrew language. Naturally, we did this without expecting any recompense.

Enlarging the School Building

This glorious chapter in the history of the Lubtch school, is unique, with no parallel in any of the history of the chain of *Tarbut* schools in Poland.

As the school was too small to accommodate all the children of the town, it was necessary to build an addition of at least two more rooms. The problem was in obtaining the necessary financing for the building, for it was hard enough just managing to maintain the school. Many meetings and consultations took place until we finally decided to ask the parents of the pupils for an additional payment towards the building costs. It was very difficult for us to collect the money, not because the parents didn't want to pay, but for lack of means. We held parents' meeting and explained the situation. They did understand but weren't able to make the payments. The parents' committee was drawn into action. They went from house to house collecting the "debt". After the amount of money that was possible was collected, we saw that it wasn't enough. Again we held meetings, and again we consulted, but there was no money. One of those days, I met with the chairman of the parents' committee, Mr. Chaim-Asher Osherovsky, and his eyes were shining: "I got some advice", he said. "Tonight we must hold a parents' meeting". At the meeting, R' Chaim-Asher said that this house doesn't give him rest, we must build no matter what! "This matter concerns the very soul of our children. If the child does not find a place with us, he will be forced to attend the Polish school, which would mean - forced conversion." He suggested that a working tax be imposed on the parents and that every household be obligated to contribute three working days to building the house. His suggestion was accepted and unanimously received. We bought building materials and hired a professional builder from the money we had collected. All the work was done by the parents in turn.

Volunteers building the *Tarbut* School

I stood in the school room. Looking outside, I saw Jews with beards and sidelocks, amongst them elderly people coming during the day, lifting up boards, pushing wheelbarrows of soil to fill the foundations of the building. I thought to myself: what compels these people to respond to the parents' committee decision? What compels them to donate from their money and to exert themselves? They were carrying out the internal, spiritual command to build a school, without which their children were likely to assimilate and become impure.

Almost the whole town came for the dedication. It is hard to describe the happiness and the self-satisfaction of their accomplishment. The new rooms, where the celebration took place, were bright and light. Everyone came in high spirits and congratulated each other. The chairman of the parents' committee, Mr. Chaim-Asher Osherovsky, could not speak from emotion. He read with an emotional voice choked with tears: "Blessed art Thou our Lord, our G-d, King of the Universe, Who has kept us alive, sustained us and brought us to this season." And the audience answered in a loud voice: "Amen!"

I gave a welcoming speech that was actually a hymn of praise to the simple working Jewish person who had left his work and livelihood and came to give a hand in building the school. After the celebration, the Chairman invited the audience to pray saying: "Come fellow Jews, let us go to the synagogue and pray, to give thanks to G-d that we were privileged to carry out this great mitzvah."

I never again saw a public celebration as joyful as this. I was fortunate to witness it and fortunate that I was privileged to tell the story of a Hebrew school in the Polish Diaspora.

A week after the dedication, a committee was set up in charge of the school house whose job was to take care of the building. This was a public primary school in the fullest sense of the word, a school that the people themselves had built with their own hands. I am sorry that I didn't photograph this occasion. It would be wonderful to see a photo where Yitzchak, the chimney sweeper, and others are working, dragging beams, from morning to evening, and building a Hebrew school in the Polish dispersion.

The Parents' Committee

I would like to mention with honor and admiration the names of members of the parents' committee who untiringly bore the yoke of building and maintaining the school for many years:

Mr. Chaim-Asher Osherovsky, chairman of the committee
Mr. Yisrael Solodocha
Mr. Chaim-Leib Levine
Mr. Chaim Bruk
Mr. Moshe Shlimovitz
Mr. Abraham-Haim Ostshinsky
Mr. David Davidovitz
Mr. Vilner

These dear people devoted their time and energy to building a school in our town. They were often prevented from resting in order to set the school on a firm foundation. I mention, with a shaking voice and with acknowledgement, their holy names, bow my head and pray for the elevation of their pure souls to eternal bliss.

A group of teachers of the *Tarbut* School, 1929
From right to left: Chaim Persky, Leah Oshrovsky, Chaim Bruk, Chuma, Alter Shmulevitch, Goldshmid

Teachers of the School who Perished in the Holocaust

With sadness and sorrow, with honor and admiration, I mention the names of the teachers of the school in Lubtch who perished in the Holocaust with all the House of Israel:

Shmulovitch, Yaakov
Petokovski, Boniah
Persky, Chaim
Sonenzon, Shalom
Rozenblum

Dear teachers of Israel, trustees of the House of Israel,

How bitter is my fate that I have to mention your names in the memorial book! For you were my loyal partners in your concern for educating the young generation. You invested physical exertion, thoughts and goodwill in your work. You lit the light of Israel in the hearts of many. You were like the pillar of fire which lit the way of the People of Israel in the Diaspora. You educated a generation aspiring to freedom and self-determination, a generation of realizers of the Zionist dream, of brave and daring Jews.

But your toil was not in vain, your dream became a reality: the land was liberated from the yoke of foreign domination. The people returned to their homeland from all corners of the Diaspora. How sad is the heart that you did not succeed in seeing it. I mention your dear names together with the other Jews of Lubtch who perished in the Holocaust, for whom you were loyal partners in their lives. May the Guardian of Israel bind your pure souls with the souls of the educators of the generations who sacrificed their lives to educate the people and to continue its existence!

About the Pupils of the Lubtch School

"Such a revenge, the retribution of the spilled blood of a child

Satan has yet to create -

And the blood will curse the depths!" (Chaim N. Bialik)

It is accepted that there are bereaved parents, that there are bereaved women, but no one ever thought that the most bereaved of all would be the few Hebrew teachers that survived. For we brought up, nurtured, and educated a generation for work and creativity, to love one's fellow-man and social justice.

Since the Holocaust, there has been no joy in my heart. The world is covered in gloom. "Darkness and no light in it...", for what is the sense of life for a Hebrew teacher whose pupils are no longer? When I recall those days when the school was joyful with the voices of children; when I remember the corner we created in a strange and hostile environment, a corner of holiness and radiance where are dear children absorbed Torah and Judaism, love of man, equality, righteousness and truth. When I recall the atmosphere of the school, the *Rosh Hodesh* [new month]celebrations, the shining eyes of those who won the *Keren Kayemet* flag for a month, it is hard to get used to the idea that all this was uprooted, cruelly and with satanic thoroughness.

A million children, Children of Israel, were murdered in the Holocaust. But for me, this is not a "number", but living children, happy and sprightly, learning and mischievous. Before my eyes stand: Benyamin Levine, Esther Levine, Solodocha, Kresilov, Chaim-Leib Kalmonovitch, Shmuel Kalmonovitch, Osherovsky, Bruk and more...

Where are you? Where are you, my children?! Who plucked you so cruelly in the prime of your life? How many talents were lost with your deaths?! Avraham Kalmanovitch, a very talented child, outstanding in every subject and especially in art. We hung many hopes on that child. Sara-Henia Boldo - a good girl, outstanding in her studies and in dance.

Your memory has not been erased from my heart, the heart of your teacher. I carried you in my heart throughout the days of the Holocaust. And when I was exiled to a distant country, I carried your blessed memory in my heart. When I finally won the right and arrived in Eretz Israel, you were before my eyes - always, and I will mourn you until my dying day.

[Pages 74-77]

The "Chorev" School In Lubtch

Translated from the Yiddish by Harvey Spitzer

"*Dos Vort*", No. 618, Vilna, 28 Nissan, 5697 (1937)

"Lubtch has a strong *Tarbut* (Culture) school, one of the strongest in the region, and despite the sorrowful consequences of *Tarbut* education (in the area of religion), who will dare oppose it?

Several local, newly married rabbinic students, however, learned in Torah, from the *"Beit Yosef" Yeshiva* (of the Novogrudek type) are setting up a *"Chorev"* school [public religious school] and are appealing in the village to Rabbi Shlomo Podolski, (affiliated with the Novogrudek *yeshiva*, and himself a leader). He comes right to the front, unafraid of any kind of attacks, persecutions and smear campaigns in the press, etc.

The result: With his brilliant talent, Rabbi Shlomo Podolksi organizes the *Chorev* School, which remains a model school for the surrounding towns and shows that nothing is impossible for work undertaken with devotion and self-sacrifice".

"*Dos Vort*", No. 636, Vilna, Friday, 3 Shvat, 5697 (1938)

A public religious school, the *Chorev* school, has been in existence in our village for the past two years. It is impossible to describe the amount of hard work and self-sacrifice that went into establishing this school. In general, creating a religious school in a place where there is a strong *Tarbut* school is not one of the easiest things. There has been no end to the trouble, slander and scourges which the founders of the local *Chorev* school have had to endure from the "national culture bearers". And, in fact, they themselves have been largely responsible for the founding of the *Chorev* school because of their unlimited insolence and license. Making a joke of everything which we hold sacred and dear, making derisive remarks even in front of children about the holy wise men of the Talmud and Great Men of Israel, which makes one shudder, hearing such mockery. Taking advantage of the opportunity that arose a few years ago when the head of the local rabbinic court, Rabbi Yitzchak Weiss, fell ill, they took over the town's *Talmud Torah* school (religious school for young pupils) - which, until then, had been operating under Rabbi Weiss' supervision and had prepared pupils for the elementary *yeshivot* - and they turned it into a *Tarbut* school without the knowledge or consent of the parents, most of whom are decent and honest Jews. Once that happened, it was too late to do anything about it.

When their wild orgies against Jewish tradition had reached their limit, however, the town's people took a step closer to creating a *Chorev* school, which offers a sufficient measure of secular studies as well as, and especially, a spiritual education of Torah and faith. To that end, we extended a challenge to the popular speaker and zealot, Rabbi Shlomo Podolski who, with his brilliant lectures, succeeded in breaking down iron walls, with the result that a *Chorev* school was created to the joy of all the parents.

On the evening of the lighting of the fifth Channukah [Festival of Lights] candle this year, a festive program took place at the *Chorev* school. Rabbi S. Zimon, opened the evening's program in the crowded auditorium, giving a report of the school's activities. His talk was rich in content and left a great impression. One of the younger pupils recited the blessings over the Chanukah lights, sang, "*Ha-narot halalu anu madlikin*" ["These candles which we light"] and then several numbers were performed in Hebrew, Yiddish and Polish. A presentation of "Jacob and Esau" held the audience enraptured.

Rabbi S. Podolski closed the evening with a brilliant lecture, mentioning, *inter alia*, that if all Jews celebrate the miracle of Chanukah as a miracle which happened "in those times", Lubtch also celebrates the miracle as happening "at this time". Like the Maccabees, who found a small quantity of oil suitable for the lighting of the Menorah, we found a small number of children and with them we kindled the "light of Chanukah". We never imagined that our undertaking would last even one day, but "a miracle occurred" and it has lasted and will continue to last. At the end of his talk, the speaker appealed to the parents to save their children from the nails of "apostasy" while it is still not too late. The evening in general and the lecture in particular made a great impression on those present to the extent that a noticeable movement is presently underway involving parents - who until now were far from the *Chorev* ideal - taking their children out of the *Tarbut* school and placing them in *Chorev*.

On this occasion, we would like to express a cordial "well done!" to Rabbi S. Podolski for his devoted work on behalf of religious education in our village as well as to the important personages: Rabbi S. Zimon, Heshel Kivelevitch (president of *Chorev*), Reuven Paretzki and to all the officials, workers and benefactors of our *Chorev* school.

We should especially like to thank Rabbi Avraham Yisrael Miskin in Buenos Aires, Argentina and to all the other benefactors there for their generous donations for the benefit of our school.

[Pages 77-78]

A "Periodical" in Lubtch

Collected by M. Tzinovitch

Translated from Hebrew by Harvey Spitzer

"*HaTzfira*" from the year 5654 (1894), issue No. 18, in the column "A head whirling with ideas" announces the following interesting items:

"In the small town of Lubtch (Region of Minsk), some young people gathered together for the purpose of giving honor to education and to stimulate others of their age to learn the R.L. (Russian language, M.Tz.) and to blow into their nostrils the breath of the spirit of enlightenment. They have begun by imitating a splendidly written periodical, and every week they prepare one issue in neat handwriting and they distribute the issues among friends and acquaintances in other small towns."

The chief writer of the above-mentioned column, Mr. Naftali Neimnovitch, who was sent some of these issues, continues thus:

"Both issues from this forged "periodical", which they've chosen to call "Pottery", were a joke to me. Within its pages can be found sorts of articles, sorts of poems, sorts of feuilletons, sorts of questions, and sorts of riddles. The intention itself is not bad, for "when scholars (authors) vie, wisdom will increase" and everyone in the young generation is stimulated in this way to learn and write, but the trouble is that the dwarf editors are still "eating *boser*" [still lack experience], have a poor knowledge of the Hebrew language, and the rules of grammar are unfamiliar to them. And therefore, instead of doing good, they are actually harming their contemporaries and it is hard to correct an error. Look, they call their periodical "Pottery" because it is like a broken clay vessel.... and he ends his article with these words: "Why are you young people in a hurry? Why will you envy Jewish writers while you yourselves didn't work hard at it in your youth as we did, and neither did you read nor change? First, "kill" yourselves in the tents of *Torah* [learning], seek *Torah* and wisdom, acquire knowledge of the world and its inhabitants, raise yourselves slowly to the heights of praise. You will then succeed in becoming useful people to your nation and country. And then, when you grow up and become old and life is good to you, you will exclaim joyfully, "Happy are we that our youth has not shamed our old age..."

[Page 78]

After The Event...

by Hilel Krosnitz

Translated from the Yiddish by Harvey Spitzer

The last rabbi of Lubtch - may his days in Paradise be bright! - was accustomed to mathematically calculating the amount of water in the *mikve* [ritual bath] and only when he confirmed that everything was properly done according to Jewish law and religion, would the *mikve* attendant let the women go in.

It had to happen, however, that Satan caused the rabbi to make a mistake in arithmetic - it shouldn't have happened, but it did happen - and the rabbi confirmed that the *mikve* was - *kasher* [suitable for use].

Later that evening when the rabbi was at last free from adjudicating a case of Torah law and had gone over his calculations regarding the amount of water in the *mikve*, that he discovered his error - it shouldn't happen to us! - that the *mikve* was unfit for use!

The rabbi was not lazy and immediately went to the *mikve* attendant, from whom he took the list of women who had immersed in the ritual bath that evening, and he then left to make the announcement. He would go to a home, knock on the window and announce:

"The *mikve* is unfit for use. You mustn't!!" He said what he had to say and went away.

He also went to Mashke Berezinsky's window, knocked on it and announced the news.

Mashke Berezinsky's answer was not long in coming:

"Rabbi, too late. It's already after the event!"

[Pages 79-98]

Rabbis Of The Lubtch Community

by Moshe Tzinovitch

Translated from the Hebrew by Harvey Spitzer

Rabbi Yosef-Moshe-Simcha Rapoport

He was the son of Rabbi Zvi-Hirsh HaCohen Rapoport, head of the rabbinical court in Mir. He received a religious education in Lithuania in the small town of Mir, which was considered one of the oldest communities in that area. Later R' Yosef-Moshe-Simcha lived in Zamut, northern Lithuania, as son-in-law of R' Yaakov, head of the rabbinical court in Krozi and some time later returned to his former surroundings. Lubtch was his first place of office as rabbi and head of the rabbinical court. There, in 5505 (1745), he preached many sermons which are mentioned in his book, "*Bigdei Moshe*".

Afterwards, the rabbi made a big jump: from Lubtch, which is in Greater Lithuania, he wandered to Zimrod (Western Galicia) to take office as head of the rabbinical court, and from there he came to Lintchna (District of Lublin). Here he became famous as a genius and righteous man until the members of the community of Untsdorf, in distant Hungary, heard about him from the great rabbis of Poland, "for this man Moshe we know what has become of him. He toiled and found success and is indeed a genius, a great rabbi of the generation", and they sent him a letter offering him the opportunity to be their rabbi, and he moved to Untsdorf.

Rabbi Yosef-Moshe-Simcha wrote and edited a wonderful and valuable book entitled "*Bigdei Kodesh*" on "*Pirkei Avot*" (Ethics of the Fathers), containing two commentaries: A) "*Bigdei Moshe*" of his own and B) "*Bigdei Kavod*", written by his son-in-law, the *Gaon* [Genius] Rabbi Yisrael Menachem-Mendel, head of the rabbinical court in Tromboli. With the completion of the book, Rabbi Rapoport printed two responsa of his own dealing with rendering decisions based on the authoritative interpretation of the law which he sent to the Gaon R' Yechezkel Landau, head of the rabbinical court in Prague, as well as a few new interpretations on the Torah by R' Moshe-Mordechai HaLevi Itingai, son of the Gaon R' Lipman of Sanuk.

The book, "*Bigdei Kodesh*" was published posthumously in the year 5566 (1806) and appeared with the approval of the Gaonim: R' Yaakov-Meshulam Ornstein, head of the rabbinical court in Lvov, R' Meir, head of the rabbinical court in Brodi, R' Yehoshua-Heschel Babad, head of the rabbinical court in Tarnopol and R' Chaim, head of the rabbinical court in Czernovitz, (author of "*Be'er Mayim Chaim*"), all of whom were lavish in their praise of the author as a great Torah scholar and an outstanding expositor of Scripture. R' Meir writes about him: "He left behind several essays on several tractates of the Talmud and his name is famous as one of the giants of his time".

Some of his children whom he raised and educated did not follow him to Galicia and Hungary and stayed rooted in their mother country. These include his son, R' Yaakov-Yokil Rapoport, who was a rabbi in Yanov, near Pinsk, and his son, R' Zvi-Hirsh, who wrote the preface to the aforementioned book. His daughter Shprintza was married to the Gaon R' Meshulam-Zalman, head of the rabbinical court in Pakroi (Zamut) and his daughter Gruna was the wife of R' Yisrael-Menachem-Mendel, head of the rabbinical court in Tramobovli.

From a document belonging to the rabbinate in Untsdorf, we see that the name of Rabbi Yosef-Moshe-Simcha Rapoport was famous. They sang his praises and his greatness in all branches of learning: "The famous genius, the great eagle, the great, broad-winged eagle, renowned in the farthest ends of the world and sea, whose mouth uttered pearls of wisdom and who was well-mannered and crowned with the crown of Torah, priesthood and kingship" and another tenure of office. The date of this document from the rabbinate in Untsdorf is Sunday, the day after the Feast of Weeks (Shavuot) 5540 (1780). He disseminated Torah knowledge there until the day of his death in 5560 (1800). The Jews of the community admired him and related to him with love and honor.

The Gaon Rabbi Eliezer Shapira

Details of Rabbi Eliezer Shapira's biography have not been preserved and the scant information that we have has come down to us indirectly from the identification of famous rabbis to the above-mentioned rabbi, who was a special descendant of the Shapira family of Vilna-Lubtch.

We know that R' Eliezer was a native of Vilna. His father, the Gaon R' Aryeh-Leib Shapira, 5461-5521(1701-1761) served as a scribe and judge in the rabbinical court in Vilna and acquired fame in the world of Torah as the author of a two-part treatise, "*Nachalat Ariel*" (based on its plain meaning) and "*Ma'on Arayot*", (based on argumentation) on the Talmud tractate, "*Sofrim*" (1732). He also wrote a book on the Torah "*Kvutzat Kesef*" (1742).

It is impossible to determine exactly when R' Eliezer served as head of the rabbinical court in Lubtch. However, it was a long time after the term of office of R' Yosef-Moshe-Simcha HaCohen Rapoport, who is discussed above. We can point out that R' Eliezer was famous in his time and was known by the great rabbis of Lithuania, many of whom were related to the rabbi who functioned in Lubtch, as we shall see further in this article.

We don't know if R' Eliezer Shapira had any sons, but it is known that he had two daughters: one was married to R' Menachem-Zundel, head of the rabbinical court in Eibnitz, and the other was married to R' Chaim Epshtein from among the notable families of Vilna, the "Jerusalem of Lithuania". R' Menachem-Zundel and his wife had a son while they were living in Lubtch and were still dependent on their father. The child was a child prodigy named Aryeh-Leib (after his grandfather), who later became famous as the genius of his generation. He studied Torah in the local study hall in Lubtch with his relative, Shmuel Bakshter, who was five years his senior, and together they went to study at the *yeshiva* in Volozhin, which was then founded by the Gaon R' Chaim. R' Aryeh-Leib achieved fame afterwards as a lion in the company of the leading rabbis of Lithuania. He was head of the rabbinical court in Iliya (where he became friendly with the Gaon, the Researcher, R' Menashe, a leading figure in Ilyia, and with his restricted circle), in Vasilishok, Smorgon and in Klavaria, where he died in the year 5613 (1853).

R' Aryeh-Leib Shapira had the merit of establishing a chain of rabbis and scholars who were active in disseminating Torah knowledge in Lithuania, Russia, Poland and independent Israel. Among them, we can mention the Gaon R' Raphael Shapira, of blessed memory, head of the rabbinical court and rabbinical college in Volozhin and his sons R' Yaakov Shapira, who succeeded his father at the same *yeshiva*; R' Aryeh Shapira, official communal rabbi in Bialystok; R' Yisrael-Isser Shapira, director of the *kolel* [*yeshiva* for married men], "*Sha'arei Torah*" in Tel Aviv; R' Moshe Shapira, (son of Aryeh), head of the rabbinical college and principal of the "Be'er Ya'akov" Yeshiva; R' Raphael Shapira (son of R' Yisrael-Isser), head of the rabbinical college and principal of the *kolel* for married students "*Tifferet Israel*" and "*Tifferet HaCarmel*" in Haifa, and R' Shimon Langbort (son-in-law of the Gaon R'Ya'akov Shapira), head of the rabbinical college and principal of the "*Gaonei Volozhin*" Yeshiva in Bnei Brak.

The Gaon R' Chaim Epshtein, the second son-in-law of R' Eliezer Shapira, was likewise a Torah personality of distinguished birth. He was the son of R' Mordechai Epshtein (R' Mordechai Gitke Toives) from Vilna and grandson of the Gaon and Kabbalist, R' Aryeh-Leib Epshtein, (author of the book, "*HaPardes*", and head of the rabbinical court in Koenigsburg, capital of East Prussia). R' Chaim lived a number of years in Lubtch after his marriage, soaked up the religious atmosphere and then moved on to Vilna.

R' Shmuel Yosef, who knew R' Chaim very well from the period of their studies at the "*Yisod*" Yeshiva in Vilna, relates the following about him: "R' Chaim did not depart from the "tent of Torah" and did not go home except to have lunch. He had a special room in the attic of the study hall of the aforementioned *yeshiva*, where he had a treasure of books and where he would sleep all week. He was tall and thin. He face always bore an expression of anger and there was never any laughter on his lips. His steps were few and measured. He was noble and refined."

In his old age, R' Chaim made *aliya* to Eretz-Israel. He settled in Jerusalem, the Holy City. Although he wasn't conspicuous among the many, the notables of Jerusalem from among the "*Porshim*" ["Secluded ones"] admired him and showed him great respect.

He passed away in the year 5610 (1850). His memory is recorded in the book, "*Toldot Chochmei Yerushalayim*" by Frumkin-Rivlin.

R' Nahum Bar Moshe

R' Moshe, father of R' Nahum, was head of the rabbinical court in Zhital, near Novogrudek. His second son, R' Chaim, went off to "explore" together with the *Gra* [Gaon from Vilna], from whom he received secrets of the *Kabbalah* [Jewish mysticism]. This family is related to the *Maggid* from Dubno and to R' Shaul Vahl, from Brisk in Lithuania who, according to a legend, was king of Poland for a day.

R' Nahum, head of the rabbinical court in Lubtch, had a famous son named Eliyahu-Chaim, who replaced his father in the rabbinate in Toretz. R' Eliayhu-Chaim became famous with his treatise "*Aderet Eliyahu*", which contains two explanatory commentaries on the laws of ritual slaughtering. Because of its importance as a guidebook for ritual slaughterers and meat inspectors as well as for rabbis in matters of ritual slaughtering and meat examination, it won the approval of the leading rabbis including R' Moshe-Avraham, head of the rabbinical court in Mir, R' Yitzchak- Elchanan, head of the rabbinical court in Novogrudek, R' Yosef, head of the rabbinical court in Slotzk, R' Shmuel-Avigdor Tosfah, head of the rabbinical court in Karlin and R' Eliezer-Moshe Horovitz, head of the rabbinical court in Pinsk, all of whom praise and extol the author and his book "in which there is a great blessing for the profession of ritual slaughtering and meat examination". This book merited a second edition in the year 5654 (1894), published by Rosenkrantz Shriftzitzer in Vilna. In the preface to this book, the author calls his father, R' Nahum, head of the rabbinical court in Lubtch, "my teacher and rabbi, Luminary of the Exile, famous in his Torah and piety, and who was also given a fitting memorial in the writings of the "*Chochmei HaEmet*". At the time of the printing of the book, the author was 70 years old.

R' Nahum's second son was R' Yaakov, preacher and "teacher of righteousness" [rabbi] in Kovno.

Rabbi Dov-Baer Yaffe

He was known by the name "Berl Toretzer" after the name of the little town of Turetz, where he had earlier served as rabbi and head of the rabbinical court. It was also written about him that he was the head of the rabbinical court in Karelitz. (Both of these small towns are near Lubtch - Moshe Ts.)

R' Dov-Baer Yaffe was apparently born in Korelitz where his father, the "Renowned Righteous Gaon" R' Yaakov, served as head of the rabbinic court. (According to "*Sefer Klilat Menorah*" published in Berditchov, 5652, he was the son of R' Natan Halevi Rubinstein, head of the rabbinic court in Dubno - district town of the Volin region). Likewise, according to the aforementioned source, R' Yaakov was the brother-in-law of the "holy, pure and famous" R' Nahum from Tchernobil, generation after generation of great rabbis going as far back as Our Teacher Rabbi Mordechai Ben Avraham Yaffe, 1535-1612, author of "*HaLevushim*" (From a letter written by R' Mordechai Gimpel, son of R' Dov-Baer Yaffe, to the Hassidic "Admor" from Toriski, who came from a home in Tchernobil, as mentioned in the same book).

We know that R' Dov-Baer Yaffe was one of the first and select pupils of the Gaon R' Chaim in his upper-level *yeshiva* in Volozhin. R' Dov-Baer's friends at the *yeshiva* were students who subsequently became famous rabbis: the Gaon R' Yitzchak, who succeeded his father, the Gaon R' Chaim in his position as head of the rabbinic court and as head of the rabbinic college in Volozhin, and the Gaon, R' David-Tuvia Rabin, the official city rabbi in Minsk, capital of White Russia. R' Chaim highly regarded his pupil Berl, both on account of his Talmudic erudition and his righteousness, and he would say of him, in the presence of his other students (all of whom were destined to become famous as great scholars) that in his direct argumentation he was like one of the "*Rishonim*" (earlier great Talmudic authorities) - the Rash"ba, and the Ran of blessed memory - and that he himself had learned from Dov-Baer how to pray with intent and devotion.

The Gaon R' Dov-Baer wrote a book of his own which contained new interpretations on the Mishnah Order "*Moed*" as well as several books with a commentary on Scripture through the simple elucidation of the text and through conceptual analysis. One of his students, R' Yisrael-Michael Yeshurun (native of Karelitz) made some of his works suitable for printing; however, not all of them were printed, although many of his writings which were in the possession of his son, the Gaon R' Mordechai Gimpel Yaffe, were found to be suitable for printing. The Gaon R' Dov-Baer Yaffe was rabbi and head of the rabbinical court in the important community of Otian. He died in Vilna in the year 5589 (1829), in the prime of life, on his way to consult with his doctors.

In his eulogy, the Gaon R' David, head of the rabbinical court in Novogrudek said, "With profound sorrow we heard about the passing of the wise Torah scholar, the sharp-minded rabbi, Dov Baer, who was a preacher of justice and a teacher of righteousness in many communities adjacent to our community and, at the end of his life, was accepted as preacher and rabbi in Otian." (See "*Glia Masechet*").

In the preface to his book, "*Avot D'Rabbi Natan*" (5593), the Gaon R' Eliyahu, son of R' Avraham, mentions the "eminent and acute Rabbi Dov, who was a preacher and rabbi in Lubtch."

Rabbi Dov-Baer's sons were: R' Yosef-Yehoshua Yaffe, head of the religious court in Toiragen (mentioned in the book "*Sh'eilot v'tshuvot Tsioni*", par.28) and the Gaon R' Menachem Gimpel, head of the rabbinical court in Dartchin and

Rizinau, interred in Petach Tikvah, Eretz-Yisrael. R' Dov-Baer's son-in-law, R' Yaakov, served as rabbi in Otian, the city of his last position in the rabbinate.

The research scholar, Rashi Fin(e), included the name of R' Dov-Baer Yaffe in a list of inscriptions of tombstones in the old cemetery of Vilna which he published in his well-known book, "*Kiriya Ne'emana*".

In the addendum of the book, "*Tsemach David*", it is written: "Dov-Baer from Karelitz, rabbi in the holy community of Otian, was renowned as a genius and righteous man who raised up many students, and his family lineage goes back generation after generation to the Gaon R' Mordechai Yaffe, author of 'HaLevushim'".

His son, the Gaon R' Gimpel Yaffe, was about nine years old when he was orphaned from his father. He may have been born in Lubtch when his father was serving as rabbi in that town. All his life, R' Mordechai Gimpel was in anguish over the fact that "most of his writings on the Torah were in my possession including his responses and essays-and most were burned in a big fire that broke out in Brizhinoi, and I didn't manage to publish the remnants of his writings which are more valuable than gold." (From "*HaRav HaMeyuchad*", by Binyamin Yaffe, Jerusalem 5718.)

The grandson of R' Dov Baer's sister was the Gaon R' Avraham-Yitzchak HaCohen, head of the rabbinical court in Jaffa, chief rabbi in Jerusalem, and Chief Rabbi of the State of Israel, who would always speak respectfully of his holy great-grandfather, R' Dov-Baer, a personality from Lubtch.

The Gaon Rabbi Yehonatan

He was known in the Lithuanian world of Torah as Yehonatan from Volin, referring to the Volin region, where the little town of Stanov, his birthplace, is located.

From the days of his youth, he was absorbed in theoretical learning in Talmud and its commentators and was distinguished by his wonderful skills, exemplary diligence, his piety and acts of righteousness. His father, a "*Chassid*" (follower of the sect of the "devout" founded by the Baal Shem Tov), as were the other people in Stanov, wanted his son to continue on the path of *Chassidism*, to go to the *Admor* (Chassidic rabbi) and stay in his surroundings. R' Yehonatan, however, aspired to be dedicated to the study of Torah, and his only wish was to go to a place of Torah learning in Lithuania. Not long afterwards, his young wife died, and so he went to study at the Volozhin Yeshiva. The head of the *yeshiva*, R' Chaim, was amazed at the student and reserved a special room for him in the *yeshiva* building. His meals were provided by the *yeshiva*. R' Chaim would go in to see him to discuss matters of Torah and the authoritative interpretation of the law. In addition to his diligence in his studies, R' Yehonatan would conduct himself with piety and with abstinence like a saint, and all the days he stayed at the *yeshiva* in Volozhin were devoted to Torah and its service.

At that time it was the custom at the Volozhin Yeshiva for the students to be sent on holidays to well-to-do families in the small towns of the area, and in this way they would renew their strength after a period of extended toil in their studies. R' Yehonatan was sent to Lubtch to the home of R' Shmuel Bakshter. R' Yehonatan's noble soul was joined to that family, which he came to every holiday, and he became a regular guest of R' Shmuel, who treated him as one of the family members.

In the year 5581 (1821), R' Chaim passed away and his son, R' Yitzchak, was appointed to replace him as head of the rabbinical court and head of the college. R' Shmuel Bakshter consulted with R' Yitzchak as to whether he should take R' Yehonatan as a groom for his daughter. R' Yitzchak answered him in these words: "I also have a daughter who has already reached marriageable age, but I would like to fulfill what is said: 'I have given my daughter to a man in the full sense of the word, and not to an angel.'..." Nevertheless, R' Shmuel gave him his daughter for a wife, since his daughter was also in agreement. Later on, R' Shmuel realized that this match was indeed not so suitable, for his son-in-law was too far removed from the affairs of this world and that he yearned only for Torah....

And indeed, while at Lubtch, R' Yehonatan devoted himself to Torah and service to God and became a shining example of holiness on his way, not only in Lubtch but also in all the small towns of Lithuania and Zhamot. However, his days were not long there as he passed away in the prime of life in Lubtch while his father-in-law, R' Shmuel Bakshter, was still alive. Many men from Lubtch who were born the year that R' Yehonatan passed away recall that they were named Yehonatan in memory of the saintly rabbi who died childless without leaving any progeny after him. The married *yeshiva* student, R' Yaakov-Moshe Direktor, head of the rabbinical court in Mosh, called his son Yehonatan, and his son later became a well-known rabbi in Israel.

R' Yehonatan from Volin is mentioned three times in the book, "*HaHut HaMeshulash*".

The Gaon R' Eliezer-Yitzchak Fried (who replaced his father, the Gaon R' Yitzchak as head of the rabbinical court and college in Volozhin), writes about R' Yehonatan, "...renowned in Torah and piety, my soul friend, (par. 23), who lived here in the holy yeshiva of Volozhin". The great genius and renowned saint, revered rabbi, R' Yisrael-Meir, of blessed memory, from Radon, author of "*Hehafetz Chaim*", who knew R' Yehonatan when he was young, brings down in his well-known book, "*Ahavat Hesed*": "'*Marganita Tava* - Containing Good Rules of Conduct' by the true genius, saint and renowned rabbi of the preceding generation from among the sages of Israel, the genius and splendor of the Jewish People, devoted to God in his steadfastness of heart and awesome deeds, from the town of Lubtch, where everyone called him R' Yehonatan from Volin."

According to one source, R' Yehonatan served a short time before his death as rabbi and head of the rabbinical court in Lubtch. However, he resigned sometime later on account of his restrictions which he didn't want to force upon the members of the community. The same source, ("*HaMelitz*", 5660-1900: Ben Ephraim), relates that one of the students of R' Yehonatan in Lubtch was the then young R' Eliezer-Chaim Meizel (who was subsequently head of the rabbinical court in many large communities in Poland). Also R' Eliezer Bakshtansky from Pinsk, a native born son of Lubtch and relative of Shmuel Bakshter, studied under R' Yehonatan and heard words of Torah from his mouth.

The Gaon R'Aharon-David Baksht

This rabbi, one of the great *Halachic* [Legal part of Jewish traditional literature] authorities in Lithuania, was the author of the book "*Peulot Adam*", which contains new interpretations of laws, remarks and philosophical thoughts on the book "*Chayai Adam*", by the Gaon R' Avraham Danzig, rabbi in Vilna. However, it was only in 5643 (1883), fifteen years after the author's death, that this book had the fortune to be published in Vilna.

The manuscript, which was in the possession of the author's son, R' Chaim-Eliezer, resident of the town of Darbani, was published at the expense of the author's son-in-law, R' Shniur Zalman, a well-to-do Jew of the Habad Hassidim and one of the important figures in Vilna. In his preface to the book, R' Shniur Zalman writes that his father-in-law had written two other important works which had remained, one entitled "*Sha'ar HaMishkal*", containing two explanations of the Rambam's (Maimonides') "*Sefer HaMitzvot*", and the other, bearing the name "*Moreh Da'at*" dealing with exegesis and ethics.

According to the following source, we know that R' Avraham-David Baksht was one of the close friends of R' Yitzchak of Volozhin. Printed at the front of the book "*Peulot Adam*" is a letter of R' Yitzchak to R' Avraham-David Baksht from the year 5586 (1826) regarding a matter of law concerning the grafting of a tree. This question was sent by R' Avraham-David in his time to R' Chaim from Volozhin, father of the Gaon R' Yitzchak. In the meantime R' Chaim died and R' Avraham-David asked R' Yitzchak if he would kindly send him the response that his father, the Gaon, of blessed memory, had written. R' Yitzchak replied that this response was not found among his father's writings due to a fire that had broken out in Volozhin. He mentions something en passant about an illness which struck him the previous year and the following summer. R' Avraham-Yitzchak is described in these words: "My beloved friend, the Rabbi, Light of the Exile, sharp-minded, reasonable in handing down decisions, astute branch of the family tree, standing with its roots."

In the preface to the book, R' Chaim-Eliezer praises R' Avraham-Zadok Boigen, head of the rabbinical court in Darbani, who encouraged him to tend to the printing of this important book of his father's, and blesses his brother-in-law (his sister's husband) with the blessing that "he should dwell in the shade (protection) of money", and this blessing, in fact, became a shield against that, and he published the book at his own expense - it is for the merit of the many and for the merit of the soul of the rabbi and author who toiled all his life in learning Torah. And indeed, this author from Lubtch revealed himself as an authority in Jewish law and an expert in handing down decisions, and in this book he often surpasses what he wrote in "*Chayai Adam*", which is intended for use by deciders of Jewish law based on the "*Orach Haim*" section of the "*Shulchan Arukh*" (Code of Jewish Law). He likewise surpasses the book "*Chochmat Adam*", which is devoted to the "*Yoreh Deyah*" component of the "*Shulchan Arukh*" written by the author of "*Chayei Adam*". Only some of the ideas were printed in his book. The rest are found in manuscript and are awaiting someone to come to the rescue and pay for the printing.

According to the preface of the book, it is known that R' Avraham-David Baksht lived a life of suffering and distress until his acceptance as a rabbi in Lubtch. He would teach his pupils for the sake of Heaven without accepting any payment in return. Apparently, the honorable resident of the town, Rabbi Shmuel Bakshter who, I seem to think, was a relative of his, helped him obtain a position in the rabbinate. And indeed, this family was famous in its importance, as the Gaon R' Yitzchak emphasizes in his letter to R' Avraham-David, "the branch of the family tree".

Rabbi Avraham-David passed away in the year 5627 (1867). A death notice appeared in the Hebrew weekly "*HaLevanon*", year 4, 5627-8, issue 25. The author of the report is the Bible scholar, R' Yehoshua Bar Elchanan HaLevi Levinsohn, a distinguished person from Lubtch.

The Gaon Rabbi Shmuel Zibertansky

R' Shmuel Zibertansky was born in Lubtch in 5578 (1818). He was the son of Rabbi Yosef, a member of the Maslovty family. He was orphaned as an infant and received his Torah education from his father's father. His splendid abilities were already evident as a child. He later came to Vilna to soak up religious instruction at the upper level *yeshiva* where he studied under the patronage of his relative, the Gaon R' Yisrael Zartcher, one of the leading rabbis of the city. The youth, whose soul craved clear and outstanding learning, soon gave proof of his great skills, rapid grasp of ideas, and amazing memory. His mind abounded with new interpretations, which made him famous as the "child prodigy from Lubtch". His classmates with whom he exchanged ideas were two "geniuses", R' Hillel Mileikovsky, head of the rabbinical court in Salant, and R' Alexander-Moshe Lapidotsohn, head of the rabbinical court in Roseini. They remained R' Shmuel's friends all their lives.

There were rabbis among the well-to-do property owners who wanted R' Shmuel as a son-in-law. The wealthy and respected R' Moshe Rodominer succeeded in winning him as a husband for his daughter, thus removing the burden of making a living from R' Shmuel so that he could continue to study Torah and become famous as one of the geniuses. And indeed, R' Shmuel became a household name in the world of Torah.

In 5638 (1878), when still diligent as a private person in the "tents of Torah", R' Shmuel was appointed supervisor of the *kolel* in the "Opatov" Beit Midrash in Vilna, which was maintained by a special fund from the estate of the wealthy R' Yudel Opatov. There, many superior students, including great Torah scholars, warmed themselves in his light. When the scholar, the Gaon R' Yaakov Barit, a rabbi in Vilna, died in 5643 (1883), R' Shmuel was appointed to assume his position, a role he performed with much success until his death on 8 *Tammuz*, 5658 (1898).

R' Shmuel's grandson, the Gaon R' Hanoch-Henich Eiges, (son-in-law of the son of R' Shlomo Zibertansky) published letters remaining after R' Shmuel's death in a special book entitled "*Olam Shmuel*" (Vilna 5661, 1901). The book contains two parts: Part I - differences of opinion, new interpretations and elucidations on subjects from the *Mishnah* [Collection of Oral Laws]; Part II - sermons and concluding remarks on various tractates of the Talmud. R' Hanoch-Henich attached new interpretations of the Torah of his own to this book entitled "*Minchat Hanoch*" (on matters relating to sacred offerings).

A eulogy delivered upon the death of the Gaon R' Shmuel may be found in the book, "*Makor Haim*" by the Gaon R' Chaim Seglovitz, rabbi in Vilna. The author knew R' Shmuel very well, having regularly engaged in give and take with him on certain matters of Jewish law. He quotes the Gaon R' Shmuel several times in this book.

R' "Shmuel from Lubtch" was known by this name within and without Vilna. He even liked being called by the name of his hometown, which produced famous personalities of Torah and spiritual leaders who were renowned among the Jewish people.

R' Shmuel once received a letter from the rabbinate in Lubtch. This was apparently around 5628 (1868) after the death of the head of the rabbinical court, R' Aharon David Baksht. According to Mr. Pisiuk, R' Shmuel served as head of the rabbinical court in Lubtch. However, he missed Vilna, returned to his family and gave up his position with the rabbinate in Lubtch. It seems that his wife and children, who were in Vilna, refused to settle in the small town of Lubtch.

The Gaon R' Yechiel-Michal Epshtein

The Gaon R' Yechiel-Michal Epshtein was born in 5590 (1830) into a distinguished family in Bobruisk (Belarussia). His father, R' Aharon, devoted his son to Torah and hung all his hopes and wishes on him. He studied at the yeshiva in Volozhin where he was the pupil of R' Yitzchak, from whom he acquired a way of learning involving methodical expertise, examination of versions and words of the early Talmudic expositors. He was especially occupied with rendering definitive *Halachic* decisions through exposure to all sources. He was 22 years old when he was ordained by the great rabbis of Lithuania. However, he gave up the rabbinate and dwelled in the "tents of Torah". His livelihood was assured thanks to his well-to-do father and father-in-law, R' Yaakov Berlin, a resident of Mir, who was also well-off, distinguished, scholarly, respected and a lover of Torah.

However, owing to conditions at the time - his father died and his father-in-law went to live in Eretz-Yisrael - R' Yechiel-Michal accepted a position with the rabbinate in Novozibkov (Tsarnigov Region). Although this city was home to numerous Habad Hassidim, the Hassidic *Admor* [rabbi] agreed to the appointment of the rabbi in his community.

He was assiduous in his learning also in Novozibkov. In 5629 (1869), he wrote a book entitled "*Or Layesharim*" dealing with the "*Sefer HaYashar*" by Rabbenu Tam. R' Epshtein's work was published by the Zytomir Press a few generations later.

He was already famous as a genius when he was accepted as the head of the rabbinic court in Lubtch and the Jews of the town rejoiced over his appointment. However, their happiness was premature. The leaders of the Novogrudek community "snatched" the rabbi away from them unbeknownst to the people of Lubtch. On the first day of Tammuz 5634 (1874), the Jews of Novogrudek welcomed him with honor befitting a king. And this incident became the topic of conversation in all the small towns of the area. R' Yechiel-Michal became a great "responder" to questions on matters of Jewish law; people turned to him from far and wide with serious questions and for the sake of obtaining rabbinic ordination.

Despite his concerns for the affairs of the community and for two additional matters mentioned above, R' Yechiel-Michal Epshtein surprised the Torah world with the writing of his great "*Arukh HaShulchan*" on four parts of the "*Shulchan Arukh*" #148; (Code of Jewish Law by Joseph Caro) characterized by its originality, independence of thought, fine planning and clear style. Designed according to the format of R' Mordechai Yaffe's "*HaLevushim*", this major work deals not only with laws in force in his time alone, but also with all subjects pertaining to *Halacha* and even pertaining to three "Orders" of the Mishneh (*Zera'im, Kodashim and Taharot*) from the first sources of Talmudic literature to contemporary deciders of Jewish law. In this book, he brings down decisions based on vague and unknown sources unfamiliar to several great *Halachic* authorities. He deciphers them in a clear and simple style which is understandable to everyone. He shows the give and take of *Halachic* clarification in the subject under discussion and thereby one arrives not only at knowing the law itself in light of its definitive judgment, but also the sources themselves, which is very beneficial even to rabbis who are experts in these matters.

Two parts of the "*Arukh HaShulchan*" appeared in print by the day of the death of the Gaon R' Yechiel-Michal Epshtein in 5668 (1908); seven additional parts were brought for printing after his death (Vilna, 1923-28) by his daughter, Brayna Volbrinsky. R' Yechiel-Michal Epshtein left behind new interpretations on the Babylonian and Jerusalem Talmud and a mass of responses which have yet to appear in print. In 1938, a continuation of his above-mentioned decisions appeared entitled "*Arukh HaShulchan le-Atid*" (Yalkut Publication) on the Mishneh Order of *Zera'im* with a preface by his grandson, Rabbi Meir Berlin, son of the "Netziv" of Volozhin, and likewise a third part (1946), published by the Mosad Rav Kook-Jerusalem.

The sons of the author of "*Arukh HaShulchan*" were R' Baer and R' Baruch Epshtein: R' Baer was a great scholar who emigrated to Eretz-Yisrael in 5666 (1906) and settled in Jerusalem. He was the treasurer of several Torah and charity institutions of the former Jewish population in Palestine. He died in 5691 (1931) and was laid to rest on the Mt. of Olives. R' Baruch Epshtein, a resident of Pinsk, is the son-in-law of the Gaon R' Eliezer-Moshe HaLevi, of the Horovitz family. He was the author of the book "*Torah Temimah*". He likewise wrote his autobiography and the life of his ancestors entitled "*Makor Baruch*" in three volumes including a long introduction in a separate volume (Vilna 5688-1928).

Rabbi Tzvi-Nahum Titkin

We do not have any special information concerning this rabbi. He was head of the rabbinical court in Lubtch after the death of Rabbi Avraham-David Baksht and he remained in that position until 5638 (1878). In that same year, he was accepted as head of the rabbinical court in Kletsk (Slutsk District) and left Lubtch.

Zvi-Nahum was a distinguished scholar as was fitting the level of Talmudic erudition of Lubtch, especially as at that time the righteous and venerable R' Shmuel Baksht was still alive and active there. R' Zvi-Nahum died in Kletsk in 5641 (1881) at the age of 61.

During the period when R' Zvi-Nahum served in office in Lubtch, his son R' Moshe-Chaim (Rabinovitz) grew up and was educated by his father, who designated a group of learning partners for him among the finest *yeshiva* students in the town. Among them was the renowned Talmudist R' Malkiel Tennenboim, the son-in-law of a wealthy Jew who owned an estate near Yarmitch, close to Lubtch. R' Malkiel would come to Lubtch to refresh himself with words of Torah with the head of the rabbinical court, R' Zvi-Nahum and he chose a fixed place for himself in the study hall in Lubtch on the days he came there. Later on, R' Malkiel was prominent as head of the rabbinical court in Lomzhe and wrote a book entitled "*Divrei Malkiel*".

Moshe-Chaim also studied in Minsk in the company of rabbis, R' Aryeh-Leib, the official town rabbi and R' Gershon-Tanhum, head of the rabbinic college (Mesivta) in the "*kloiz*" [synagogue] in Limks and likewise with R' Shmuel Zibertansky (native of Lubtch), and R' Eliyahu-Eliezer Grudzhensky - both of whom were rabbis in the city of Vilna.

R' Moshe-Chaim was a distinguished Talmudic authority and was considered a giant in Torah in the circle of the younger generation of rabbis. He emigrated to America where he guided the new spiritual leaders in the traditional ways of Torah. In 5648 (1888), he was rabbi and leader of a congregation in the Brownsville section of Brooklyn, New York and established regulations for strengthening religion, exalting Torah and the honor of the rabbinate. R' Moshe-Chaim had the merit of living a long life and he died in 5692 (1932), at the age of 82. He left behind works on all subjects of Torah.

R' Moshe-Chaim always remembered his hometown of Lubtch and would often send sums of money for the benefit of religious and charitable organizations in the town.

Rabbi Yitzchak HaLevi Bonimovitch

We have no information regarding the biography of Rabbi Yitzchak HaLevi Bonimovitch. He may have been born in Volozhin if we consider the fact that this name was common in that town in those days and that several people bearing that name were heads of the community and town workers.

R' Yitzchak was accepted as rabbi in Lubtch after R' Zvi-Nahum Tiktin moved to Kletsk. In 5659 (1899), he was very active on behalf of the town and devoted himself with great energy to the rehabilitation of the "burned ones", those who were burned in the great fire that broke out that year in Lubtch.

Certain details of that fire, an event which served as a date marker in the history of Lubtch, can be found in the daily newspaper, "*HaTsfira*", issue #117, of the year 5658 (1898). There we read: "Yesterday, God's hand was evident in the city. At twelve o'clock a fire broke out and consumed more than 150 homes and buildings including a synagogue, and two study halls. The public bath, post and telegraph office and the pharmacy were also burned to their foundation. More than 200 families whose homes were reduced to embers are suffering want and hunger. The condition of these unfortunate people is awful and it is impossible to describe the disaster which befell them so suddenly." This report is signed by A.Ch. Itzkavitch from Delatitch, who appeals "to the generous among the people to hurry to the welfare and aid of the "burned ones", adding that "every donation, even the smallest, will be accepted with many thanks".

In the newspaper "*HaTsfira*", issue #182, the head of the Lubtch rabbinical court, Rabbi Yitzchak HaLevi Bonimovitch, appeals directly to public opinion in Lithuania and Russia asking for help for the victims of the fire of our town in the following words: "A appeal for aid! The voices of the moaning of the victims of the fire in our town will reach Heaven. It is impossible to describe in words the extent of the affliction, misfortune and distress which befell this city, as the victims were unable to save any of their belongings, lacking even slight relief, and they have nothing to feed themselves or their children. Also the study halls and synagogue, which were built for our prayers, were burned down to their foundation, and there is no place to pour out our prayers before God the Merciful on the High Holy Days, which are coming upon us for the good".

"Please, merciful sons of merciful fathers, take pity on the souls of the misfortunate who are wandering around the streets of Lubtch. Bear in mind that the days of autumn will not be long in coming and that there is no place of refuge for those stricken by the disaster to hide from the cold and from the terrible lack of food and clothing in every corner to which we turn- in our city. Please hurry to our aid! And all who have pity will themselves be pitied and will acquire wealth in their homes, and their charity is everlasting".

This special emotional appeal of Rabbi Bonimovitch made a great impression on the Sons of Israel in the near-by communities and on certain individuals among the generous people in other places. In connection with this, we read in "*HaTsfira*", # 206, the following: "On behalf of the poor people in our town who were victims of the fire", Chaim Bonimovitch (apparently the rabbi's son) expresses his special thanks to the honorable gentlemen: "the respected citizen, Dr. Shapira, and Pan [Sir] Beiten for not sparing any effort and toil in raising money and collecting food from the estate owners - hundreds of rubles which will be divided among the misfortunate to help them in every way possible, and yet their hand is still outstretched. And may the blessing of the poor, who are awaiting the Lord's salvation and the aid of men, come upon them."

One of the sons of Rabbi Yitzchak HaLevi Bonimovitch was R' Aharon HaLevi, head of the rabbinical court in Shatsk (Slutsk District) from 1884 to the day of his death in the month of Tammuz 5674 (1914), some twenty days before the outbreak of the First World War. The Orthodox Hebrew weekly, "*HaModia*", which appeared then in Poltava (Ukraine), carried this news report. Special emphasis was placed on the fact that the late rabbi was "the son of the Gaon R' Yitzchak HaLevi (Bonimovitch), head of the rabbinical court in Lubtch."

Rabbi Yitzchak HaLevi Bonimovitch (R' Itchele)

Rabbi Meir Abovitz

He was born in the small town of Shniadova (Lomzhe District) in 5636 (1876). He received his Talmud education at the *yeshivot* in Lomzhe and Radon as well as in the *Kolel* [school for married men who left their wives to study] in Kovna. He was ordained for the rabbinate by the "Gaonim": R' Moshe Danishevsky, head of the rabbinical court in Slobodka, R' Hirsch Rabinovitch, head of the rabbinical court in Kovna, and R' Malkiel Tennenboim, head of the rabbinical court in Lomzhe. He served as head of the rabbinical court in Delatitch and later in Lubtch after the death of the previous rabbi.

However, Rabbi Abovitz served for only a short time as head of the rabbinical court in Lubtch. In the fall of 5675 (1915), during World War I,

Lubtch was destroyed to its foundations. The Jews who were living there became war refugees. They were uprooted and wandered to other places. Rabbi Abovitz found a place of refuge in Novogrudek, which was then occupied by the Germans. He remained there afterwards and was active in the rabbinate for many years - until 5701 (1941) when World War II was raging.

Rabbi Meir Abovitz was a great rabbi, highly respected in the districts of Polish Lithuania and represented the glorious rabbinate of Lubtch with honor. He was also a great scholar of the Jerusalem Talmud, something which was uncommon among other rabbis, even the most well-known among them. He won recognition and great renown in the rabbinical world with his book "*Pnei Ma'or*" on both Talmud tractates of Shabbat and Eruvin in the Jerusalem Talmud (Vilna, 5686, 5698) In this book, the author mainly explains remarks by the Gra [the Gaon from Vilna] pertaining to his elucidation of the Jerusalem Talmud. He is aided in several places by substitutions of texts brought down in the book "*Ahavat Tsion ViYerushalayim*" by the sage, R' Dov Baer Ratner from Vilna. Likewise, he attached to his book "*HaNer HaMa'aravi*" by the Gaon R' Yosef-Shaul Natansohn, and "*Eyn Mishpat*" by the Gaon R' Mordechai-Zev Itinga, in addition to the two above-mentioned tractates of the Jerusalem Talmud. He also added to his book, "*Pnei Ma'or*", pamphlets entitled "*Shvivei-Or*", containing remarks, completions and additions next to each tractate.

R' Abovitz lost many of his writings in Lubtch on the day the Germans occupied the town during the First World War. Nevertheless, new interpretations of his, on most of the tractates of the Babylonian Talmud as well as on the majority of the tractates of the Jerusalem Talmud remained in his possession. Close to his death, on the eve of the dreadful Holocaust, his book of discourses, "*Kochavei Or*" also appeared (Vilna 1938). It contains sermons, elucidations of legends and explanatory discussions given at the conclusion of a tractate of the Talmud or an Order of the Mishna. Included also are his remarks on the "*Azharot*" of R' Shlomo Ibn Gvirol, referring to the 613 commandments in poetry form (recited on the Feast of Weeks in many Sephardic congregations).

Rabbi Meir Abovitz was a loyal Zionist, devoted to the *Mizrachi* [religious Zionist] movement and participated in its conferences and congresses. He was also active on behalf of the Jewish National Fund and the *Keren HaYesod* and took part in special fund raising drives for the benefit of the renewed Jewish settlement in Eretz-Yisrael.

In 5679 (1919) Rabbi Abovitz took part in a meeting which took place in Vilna to establish the *Mizrachi* movement. Most of the rabbis and rabbinic judges of the "Jerusalem of Lithuania", including R' Yitzchak HaLevi Rubinshtein, R' Hanoch-Henich Eiges and R' Meir Karelitz took part in the meeting. He signed a manifesto presented by a group of rabbis in Polish Lithuania appealing to others to join the *Mizrachi* movement, emphasizing the great need "to develop branches and associations in all cities near and far in Lithuania which will work for the benefit of the building of our people on the mountains of Zion and to correspond in writing with the rest of the *Mizrachi* centers", and [they called] "on the central committee to try to improve the education of our children according to the spirit of the written and orally transmitted Torah and to plant in their hearts faithful love of our Torah for our people and our land".

He also participated in the first conference of *Mizrachi* rabbis in Greater Poland which took place in Warsaw in the summer of 5683 (1923). He signed a manifesto on behalf of the *Mizrachi* rabbis in Poland (Elul 5683) encouraging Jews to join the *Mizrachi* movement, emphasizing the great value of the movement "which aspires to strengthen the Torah and the revival of Eretz-Yisrael, the Jewish People, and the language of Israel wholeheartedly".

Rabbi Abovitz helped found the *Mizrachi* branch in Novogrudek - the only religious organization in the city - and greatly endeavored to strengthen national-religious education in that city as a safeguard against the influence of secular schools that had sprouted in and around Novogrudek after the First World War. He also set up a lower division yeshiva in Novogrudek (1922) which was permeated with the religious Zionist spirit in the style of *Mizrachi*. He likewise established a *Shas* society next to *Mizrachi*.

Despite his being a loyal Zionist, Rabbi Meir Abovitz was accepted as well by the rabbis in the area who tended towards *Agudat Yisrael* [ultra-orthodox party]. The Gaonim R' Chaim-Ozer Grudzhensky from Vilna, R' Zvi-Hirsch Kamai from Mir and R' Elchanan Vasserman from Baronovitch considered him to be a great person, both crowned with Torah and God-fearing.

The son of the Gaon R' Elchanan Vasserman, R' Simcha (lives in the USA), was R' Meir Abovitz's son-in-law. In his father's book, "*Kovetz Shiurim*" (published in Israel), R' Simcha points out that his father-in-law, R' Meir Abovitz, died on 7 *Tevet* 5701 (January 6, 1941), had the merit of dying on his bed and was buried in Novogrudek.

Rabbi Yitzchak Weiss (Veis) - May the Lord Avenge His Death!

He was a native of Yanova (Grodno District). He received an outstanding Talmudic education. For a number of years he attended R' Yosef Yozel's *Musar* (Ethics Movement) Yeshiva in Novogrudek. He then studied at the Mir Yeshiva for some time and was a close friend of the Gaon R' Eliyahu-Baruch Kamai, head of the rabbinical court and rabbinical college of this town. He was a son-in-law of the Gaon R' Meir Abovitz, head of the rabbinical court in Lubtch and took his place in the rabbinate of that small town after his father-in-law was accepted for a position in the rabbinate of Novogrudek and settled there.

R' Yitzchak Weiss was considered an outstanding and innovative student according to the style of learning of the Lithuanian *yeshivot*. His way of learning in understanding the secrets of the various topics of the Talmud according to the explanations of the early Talmudic authorities was based on the approach of his teacher and rabbi, the Gaon R' Raphael-Alter Shmuelovitz (also a native of Lubtch), head of the rabbinical college in Novogrudek. He had some written lessons of his above-mentioned teacher and rabbi on various tractates of the Talmud, and many of the Mir Yeshiva students came to him in Lubtch to become "intoxicated" with the learning method of both R' Alter and R' Yitzchak.

For some time R' Yitzchak maintained a group of *yeshiva* and Torah students in Lubtch who were blessed with special ability and who learned diligently under his guidance in the local study hall. He saw to it that they had lodging and food. He would sometimes come to the Mir Yeshiva to participate in the Talmudic give and take with the famous *yeshiva* boys and rabbinic college students. The following real-life description of R' Yitzchak may be found in the preface to the book, "*Imrei Da'at*" (Jerusalem, 5722, 1962):

"I have a holy obligation to recall the memory of my childhood friend, the *Gaon* [genius], and wonderful innovator of *halacha* and ethics, R' Yitzchak Weiss, the Lubtch rabbi, who was called at the "Yitzchak Yanover" Yeshiva, may the Lord avenge his blood!"

To our sorrow, not a trace remains of his family. We became friends forever in a written contract for Torah and work, and we shared our expenses. We went into seclusion in summer as well as in winter in some village where we spent days and nights undisturbed. After we each got married, we moved to the *yeshiva* in Baronovitch. Later we decided to seek positions in the rabbinate. Together we studied the rulings of the deciders of Jewish law and in the same week he got a position in the rabbinate of Lubtch and I in Horodishets. May his memory be blessed and may the Lord avenge his blood!

The writer of these lines is Rabbi Yitzchak Veinshtein from Zhetil, who was head of the rabbinical court in Horodishets, spiritual director of the Volozhin Yeshiva and head of the rabbinical court in Vishniva and now a resident of Jerusalem.

It is worth mentioning that with all R' Yitzchak Weiss' devotion to Lithuanian learning and to the aims of the *Musar* movement in Novogrudek, he was cordial to religious Zionism and contributed to the Zionist fund and *Mizrachi* fundraising drives. He likewise engaged in propaganda to encourage young people from the small towns to go on *aliya* to Eretz Yisrael.

[Page 98]

Reb Itchele's Curse

by Yitzchak Shlimovitch

Translated from the Yiddish by Harvey Spitzer

Year after year, the Jews of Lubtch were involved in law suits with the gentiles over their claim to the pasture fields by the Neiman River. Meanwhile, the gentiles inflicted great harm on the animals: they would drive the cows away from the pasture, beat them pitilessly and even cut off their udders.

One night, a fire broke out on Delatitch Street, where the gentiles lived. Their sheds containing stored crops from the fields also caught fire. On that very same day, the gentiles had cut the udders off several cows belonging to Jews. The Jews had apparently forgotten about that and eagerly helped the fire fighters put out the blaze.

The rabbi at that time, Reb Itchele, seeing now hard the Jewish boys were working to extinguish the fire, said to them:

"Children, don't exhaust yourselves! If their property burns down every year, they'll forget about us." Since then, not a year has gone by that there haven't been fires among the gentiles on Delatitch Street.

My father, from whom I heard this story, used to add: – The *zaddik* (righteous man) had put this curse on them.

[Pages 99-104]

That's How We Lived...

by Gershon Jankelowitz

Transcribed and expanded by Greta (born Grunia) Katz (nee Jankelowitz) for her father Gershon

Translated from the Yiddish by Harvey Spitzer

My father, Hershel Zvi, was a country man and lived in the little village of Zaluzshok, near Ostashin. At that time, many Jews lived in villages, owned small stores and taverns, bought up products from the gentiles, sowed fields and gardens and struggled to make a living.

Although we lived among gentiles, we kept our "*Yiddishkeit*" [Judaism]. We prayed three times a day, obeyed the dietary laws, sent our children to study with teachers or brought teachers to our homes, observed the Sabbath and, on the holidays, we would go to the small towns ("*shtetlach*") to celebrate the festivals together with all the Jews.

Certainly, all the stories which were told about the country people were exaggerated. Perhaps the country folk were a little more primitive, more naïve than the city people. There were also a lot of ignorant and coarse people, but they could just as well be found in the cities, but no one told stories about them and put their every word on display.

The rhythm of life flowed by quietly and peacefully with its small worries and small joys. People made do with little, didn't have great aspirations and thanked God for giving them life and a piece of bread.

But suddenly, a decree was issued by the Czar that the Jews must leave the villages and move to the small towns. My father, may he rest in peace, harnessed the horse to the wagon, placed a few things on it, seated mother and her 5 sons and 5 daughters, said goodbye to our Gentile neighbors and left for my grandfather's home in Lubtch.

Gershon Jankelowitz

Chaya-Basha Jankelowitz

My grandfather, Yoske Yisrael-Isaacs, was a rich landlord and owned a big place and fields in the small town. When my father arrived and began to cry: "What should I do now with my family?", my grandfather calmed him and said: "You know, my son, I divided the inheritance while I'm still alive among your brothers and sisters, and I won't do you an injustice either. Take the backmost place for yourself with a small field, build a house, plant a big garden with vegetables and God will help you".

Father followed his advice and we became residents of Lubtch. But, as we didn't have any income, my father became a "village traveler". He would borrow merchandise from Shlomo Chazkels and sell it to the peasants in the surrounding villages. In addition, he would lay out 3 rubles in cash to buy products from the peasants. Every Sunday they would settle their accounts and borrow more merchandise until the following Sunday. That's how Jews did business at that time and, thank God, made a living. Trading consisted mainly in buying and selling linseed, flax, cattle, horses, mushrooms, hog bristles, small hides, fowl and eggs.

At the beginning of the [20th] century, 400 Jewish families were living in Lubtch and of those, 100 families were "village travelers", going out to the villages on business. The rabbi at that time was Rebbe Itchele, a superlative scholar and great *zaddik* (righteous man). His salary was 10 rubles a week and when the people wanted to add two more rubles to his pay, he refused to accept it. The rabbi's salary came from a tax on yeast and slaughtering animals. The *chazan* [cantor] was called Reb Meyer-Ozer, and he had a very pleasant voice. In general, one must remember that the Jews of Lubtch were connoisseurs of singing. They were ready and willing to pay a lot for a good cantorial "piece". How many small towns allowed themselves the luxury of maintaining their own *chazan*? But, let's get back to that time. The rabbi used to pray in the red study hall. There were also, of course, scholars and actually good scholars: Moshe-Mordechai from Novogrudeker Street, Reuvke the Scholar and others.

When Rebbe Itchele passed away, his son, Rebbe Yosef-Eliahu succeeded him as rabbi of the village. However, some of the Jews in Lubtch didn't agree and demanded that another rabbi be appointed- Rebbe Hirsh, the brother of Reb Moshe Rabinovitch. A fire of contention broke out, and finally there were two rabbis in Lubtch. The taxes on yeast and slaughtering continued to support both rabbis.

When I was supposed to get married, it turned out that my fiancee's relatives were followers of Rebbe Yosef-Eliahu, whereas my family belonged to the other side. My fiancee's relatives announced that if Rebbe Hirsh officiated under the *chuppa* [wedding canopy], they wouldn't attend the wedding. Their ultimatum made us very sad, but I wouldn't give in. Of course, Rebbi Hirsh did, in fact, marry us under the *chuppa,* and my fiancee's family did attend the wedding (did they really have a choice?), but the next morning my father-in-law went to pray in the other study hall and didn't bring me into *shul* as required by custom. Therefore, we refused to go to the "sweet ginger cake and brandy" ceremony at my wife's family's home. Some good friends, however, got involved and made peace in the family at the sweets table. These were the kinds of problems that concerned us at that time. It is really hard to conceive of the great change that has taken place in Jewish life in the course of the last two generations.

After my marriage, I had to worry about providing for my wife and our children, who came into the world one after the other - may they have long lives! I rented orchards, had a dairy farm, traded in whatever was allowed and nevertheless could hardly make a living.

When the First World War broke out (1913), we were driven out of the town. We spent the entire war years wandering through various villages around Novogrudek. After the war, we returned to Lubtch, but the village lay in ruins and we had to start all over. We were hungry and suffered a great deal until we managed to get back on our feet.

The situation in Poland got progressively worse. A serious economic crisis accompanied by blatant anti-Semitism oppressed us and also provided warning about the future. Jews started to seek out countries for emigration. They would go anywhere if only to get away from Poland and from the smoldering volcano-Europe.

In 1930, I left Lubtch for South Africa. Four years later I brought over my children just before the onset of the bloody deluge.

[Page 104]

For the general good...

by Shalom Leibovitch

Translated from the Yiddish by Harvey Spitzer

Jews in Lubtch generally enjoyed neighborly relations with the gentiles in the village. However, there were instances where they tried to abuse us. Naturally, we wouldn't let them.

One Sabbath day, the gentiles took their herds up to graze on the *vorek* [meadow], which belonged to the Jews.

Obeying the rabbi's orders, we went out to the *vorek* and chased off the gentiles with force. We wouldn't allow Jewish property to become ownerless. The gentiles thought that we wouldn't react on the holy Sabbath, but they were mistaken. The rabbi permitted it, having the general interest in view.

[Pages 105-110]

The 1915 fire in Lubtch

By Yitzchak Shlimovitch

Translated from Hebrew by Harvey Spitzer

Yitzchak Shlimovitch

People in our village spoke a great deal about the war. The "statesmen" and the "strategists" would gather in a corner of the house of learning and discuss the war for hours at length. As was the custom, there were "Russian" and "Germans", that is, those who supported the Russians and those who sided with the Germans. But, when the war was already knocking at our door, the "statesmen", who followed the progress of the war on their hand, did not know what to think. And even when the first refugees began showing up around the high holidays, they still assured us that "it will not come to us". It was simple and clear: a forsaken village, 30 miles from the railroad line, what do armies have to do here?...

At the conclusion of Yom Kippur, when Jews were sitting down and breaking their fast, a loud noise of heavy wagons and horseshoes was suddenly heard. Our house was on a street which cut across the entire village. We went out to see what was going on. The whole street was filled with several rows of wagons harnessed to four and six horses which kept on moving ahead. No one could sleep at all that night because of the noise. This went on for two full days without a stop. An entire army with all its weapons and soldiers was passing through: foot soldiers, horsemen, adjunct divisions and "provisions". At the side of the road, exhausted and thirsty soldiers walked along in disarray. Many of them were wounded, with bandages covering their body parts. Some would run into the houses asking for a piece of bread or a drink of water. When there was only a small loaf of bread remaining in our house, which we wanted to keep for ourselves, a soldier came in just then asking for bread. Father told him that we had only that single, small loaf and that he couldn't give it away to him. The soldier raised his gun and pointed it at father's chest and called out: "If you don't give it to me, I'll put a bullet right through you!" And this wasn't the only such case.

In the morning on the eve of the holiday of *Sukkot* [Festival of Tabernacles], a Russian colonel came into our house. He was a tall, slender man with a long, gray beard and a good-natured expression of true intelligence on his face. He asked if he could buy a fur coat. We handed him a coat and he put it on. He asked the price and paid. This made a great impression on everyone. After the terror of the Cossacks, who took everything without money, besides honoring us with beatings, this was certainly a surprise and my father started to cry. The colonel placed his hand on father's shoulder and said:

- – Don't cry, little uncle, you needn't. The Germans will actually soon be here, but don't worry. If they go another seven years the way they have been going, we will lose some territory, but their feet will become swollen as they move on and they will fall.

The two days of *Sukkot* went by in ever-growing fear. The village was under the command of the Cossacks, who took over in their own way. On the second day of *Sukkot*, in the daytime, an airplane flew over. People said it was a German plane and that it would drop bombs. There was a panic. People went down into the cellars to find shelter, but the plane went away and nothing happened. An hour later, two explosions shook the village. There was great confusion. No one knew what to do, where to run. With fingers shaking from fright, people began harnessing their horses to wagons and hurried out of the village onto the *vorek* [meadow], between the Neiman River and the study halls. That evening, someone came to tell us that the first bomb had hit Binyaminke's cellar and that there were dead and wounded.

Binyaminke, the rich wholesale grocer, was a whimsical Jew, stubborn but very smart with various ideas. A story was told about him: One morning he unloaded a few barrels of herring in his store. A neighbor who was just then passing by noticed that sauce was leaking from one of the barrels. The Jew did not waste a second, put out a finger and began licking the sauce. When Binyaminke saw this, he began shouting at the Jew: "Oy, Reb Meir, you are a Jew, a *nasher*!" [lover of dainty foods, a gourmand].

A few years before World War I, Binyaminke's house burned down together with other houses. When re-building his house, Binyaminke said: "This time I'll build my house in such a way that if there's another fire in the village, my family and I will sit calmly in the cellar, drinking tea." He did, in fact, build a house with several floors, the loveliest brick house in the village, and he saw to it that it had a very strong cellar besides. When the airplane was flying over the village, he gathered his family and neighbors together and they went down to the cellar to seek protection. As fate would have it, precisely his house with the cellar was the first one to be hit and produced the first Jewish casualties in the village.

When night fell, fires could be seen. The sky was red in several places, indicating that the surrounding villages were burning. After midnight, the staccato sound of machine guns and rifles was heard. From time to time, cannons also thundered. Fright and panic increased. Jews with stronger nerves calmed the general populace and people were told to recite psalms, which was accompanied by the wailing of women and children. The whole time, soldiers kept on running away in order to get to the other side of the Neiman River. An airplane appeared and dropped bombs. The bridge started to burn, but the Cossacks ran through the fire on their horses, while those on foot went into the water.

Fires, which the Cossacks purposely set, began to break out in the village. A quarter of an hour later, the village was burning on all sides. The heat was so intense that we could not stay in our place, so we moved to wherever there was moist grass. Bullets were flying over our heads and hit the wagons, wounding horses and many people as well. We all prayed to God to save us from the great danger.

Suddenly, the shooting subsided. From afar, we could see the steel helmets of the approaching German soldiers. They soon, in fact, reached us and ordered us to "disappear" as quickly as possible on the other side of the village, closer to the smaller villages because the battle was still going on. We started on our way at once and hid out in one of the smaller villages.

When we came back home the next day, we found only chimneys and ovens, our houses having been destroyed by the fire. We had no other choice but to take up our walking sticks and set out on the difficult way of war refugees.

Our Culture Club

At the end of the war, we returned to the burned down, devastated place which was once our village, Lubtch. It took some time until we re-built our house, as did many other Jews from Lubtch who had wandered from place to place during the war years and had, at the first opportunity, come back to re-build their homes on the ruins.

The children, who had grown up during the war years and had become young men and women, barely knew one another and felt like strangers. They slowly began to get closer, to talk and meet in the evenings. A club was created which had the pretension of setting the cultural tone of the village and did, in fact, help set Jewish life on a new, more modern foundation.

The following people belonged to the club: Berele Kabak, Reuvke Berkovitch, Chaim Bruk, both Shapiros, Aba Rozovsky, my male cousins Yoel and Kushe, my female cousins and others. Our meeting place was at the home of one of our members, Bashke Shimshelevitch (Shia-Niames). Their neighbors, Sheinke Gelfand and Rashke, and Chaim Bruk's two sisters also came to the meetings.

Aba Rozovsky aspired to be a poet. He did, in fact, write lovely poems which he read aloud to us with great pathos. One of his poems has remained etched in my memory to this very day. It goes something like this: "A Jewish mother tells her son about the "Sambatyon" River and about the Jews who live there and that no one ever dies there. When the child gets older, he comes to his mother with a complaint: he is studying geography in school and has not found a place called "Sambatyon" on any map. "You foolish little child", answers his mother. "No one knows where it is located. No one dies there because, in fact, our people have not yet set a foot in there".

At the end of 1921, two sisters, Leah and Frumke Osherovsky, came into the village. The small children would always gather around them. Dear Frumke liked to occupy them like a good nursery school teacher. It was then that we thought about organizing an elementary school. We set up the school in a part of the white house of learning which had been repaired. The first two teachers were Chaim Persky and Leah Osherovsky. Money for the school and for the repairs was provided by the *Yekopo* assistance organization in Vilna. Incidentally, I would like to mention that this was done at the initiative of my father and Tuvia the *Shamash* [synagogue beadle] (Shimshelevtich), who devoted a lot of time, effort and work to bringing this plan to fruition.

We also set up a library, and right away many loyal readers of Yiddish and Hebrew showed up to borrow books. The first books were also received from *Yekopo* in Vilna. If my memory serves me correctly, the first organizing committee of the library consisted of the following members - Chaim Bruk, Berel Kabak, Bashke Shimshelevitch, Reuvke Berkovitch, Rashke, the blacksmith's daughter, Sheinke Gelfand and my humble self.

I left Lubtch in 1923.

[Page 110]

A Comedy

Translated from the Yiddish by Harvey Spitzer

The founding of the Beitar academy took place in the fire brigade coach-house. Shlomo Kalmanovitch stood at the door and let the people in.

A teenager comes up and asks him:

– Shlomo, what's taking place?

– A Trumpeldor comedy, Shlomo replies....

[Pages 111-114]

Small Towns of Houses and Trenches

by Moshe Kaganovitch

Translated from the Yiddish by Harvey Spitzer

(From a journey through the Vilna provinces)
Published in "Moment", No. 210
September 8, 1932

Lubtch and Delatitch are two small towns on the Neiman River, which flows here along the streets of both towns, adding much charm and beauty. Both towns were re-built on their ruins in the first years after the war (1918-23). The German-Russian front extended along both sides of the river for a couple of years. The entire population was evacuated and found a place of refuge in the outlying, surrounding villages.

After the war, Jews from both small towns returned to their homes, as did the peasants, and with industry and perseverance began to re-build the town and cultivate the black, fertile, blessed earth of this region. The residents have a lot to tell about those first days when they stayed temporarily in trenches and were exposed to all kinds of dangers. Many people were killed while digging and plowing, from the shrapnel, grenades and bombs which had remained stuck in the earth. They managed to build small houses and stores thanks to the help of relatives in America and a large loan from the Vilna relief organization, *Yekopo*. Today 450 families live in Lubtch, 300 of which are Jewish.

Delatitch is much smaller and looks like a big village. Located 5 kilometers from Lubtch, it gives the impression as being a suburb of the other. It is, in fact, joined to the Lubtch community and uses their religious articles. During the first years, many Jews made a living from the previous war by dealing in barbed wire, railroad equipment and various parts of the trenches until the higher military authorities declared these to be military property and prohibited anyone from taking them apart.

The big cement trenches extend here along the Neiman River. Even today, many trenches can be found in the small towns between houses, stables and sheds, and the population makes use of them for practical purposes such as for storing potatoes, etc.

The soil here, as said, is very fertile and black without any stones as nowhere else in the entire Vilna region. Much business is done in grain crops, flax and linseed, which grow very well here. "Dutch" cheese is produced here and is shipped from one end of Poland to the other. In the big centers, it is known as "Lithuanian" cheese. The cheese concessionaires, who get their milk from rich landlords, have, in the past few years, lost their wealth due to the enormous decline in the price of cheese which has surpassed all possible calculations (1.70-2.00 *zloty* last year).

I was in Lubtch at the time of the annual fair, the *Ilia*, when people used to really take in a lot of money. Today, however, the storekeepers in Lubtch are standing with folded hands in the middle of the fair. The peasants haggle, look at the merchandise, admit it's cheap but still go away without buying anything. Therefore, prices on everything are unbelievably low: 60 cucumbers were selling for 10 *groschen* and cherries at 8-10 *groschen* a kilo.

The general impression is that although Lubtch and Delatitch have been hard hit by the terrible crisis, the material situation of the Jews, in comparison to those in other small towns, is quite satisfactory. This is true because they have few expenses and everything is ridiculously cheap. People have vegetables and potatoes from their own gardens, and the standard of living has always been low. Likewise, people are involved in various businesses at the same time: cheese concession, retail stores, trading in grains, etc.

Besides all this, Jews of Lubtch have a reputation for being stingy, so they have, in fact, held on to the capital they acquired in the good years.

Lubtch has a cooperative bank, charity fund, a few organizations and clubs (*Hashomer Hatzair, Hechalutz, Beitar, Poalei Zion*), a *Tarbut* school (five grades) and a very active dramatics club which brings the town's youth together and is truly a social and spiritual asset. In the summer, however, these groups are practically all dead because the young people are busy helping their fathers in the gardens, cheese concessions and stores. Besides, the lovely Neiman River attracts them for bathing and having fun.

Now that winter is coming with its long nights and cold, dark days, when frost turns the frolicking waters of the Neiman River into chains of ice, only then do the young people participate in the activities of the organizations and clubs which also serve as rendezvous places.

Lubtch and Delatitch, with their wooden houses and trenches, then take a rest until spring, when the Neiman River announces the coming of the joyful, lively part of the year-summer.

Brought for printing: **Moshe Tzinovitz**

[Page 114]

A Red-Headed Bride...

by Chaim Yankelevitch

Translated from the Yiddish by Harvey Spitzer

Yenta luckily became a bride. It's easy to say "became a bride", but, in fact, a lot of effort, time and talking were required before the matchmaker succeeded in convincing the prospective groom and his parents - and winning their approval for the match.

Only afterwards did the real episode of bargaining and promises begin. How else? A table and chairs, sofa, beds, a couple of years free rent, and many other things just, in fact, as the saying goes: "Promises and love don't cost money".

But what can be done about the bride's hair? Yenta, poor thing, was punished by God - a girl with flaming red hair - a red-head. Little by little, people mumbled the truth. They're afraid the prospective groom will change his mind and that will be the end of the match.

When he heard about his, the groom-to-be called everyone together and calmly said:

A red-headed bride, it doesn't matter. Being with me, her reputation will be blackened...

[Page 114]

"As Is"

by Hillel Kroshnitz

Translated from the Yiddish by Harvey Spitzer

Meite Kasmeievitch's mother tells a few fortunate women that her daughter is being wooed by a young man from Radon. Actually, he is really not young, but he is rich and ready to take her daughter without a dowry of any kind. He'll take her "*kak stoi*", meaning "just as she stands and walks".

[Pages 115-119]

The Hidden Light of the Jewish Mother in Lubtch

by Chana Dichter

Translated from the Hebrew by Ann Belinsky

Chana Dichter

I arrived in Lubtch towards the end of 1933. I came there after working three years at the *Tarbut* school in the capital, Warsaw. On the way, my thoughts about the town were gloomy. I thought that I would lead a miserable and boring life in this faraway corner. The region is sure to be undeveloped, I thought, and the residents, like in all small towns, are busy making a living to the last of their strength and not free to develop a spiritual or intellectual life. But to my great joy, my thoughts did not turn out to be true. The people were friendly. The teaching staff at the school was large, responsible and dedicated. The school building was spacious, bustling with healthy, happy children enjoying a complete Hebrew education.

A dedicated and responsible parents committee was active in the school. I and the other new teachers met with the members for a prolonged discussion on the first Sabbath that we spent in the town. These were traditional people who went to the synagogue, as was their custom, for morning prayers, returned leisurely to their homes, tasted the Sabbath foods and only after that, met with the new teachers to get to know them close-up. The conversation was agreeable and pleasant. I immediately felt that we had a common language and that with combined strengths we would establish the Hebrew school in Lubtch. They finished with a promise: "We promise the teachers a fair salary, so that you can dedicate yourselves with a quiet heart to your pedagogical work." I was amazed - where did these Jews have such a correct attitude, being so far away from the pedagogical centers and busy with their daily battle of existence? But these are good Jews, who carried in their hearts the national obligation and heritage which they had received from their forefathers. From that time on - I dedicated myself to the school, to the children and youth and especially to the mothers. After a short while, I was integrated into the pageant of Jewish life in Lubtch, sharing the worries of both parents and children.

In order to get to know each of my pupils at close hand, I began to make home visits. I wanted to see the conditions of the housing and their way of life. When I returned to my room, I would write down my impressions. The picture was very dismal. Especially heart touching was the hard life of the Jewish mother. I saw her suffering, and her silence bore witness to the acceptance of her lot in life - "this is my fate!" I understood her feelings - she stands confused, without education and without experience, opposite the new stream which she did not know. The only thing that remained was the motherly instinct that nature had given her, with which she knew that she had to give all that was necessary for the education of her child. Of course it was too little, and her worries were many: at home there were a number of children, there was penury and crowding; the father, a craftsman who usually worked at home; and the mother, helping him in the troubles of earning a livelihood. At home there is noise and commotion, each one disturbing the other without meaning to. Material assets are meager, and all the heavy load of educating the child and providing his material and spiritual needs "fell" on the mother's head: to prepare food, to make sure he has new, clean clothes. To provide books and study materials and to make sure he is healthy and advancing in his studies.

Group of pupils of the *Tarbut* school at a gymnastics lesson

This way of life of the mothers robbed me of my rest. I began to search for a way to help the busy mothers. For this, I organized a three-pronged program:

A. To have a general meeting every Friday evening. At these meetings I discussed subjects related to the changes that had occurred in the life of the women in Eretz-Yisrael: the status of the woman in society and her struggle for equality and independence in all walks of life. I especially dwelled upon new educational methods.
B. Every Jewish festival, I organized a party to give the Jewish mothers knowledge about the essence of the Jewish festivals and their educational value for the children.
C. To have a monthly parents meeting: at these meetings, we solved individual problems with which every mother was wrestling.

A recurring phenomenon was that after each meeting or party, the mothers would not hurry to return home. They wanted to remain in that framework a little longer; perhaps they would get what was needed for their children's education. And indeed they got much. The meetings usually ended late at night. It was dark outside and the way to my room was quite long, but all of them continued to walk together with me. They did not notice the cold, the rain and the wind until they parted and each went her own way home.

I realized that these meeting had become the content of their lives. They gave them the chance to talk about all and everything, to remove heavy stones from their sad and loving hearts. Here they would find support and encouragement, help and advice.

Parents Meetings

The women came into my room bringing many problems with them. I loved to look at their faces: when they entered, they did not dare sit down, they didn't know where to start, and sometimes they feared to ask. I knew that their behavior derived from modesty, so I would be the one to start the conversation. I told the embarrassed mother about her child, about his scholastic achievements. I brought examples of proper education. I told her that God cared about her and had given her much wisdom and eternal knowledge and that was the mother's heart: a heart which senses every change in the child's life. She must show the child that she understands everything he is reading and learning: she must supervise him when he is doing his homework and listen patiently to what he has to say. In this way the child will realize that her eyes are observing his ways and supervising his education, while being concerned and assisting. The mother left this meeting with a sense of security, belief in her strength and feelings that now she would know how to act.

The mother began to maintain the family framework, placing more emphasis on the cultural pattern of the Jewish festivals. She lit Sabbath candles according to the number of her children, and in the house there was a very festive atmosphere. On the table was a sparkling white tablecloth, kept only for this purpose. On every Sabbath and festival, she would make special food to improve the "taste of the festival."

The mother of Leib Kalmanovitch said to me: "Teacher, if you knew how much effort this costs me. But since our conversation, the role of the home has become clearer to me. I previously thought that traditional education is not enough to educate the child. Now, I understand everything, that this (the role of the home) is the basis of a good Jewish education. In this way I bind the hearts of my children to their people and their Torah." I escorted her to the door of my room and a warm handshake separated us, but in my heart this conversation left much light and hopes for a good future.

One of the mothers couldn't come to these conversations. This was the mother of Daniel Ayzikovitsky. This young woman was paralyzed and bedridden. I understood her soul and came to their house. I brought with me the list of grades, the child's exercise books and a smile. A tremor passes through my body to this day when I remember this woman. Her image comes before my eyes; her pale face expressed deep sorrow. Two blue eyes, big and deep, protruded from her face. Her eyes searched me and tears flowed, protesting against the injustice of her bitter fate. I sat down beside her and told her gently about her delicate son. She did not speak, only from the movements of her body, did I understand what was on her heart. I comforted her - "Don't worry, God gave your son a good, wise heart, a good mind, and independence. He is making his way in life with confident steps." She stroked my hand: this was the thanks of the unfortunate woman. I visited her without fail once a month. I knew that this visit would bring a ray of light into her dark and despairing world.

I want to tell more and more about these women, but to my great sadness, time and the troubles of Israel have made me forget their names. But I carry with me the purity of their actions and the extent of their sufferings. I have unfolded but one drop in the lives of the mothers of Lubtch, women who brought up their children in sadness and in poverty, in lack and in worries. They saved from their mouths so that their children would be satiated. How terribly sad that they did not merit during their lives to enjoy the fruits of their heavy and difficult labor! But their hidden light lights up that period of my life.

It was Sabbath evening. I lectured about the new ways of education in Erctz-Israel. It was eight o'clock. From every corner of the town, men, women and youth streamed to the school auditorium. The hall was completely full. Sometimes the electricity, which didn't work well, went off, but no one noticed the failure. They sat patiently for a long time until the electricity was restored.

I raised the subject of the new image of the mother in our country: there, in Eretz-Israel, the child was educated for hard work and bravery. There they instill confidence and courage in him. The new generation needs to fight for every piece of land until the people of Israel achieve political independence. There the new lullaby was created - the song of work and creativity, the song of plowing and reaping.

The conversation continued for a long time. I looked into the eyes of those present. I searched for a sign, a drooping of the eyelids, for they had come after a difficult week of toil, after preparing for the Sabbath. But their faces expressed freshness, concentration and alertness. Here and there was a silent sigh.

I finished my talk. There was a deep silence in the hall. No one moved from his place. I said, "Shabbat shalom!" But everyone stayed in their seats. Suddenly I heard a woman's voice: "Thank you for the pleasure you have given us tonight. We have learnt a new Torah (teaching), and from its light we will teach our children."

We left the hall. It was a dark and murky night, but a great beam of light along the path illuminated my way: this was the hidden light of the Jewish mother in Lubtch.

[Page 120]

My Dear Mother

by Itzik Manger

Translated from the Yiddish by Harvey Spitzer

The holy Sabbath longs for your noble hands
(In the brass candlesticks, burned out Sabbath candles)
Death has long since cast a shadow on your face,
The mothers from the Bible grieve by the wall.

The "golden kid" under my destroyed cradle
My soul yearns for your lullaby,
The golden peacock flies with broken wings
And carries in its beak the false ring "happiness".

But God is here, the God from your cried out nights,
You told me He is great and unjust
Because He torments His creatures on the earth.

Your belief and your complaints still resound in me,
When I now think of your grave and I think of you
And pay you back the tears which you shed.

[Pages 121-134]

I Remember My Village Delyatichi (Delatitch)

by Mina Brenner

Translated from the Yiddish by Harvey Spitzer

Mina Brenner

I was born in Delatitch. I don't remember, however, whether it was after the first fire or after the second because the village often burned down and people would date all important events according to the fires, and my birth, too, was dated in this way.

I remember one such fire to this very day as though it were just yesterday because I was then already ten years old. My parents had just gone away that very day and we, six children, were alone at home.

Suddenly, the church bells started ringing and thick smoke clouded the sky. Church Street burned down first. Long tongues of fire jumped from one straw roof to another, and soon the market place, Karelitch Street and Keider Lane went up in flames.

My older sister took our little brother by the hand and brought him to our grandfather's. However, by the time she got there, grandfather's house had also caught on fire, and so she went with our little brother to the bank of the Neiman River.

My younger brother drove the cows out of the stable and another brother tied up the bedding. I followed suit and wanted to catch our hen but, as if to spite, she hid in the henhouse under a big baking oven. Hens were generally free to wander in the house and when it came time to lay an egg, they would jump up on the bed, clucking. We would cover them with a small cloth and a few minutes later, they would lay an egg and jump off the bed. I lay down on the ground and drove the hen out with a stick, but she only hid deeper in a corner of the henhouse. The flames had already reached our house and the smoke began to choke us. Suddenly, a few strong hands lifted me off the ground with a shout: "Run away! Leave the hen alone, run away!" On the way to the Neiman, I had to run through the market place which was burning on all sides with a hellish fire. There was a tavern in the middle of the market place, and when the brandy caught on fire, flaming streams spewed forth.

At that time, a widow named Beila the Cheese Maker lived in Delatich. It was said that she was a rich woman and when her husband died, she placed her belongings in my grandfather's shed. During the fire, she ran there to save her things. She ran into the shed when the gate had already burned down and she was engulfed in the flames. No one heard her shouts as she turned into a living bale and was killed together with her belongings.

The Jews from Lubtch at once sent in wagons loaded with food for those whose homes had burned down, and they helped in any way they could, although they were not wealthy either.

In a short time, the homes were rebuilt. They were much more comfortable and more modern for that time. Some people built with their own means, some had insurance money, while others received help from relatives in America.

*

Delatitch was a pretty village surrounded by woods, gardens and orchards whose lovely fragrances were really intoxicating.

Friday evening, after the shops closed and the weekday hubbub came to a halt, candles would brightly light up the Jewish homes and the men, wearing their finest Sabbath clothes, would walk to the synagogue at an unhurried pace and with measured steps to welcome in the Sabbath.

When they returned home from the synagogue, the singing of "*Shalom Aleichem Malachei Hasharet*" was carried through the open windows. That lovely melody was sung by Gershon the Teacher and his children to welcome in the Holy Sabbath. His son, Moshe, with his strong and pleasant voice, outdid all the other children. Another Jew who had an excellent voice was Shabtil the Butcher, the prayer leader on the High Holidays. When Shabtil stood before the altar and began the prayers, the synagogue walls would actually shake. The worshipper's eyes would swell with tears and they would beseechingly submit their requests before the Almighty, confident that they would be heard.

Moshe the town clerk lived next door to us. His wife had a store in the market place. Moshe's job was to record births and deaths, prepare passports and announcements - true or false - whenever necessary to help another Jew out. There was also a mailbox in Moshe's house for mail, which was brought from Lubtch everyday in a wagon. A harness with a bell was put around the horse's neck. The ringing of the bell was a sign that the mail had come and that you should go and pick up your letter. For five kopeks, you could go back to Lubtch on the wagon with the mailbox.

I was often at the home of the rabbi of Delatitch, whose daughter Shoske was my girlfriend. Besides deciding a question of religious law such as what to do if a dairy spoon fell into a meat pot, or settling a dispute on the basis of Torah law, the rabbi had a "monopoly" on selling yeast and salt. His wife, the *rebbitzen*, was also involved in the business and they actually made a living from this. In this way, the rabbi was not dependent on synagogue officers or rich people in the village. He only had to ask God to see to it that the Jews in Delatitch had enough to eat and that they wouldn't have to go without salt and yeast...

Delatitch was built like all the small towns in our area: In the middle of the town was a market place in which there were a row of stores, a tavern where the gentiles got drunk, a few streets as well as the road leading to Lubtch and to Yordika, which was situated close to the Neiman River. Around Passover, when the river flowed with a strong current, there was no way to get to Yordika. Rivkah lived there with her four daughters, Sonia, Mina, Itke and Devorah. They made a living selling bagels. The daughters were intelligent girls, they spoke "intelligently" and we were envious of them. Mina and Itke were killed in the Holocaust.

The market place and surrounding streets were inhabited by Jews. The gentiles lived in the outlying parts of the village. Our neighbors were Christians and we lived on best terms with them. On the Sabbath, they milked our cows, extinguished the oil lamp, and in the winter, they heated our oven and did whatever gentiles were allowed to do for Jews on the day of rest. And yet there was hatred between the two peoples, although one could not get along without the other.

Whenever there was a Christian holy day, and a religious procession with music passed through the village, we Jewish children were kept at home, as our parents were afraid to let us go out into the streets.

As much as we hated one another, mostly on account of religious fanaticism, this did not keep us from being connected in our daily living. All week long both sides waited for Sunday's market, when the peasants from the surrounding villages would come and sell their wares to the Jews. On that day, the market place came to life: people bought and sold and got bargains from each other, gentiles reviled one another, cursed "their mother" and grandfather's grandfather, horses neighed, sheep bleated, drunken gentiles sang in the tavern. The market place was filled with voices and shouting. Jewish shops were crowded with peasants who haggled for a long time over prices and merchandise. The shopkeepers watched the "uncircumcised" gentiles with "seven eyes" lest they take something without paying for it. We thanked God for providing a living for His People Israel.

Like all Jewish small towns, Delatich had a study room [Beit Midrash), a *mishnayot* [oral laws] study group, an "*Ayn Yaakov*" study group, a group for people reciting psalms and many teachers. There was no shortage of beggars either. On the street leading to Lubtch, stood a public bathhouse and a ritual bath crowded with Jewish paupers from all over the country seeking alms.

Several great scholars lived in our village and it was said that they could exorcise a "*dybbuk*" [spirit of a dead person]. To this very day I recall an incident that occurred in Delatitch which I heard told about at my mother's sewing table:

One day a Jewish woman came into the village with her daughter. Suddenly, the girl collapsed in the middle of the market place and began hitting her head with her hands and screaming in a wild voice: "Will you go for a drink of water at Neche's house without reciting a blessing?" When the *dybbuk* left her, the girl stood up, exhausted, perspiration running down her face. The Jewish woman related that a year before the girl was still healthy and as quiet as a dove. It seems that the mother and daughter had spent a night in a stable where there was a cow. In the middle of the night, the *dybbuk* came out of the cow and went into the daughter. As there were scholars living in Delatitch who knew how to drive away a *dybbuk*, her daughter would be helped and her haunted soul would be repaired. I don't know whether the girl was actually helped, but from that day on, I have run away from cows as if from the greatest danger.

For this reason, it is actually possible that our small town was crowned with the nickname "Delatitch's crazy people". The fact is, there were several crazy people in our village. The one I particularly remember was Shaya with his son Zaydel.

Shaya was a great scholar and his wife wasn't quite normal either. When Shaya was overcome with troubles from a bitterly hard life, he suddenly came out with harsh words against all of mankind. People pronounced him crazy, and when the community decided something about someone, absolutely nothing could change this decision.

In my time, young people from respectable families didn't have the opportunity to take up an occupation or profession. Nor did they want to have a simple trade, as a tradesman was a stain in the family. Parents wanted their sons to be educated or merchants. In our village there were rich lumber merchants as well as lumber agents. Both my grandfather, Avraham Rabinovitch, and my father, Berel, were agents. Rachel Manes and her son Herzel were lumber merchants. People said that she had a "man's head". She managed the business better than her own son. My mother, Esther Chiene, was a seamstress and employed a few workers. They would work until late at night mainly just before a holiday. My mother was a "woman of valor" and helped bear the yoke of earning a living. And every year there was an addition to our family.

It was a hard life in every respect. Water was carried in pails attached to a yoke. It was trouble enough in the summer, but in the winter, in the freezing cold, when the well was completely covered with ice, you were risking your life. And when you finally pulled the heavy pail out of the well and fastened it to the yoke, your foot suddenly slips and all the water spills out of the pail and you have to draw up water again with your frozen hands. There was actually a water carrier, Vassily, who brought a yoke of water to your house for a few *kopeks*, but when Vassily got drunk - which happened often - we had to be harnessed to the yoke ourselves.

With the coming of winter, came the episode of heating the house. A good householder prepared wood for the winter during the summer. The wood could dry out and that was trouble enough. But those who would buy wood in the winter - when the wood was wet and burned poorly - were not to be envied. When you heated the oven and closed up the chimney, you went around more than once with your head filled with charcoal fumes. It was forbidden to open a window, and it was actually impossible to open a window because right after *Sukkot* a second window was put in - a double window! Wadding was placed between the windows, and an immeasurable quantity of pieces of colored paper was poured into the spaces between the two windows. People would also put various charming ornaments between the windows such as chicks and ducklings, etc. all fashioned out of wadding. We sealed up the cracks lest - God forbid - a breeze should blow in. Just one casement window with a small opening could be opened to let in some air. But who could allow himself such a thing? - except for the "progressives", who were called "snobs" in Delatitch because otherwise it would not become them to open a casement window.

As the cold weather set in, the windows were adorned with wonderful "frost flowers" - simply to look at and enjoy. But no sooner did the windows begin to freeze over than the barrels of water also began to freeze. We finally had to begin to make the house much warmer so that the ice would melt. Meanwhile, we sat around the golden oven just like chicks under the hen's wings. The oven produced a gas from the pitch wood with the odor of a greasy essence, which gave us a headache. We ran to the "paramedic" ("*feldsher*") and he would advise us to wash our head with warm water. Finally a remedy was found: as soon as the chimney was closed, we went outside into the fresh air. And that method actually helped.

The "paramedic's" wife, Yocheved, was a midwife. She helped the women bring their children into the world. And soon as she delivered the child, she washed it and wrapped it in swaddling bands so that the baby could not move its hands and feet. The baby's crying was of no concern, for if babies move about, they'll grow up with crooked hands and feet.

Her husband, Meir the "paramedic" served as the doctor: he used to give castor oil, Glauber's salt, tansy for the children, etc. If someone complained of a pain, cups were placed over the painful area, sometimes broken cups or leeches. If you had a fever, they placed a bladder with ice on your forehead, and if that didn't help, they went to conjure an "evil eye". If you needed a real doctor, you would have to travel to Lubtch or Novogrudek.

When I was six years old, I was given my first reading instruction with Shabtil the Teacher. His method of teaching was very simple: the letter "*vov*" was a little line with a head, a "*yod*" was a small dot etc. This is how I learned to read. Shabtil the Teacher was old and skinny, and when he was teaching the children, he would fall asleep and have a good snooze. Naturally, the children were delighted.

When I was a child, I imagined that the world was a stepladder. The first rung was Delatitch, the second rung - Lubtch, after that came Novogrudek, Minsk, Warsaw and at the very top was America - the end of the world. That was the time of the great emigration to America. We spoke about America while eating and lying down to sleep. People borrowed a few dozen rubles to send their children to the "golden land" in the hope that they would bring one another over. And that's what actually happened. As soon as someone made a nest and settled down, he would send for his family. From our family, my father's brother, Shlomo Rabinovitch, left for South Africa and later brought his four brothers here. Shortly before WW I, my uncles brought over my older sister, Vita Rachel.

Time doesn't stand still. Delatitch also woke up: Modern teachers came and the children began learning Yiddish, Russian, arithmetic and history. Older children were sent away to foreign countries and they sent back help, thanks to which the material situation improved. The Jews in Delatitch celebrated weddings, circumcisions, redemptions of firstborn sons, and lived in hope of leaving the village and being re-united with their children abroad.

There was no *yeshiva* (rabbinic seminary) in Delatitch. Anyone who wanted to study in a *yeshiva* had to go to Novogrudek, to Rabbi Yuzel's yeshiva, where one followed the "*Mussar*" tradition. The *yeshiva* boys would come home on every holiday and would be welcomed with the greatest respect. Rabbi Yuzel often came to the woods in Delatitch, where he had a house. He would sit and study Torah there. A *yeshiva* boy would pass him food through an open window so as not to cause him to lose a minute of Torah study.

The awakening of Yiddish life also reached Rabbi Yuzel's *yeshiva*. The boys began to read Yiddish books and newspapers and to become interested in social and national events in Jewish and general life. As a result, they moved further and further away from the *yeshiva*, with its strict rules. Some of the students became anti-religious and even strongly militant. Those, however, who remained in the *yeshiva*, eventually outdid one another in their fanaticism, including Rabbi Yuzel himself.

The First World War

At first, Delatitch almost didn't feel that a terrible war was in progress, only that some men had been drafted into the Czar's army. From 1914 to 1915 the town's population led a normal life without any special earth-shattering occurrences. I also remember that a great debate took place in the study room. One side supported the Russians and the other the Germans. The arguing was so bitter as though the two opposing sides were really enemies. Towards the end of 1915 there was a great commotion in the village: the fish in the Neiman River were lying nearly lifeless in the water, with their stomachs down. People explained this phenomenon in hundreds of ways: Some said that the enemy had poisoned the fish, while others maintained that the end of the world had come and that before the advent of the *Moshiach* [Messiah], all the fish in the waters would fall asleep except for the Leviathan [whale], which would remain for the great meal in Messianic times.

Shortly afterwards we found out the secret: The government had issued an order for the breweries to spill their alcohol into the Neiman. For a few days there was no lack of fish in the village. You simply had to go down to the river and take them out with your hands.

We had not yet managed to digest the fish when soldiers began marching. For three whole days and nights one heard - incessantly - the heavy steps of the soldiers, who were crossing through Delatitch to get to the other side of the Neiman River. They were given a few hours to rest in the houses. They were dead tired and fell down to sleep wherever they could if only to have a little rest. They didn't have any time to rob or harm the population. Before leaving the village, the last soldiers ordered the civilians as well to go across to the other side of the river. We considered what to do, but there wasn't too much time to make plans. We were afraid that the bridge would be taken down and that we would remain in enemy hands and who knew what the enemy would do to us. People were terrified. We quickly got some food and warm clothing together. It was just the time of the *Sukkot* holiday when the nights became longer and colder and no one could know how long we would have to be outside under the open sky.

The Germans came into the village. The Russian army took up positions on the other side of the Neiman River, and we were in the middle between the two combating camps. Shells were flying over our heads. We only saw fire and heard the cries of the wounded. Naturally, we kept on running without stopping like hunted animals. We often fell down, got up and ran further just to get out safely. When the fighting subsided and the shooting and fire had stopped after three days of heavy fighting, we returned to the village, which remained in German hands.

Coming into the village, we found out that Zelik the Shoemaker had not run away with the other residents of Delatitch but had hidden in the study room. When the Germans entered the village, they took him for a spy and wanted to shoot him in the market place. A large delegation of returning village Jews approached the German commander and worked for his release.

All the houses were occupied by the Germans. The commander took over our big house, and we were given just one room. Two days later, all the civilians were ordered to leave Delatitch within four hours and go to a neighboring village for a few days. We took food provisions for a couple of days, locked up everything, left the key with the commander - in sure hands - and went to a village three miles away.

Three days went by, a week, and we were still forbidden to return home. As we were unable to buy food, we dug up potatoes in the fields and sustained ourselves in that way. It had never occurred to anyone to take along salt - a cheap enough item -, but what kind of taste do potatoes have without salt? Besides this, we had a stomach "disturbance". Everyone without exception was groaning from abdominal cramps and it was impossible to get a remedy for that.

We were all infested with lice, like little ants, from sleeping in filth and in tight quarters on straw in barns. It was simply impossible for us to stay in the neighboring village any longer. As we were prevented from returning to Delatitch, not knowing when it would be possible for us to go back, we had no other choice but to walk to Novogrudek, nearly 30 kilometers away. My father wasn't with us. He was in the area of Svalk, where he worked in a forest and we had heard nothing from him. My mother and her small children started on the way. It took us two days to reach that town.

There was a flood of refugees in Novogrudek from Lubtch, Delatitch, Silev [present day Vselyub] and other surrounding small towns and villages. As the town could not accommodate so many refugees, a committee was formed to send some of the refugees to other places. It was difficult, but we managed to get permission to remain in Novogrudek, where we stayed until the end of the war in 1918.

As soon as the war ended, we went back to see our village and to decide what to do. When we entered Delatitch, it seemed as though we had fallen into another world. The whole village was dug up and cut up by trenches. Some of the houses had been taken down to make room for trenches and bunkers. It was really a subterranean village which extended all along the Neiman River from Lubtch to Delatitch and beyond. When Yankel Baksht noticed this, he exclaimed: "Anyone who has not seen Delatitch as it looks now, has not seen the world!" We decided on the spot to return to our homes and begin to build our lives anew, as it has often happened in our long history after every period of destruction and expulsion.

Life became much more pleasant. We already had electric lighting both in the houses and in the streets, but people also need to eat. The fields hadn't been cultivated in three full years, so there was little food to buy. We had no other choice but to take up our wandering staffs and go in search of another place where we would at least have a small piece of bread to fill us up. That was enough for us because we didn't have very great aspirations at that time.

My recollections of Delatitch are cut off here. What I experienced later on, my wanderings through towns and villages in the post World War I chaos, all of these troubles and dangers are really unforgettable, but they no longer belong to the period of my life in Delatitch.

I would like to recall the sacred memory of my sister Zvia and my brother Aharon, the first two victims in my family during World War I.

*

Throughout my life in satiated and wealthy South Africa, I have always remembered my little town, Delatitch, remembered it with sorrow and yearning, as a person longs for the beautiful years of his youth which were taken away in the flames and smoke of wars.

[Page 134]

No One Leaving and No One Coming

by Hillel Kroshnitz

Translated from the Yiddish by Harvey Spitzer

Yoske Yedidovitch went to take a look at a prospective bride. It was a rainy, autumn day when the cold penetrated your bones.

His father warned Yoske that if he were asked for some news, he should answer that on the street "no one is leaving and no one is coming". This means that in such weather, there is no one outside, so no one knows any news.

Yoske decided to have a little fun, and when someone asked him:

"So, what's going on, young man?", Yoske didn't give it too much thought and answered:

Outside there are now two people "not leaving" and two "not coming".

Nothing became of the match and Yoske remained an old bachelor.

[Pages 135-141]

Lubtch Until the First World War

E. Sampson
(Eliyahu-Moshe ben R' Yehoshua-Yaacov Shimshilevitz)

(Originally translated from English to Hebrew by T. Shimshoni)

Translated from the Hebrew by Ann Belinsky

E. Sampson

Lubtch was a typical Jewish town, in the jurisdiction of the Russian Empire. After World War I, it was included in the Polish Republic. From the municipal point of view it belonged to the Novogrudek section - in the Minsk district. Lubtch lies next to the banks of the Neiman River, whose waters flow to the Baltic.

Like other towns in Russia of those days, Lubtch was built around a wide square, from which streets branched out towards the neighboring villages; every street was named after the village towards which it went.

Most of the town's inhabitants were Jews, only about ten percent were orthodox Christians, who lived at the end of the streets, as if they were not part of the community. When the area passed over to the Polish rule, they sent a considerable number of Polish citizens, Catholics from west Poland, to give the area a Polish color.

The shops and storehouses were concentrated in the square, which was the center for business. Once a week a market was held here, and the farmers from the surroundings brought their produce to sell and barter.

The houses in the town were built from wood. The roofs of the some of the houses (mainly of the gentiles) were covered with straw and were an immediate fire hazard. Every house included a large living room, two or three bedrooms and a kitchen, wherein stood a large oven for cooking and baking. A smaller and decorative oven was built in the middle of the house in order to heat the house during the cold winters. A *succah* [tabernacle] and a cold storage cellar were also part of the main necessities of every house. Behind the house stood a structure which was used as a workshop or a place for keeping animals: a horse, a cow, a goat etc.

There was no supply of electricity or gas to Lubtch, and candles or kerosene lamps were used for lighting. Logs of wood were used for heating. During the German occupation, in the First World War, a primitive electric power station was erected, which continued to work after the ceasefire and retreat of the Germans from the area. This power station supplied electricity for lighting, usually from darkness until midnight.

There was plenty of water from the wells which were dispersed in all corners of the town. Pumping water from the wells was not an easy task - it was difficult to carry the buckets in our hands or on our shoulders, and especially dangerous during the winter, when the well was covered by a layer of ice.

The weather was usually pleasant, hot in the summer, cold in the winter. Spring was delightful - we heard the chirping of birds returning from their migration, trees budded and the intoxicating scents of the flowers filled the air. In the spring and summer, rain fell from time to time, but despite this, it was warm and enjoyable.

Autumn brought with it the cold and the heavy showers, turning the streets of the town into streams of mud, making them almost impossible to cross. A start was made to pave the streets with stones, but the work had not yet been finished by 1939.

The Neiman River was frozen for three months of the year, and served as an excellent place for the youth to skate. In March, when the snows thawed, the river overran its banks and flooded the nearby meadow and reached the houses. In the summer its waters were cool and quiet, and bathing was a pleasure. To sail on the river in small rowboats in the evenings to the light of the moon and sparkling stars was romantic. On Fridays, many swimmers of all ages swarmed to the river, not only to swim, but also to wash and purify themselves in preparation for the holy Sabbath. The women - as befits proper daughters of Israel - washed separately, at a recognizable distance from the men. Bathing suits were not known in those days.

No industry existed in Lubtch, so in any case there was no working class as such. In the town there were a number of craftsmen such as tailors, bootmakers, carpenters, who supplied the needs of the population. The best of these emigrated to the United States or to England, where they proved their abilities, by establishing a large industry of readymade clothes. Simplest clothes were made at home, and knitting of socks and gloves was a woman's job. The standard of living was primitive. Food, fresh and healthy, was home-made: black and white bread were baked at home; milk, butter and cheese were also home-made; almost every house had a cow, potatoes were plentiful, and kept in the cold storage cellar of the house all year round.

The shops were mainly in the market square and were managed by the women. Most of the men were busy with small trade. Since flax, flax seeds and grains of various kinds were the main produce of the district, the merchants would travel around to all the villages in the area and buy the farmers' produce. Trade in flax and flax seeds, especially in the autumn and winter months, occupied most of the Jewish population who made their livelihood in this business. Many houses were used for sorting the different types of flax; every type was parceled up into bundles which were then sent to the closest railway station, and from there sent to different parts of the country, and also to neighboring countries.

The Neiman River was used as a transport artery during the autumn months. The grains and seeds were transported in ships and freight boats to Germany and other countries. They also used the river for transporting logs which had been cut down from the thick forests which covered the area. Transfer of logs via the Neiman was the cheapest means of transport. Trade in logs was an honorable job and several of the town's inhabitants found a livelihood as secondary tradesmen or agents. The log traders came from larger centers.

Lubtch was not considered to be a rich town as it had no wealthy people and the inhabitants made do with little. There was no railroad line in my time, and moving from place to place was by horse and cart. It is hard to believe, but in Lubtch there were people who had never seen a train engine or heard its whistle. The paths were not paved and in the summer they were used by horse and cart. In the winter, when the paths were covered by snow, people used sleighs. The "wagon driver" was the connection between Lubtch and the environs. He took people to the neighboring centers - Novogrudek and Ivyeh. The Germans, who held Lubtch during the First World War, built a narrow iron railway line - the *kleinbahn*.

Although the waves of revolution and the spirit of uprising against the Tzar had spread all over Russia, and the influence of education was clearly seen in the life of the Jews in all the towns of Europe, the gust of the wind of enlightenment had not yet come to Lubtch. The Jews there led a conservative way of life; the basic tenets of religion were unshakeable and stood above every doubt. The life of the society ranged around three synagogues; the red, the white (according to the colors of the bricks) and the wooden synagogue, which was called in Yiddish *"Der hiltzener Bet-Midrash"*. The red synagogue was for the extremists, the white - for the petit-bourgeois status, and the wooden synagogue was attended by the youth. The synagogues were open for *shacharit, minchah* and *maariv* [morning, afternoon and evening] prayers, for studying the Talmud after the prayers, and for general discussion. The wealthier congregants were of course the "seat holders" in the synagogue. The price of a seat (*makom*) was according to its location. The *makom* was considered to be of value, and became the unique property of its owner and passed from father to son by inheritance.

The Rabbi was the spiritual leader of the community and the "*strosta*" (*muchtar*) was the civilian leader and chosen in local popular elections.

The needs of the community were financed by the taxes imposed on various things such as candles and yeast. The right to sell them was bought as a concession, and the vendor had the exclusive right to sell these commodities.

In the town there were a number of societies for mutual help, amongst them "*Agudat Achim*" - for disseminating friendship and brotherhood amongst all. My father was chairman of the *Agudah*. I took part in the "*Bikur-Cholim*" *Aguda*, most of whose members were youth who volunteered to help the sick. An important institution was the "fire-brigade" society, whose members were all volunteers; since fires in Lubtch broke out very often, they had lots of work.

The Jewish population was mainly divided into two ruling families, Shimshilevitz and Kivilevitz, who were in dispute about all sorts of things, but in the end solved their problems in a friendly way.

Security, law and order were the responsibility of the government, whose representatives, the policemen, wielded a lot of power. The population was under their jurisdiction and subject to their judgment, whether for good or for evil, but it was possible to settle almost every problem with a "present". For example: the commander-in-chief of the local police "happened" to pass by our house at the time when workers were repairing it after it had been damaged by fire, and sent a policeman to tell us to stop their work. In reply, my father sent a "present" to the commander, a wagon full of hay, and naturally the work did not stop.

In Lubtch, there was a post office. Letters were sent and received every day. A letter received from a relation in a far-off country, was considered a great occasion. It was easy to send or receive a telegram. It is surprising that such a scientific way of communication had arrived in a remote town such as Lubtch in those days.

The inhabitants of Lubtch did not have a high standard of culture. There were a number of scholars in the town who were experts in Talmud and who studied their lessons day and night. The Jews were religious, God fearing and accepted their beliefs with no reservations; going to the synagogue became a habit and an acceptable thing to do. The Sabbath or a Holy Day was a day of rest and joy. The laws of *kashrut* [the Jewish Dietary laws] were kept scrupulously. Very important matters affecting the world did not bother the quiet citizens. Only two or three people received newspapers from Vilna, Warsaw or Peterburg, and passed on the news to the others. It is no exaggeration to say that events such as the death of Tolstoy, the murder of Stolifin or the Baylis trial were not valued as they should have been in the town.

The spoken language was Yiddish, although many knew a little Russian, which was necessary for commercial negotiations with the farmers of the area, or to speak to representatives of the government. Almost all knew Hebrew, but didn't use it as a spoken language; the educated young generation used Hebrew in writing important letters or documents.

Education of the children began at the *cheder*. There were three levels of study: the first was for beginners- boys and girls together learnt the same alphabet and got as far as reading the Pentateuch (Five Books of Moses); at the second level they studied Bible and the Hebrew language, but only boys aged 8-12 participated. The third level was the "*yeshiva*", an institution for Torah study, where they continued to study Bible and Talmud. In Lubtch itself there was no *yeshiva*, and whoever wanted to continue Torah studies had to travel to the Mir or Volozhin *yeshivot*, which were not far from Lubtch.

The educational method was not unified: the *chedarim* were managed by *melamdim* [elementary school teachers] who mostly knew the material to be learnt, but were not authorized to teach. Each taught according to his own methods. Although education was not compulsory, all the children in the town took part in the lessons. Secular studies were not taught at all at the *chedarim*.

Children of the Gentiles went to the state elementary school. But there was no obligatory law of education, and thus few studied and there was much illiteracy. The Jewish children, who longed to receive secular Russian education, had to take private lessons. Few of my age had the option of studying in the school at Novogrudek, where the pupils got a good overall education. That was a good state school, organized and well equipped. The pupils were accepted only after special entrance exams; the teachers, all non-Jews, were authorized and dedicated to their job. I was one of the fortunate children who studied there.

In Lubtch when I lived there, there were no people of the free professions. The doctor was a general doctor. There were no local youth who had become doctors. Young doctors came for several years in order to acquire medical practice. One of the doctors I remember still is Doctor Shapira, who was an excellent doctor. But he too moved on to Vilna, after he had acquired experience in Lubtch, and continued with a medical practice there, until he was murdered by the Nazis, in the second World War, The pharmacists helped the doctor. There were no lawyers in the town and no one felt their absence.

Disputes were solved by the local police with the help of a suitable bribe, as I have mentioned above.

The Zionist idea came late to Lubtch. In the houses of the Jews it was possible to find the photos of Moses Montefiore, Baron Hirsch and Captain Dreyfus., but no photo of Dr Herzl was to be found. Nobody had read "The Jewish State" by Herzl, nor had they heard of Nordau. Literature by Bialik and Ahad Ha-Am was not known to them.

I remember a visit with my father to the synagogue on the eve of Yom Kippur. On the table stood bowls for charity, every bowl had a note on which was written the aim of the donation. On one of the bowls was a note on which was written "for buying land in Eretz-Israel". The coins which the Jews placed in this bowl found their way to the *Keren Kayemet Leyisrael* [Jewish National Fund]. Engraved on my memory is the action of Getzel Ostshinsky, who had returned from a visit to Eretz-Israel. When his friend Aryeh-Leib Nochimovsky (the grandfather of Yisrael Nochimovsky) turned to him with a question about the possibility of managing to live in Eretz-Israel, Ostshinsky answered him: "It's not for you, for you are a business man". Ostshinsky was an enthusiastic lover of Zion.

I think that much changed in Lubtch since 1913, when I left the town of my birth. In the period of World War One, it was completely destroyed by both the German and Russian armies, during times of invasion and retreat. After the peace pact, most of the inhabitants returned and rebuilt it. When I visited there in 1939, they were living in fear in the threatening shadow of Hitler. Many turned to me and begged me at least to take their children to England. I wanted very much to help them but stood helpless in the face of their despair, and was powerless to save them.

After I left Lubtch, a big change came about, and the advances in technology didn't pass them by either. A number of institutions had telephones and radios. All the inhabitants were enraptured to hear the news, especially from overseas. Newspapers in Yiddish and Hebrew were sold, and their content was a source of discussion. A modern school with an authorized teacher, sent from Warsaw to administrate the school, gave the pupils the Hebrew language; vocational education was given preference.

With the help of the "Joint", a cooperative bank was set up, on a non-profit basis. My father was the chairman of the bank, whose activities were carried out with energy and talent, and were of much help to the inhabitants.

The Zionist idea permeated all levels. Matters pertaining to Eretz-Israel were subject to public discussions and arguments. People prepared themselves for *aliyah* to Eretz-Israel and indeed many came there and settled in its cities, *moshavim* [communal cooperative settlements] and *kibbutzim*. If the people of Lubtch had known that the second much loved President of the independent State of Israel would be from the Shimshilevtich family, no doubt they would have been bursting with pride.

[Pages 142-144]
The Pastoral Picture has Vanished and is No More

by Chaya Vilner-Bruk

Translated from the Hebrew by Ann Belinsky

Chaya Vilner-Bruk

A town like any other town, in its center a market place with rows of shops; the market is bustling and alive with people; traders and peddlers negotiating with each other in loud voices, wishing to make a good deal and find a compromise agreed on by all. From the marketplace, the streets led out to the edges of the town - where the Gentiles lived.

Despite this, there was a special character about the town. It was picturesque, and sometimes seemed to have been painted by a master artist, or have fallen out of a book of legends, because of its special topographical placing.

Behind the one-storied buildings, forest trees made a verdant wall, with their canopy reaching skywards; the blue waters of the Neiman River babbled merrily, and it seemed as if the river embraced the whole town. The meadow between the Neiman and the forests was colored in fresh green colors that aroused the strong desire to roll over and be mischievous in them. Next to the Neiman stood the castle, adding loftiness to the scene.

The river was noisy with bathers. A short time before the Holocaust, a "plaza" [bathing beach] had even been erected, yellow sand had been spread and various kinds of equipment had been installed for the convenience and fun of the bathers there.

Rowboats drifted on the Neiman; often songs of yearning and longing were heard from them. The youth sang from their heart's desire to the pleasant sounds of mandolins. Often they would float in silence, while listening to the rumbling of the waves and the beating hearts, disturbed only by a fish leaping out of the water into the air.

Many legends are connected to the Neiman; amongst them the legend telling about how every summer the river demands human sacrifices. And indeed, beneath its quiet waters and its innocent appearance, people would disappear every year in its murky depths, something that caused general mourning in the town, and a temporary withdrawal from bathing in the river. But slowly, the river's iniquity was forgiven, as one forgives a sinning baby, for it was hard not to bathe in its pure, cool waters, seducing one to enter and freshen up on the burning hot days.

Boat ride on the Neiman, Shavuoth, 1926

From right to left: Avraham Bruk, Gotel Shimshelvitch, Perla Yankelevitch, Nachum Shlimovitch, Risha Nachimovsky

The gentile women in bright clothes were seen washing their garments in the waters of the river, while talking and giggling as only women know how.

When winter came, the landscape changed, the river froze over, and everything was covered in pure white sparkling snow. The pine needles peeped out and became silvery from the snow which piled up on the branches of the tree as if to hint: "The Lord of Winter cannot daunt us"; the snow-covered castle looked like a white mountain. It seemed that the town was cut off from the whole world, from the point of view of "the end of the world". Even the little train (*kleinbahn*) remained stuck more than once in the snow, somewhere in the middle of the way, and didn't arrive.

The railroad station was located at the end of the town at the foot of Castle Hill. It was an important meeting place in the town. Towards evening, people would come to welcome the visitors who had arrived from far away, or just out of curiosity to see who was coming on the train, to breathe and absorb the strange smells of the fascinating distant regions. An important reason to come there was that, with the arrival of the train, came the mail they were expecting., - maybe there would be luck and a letter would be delivered from the legendary distant "Golden Land" of America, or from the land of the yearning of the forefathers - Eretz Israel.

Newspapers also arrived by train. They told wonderful stories about what was going on in the wide world. The station was a place for discussions by those "who knew" about politics, who would carry on with obvious self confidence about any and every subject. Jews, weary and preoccupied with the burden of making a livelihood, did not give up on going to the train station and to the post office, and not only in order to peep at the newspaper.

The area of the synagogues was always bustling with worshippers on Shabbat and Holy Days; every synagogue and its nickname, every synagogue and its congregation who came also on weekdays, "to catch" a prayer, S*hacharit* in the mornings, M*a'ariv* in the evenings.

A special event was with the arrival of the "*maggid*" [preacher] to the town. I remember being present when one of the "*maggidim*" gave a sermon. He had a majestic appearance, with a long silvery beard. At the "White" synagogue where he spoke, sat Jews studying the Talmud with a tune; around the preacher a group of people sat, thirstily taking in every word he spoke.

The preacher spoke with pathos, alternatively raising and lowering his voice - in order to make his message easy to understand and to wake the drowsy. He spoke with passion in praise of a rabbi, a great righteous man of Israel.

In the women's section of the synagogue, sat several old ladies who never stopped weeping loudly, even if they didn't understand the sense of the preacher's words, even without knowing if the rabbi was alive or dead. The tears flowed from the depths of their Jewish heart, full of sadness and worries.

The smoke of the approaching conflagration was already starting to rise, but the people of Lubtch did not yet feel the flames of rage which were advancing and would soon destroy them.

It is hard to believe that the pastoral picture has disappeared and is no more. In my imagination the blue of the Neiman has become a burning purple - the blood of the martyrs who were murdered and butchered...

[Pages 145-147]

The Castle in Lubtch

by L. Perkofchik
(From the newspaper, "Golus Radzimi", Minsk, Sept. 1969, P.8)

Translated from the Hebrew by Ann Belinsky

At the end of the 15th century, the Lithuanian knight (the Count), Alexander Kazmirovitch, (as is written, emphasized and sealed in the Document Seals) - gave the castle and its surrounding land as a present to his secretary, Fyodor Kharptovitch, But the aforementioned document, while interesting and broad in scope, does not discuss the history of the existence of Lubtch. The settlement of Lubtch had already existed in the middle of the 12th century. The exact date of the building of the Lubtch castle is 1281. This date was found on a bronze chandelier discovered in the courtyard of the castle.

Thanks to the castle and the market days and fairs that were held in Lubtch, the town strengthened and its inhabitants became wealthy. Many merchants came to the fairs and paid taxes to the owners of the castle. It is known that at the end of the 16th century, Lubtch was granted permission to rule itself. The town's symbol was then a half horseshoe with crosses and three goldfish. At the same time, the first printing office in Lubtch was founded, in which monks would print their holy books. As property of Kharptovitch, the castle passed with part of its lands to the well-known nobleman, Jan Kishka and, from him, the castle passed into the hands of the Radziwils at the beginning of the 17th century. It is thought that the building of the castle from stones had already started during the days of Kishka and was finished by Bogoslav Radziwil, who received the castle as part of the dowry of his wife Hannah.

In the first half of the 17th century, the castle stood, built from smooth stones, surrounded by the waters of the Neiman River. In the Lubtch museum there is a drawing of the town and a photocopy of the document describing the castle of the knights (counts).

During both World Wars, the front gates of the castle and the tower on the Neiman River were destroyed. But the strong walls of the central wing remained intact. At their base, the rooms were reconstructed and are now used by the high school. This comfortable and spacious two-storied mansion has high windows in the walls.

Cedar and elm trees flourish on the wide area around the castle. In the courtyard surrounding the castle, which is fenced in by walls up to the gate of the palace, there is a deep moat with strong walls. There is one underground bridge, mentioned in the days of early Lubtch. On the hill of the castle and around it, where there were ruins, stretches an ancient park with rare trees.

The Castle and Tower in Lubtch

The most interesting structures in the castle are the four towers in the four corners of the castle which constitute a very important monument. The towers, with arcades and square shapes, are covered with grey stone. When the castle was reconstructed, another tower was reconstructed from unworked stone and bricks. This was the second tower and is of majestic appearance, no less so than the other towers. Under the tower is a large cellar and above it are three stories with small, narrow windows and rooms used for different purposes.

The castle in Lubtch on the Neiman can serve as an historical document in the colorful antiquities of Byelorus and as a witness to its special character in the Middle Ages.

[Page 147]

Frosty Weather in the Summer

Collated by E. Eliyav

Translated from the Hebrew by Ann Belinsky

It is worthwhile mentioning an important historical item that occurred in the environs of Lubtch-Ivyeh, in the years 5570-2 (1810-1812), which I heard from my old grandfather R' Eliezer Kashtzar, may he rest in peace.

He told me that they found an entry in the "Record Book of Ivyeh" [*Pinkas Ivyeh*], where it is recorded that at the beginning of the nineteenth century, a cold spell hit White Russia (Belarus) which reached 40-45 degrees below zero. Abundant snow fell until after the Festival of Passover; the frost was so strong that the water in the Neiman River remained frozen until the summer months. Many people died from the cold.

In order to commemorate the exceptional event, people from all the surrounding towns met on the "Lag B'Omer" Festival from Lubtch, Delatitch, Mikolavia and Ivyeh, among them also heads of the Christian sects. They gathered together on the ice of the Neiman River, by Mikolavia, and drank "*lechaim*", "to life!".

The event was commemorated in the record books of Ivyeh, Lubtch, and Delatitch.

[Page 148]

Secretaries of the branches of *Hashomer Hatsa'ir* in 5691 - 1931

Right to left: Alter Leibovitch, Chaim Yankelevitch, Kaila Shmulevitch, Mordechai Kivilevitch, Henia Bakst, Moshe Persky, Gittel Zalikovsky

A group of youths

[Information from Allen Katz:
Standing first on the left: Greta Katz (nee Jankelowitz) - Gershon and Chaya-Basha's daughter.
Standing 4th from left: Barney (Beryl) Jankelowitz (Greta's brother)
Standing 6th from the left: Solly (Solomon/ Shlomo) Jankelowitz - first born child of Gershon Jankelowitz]

[Pages 149-156]
The Branch of "HaShomer Hatza'ir" in Lubtch

by Hillel Shmulovitch

Translated from the Hebrew by Ann Belinsky

We were children, about 10 years old, when we returned to Lubtch, immediately after the First World War. The town was cut up with trenches, burnt, and wolves prowled around in the middle of the day.

Lubtch was used as a front line in the First World War. The topographical situation of the town - the Neiman River and the forests surrounding it, was well suited for the digging-in of the fighting camps. In the town itself the Germans built concrete fortifications with little windows for shooting, and in the forests, the Russians made fortifications of wood. The wide meadow that stretched from the Neiman to the town - the "*Varak*" [meadow]- turned into no-man's land, mined and fenced with barbed wire. Inhabitants of the town turned into refugees, awaiting the day when they could return to their homes.

With the conclusion of the war, the inhabitants began to return to rehabilitate it from its ruins and again life became cheerful, with Jews working for their living and the voices of children resounding. Despite the difficulty of earning a livelihood and the poverty, they built public institutions that were vital for the community: synagogue, *mikveh* [ritual bath] and school - prayer, purity and education- the bases which were the foundation for Jewish life, and thanks to which Judaism existed, despite the hardships, the suffering and the penury that were part of our people's lot in the Diaspora.

The youth of the town built a library, at first located in the house of the teacher, R' Eliezer Kalmanovitch, around 1922.

The town was distant from the centers of trade and culture; the river and the forests "hid" the stormy mood of the period from the inhabitants. Life in the Jewish streets in Lubtch continued to flow slowly and quietly, and this was during a period when the spirits of the youth in Poland were fomenting, especially the youth of the national minorities. Many were arrested and sent to prison for several years. There were no signs in the town of the famous workers party the "Bund", or of a communist cell among the Jewish youth, despite the fact that there were strong active communist organizations in the district. In this way we were "out of the boundaries".

Only the Zionist movements came to Lubtch, albeit relatively late, but they did arrive. This is because the roots of Zionism suckled their strength from the prayers in the synagogue, the *cheder* and the *yeshivot*.

Hillel Shmulovitch

In the town, the Hebrew "*Tarbut*" school was founded, where the children were educated in Hebrew according to the new pedagogical method, by qualified teachers. Chaim-Asher Oshrovsky worked very hard for the school, seeing it as his life's investment.

In 1925, when the Hebrew University on Mt Scopus was founded, we celebrated this event in the *Tarbut* school; the teachers emphasized the historical importance of the event. We saw the university as a pillar of fire that would pass in front of the camp on its way to national redemption.

In the town there was a Polish elementary school, where some of the Jewish children studied, as one did not pay tuition fees there. The Jewish youth who attended this school also received a nationalistic education in the Zionist youth movements.

About 1924, the *Hechalutz Haklali* [General Pioneer] and *Hechalutz HaTzair* [Young Pioneer] youth movements were started in the town. Members of *Hehalutz* worked a large vegetable garden which was used as a training farm. In 1926, the first of the implementers of the goal of the "*Hechalutz Haklali*" emigrated to Eretz-Israel.

The cultural life in the town develops, the library is enlarged, a drama circle is formed and also the fire-brigade and the orchestra are organized. But the youth are still wondering, looking for their way. The economic situation gets worse. This is the beginning of the infamous Garbsky period. The Poles set up a flax cooperative, something which upsets the livelihood of many Jews. The burden of taxes gets heavier and trade lessens, the pressure and the poverty increase and the Jews arrive at a point of starvation; the anti-Semitism increases and no-one knows from where salvation will come.

Lubtch Branch of *HeChalutz HaTza'ir* in 5685 (1925)

As troubles mounted, the activity of the pioneering movements increased. In 1927 the Hebrew literature club was set up, guided by the teacher Alter Shmulovitch; the club had about 25-30 youth, graduates of the "*Tarbut*" school. The club dealt with Hebrew literature and from time to time one of the students was asked to prepare a lecture. Following the lecture, arguments and disputes arose about the problems of the nation and ways to promote its revival. Searches for the way of creating the renewal of the ancient homeland found their solution only with the setting up of the *Hashomer HaTza'ir* [Young Guard] movement.

In the summer of 1928, the branch of the *Hashomer HaTza'ir* was founded in Lubtch. The movement immediately drew the best of the youth to it, life became more interesting and it seemed that there was something to live for, and something to fight for.

The branch was founded by the initiative of a group of youth, aged about sixteen-seventeen, who were looking for ways to express their yearnings and hopes and for some reason didn't find this in the *HeChalutz HaTza'ir* youth movement. At one of the formative meetings that took place in the yard of our house, where the participants included Mordechai Kivlevitch, Chaim Sonenzon and myself, it was decided to establish the group. An important determining factor was that in Novogrudek, on the initiative of the teacher Piltzky, a Hashomer HaTza'ir group had been established there. We decided to invite Piltzky to come to us and after we heard an explanatory lecture from him, the group was established, and we were roped in by youthful exuberance to be leaders. The first head of the group was Nachum Shlimovitch and after he left, the responsibility fell on the young group leaders only. Many problems lay before us, but the central problem was operation of the leadership program, organized by the *Galil* [district] leadership and the main leadership. For this mission we were helped by the town library and by the support of many of the teachers who aided us with their knowledge and advice. By undertaking this activity, the group gained an honorable place in the town, as many parents began to understand that there was deep significance in the activity of their children and that it was not only for amusement.

Lubtch Branch of *HeChalutz* in 5685 (1925)

In 1930, several older members of the group went to the seasonal training course. Their aim was to get to know older members of the same level from the *Galil* district, and to see what physical working life was like. We began to act with regard to going to the training course. We made lists of the members who would go, taking into consideration their activity in the group and the promise to have suitable leadership and leaders. The first to leave for the training course was the member Yisrael Mendelovitz. The group became based with about 150-180 members. It had an educational library and the main thing was that it had a dedicated active and alert group of leaders. The group took part in meetings of the *Galil* district and was outstanding in its activities. Preparations for aliyah to Eretz-Israel began to bear fruit. Any older member who refused to go to the training course and to realise the principles of the movement, was exiled from the Movement.

Founding Members and Leadership of the Lubtch Branch of "HaShomer HaTza'ir" 5694 (1934)

Aliyah to Eretz-Israel was the solution for the youth who felt an atmosphere of suffocation and of no way out. A heavy financial crisis was going on in Poland in the years 1932-1935, and the Jews were heavily affected. The youths wandered around with nothing to do, literally, and many Jews were unemployed and suffered from impoverishment. The police and the regional council increased their oppression of the Jews, and the worst was the lack of hope and a way out. This crisis brought many to the gates of the youth movements. Activists in *Hashomer HaTza'ir* increased their activities and tried to penetrate as many levels as possible. Several of those activities were:

a) A dancing party for all the inhabitants, with the participation of the firemen's orchestra. The proceeds were dedicated to the *Keren Kayemet-LeYisrael* [Jewish National Fund - JNF]. The dancing parties gave an opportunity for meetings amongst the Jewish youth and the Belarussian youth. Since the district, which was inhabited by Belarussians, was conquered by Poles, who occupied all the key positions, their relationship to the Belarussian inhabitants of the place was not much better than their relationship to the Jews. There was much agitation amongst the Belarussian youth. The national awakening was a unifying factor between the youth of the two peoples. The Belarussian youth, mainly communists, came in hordes to the dance parties, which were followed by other meetings.

Flower Day for the benefit of the *Keren Kayemet LeYisrael* (JNF)

b) The Jewish National Fund served as an important base for education in the youth movements. A JNF fundraising committee was set up. The JNF chairman, the teacher Chaim Persky, authorized our decision to have a bazaar, whose proceeds would be dedicated to redemption of the land. The teachers, the town leaders and especially the youth from all the youth movements were roped into this activity. The organizing committee went from house to house in the town and even went to neighboring towns to get people to donate. The success was great; the hall was too small to contain all those who came and the proceeds were over and above all expectations - the amount of one thousand Polish *zloty* was raised.

c) Organization of a Trade Union.

Amongst the members of the group there were children who worked as apprentices of tailors in conditions of exploitation; many hours of work, a minimal wage and often unfair relationship. A spur to action was that the youths and the workers could not study Hebrew in the evenings before leaving for the training farm, and the few that managed to get to the lessons didn't absorb anything because of tiredness.

At a meeting, the employers even refused to discuss an eight-hour working day. The leadership of the group called for a meeting of the committees of *HeChalutz* and the *Poeley Tzion* political party (Tz. S.) and it was decided to undertake a cooperative effort. The first stage in the struggle was to prepare the workers themselves, to explain to them the essence of the struggle and that they would have to stand up against many difficulties, such as being fired from work, threatened and even enticed with a raise in salary. We promised them that at the end of the struggle, all would return to work.

As they had been asked to do, the workers announced to their employers, that they would not work any more than eight hours a day - here the struggle began. The employers fired them and threatened. Many jobless young people wandered around the town, but no-one took the place of a worker who had been fired; they behaved exemplarily, which toughened and strengthened the organization. A lecturer from the trade union was brought from Novogrudek, and his lecture added to the unification of the striking workers.

When the employers understood that threats would not defeat the workers, they began to use violence - they broke into houses and shouted threats at the worker's family, even at parents who were not at all involved in the issue. They threatened me that they would turn me over to the authorities and told my brother Yaakov, who was a teacher at the *Tarbut* school, that he would be fired. When the threats did not work, they turned to action: my brother and I were taken to the police and my father's trade license was taken away. I was accused of organizing the workers, even though I myself was not a worker - a serious political crime in Poland. In my defense, I claimed that the workers needed to have a free evening to learn Hebrew, and to prepare for their aliyah to Eretz Israel.

After we were released from detention, the family met together to discuss the situation, and it was decided that we would not stop the struggle, even if the whole family would suffer. (My parents approved this decision). The threats, the shouts and the bruises did not stop for a few more weeks, but the trade union arose and became a fact. An eight-hour workday was established, all the workers returned to their previous place of work and no-one suffered. Everyone was happy about the improvement in work conditions, and proud that they had undertaken the struggle and won.

Adolescent youth, sixteen and seventeen years old, with the help of some other twenty-year olds, organized themselves and went out to struggle against the "employers" who themselves were workers, working hard to make a living for their families.

In September 1935 I made aliyah to Eretz-Israel and thus realised the principal goal of the ideology of the *HaShomer HaTza'ir* youth movement.

[Page 156]

Wealth Passes On, One Must Remain a *Mentch*...

by Gershon Jankelowitz

Translated from the Yiddish by Harvey Spitzer

A Jew named Bere Litshitzer lived in Lubtch. He was the son of very rich parents. When Bere got married, his parents scattered sweets on the streets to lead the bride and groom to the wedding canopy from their house to the synagogue. Afterwards, they distributed the sweets among the poor people.

Some time later, when nothing remained of his wealth, Bere became a very poor man. But

Bere remained the "*mentch*" [decent and responsible person] he had been: he didn't cry or complain, kept the religious traditions and quietly and calmly bore his hard life and even liked to make a joke at his own expense.

One day on his way to pray at the synagogue, Bere stopped by our house and said to my mother:

— Chaya Sarah, just listen to what happened at my house. My chicken has gone crazy.

My mother looks at him as though he isn't from this planet and asks:

— Bere, what are you chattering about?

Bere laughs and finishes:

— She looks for crumbs under the table. Since there's no bread on the table, what can she find under the table?

[Pages 157-162]

The Dream Has Remained...

by Mina Kroshnitz (Faivishevitch)

Translated from the Yiddish by Harvey Spitzer

Most of us were children of poor homes. The burden of making a living weighed heavily on our parents and made them old before their time. It stole their joy of living and caused them endless worries. My father and mother would often sigh, and sadness gnawed at their heart. Only on the Sabbath, holidays and on joyous occasions would they be relieved of their worries and harsh thoughts. Then their spirit would be ennobled and uplifted, and a bright smile could be seen on their faces.

Mina Kroshnitz (Faivishevitch)

Of course, their moods would be conveyed to us their children. Our childhood joys would be extinguished under the worried look of our parents.

We were young, however, and that was our greatest asset. We clung to our youth and drew happiness from it as if from a well.

The *Tarbut* school, where we received an elementary education, was a bright home for us. The teachers, almost without exception, were cordial and good, and although strict, they were our educators and guides. They got us involved in Zionist activities: throwing a few *grush* into the *Keren Kayemet* [Jewish National Fund] collection box, and taking part in other JNF activities, which made us aware of belonging to the camp of builders of the new Land of Israel. Singing songs in school of the new pioneers and reciting poems of our national poets deepened our nationalistic feelings.

It was therefore only natural that we should be members of the various Zionist youth movements which existed in our small town, mainly *Hashomer Hatsair* [Young Guard], which was the most important educational youth movement in our small town as well as in all the surrounding towns and villages.

The *Tarbut* school also served as a local chapter for the cell. We were given a few rooms where we would meet and conduct our activities. Who can today, after so many years, transmit so much warmth, joy and hope which our local chapter gave us?

Various sayings of an educational nature spoke to us from the walls, which were decorated with pictures of personalities and national heroes who were an example for us of how to live and serve our people. We would make different kinds of chains cut out of colored paper with which to decorate the rooms so they would be prettier and more attractive. The cell was the beautiful home we dreamed of.

In the evening, we would listen to talks by educators and group leaders: Motte Kivelevitch, Haim Sonenzon, Hillel Shmulevitch, Gittel Movshovitch and Moshe Persky. After every talk, we would comment on what we heard and, on many occasions, the talk would turn into an argument. These talks broadened our view of life, opened new horizons and strengthened our spirit.

Later, we would sing for hours on end, song after song, without stop. Oh, how many songs we knew by heart! Every song left its impression and effect. Here a slow, dreamlike melody makes us yearn for the lovely nights of Canaan and for the Jordan River, "which murmurs its secrets in the stillness" and here a vigorous melody stormily bursts forth with a resounding echo, Yula - Yulala! We can no longer sit in one place; hand in hand, arm in arm, we start dancing with fervor and enthusiasm until we fall down exhausted, dripping with sweat.

One of the most enduring memories was taking part in a training course ["colony"] during summer vacations in the area of Nalibak by Lake Kroman.

For us, the "colonies" were the first step towards independence and training for the collective settlements, the first stage which prepared us for pioneering life in Eretz-Israel [the Land of Israel].

During our stay in the "colony", we put into practice the scouts' command: we lived in the lap of nature, came into contact with the forest and its creatures which we came to love. We also loved one another and we saw ourselves as children of one family. We would dig a depression in the ground for a place to sit and make an earthen table in the middle. We would sit around the table until late at night and sing. Later, we would light bonfires, dance around the fire and sing:

"We sing songs around the fire,
The night is dear
We're not getting tired"...

We would return home from the "colony" burned from the sun and wind, well rested and with renewed strength for the coming school year.

Group of members of *HaShomer HaTza'ir*, 1931
[Information from Allen Katz: Middle row kneeling 4th from right - Greta Katz (nee Jankelowitz)]

Friday night: Sabbath candles burn on the table. The little flames flicker and move as though they would like to be living creatures. The family sits around the table: father and mother, my little sisters and little brother. There is often a Sabbath guest whom father brought home from the synagogue.

Father makes *kiddush* [sanctification of the Sabbath over a cup of wine] in a loud voice. He has a pleasant voice which is a delight to hear. Father generally enjoys singing a good piece of cantorial music. And he puts a lot of feeling into the kiddush. We respond in chorus: Amen!

When we've finished eating our Sabbath supper and have waited for father to recite the grace after meals, we quickly leave the house. It's more crowded in our chapter's cell than it is all week. You can hardly get in. Tonight, a meeting of the whole cell is taking place with the representative of the "National Defense", who has come for a visit.

The guest talks about the situation of the Jews in Poland, their lack of rights and lack of expectations. He tells about the achievements and activities of the movement in Palestine and about the tasks and duties of the *Hashomer Hatza'ir* youth. We are proud of our movement and with the responsibility which we bear for the destiny of our people. At that moment, we are prepared to make the greatest sacrifices for our people and country which is meanwhile more a dream than reality.

My parents Rachel and Yehoshua-Yaakov Faivishevitch

After the talk, we stand in rows in the schoolyard, group by group, level by level, for the closing ceremony of the formation of the guard. Then we hurry off to the Neiman River.

The river lies extended in the moonlight like a silver ribbon. A slight breeze combs its surface and brings out its beauty as if by magic, captivating the eye. We climb into rowboats. The vessels cut through the water and our singing pierces the deep stillness of the night.

*

It's already two o'clock in the morning. I quietly open the door and try to walk on tiptoes so as not to awaken those who are asleep. Father and Mother, however, having already woken up from the first part of their sleep, are lying on their beds absorbed in thought in the darkness. Their thoughts do not give them rest. Mother asks:

— Mineleh, is that you? What time is it?

I answer quietly, hardly audibly:

— Yes, it's me. It isn't late yet.

A big pot of carrot stew stands on the outer part of the oven in the kitchen. In the moonlight, I fill up a plate with stew, a cow's foot and a small piece of *challah* and sit down to "have a meal" The taste of the stew passes to all the limbs of my body. I chew the food quickly and the plate is soon empty.

Without forgetting to brush my teeth, I take off my jacket and white blouse with the blue *Hashomer Hatza'ir* necktie and get into bed. It doesn't take long and I fall soundly asleep.

In a dream, I see the Jordan River and the mountains of the Holy Land with a bright blue sky above. No one can be as happy as I am.

I've had this dream for so many years and feel comfortable with it. It's good to dream even when you're awake.

[Pages 163-166]

Youth Movements in Lubtch

by Chemda Simchoni (Movshovitch)

In memory of my sisters Shayna and Eshka and my brother Yosef - members of *Hashomer Hatza'ir*

Translated from the Hebrew by Ann Belinsky

"Hashomer Hatza'ir"

In Lubtch there were 3 youth movements: *Hashomer Hatza'ir, HeChalutz* and *Beitar*.

I will especially write about *Hashomer Hatza'ir* since I was educated in this movement and also was a leader there, and I knew it closely.

The *Hashomer Hatza'ir* Group in Lubtch was founded in 1928; a long time after the *Hashomer* movement was active in the large cities. It had impressive achievements despite the fact that the town was distant from Jewish centers, its youth almost never met with youth from other cities, and organization of the youth movements in our town was started late. When the *Hashomer Hatza'ir* group was founded, it began to flourish, and the young people came to it gladly, since they were thirsty for social secular frameworks and for Zionist activities.

Chemda Simchoni (Movshovitch)

The ideas of the *Hashomer Hatza'ir*, that educated towards socialism, collectivity, Zionism, Hachshara [training farms in that region preparing for life on a kibbutz] and Aliyah [immigration to Eretz-Israel] charmed the youth. Wearing a uniform was mandatory, in order to equalize the poor and the rich. The spoken language was Hebrew, which we knew to speak anyway, thanks to the welcome activity of the "Tarbut" School in our town.

We didn't have experienced leaders. We acted daringly and even with youthful passion, and we educated the younger ones amongst us with much devotion. Today it is hard for me to understand where we derived the courage to act and teach when we were not even 18 years old.

From time to time, an older member from the provincial administration (*Hanahagat Galil*), from Baronovitch would visit us; during these meetings the group would celebrate, everyone came in wearing white shirts, songs were sung with much gusto and called for awakening and self-realization. The singing was followed by a discussion centering on the ways of the Movement, on life on the kibbutz in Eretz

Israel, on the *Hachshara* [Training, training camp] and on the Workers Movements.

The Movement succeeded in bringing the youth (some of whom had never left the town limits) together with youth from other towns, by organizing joint summer camps and work camps which formed the basis of *Hachshara* groups and *Aliyah* groups.

It was not easy to convince the parents, who were traditional, to allow their children to go to the camps. A young person who left his house was considered to be going to a "bad culture". We had to go from house to house, explaining, promising and lobbying until the parents consented, even with a heavy heart full of worries.

The youth - they too were anxious and excited in anticipation of the meeting with the unknown, and with a heart full of hope awaited the future: for changes in their way of life, for the revolution in values of life, while wishing to realize the ideals that they had been educated towards in the Movement.

The first meeting of the Lubtch group with members of the group from Naliboki took place by the Kromanitza. This meeting made our hearts beat, we set up a camp in the nearby forests, we sang songs of longing for Zion and danced around the bonfire, which inflamed the youth with feelings of friendship and desire to live shared lives.

A determining meeting for graduates of the Lubtch group was a meeting with the Baronovitch graduates: there the idea of self-fulfillment and aliyah to Eretz Israel ripened.

The importance of the youth group was that the youth, who previously lived in an atmosphere of generations of torpor, was awakened to search for new ways; the apathy disappeared, they left the yeshivot in order to learn a trade and to work in productive occupations; they began to look for new paths, in order to change the existing ones and many made aliyah to Eretz Israel.

The *Hechalutz* Youth Movement

The *HeChalutz* Youth Movement was aimed at young people who were older than 18 years old.

The graduates of *Hashomer Hatza'ir* also joined the *HeChalutz* Movement, despite the fact that they were younger than 18, because they could not wait to make aliyah to Eretz-Israel and their turn to make aliyah was hastened in this way.

Hashomer Hatza'ir and *HeChalutz* succeeded so well in installing the desire of the youth to make aliya, that many of the *HeChalutz* members that did not get "certificates" left for Eretz Israel as tourists and remained there illegally. Others arrived as illegal immigrants by different schemes.

The committee of the *HeChalutz* branch with the comrade Bresslavsky from Eretz-Yisrael, in 1931

Sitting from right to left: Moshe Bakst, Avraham Leibovitch, Mordechai Kivilivetch, Y. Bresslavsky, Leah Osherovsky, Bilka Zalikovsky.
Standing: Chaim Yankelevitch, Leibeh Kivilevitch, Simchah Chaimovitch

The Beitar Movement

I cannot expand on *Beitar* in our town as their "Guidelines" by which they acted in the movement were completely strange to my way of thinking. I was a fanatic for the ideology of my movement, and not interested in *Beitar*, which basically was against the Workers Movement.

The *Beitar* Movement was active in Lubtch, it succeeded in attracting a group of young people from the town, and gave them a completely nationalistic education, in the spirit of the Zionist-Revisionism of Ze'ev Jabotinsky. They also underwent army training (without weapons). At some stage a *Hachsharah* kibbutz of *Beitar* was set up in Lubtch, to which youth from different parts of Poland arrived. The "kibbutz" fought hard for its existence economically and was eventually forced to close down.

It is a pity that only a very few individuals from this movement, youth of our town, succeeded in making aliyah to Eretz Israel.

[Page 166]

The Mathematicians...

by Gershon Jankelowitz

Translated from the Yiddish by Harvey Spitzer

Velvel had a son-in-law, Yisrael, who was his partner in business. Neither of them could read or write.

After a day of business, they would both make an account which consisted of making little notches on the chimney of the baking oven.

It would often happen that Gittel, Velvel's wife, would come and ask:

— Velvel, give me a little money to buy food for tomorrow.

Velvel, deeply engrossed in doing his "arithmetic", would lose his patience and scream:

"I'll soon give you a smack, you'll have a little money. You spoiled our arithmetic."

And back to the beginning and new little markings on the chimney.

[Pages 167-169]

The Trial

by T. Shimshoni

Translated from the Hebrew by Ann Belinsky

The event described below really did happen. I was a witness to the goings-on, and I remember it as if it just now happened. It was on a Sabbath morning. I was a child and I slept late, while all the Jews of Lubtch were in the synagogue. When I looked out the window towards the market square, I saw workers bringing a wagon filled with wood and boards which they started to unload in the market opposite our house and immediately began building a kiosk. Afterwards it turned out that the kiosk was erected by a Polish merchant named Roman, who owned a shop selling strong drinks and spirits (It was the only shop in the town belonging to a Pole; all the others were owned by Jews). Roman intended to put up a kiosk in the market square and to sell sweets. Because he knew that the Jews in the town would oppose it, as it was in a public area open to all, he built the structure secretly in one of the courtyards on the Street of the Gentiles. He chose to erect it exactly on the Sabbath day, so that by the time the Jews in the town, who were in the synagogue, realized what was going on, it would be already completed.

T. Shimshoni

The matter was found out by the members of the congregation, who came out to see what was going on, wrapped in their prayer shawls. Very quickly many Jews gathered around the workers, and an argument burst out between the Jews and the gentile workers, who did not understand why the Jews were so angry, and who were not really a side to the dispute, but had just been hired by Roman to do the work for him. Several hotheads amongst the Jews would not let the work go on and started to dismantle the walls. Roman arrived at the place with a number of policemen, and it seems that they had anticipated this development. The Jews dispersed to their houses, the work was stopped, and a police guard was left to make sure there was no more dismantling of the kiosk or interruption of its building.

The next day Roman brought photographers and journalists from Novogrudek, the largest town in the district, to take pictures of the wreckage. The Novogrudek newspapers published articles of anti-Semitic nature, accompanied by photos of the destroyed kiosk, in which they protested against the Jews of Lubtch preventing a Pole from building a kiosk.

A few days later, a policeman appeared at our house, showing an arrest warrant for my father, together with two other Jews, and they were accused of causing damage and worse, of racial incitement - an accusation that was extremely serious. The accused were taken under guard to the regional prison in Novogrudek.

The rumors of the arrest came to the attention of the city leaders in Novogrudek, who leapt into action. They appealed to the authorities and after much effort, managed to free the prisoners on bail. At first they agreed only to free my father, but he refused to leave until the others who were arrested with him were freed too. In the end, they were released together and managed to return home in the evening, as the holiday was beginning. I remember that all the people in the town waited for their release with bated breath.

The suspects were served with an indictment, as they wanted to turn the trial into a showcase. Behind Roman stood his brother, head of the Novogrudek Criminal Investigations Department. The Jews were accused of a serious crime and if found guilty, a heavy punishment awaited them- years of imprisonment. The trial caused my father much blood and money: he hired a famous lawyer from Vilna, whose name was Petrosvitz, a Christian, a professor of law at the university, to supervise the defense. A Jewish lawyer from Novogrudek, Zladovitz, was also hired to prepare the defense. All of the financial load fell on my father's shoulders, as the other two were poor and had no means to help with the defense expenses.

The day of the trial arrived. Many Jews from Lubtch traveled to Novogrudek to be present at the trial.

The first witness was Roman himself, who proudly mounted the witness stand. He gave evidence confidently and brazenly, even though he himself had not been present during the dispute. He described my father as head of the inciters and as one of the heads of the community to whom all listened, and that he was to blame for the destruction. Afterwards the workers appeared. In their testimony to the court, they reneged from their statements at the police station and claimed that my father did not participate in the argument, but arrived on the scene later. They did not identify any of the accused, and couldn't indicate who caused the damage. When the prosecutor asked why they were now saying the opposite of what they had said in the police station, they answered that they were told by Roman what to say, but now, since they had vowed to tell the truth, they were telling the truth, as their fear of God was greater than their fear of man.

The last witness that the prosecutor called to the stand was a Pole, a known drunk who determined the direction of the trial. On the witness stand, he started describing how the Jews attacked the structure and wrecked it. In his speech, he enlarged on the part my father played in this action, saying that he saw Yehoshua Shimshilevitz walking, wrapped in a prayer shawl, shouting, "*Mi shul ari*", and the Jews immediately began the destruction. This witness was the last of the witnesses for the prosecution.

When it came time for the defense to give its arguments, the lawyer Petrosvitz stood up and declared that he would not bring any witnesses for the defense because, in his opinion, there was no basis for the accusations, since one could not believe the last prosecution witness because, in his opinion, the witness's words were blatant lies. He explained to the court that the meaning of the words, which were not, "*Mi shul ari*", but rather, "*In shul arein*" ("Time to go into the synagogue"), a call to enter the synagogue, which was a sign of the approaching holiday or Sabbath.

Then he explained that it is a custom of the Jews that the *shamash* (beadle) walks through the streets of the city crying out "*In shul arein*" - a sign that the time has come to close the shops, light candles in the homes and come to the synagogue to pray. They are also called to the synagogue when a *hazan* [cantor] or *maggid* [orator], has arrived in the town, and the Jews are called to come and listen to the *hazan* or listen to the *maggid's* sermon. As already mentioned, this calling out is done by the beadle, who is usually a poor Jew. The calling was done on weekdays, and never on the Sabbath or holy days, and it was therefore impossible, continued the lawyer, that an eminent and respectable person like the accused, Yehoshua Shimshilevitz, who was a well-to-do businessman, head of a bank, would go out and call out "*In shul arein*", especially not on the Sabbath.

Since the prosecution's case was based mainly on the testimony of the last witness, as he was an "eyewitness" and his testimony had been shown to be false, the lawyer requested that the accused be cleared of any blame or suspicion.

The accused were found not guilty and released to Roman's great sorrow and to the happiness and joy of the Jews of the town, who succeeded in overcoming Esau's plotting against them.

[Pages 170-171]

Episodes from the Town

by Eliyahu Sampson

Translated from the Hebrew by Ann Belinsky

A train in the town was a source of income and prosperity. The clerks of the Russian government, who knew that the towns wanted trains, would receive bribes from the Jews, in exchange for empty promises. One day a Russian clerk came to Lubtch, representing himself as a commissar with the rank of General. He summoned representatives of the Jewish community, showed them plans of a railroad which would connect Lubtch to the surrounding towns. The Jewish representatives requested that a railroad station be built in their town. The General claimed that it would not be easy, but for a fair sum of money, it could be arranged.

The matter was brought to the knowledge of the inhabitants, and the Jews of Lubtch agreed to pay. Every household contributed according to their means; the General accepted the money, promised that the station would be built in Lubtch, made his farewells to the community and went on his way. Since then, no one has seen either him or the station.

*

One day a handsome Jew with a majestic appearance came to the town. His beard was carefully tended and he spoke a little Hebrew and fluent Yiddish. The Jew lodged in a hotel for several days, and all the Jewish townspeople wondered what his business was here. In the synagogue, he was honored by being called up to the Torah and the important people in the congregation saw it as an honor to invite him to their homes. The guest promised donations to charity foundations, was shown around the town, found out its deficiencies, and promised to help in fixing them. The Jews of Lubtch were very happy, as it seemed that their town had gained a new Moses Montefiore. They tried to make the guest's stay as pleasant as possible. He lived a sumptuous life for several weeks, then left-and with him, all the promises flew away.

Such was the nature and naivety of the Jews of Lubtch.

*

A story about a young Jew who emigrated to America. He remained there a year, two years and returned to Lubtch with a few dollars in his pockets. This same young man came to the synagogue dressed grandly: a nice coat, a top-hat, a bright white shirt, and a handsome tie. All the girls in the town ran after him and the matchmakers knocked on his door. On the Sabbath he came to the synagogue, sat by the eastern wall, took a *tallit* [prayer shawl] out of a bag and wrapped himself in it. When he was called to the Torah, and the *hazan* recited a prayer for health for his father and mother and was about to say a similar prayer for his wife, the youth said he was not married. If so, where is the *tallit* from? There was a tumult in the town: he has a wife in America and here he is seen with maidens.

The youth was invited by the rabbi to explain the matter. He swore that he had no wife and that he had never been married; and that in America everyone puts on a *tallit* during prayers. There was an exchange of letters from the rabbi of Lubtch and the rabbis of New York in order to find out if he was a bachelor or not, but the young man had disappeared from the town.

Planting a grove on Mt. Hazon by the Jews of Dublin in the name of Eliyahu Sampson - from the businessmen of Irish Jewry. E. Sampson appears in the photo

A story of a Jew named Tuvia. When he was asked what a Jew lives from, he would answer: "What does that mean? From poverty, of course!"

[Page 172]

The Request is Heard...

by Chaim Yankelevitch

Translated from the Yiddish by Harvey Spitzer

News reached the town that the Governor, in person, was coming on a visit. The community leaders meet and consider how to greet the important guest. Bread with salt would be brought to him, as is the custom, but they must also use the opportunity to put forth requests. And there is no lack of things to ask for: the Jews in Lubtch live in their houses without having property rights and must therefore pay the Polish landlord taxes. It is a heavy yoke to bear and they can be ordered to leave their homes for any reason whatsoever. But who has the courage to make such a request of the high authority?

Congratulations! The Governor has arrived. The Jews, dressed in their Sabbath attire, welcome him with great honor. A delegation of town leaders goes over to meet him, carrying bread with salt. They stand there submissively, with their hats in their hands, and put forth their request: "The cemetery has become too small. The dead are being buried right up to the fence. Therefore, we are asking that His Honor allow us to enlarge the cemetery a few feet on every side and may he be blessed for his goodness!"

The Governor listens to our request very seriously. After all, since it concerns a place to bury Jews, the authorities must, in fact, show the little Jews that they are relating to them in a fatherly way, and that their request has fallen on sympathetic ears:

"Fine", answers the Governor, and a graceful smile spreads across his lips.

The Governor and his attendants have left. The Jews of Lubtch can't stop talking about the great act of kindness which he bestowed upon them and, in their eyes the Governor has grown in stature into one of the "Righteous Gentile".

[Pages 173-174]

Only the Memories are Left...

by Sara Avrahami

Translated from the Hebrew by Ann Belinsky

I grew up in a traditional, warm Jewish home whose door was open to all. My parents taught me to love and help all and, by their actions, they were an example to their children.

My mother - Golda - was a quiet, modest woman, looking after the ways of her household with worry and dedication, helping the needy and often giving charity secretly.

My father - Yehoshua Shimshilevitch - was a diligent, energetic man, involved with people and loved by them. He made a living by trading in flax. He also found time to work and be active for the benefit of the public. He was one of the founders of the bank in Lubtch, and directed it for many years. The bank helped many of the population and gave a lot for the development of trade and craftsmanship in the area.

In our home, the following groups held their annual dinners: "Morning Psalm Chanters", "Learners of Talmud Between *Mincha* and *Ma'ariv* Services", and the "Burial Society". The preparations for the meals were many - Shayna the cook and her daughter were invited to oversee the work. To their aid came the *gabbays'* [beadles'] wives: Beyla Tchatchkes, Shifra Rabinovitch (Payes), Chayka and Rivka, and all of them took the trouble to prepare the festive meal. All the town honorables participated in the meal, which continued until the early morning hours. The time passed in eating and drinking, and in particular in discussion, arguments and speeches on current events.

Sara Avrahami

When we moved to the center of the town, our home became a meeting place for important townspeople, especially during *Elul* [month in the Hebrew Calendar] after the *Ma'ariv* prayers, on Saturday night after reciting *Havdalah* [ceremony recited at the termination of Shabbat and holidays]. In the middle of the room was a large table where the guests would be seated, next to steamy cups of tea which my mother prepared from a boiling samovar. Next to the table one would hear Sabbath songs, arguments and discussions about town matters. Sometimes one would hear a complaint, spoken in good temper. They were especially annoyed that my father, Chaim Bruk, and Chaim-Issar Kavak had traveled to welcome a young rabbi who was accepted for a position in our town, but part of the townspeople were not happy with him.

There was also resentment about the many expenses and that the community fund was empty. "Nu?" - said someone - "if Meir Pisuk from Rovna would come this year to be "gathered unto his fathers", it would be possible to repair the fence of the cemetery".

Trade was carried on mainly after the festival of Sukkot, during the winter months. Mainly agricultural produce was traded, both animals and plants, of which the area was aplenty: flax, linseed, grains, hog bristles and produce of the chicken coops and dairy sheds. Trading took place mainly on market day, which was every Tuesday, in the town. The Jews bought agricultural products from the farmers, and the farmers bought their necessities from the shops of the Jews. There were merchants who went out on horse-driven carts to trade with the farmers in the villages.

In the summer there was not too much work for the merchants. In their spare time, they would sit on the thresholds of their shops, telling stories and jokes. I remember till this day a story they would often tell, to the laughter of the listeners.

In the corner of Binyamin (Yaakov Shimon's son) Yedidovitz's shop, stood a large barrel of sunflower seeds. Every time that Leibe (Shaya's son) Nochimovsky, entered the shop, he would take a fistful of seeds and hand them out to all the idle people in the shop. What did they do? They played a prank on him: Binyamin exchanged the barrel of sunflower seeds for a barrel of sweet, thick, sticky syrup. When Leibe Nochimovsky put his hand into the barrel, he found it hard to pull out, and all those around laughed heartily.

Many years have passed, but how cruel is the fact that from our town only a few memories remain.

[Pages 175-178]

Educational and Cultural Institutions in Lubtch

by Chanan Boldo

Translated from the Hebrew by Ann Belinsky

In 1910, on the initiative of Ben-Tzion Shimshilevitch it was decided to build a library in the town. Since there were no means for purchasing books, it was also decided to start up an amateur group, whose income would go towards purchasing books.

The first two shows ("Goliath the Philistine" and *"Dar Yeshiva Bocher"*) funded the purchase of some of the Yiddish and Russian books. In this way, the basis for the library was built. The first librarian was Ben Tzion Shimshilevitch, and I was chosen to be the secretary.

From 1914-1920, I was away from the town. When I returned, I leased the dairy for producing hard cheeses, for 2 years. At the end of this period, I bought a flour mill on Delatitch Street, and my income was ordinary.

Now, when I could get away from the worries of an income, I started to act for the good of the public: The first priority was a school and indeed we received from the community a plot of land next to the synagogue (*Shulhoif*). With the initiative and endeavor of Mr Osherovsky, the money for the building for the school was raised: an attractive building with 7 classrooms, a teachers' room, a library and a hall, where adult and children's shows could be put on.

In 1924, the school was inaugurated, and represented a spiritual centre to the community, until the 2nd World War broke out. The teacher Mr Reiss was appointed headmaster, and amongst his pupils, I remember Mr Goldschmid (from the town of Baksht) and Mr Chaim Persky.

Under the leadership of Mr Idel Kesmayevitch, and after him Mr Berkovitch, a voluntary fire brigade was formed. With the help of donations and the governmental participation, a large building was built next to the market, with the equipment needed for extinguishing fires.

In 1929, an order came from the officer of the Novogrudek Region (*Strosta*), to choose a community committee that would organize the management of the Jewish institutions in Lubtch. Their job was to appoint religious officials - a ritual slaughterer, cantor and rabbi, to care for people in need and to be recognized representatives of the Lubtch Jews - the towns of Delatitch, Karelitz, and Nagnivitza-Niechtet also belonged to this committee from the point of view of administration and representation to the authorities.

The community committee was appointed for 4 years. The inhabitants were taxed to cover the debts - expenses of the committee, and for various services that they received.

The Fire Brigade Band

Among the first town officials were: Chaim Bruk (chairman), Yisrael Soloducha and others.

The second committee included: Elchanan Boldo, Yitzhak Berkovitz, Dov Gissin, Reuven Bortzky, Rabbi Yitzhak Weiss, Rabbi Werner from Karelitz, and Mr Kaplan from Karelitz.

On the initiative of Yehoshua Shimshilevitch, in 1925 the Jewish Cooperative Amami Bank was established in Lubtch. Its directors were: Chaim Bruk, Moshe Tunik, Itche Notta Yedidovitch and Elchanan Boldo. From the Institution for Aiding Injured for the 1st World War (*Yakapa*) in Vilna, basic capital was received, a total of 5000 *zloty* as well as bank shares.

The bank gradually developed, and had an influential effect on the commercial and financial life of the town. Bank loans were given (for 2 months, the inhabitants were careful to pay their debts, worrying that the banks might suffer) and it was never necessary to open court proceedings. A way was always found in order to help those who had difficulty in paying back their debts.

Chanan Boldo

The bank thrived, until World War II broke out in 1939; one must remember the important contribution that the book-keeper, Mr Moshe Persky (May the Lord avenge his blood), made to the development of the bank.

With the Soviet invasion in 1939, private businesses were nationalized. My flour mill was nationalized also, and I was requested to sign a document declaring that I forgo the mill on my own free will. During the German invasion, I and my family left Lubtch for Novogrudek.

When we were put into the ghetto, I was put in charge of fencing in the ghetto. While making the fence, I left a breach which could be easily opened. When hair-raising rumors that the Germans were annihilating all the Jews began to reach our ears, I started to cultivate ideas of escape; a letter that was sent to me, wherein I was warned about the dangers of annihilation - fell into the hands of the *Judenrat* [Jewish Council] and a guard was put on my house day and night. On the advice of my wife, we started cultivating a garden by our house. When the Judenrat saw that, they thought that I did not intend to run away, and took away their guard.

One rainy night we ran away (I, my wife and children) through the breach in the fence. That same night we arrived at the house of a farmer, in the area of the village Hota; he was a peasant who loved people, and who with self-sacrifice, hid us until the long-awaited day of liberation.

[Page 178]

Wealth...

by Gershon Jankelowitz

Translated from the Yiddish by Harvey Spitzer

There was a man in the village, a horse dealer, Binyamin the Redhead, with his wife, Merke. He was neither a very rich man nor a beggar and just managed to make a living.

One fine day, Merke's uncle came on a visit from America. Hearing that her uncle was already on his way to their house, Merke shouts to her husband:

- Binyamin, take the horse and cow out of the stable. My uncle will notice them and will see how rich we are and won't leave us any dollars.

[Page 179]

The community committee of Lubtch-Karelitz in 1934 (5695)

Sitting from right to left: G. Yellin and P. Kaplan (Korelitz), R' Yitzchak Aharonovsky (ritual slaughterer and inspector), the Rabbi Yitzchak Weiss, the Chazan Tobolsky and R' Tuvia Shimshilevitch.
Standing from right to left: The first is unknown, B. Bossel and L. Prevlozky (from Karelitz). Berel-Hirschel Gishen, Yitzchak Berkovitz, Avraham-Chaim

[Pages 180-181]

Memories of My Town

by Rachel Engel

Translated from the Hebrew by Ann Belinsky

Rachel Engel

After the 1st World War, we returned to our town Delatitch. The economic situation was bad, and even between the closest neighbors there were competition and bitter arguments over their livelihood; but this did not cloud the friendship between families, as there was a strange distinction between economic arguments and national brotherhood. We were a small group of Jews in the locality and we knew that we must be united in feelings of friendship and lend a helping hand to our fellow man, otherwise we would be worn down within the unfriendly, gentile environment.

My parents made their livelihood from making yellow cheese, as did our neighbors Berel and Pia Yankelevitch. We fought over customers and we tried to restrict their ways, but the correct, neighborly relations were not impaired. I remember their house that stood opposite ours. On Saturday nights, Berel would take out his gramophone (the only one in Delatitch) on the verandah, and play cantorial selections to all the street; the brothers Avraham and Moshe would approach Berel's house, "helping" the *chazzan,* and their voices would spill out into the darkened street.

I would often visit the Cohen family, our neighbors. Beilka their daughter was my friend. I loved the mother of the family, Simka, a clever woman, with a developed sense of humor. Her smile always greeted those visiting their house, and her goodheartedness gave a pleasant atmosphere and peaceful feeling to the house.

We fostered ties of friendship and commerce with the town of Lubtch. We felt ourselves part of the Lubtch community, and visited there often.

Only a few Jews lived in Delatitch, but despite this, we took pains to develop a Jewish way of life in the place; the children received traditional education; we made sure that we kept the traditions and the mitzvoth of the Torah, both on weekdays and on Shabbat and holidays.

During the 10 Days of Penitence - Joseph Cohen was the prayer leader, before the Ark, and would pour out his prayer to the G-d of Israel, Father of Mercy, with all the congregation respectfully answering after him.

Rabbi Yaakov Baksht was then the Rabbi of the community. Every problem concerning kashrut or the community we would refer to him, and he would give a decision.

Our synagogue was large and spacious, and the community life of the Jews of the town was concentrated within it. There, my stepfather, R' Yisrael Berkovsky, would say psalms with the Jews of the community, on Shabbat between *Mincha* and *Maariv*. As *gabbay* [sexton] of the Synagogue, he would look after all necessities there. In winter he would prepare wood for lighting the fires, even before he prepared wood for his own house. Inside the synagogue we began to study with a *melamed* [elementary school teacher], and we would also play there. I remember on a certain day we were running around wildly and yelling in loud voices. All of a sudden the doors of the synagogue opened and R' Slonimsky strode in shouting in Yiddish "*Arois! Arois*"! (Out! Out!).

Beggars would come to the synagogue to spend the night. Sometimes, even whole families with their children came. My mother would prepare hot food for the children of the poor and hurry to bring it to the synagogue, to keep the unfortunate children warm.

[Page 181]

A Wedding

by Chaim Yankelevitch

Translated from the Yiddish by Harvey Spitzer

Grandmother and Grandfather went to a wedding. As is the custom, they will bring us back portions of pies and sweet ginger cake. We go to bed happy, confident that in the morning the delicious treats will be awaiting us.

We get up early and look around for the pie and cake, but it's only a dream.

— Grandpa, so?...

Grandpa sighs:

It was a sumptuous wedding, fish and meat and all kinds of delicacies such as an eye has never seen....

[Pages 182-183]

A letter from the Mendele Library in Lubtch

A letter from the Mendele Library in Lubtch (ctd). (The library seal bears the words "The Jewish Public Library in Memory of Mendele Mocher Sefarim in Lubtch, State of Grodno.") The same is written in Hebrew on the seal

[Pages 182-183]

A LETTER FROM THE MENDELE LIBRARY IN LUBTCH

Translated from the Hebrew by Harvey Spitzer

Public Hebrew Library
In memory of Mendele-Mocher Sefarim
In Lubtch, State of Grodno
October 22, 1931
No. 15

To Mr. M. Pisiuk

Dear Sir:

During his last visit to Lubtch, His Honor expressed a wish to visit our library, seeing that His Honor (was eager) to visit his native land and especially our institutions, the main thing being our library. His visit, then, gave us much pleasure and (stimulated) our desire to show him what we had accomplished during the last ten year since the founding of the library. However, to our great sorrow, due to the unexpectedly (late) hour, His Honor did not manage to visit the library. And before his departure, he promised to donate five volumes of his important memoirs for our benefit. .

This week, Mr. Chaim Brozi, head of the community, turned the books, splendidly bound and written on excellent paper, over to our possession. May His Honor accept our endearing thanks for his generous donation. May God strengthen him and grant him a long life and may he be worthy of working many more years for the public benefit.

Dear Sir, we consider it our duty to provide him (you) with details of the history of the development of the library as well as the current situation, (which will prove) how much energy and toil we invested in the library until we established it on the required height on which it presently stands.

Ten years ago, when we started re-settling in Lubtch after the Germans were driven out, we found our little town burned down and abandoned. And there we were dealing with same question of whether or not to set up a library. I remember that the first meeting was at the study hall (synagogue) and there were about 10 people present. However, in the course of time, the library developed. At first, we didn't have a room and we used to move from house to house. After the school was built, we finally had a permanent hall. Still, it wasn't easy for us to organize such a big library. However, thanks to our efforts, we overcame the obstacles. This is how things stand at present: the library contains about 1,500 books, many of which are valuable and 35% are Hebrew books. The library operates by its own authority and is named after "Mendele Mocher-Sefarim" and we don't get any support from the management or from the State. Whoever cannot afford to pay the borrower's fee receives his books free. The readers' fees only pay for binding of books and many publications (expenses). We raise money by arranging dramatic parties, literary trials, lectures, raffles, etc. We _____ from various expenses and we pay the next-of-kin with promissory notes and _____ I'm happy to point out that, to this day, not one promissory note has been disputed.

Recently, however, the situation has worsened and we are facing a very difficult test. We haven't been able to purchase a book in nearly a year. Above all, we need to build a special bookcase. The books are kept in two bookcases and there isn't enough room to hold all the books. And so we've decided to build another bookcase, specifically for this purpose, but there isn't a penny in the cash-box. Thus, we are turning to His Honor with a request for support. The bookcase is an essential item and with this donation, we will be able to build a bookcase which will remain an everlasting memorial: Mr. Pisiuk's donation. Of course, we_____. We shall continue ____ and we shall again try to order books. We emphasize the importance of building the bookcase, for books are rolling off the shelves due to lack of space. And the donation will be a thing of _____. We're sure that His Honor will consider the importance of the bookcase and will accede to our request. Our thanks are explicit. We are awaiting His (your) reply, expressing an obligation to help.

Sincerely,

    In the name of the library committee, Yankelovitz
Chanan Szmiglowicz

Library Seal:
The library seal bears the words in Yiddish "The Jewish Publich Library in memory of Mendele Mocher Sefarim in Lubtch, State of Grodno. The same is written in Hebrew on the seal.

Lubcha _____ _____ ,Novogrudek 18
PS If it is not too difficult, please send us more copies of your books and their _____. If it is not possible, (at least) try to fulfill our main request.

[Pages 184-185]

Remembrances

by Rose (Reiche - Bayla) Ballot

Translated from the Yiddish by Harvey Spitzer

As though in a dream, I remember our little town in 1904 when my father, Yehoshua Ovsayevitch, left for America.

My father was a blacksmith, and his workshop stood at the very end of Delatitch Street on the way to the Voinover synagogue. The evening before his departure, father sat us - his four daughters and mother - around him and for hours on end sang songs expressing separation, longing, promises not to forget and faithfulness. Our parents were crying loudly and we couldn't understand why grown-ups need to cry.

The day Lubtch burned down is engraved in my memory. The fire started when a caldron with tallow caught fire at Neshke the candlemaker's shop. She was Nota Mordechai's daughter. On that day, 32 houses on Otshookevitch Street were destroyed by the fire. In the great tumult, I grabbed my uncle's little girl, a year old, and ran to the river, carrying the baby in my arms. I understood that there was nothing that could burn at the river. The baby was screaming. I sat there with her until the evening, when the fire stopped. Meanwhile, people noticed that we were missing and they already lamented the fact that we had burned to death in the fire. One of the neighbors noticed us by the river and brought the news back to the family. We were considered as having been resurrected from the dead.

Otshookevtich Street was quickly rebuilt and life went on. In Lubtch, however, many changes occurred, one of which was the establishment of a Yiddish public school where one was not required to pay tuition. The founders and directors of the school were several intelligent girls who were eager to do social work, to spread light and knowledge in Jewish life and educate the young generation in the spirit of modernity. The girls really undertook a pioneering task and it is a sacred obligation to recall their names: Sarah-Chanah, daughter of Shlomo Moshe Niankever, Yache, Reize, daughter of the dry goods merchant, Sarah Zlata, daughter of Leibe the tailor and both daughters of Rabbi Yosef Eliahu, the subsequent rabbi of Lubtch.

Girls alone attended the public school. Lubtch at that time was not ready to send boys to a modern school instead of to a traditional *cheder*, besides the fact that they would be studying together with girls. This was too progressive for our little town. We studied Yiddish, Russian, Bible, composition, arithmetic and learned to sew and embroider. From time to time, Yaakov-Meir, the teacher and Berel, the miller's son, would give lessons. The school closed down after three terms, but its influence lasted for many years and undoubtedly gave a tremendous push forward to the intellectual development of Jewish life in Lubtch.

The winds of revolution which were blowing and convulsing great Russia, also reached Lubtch. Illegal party cells sprang up in our town. My older sister, Dvoshe, joined the "Little Union" and mother hastened to send her off to America as quickly as possible.

Only a few individuals remained from our widely-branched family. World War I took its toll and those who survived were later murdered by the Nazis and their collaborators.

[Pages 186-188]

The National Spirit of the Jews of Lubtch

by Avraham Shavit-Faivoshevitch

Translated from the Hebrew by Ann Belinsky

Avraham Shavit - Faivoshevitch

The residents of Lubtch were God-fearing traditional Jews, but the national spirit beat in their hearts. In the *cheder* of Rabbi Asher Hamelamed, and in the *cheder* of R' Yudel Hamelamed, the small children learned, in addition to the Chumash and Gemara, the history of the Jewish people from the book by Dubnov, Hebrew grammar from Pines's book, and language from Gordon's book "*HaLashon*" [The Language]. The language of teaching in the *cheder* was Hebrew, and this was many years before the Balfour Declaration.

There were children who spoke Hebrew between themselves even outside the *cheder* and school. On Shabbat afternoons, the teacher Haim Persky would go for his customary walk along the main street, and would make lively conversation in Hebrew with another teacher, in an especially loud voice, which made the children very happy and gave them the impetus to imitate him.

The Jews of Lubtch mourned the Destruction of the Temple and the desolation of Eretz-Israel. The Book of Lamentations was soaked with the tears of the worshipers. There was a custom there to go to the local cemetery on *Tisha B'Av* [Hebrew date]. The children would gird themselves with wooden swords, made by their parents. At the cemetery the parents would take the swords and break them. I remember that in answer to my question "Father, why did you break my sword?" he answered: "In remembrance of the Destruction of the Temple".

Stories of the heroism of our people were told by our parents with enthusiasm and emotions of pride.

Four Zionist organizations were active in our town: *HeChalutz; Poalei Tzion TZ.S.; HaShomer Hatza'ir* and *Beitar*.

Sometimes, even within the walls of the synagogue, mass Zionist meetings were held. The sexton would announce the event in the streets of the town. On the walls of the houses were large posters written in extra-large letters ("*Kiddush-levana*"), calling all residents to the meeting.

The desire to make aliyah to Eretz-Israel beat in their hearts. I remember the looks of the people when I came to part from them, before making aliyah to Eretz-Israel in 1934; their eyes expressed happiness, jealousy and yearning. My parents asked me to try and bring them there too, after I had gotten settled there. My grandfather, R' Eliezer, said: - "To make aliyah to Eretz-Israel I will not be privileged, as I am old already, but please, send me at least an ethrog, that I will be privileged to bless a fruit from the Holy Land in the Succah".

In Lubtch there were a number of institutions for mutual help, among them *Linat Hatzedek* [Overnight charity], in which I was active. Members of the institution helped families where there was someone who had been sick for a long time, - helping the sick person, sitting with him at night, caring for and looking after him, in order to lighten the burden on the family so that they could renew their energy.

The Committee of the *HeChalutz* Organization in Lubtch with the previous committee, before their aliyah to Israel -1926

I remember Chaim Bruk, who tried to help anyone in need. He was active in the Zionist movement, and enthused many with the Zionist ideal. Chaim Bruk was a leader of the community and a lobbyist for any matter that needed to be brought before the governmental authorities, such as asking for licenses etc.

With his adherence, his diligence and his pleasant personality, he knew how to settle arguments, usually for the best.

Avrahamke "*Der Svirer*" was a pious Jew, who worked all his life in carpentry. As he had no sons, he saved penny upon penny all his life, in order to be able to take on the work of *Gmilut-chasidim* [Giving charity] in his old age, so that he would not arrive at the "world to come" empty-handed. Anyone in need would receive a loan without interest. Avrahamke would keep accounts, and appear at the houses of those late in paying back the loan, and gently remind them that the time for returning the loan had arrived. This he did in order to keep on helping other people in need.

- -

Many years have passed since I left my home, years of work and labor, but I will never forget my hometown.

[Page 188]

Real Horseradish

by Chaim Yankelevitch

Translated from the Yiddish by Harvey Spitzer

A young Lubtch son-in-law, getting food and board at his in-laws' house, sits at the Sabbath table and, with a hearty appetite, eats the various foods which his mother-in-law brings to the table.

When she served the gefilte fish, the son-in-law stood up, put his arms around his mother-in-law and placed a kiss on her face. He did the same thing when she served the plate of meat.

The father-in-law can no longer keep from wondering, and asks:

— What is all this sudden kissing your mother-in-law about?

The young son-in-law answers:

— I like to use horseradish with fish and meat, and just today there is none on the table.

[Pages 189-194]

Lubtch on the Neiman

by Dov Kabak

Translated from the Hebrew by Ann Belinsky

In the land of White Russia, by the banks of the Neiman, lies the town of Lubtch, surrounded by tens of Byelorussian villages. It is a small town, located 21 kilometers from the regional city of Novogrudek and 30 kilometers from the town of Mir (whose *yeshiva*, "Yeshivat Mir", was famed as a center for Torah learning, where many desired to learn). Lubtch also had a close and good relationship with the neighboring town of Delatitch.

Lubtch was a small town, mostly populated by Jews who led a traditional life within a Christian environment. These were innocent Jews, good hearted and pious: lovers of the Torah and of learning, even the poorest of whom learnt in the *cheder* (religious elementary school) and absorbed the Torah, reverence and traditional Jewish values.

When I think back on the life in the town today, in an era when we are surrounded by the benefits of modernization and technological improvements, it seems as if fifty to sixty years ago time stood still in Lubtch. The tradition and customs were strictly kept and it was clear that they should be kept that way in the future. Life passed slowly and lazily, without much tumult and far-reaching changes: the same leaders, the same values, even the same occupations.

The inhabitants made a living mainly from commerce, mostly as small merchants who toiled to make a living. There were no rich people in the town. Most of the population was poor and made do with little, accepting God's judgment while praising and thanking the Creator.

Dov Kabak

The Jewish communities in the Polish Diaspora were surprisingly similar to each other. Nevertheless, each township had it own special character due to the influence of the ethnic-geographical environs, and the distance from the Jewish cultural-spiritual centers, etc.

Lubtch was influenced by two factors which were also the main sources of income for the populace:

A. The River Neiman; B. The rural-agricultural environment:

A. The Neiman

The Neiman flowed by the town, the sound of its waves singing a song of distant places. It served as the artery of transport and transportation for thousands of rafts loaded with logs from the forests that surrounded Lubtch. The Jews living there were the main suppliers of food and clothing to the rafters and those working at sawing.

**[Chaim Yankelovitch standing on] a timber raft on the Neiman.
In the distance - the castle**

A visit by the wood dealers was the source of livelihood for several hotels. These visits brought with them a fragrance of far away places, a new a modern ambiance that pulled the town out of its frozenness and drowsiness.

Agricultural produce was transported on the Neiman from the surrounds: the small "batten" boats made their way to Germany, carried by the currents, loaded with cereal grains, oil-producing seeds, and flax. On their return from Germany, they would carry kerosene, various fats and good quality flour.

The Neiman also left its mark on the social life in the town. It was a place for holiday making and celebration, concealing and unending wealth of surprises and entertainment: in the summer is was a pool of cooling and refreshing water, while in the winter it served as a frozen area for ice skating. The local young residents saw it as a place for social meetings, and the older people would also go there happily when they had some free time.

B. The Agricultural Surroundings

The town dwelled within a farming countryside, and twice a week the farmers of the area would come to the town with their produce.

Every Sunday, the farmers would come to the Russian Orthodox church that dominated the highest point in the town. The farmers would combine goodness with efficiency and, when arriving for the prayer service, would bring their meat and dairy and vegetable produce to trade among themselves.

Besides the Sunday market, there was also a weekly Tuesday market: the farmers would fill up the open area with the sound of the commotion of people and the bleating, mooing and neighing of farm animals, with sellers and buyers busily handling and checking the merchandise. Our "Israelite Brethren" were also part of the tumult, buying produce from the farmers for their own needs and commerce, and providing the traders with necessities.

Most of the inhabitants were merchants, shop-owners and peddlers. Because of the rural surroundings, there were many grain and flax merchants as well as cattle and horse dealers.

Dozens of the town breadwinners would go out to the surrounding villages and buy all they could from the farmers, and would sometimes be away from home from Sunday until Shabbat.

Many houses next to the marketplace served as "*sheink*", small taverns where the farmers would pass the time on market days drinking vodka, while eating salted fish with sugared tea.

The place of the "holy vessels" [religious ministrants] was not missing from the various ways of earning a "livelihood". In our town there were two rabbis who detested each other. What one called *treyf* [unfit for eating], the other called *kosher*, and they would overturn worlds in order to discredit, slander and put the other to shame.

*

During the First World War, several days before the Germans arrived at the town, the inhabitants abandoned their homes out of fear of fires (since most of the roofs were made of straw, the fear of fires was enormous.) and concentrated in the meadow behind the synagogue. Some of the farmers from the area fled with the retreating army, but the Jews remained there, since they thought that the Germans would not get to such an out-of-the-way place.

In the meanwhile, the Cossacks went on a rampage. They caught women and girls in order to behave wildly with them and they came with demands for money, threatening to burn down the town if their requests were not answered. The Jews joined together and whenever they saw the Cossacks, they would begin shouting together "*Gevalt!*" ["How awful"], something which chased the Cossacks away.

The hopes of the Jews were dashed, however, as the Germans arrived there exactly on Shabbat. The town was completely burned down and the inhabitants exiled. The River Neiman became the frontline of the fighting between the German and Russian armies until the end of the war in 1918.

In 1930, Lubtch was conquered by the Polish army. The residents began to return to it, to rebuild and restore it.

A new spirit throbbed in the town: general knowledge and especially the spirit of Hebrew education began to pulsate in the hearts of the youth who returned from the large centers of culture and made sure that this spirit was nourished. Public institutions were built to educate and serve the idea of the national redemption. The following were established: a public primary school, a large public library and kindergartens. The dispute between Yiddish and Hebrew culture was abandoned, and in its place it was decided that the general studies would be taught in Yiddish. For this purpose, I made contact with the "*Tzisha*" society in Warsaw, and they sent a headmaster for our school.

In 1921, Yisrael Rubin (Dr. Rivka'i) from "*Tzisha*", visited Lubtch. The school in our town made a deep impression on him, and in the summer of his visit he wrote that it was wonderful that he found progress in the school, although the life in the town was administrated as it had been done tens of years ago.

The school was affiliated over time with the chain of *Tarbut* schools in Poland. Under the guidance of Shmuel Shapiro (his sister Lyuba is living in Israel), a dramatic society was set up; from its proceeds the public library was built with Hebrew and Yiddish books.

The founding of the public bank aided in the development of the town. Its primary aim was to help the needy. As a member of the management of the bank, I can bear witness that many of the residents were in need and were helped by the bank.

Zionist movements including *HeChalutz* [The Pioneer], *Poalei Tzion* [Workers of Zion], (Zionist Socialists), *HaShomer Hatza'ir* [The Young Guard] and *Beitar* [Brit Trumpeldor] brought a new momentum to the town. Because the youth were already infected with the bug of Zionism (many thanks to the blessed work of Chaim Bruk, an ardent Zionist who influenced many youth), the movements began to organize farming training activities. Most were sent for training on Kibbutz "*Shachariya*" in Baronovitch. Seventy-five youths, girls and boys, made *aliya* [immigrated] to Eretz-Yisrael [Palestine] and thus were saved from the claws of the Nazi monster.

The Public Library Committee in 1930
From right to left: **Avraham Bruk, Yaakov Shmulevitch, Nachum Shlimovitch, Dov Kabak, Chaya Nignivitsky, Yunis Itzkovitch, Chaim Persky**

The Jews of Lubtch are no longer, but their images hover over our eyes, and their memory is carried in our hearts. Their voices cry out from the depths of oblivion: Remember what the Nazi Amalek did to you!! Remember because we were murdered and not given the opportunity to drink completely from the Cup of Life!!

[Pages 194-199]

Lubtch Foods

by K. Hilel

Translated from the Yiddish by Harvey Spitzer

Jews from Lubtch, like most of the population of that region, liked to eat fatty foods. There was simply a cult for fat: fatty meat, fatty chickens, fatty geese and ducks, goose fat, beef fat, fried chicken fat, fatty stuffed derma, fatty membranes, fatty puddings, fatty soup, a fowl's throat stuffed with fat, a fatty piece of breast meat, calves' feet jelly, and even a fatty bone.

Food, cooked, fried or baked with various kinds of fat, were the most delicious: cutlets, latkes, blintzes, pancakes, potatoes, mushrooms in butter, puddings, "blinis",

Passover

Matzah balls with goose fat, Shavuot (Feast of Weeks) *babke* cake dripping with butter, butter rolls, etc. Today, who still talks about a good piece of sausage, a fatty herring, and certainly a fatty fish right out of the Nieman River?

And since we're still on the subject of fish, we should, in fact, mention the different kinds of fish which the Jews of Lubtch served on their tables: First of all, there was pike - the king of all kosher Jewish fish. After pike come carp, various species of local fish - and the cheapest fish of all, called the "poor man's fish", smelling like swampy ponds. Besides these, people would sometimes allow themselves a luxury and buy a smoked herring and, in fact, a herring with the addition of herring sauce in which to dunk hot, boiled potatoes.

Yes, potatoes. What delicacies mothers in Lubtch used to make from them! Potatoes in their skins, peeled potatoes, fish potatoes (without fish), potatoes with beans, dairy potatoes, potato soup with fish, mashed potatoes, baked potatoes, potatoes cooked in Sabbath meat stew (*cholent*), potato pancakes (*latkes*), potato pudding with egg yolks (*kugel*), roasted potatoes, fried potatoes, pancakes made from potato gruel, potato dumplings (*kneidelach*), dainty potato stew with plums, dainty carrot stew with potatoes or potato dumplings (*tsimmes*) and, in fact, the entire set of potato items made with flour just as the song goes:

"Sunday potatoes, Monday potatoes
Tuesday and Wednesday, again potatoes"...

Flour was also widely used in Jewish cuisine: rye flour for baking delicious rye bread was also good for real, honey- sweetened gingerbread (*lekech*), wheat flour for baked goods, noodles (*lokshen*), dough crumbs (*farfel*), small triangular cakes of batter filled with chopped meat or cheese (*kreplach*), and soup almonds which mothers used to make by themselves. Coarse meal, with a bitter taste, to bake dark brown "poor man's" challah and cake; buckwheat meal for making for matzah balls, pancakes (*latkes*) and for baking a "*gutman*" on a tin sheet and finally a certain kind of meal which had to be toasted a little over a fire before use, to make Sabbath gruel (*kasha*) and delicious matzah balls and pudding (*kugel*) — "royal treats".

With regard to puddings, there were also different kinds of different ranks: a noodle pudding made with fat and a noodle pudding with cheese for the Feast of Weeks (*Shavuot*) occupy first place. Next comes a pudding made with flour and filled with fruit. This is followed by a "poured out" pudding made with flour, eggs and fat, a potato pudding, and a pudding in the shape of a stuffed neck of a fowl.

Loaves of White Bread (*Challah*) and Baked Goods:

Braided loaves of white bread made in the shape of ladders or in the shape of a hand with fingers, "strudel" filled with fruit; fancy egg cakes for which one had to beat the egg whites a long time until they became stiff, honey sweetened gingerbread, babka, little almond breads, cheese cakes, hard and crunchy egg cakes (*kichelach*), small rolls made with butter, and small rolls filled with cinnamon, *Hamantaschen* (three cornered rolls of bread stuffed with ground poppy seeds and cinnamon), little balls of honey dough (*teiglach*) loaves of white bread (*challah*) made with oil and baked items made with coarse meal. This is just a part of the variety of goods baked in Jewish homes in Lubtch. To this we must add the dry cakes, and the shiny, toasted bagel and certainly the egg bagel. Oh! Oh! What a taste they had!

Holiday Foods

Sabbath: gefilte fish, radishes with chicken fat, chopped liver with onions, onion stew, *tsimmes* (dainty stew of vegetables) *cholent* and potato or noodle pudding (*kugel*).

Passover: matzah balls, fermented beets, matzah "*farfel*" pudding, *cremzlach* (little cakes baked dry in a pan), matzah meal *pampushkes* (pancakes), mashed potato and egg pudding, fancy cake made with potato starch and eggs, dainty stew of prunes.

Shavuot -Feast of Weeks: cheese blintzes, babka, cheese cake, butter rolls all served with a good glass of chicory with milk.

New Year: challa in the shape of a ladder or hand, honey coated dough balls (*teiglach*) - a symbol for a sweet year.

Eve of Day of Atonement: when one performs an expiatory ritual with a sacrificial fowl, called "beating *kaparot*"; *Hoshana Raba* (sixth day of Festival of Tabernacles), when one beats willows on the ground, and *Purim* (Feast of Lots), when one beats Haman, and it was the custom to eat *Hamantaschen*, small triangular cakes containing chopped meat or cheese. And scoffers would add that these cakes could be eaten as well whenever one beats his wife!

Purim (Feast of Lots): "*Hamantaschen*", honey coated dough balls(teiglach) and certainly the real Purim banquet.

Chanukah: potato pancakes or pancakes made with wheat or buckwheat meal or, in fact, both mixed together and fried in sizzling goose or chicken fat.

When we baked bread, we also cooked a "*kaslucha*", a mixture of sour leavened bread and sugar- a finger-licking delicacy…

And a buckwheat porridge of meal whitened with milk, a fatty onion stew cooked in sweet and sour sauce; chopped eggs and onions, chopped herring in wine vinegar. We ate all foods and enjoyed them in Lubtch. We can't forget their taste, for which today I would gladly give up the best, medium rare "steak".

And a dish of *shtchav* (sorrel), whitened with yolks and sour cream with chopped up scallions, fresh cucumber and sweet beets. And the earthenware jars, set aside, of butter milk and sour cream, the sour liquid which remains in the barrel after butter is churned, and just a glass of self fermented juice of pickled cucumbers having the good taste of dill, caraway and garlic - and even more so when whitened with sour cream. It
is really so refreshing!

Indeed, and preserves of raspberries, ("may there be no need for them!") cherries, gooseberries, pears and even of radishes - yes, of radishes-, cowberries and whortleberries. And besides these, we must add the big bottles with blackberries, cherries and raspberries, which also served as a medicinal cure.

Blackberries, raw or cooked, garnished with sugar and starch, red berries served with sugar and sour cream, small radishes with cucumbers, salad greens and scallions from one's own garden mixed with buttermilk, with slices of black, rye bread spread with butter. Just remembering this makes one's mouth water.

All of these were the foods that our mothers and grandmothers prepared, giving up a lot of their time, energy and health. Foods the Jews of Lubtch enjoyed and which also produced physically healthy generations.

And as we're already mentioning the various foods, let's also mention the cooking utensils, instruments and vessels which our mothers and grandmothers used for their work. In doing so, it should be noted that some of the names originate in White Russian and have been Yiddishized:

boike – a small barrel for churning butter
deinitze – a milk pail
deizshe – a small barrel for kneading dough
dreifuss – an iron tripod (stand) for cooking
volgerholtz – a wooden instrument for turning wash in a wash basin
voyik – a kind of lever or anchor for drawing buckets out of a well
vilke – a half- rounded fork for putting pots in the oven
vechetch – a rag for scouring and cleaning pots
zaslinke – a piece of tin for closing or covering the baking oven, an oven-lid.
zipele – a thick sieve for flour or meal
tarke – a grater
tshohon – a small pot made of "tshohon" (cast iron)
yoshke – a chimney cover, a damper
ladishke – an earthenware jug or pitcher
lopete – a small board with a stick, like an oar, for placing food in oven for baking
lokshenbret – a board for rolling dough
liak – a small pot with a narrow opening for boiling water
multer – a wooden instrument for kneading dough
stupe – a wooden pestle for grinding matzah.
skorvede – a frying pan
pomoinitze – a bucket for dirty water after use
pomele – a broom for cleaning the oven, an oven mop

fendel – a small pan used mainly for cooking fish
pripetchik – forepart of an oven, a place for cooking by an oven
tzuber – the lower pestle made of wood, a tub
kotchere – a piece of bent iron with which to scrape pots from oven
katuch – a place under a baking over for keeping chickens
katshelke – a round stick for rolling dough, a rolling pin
kvart – a tin cup serving as a measure (quart) for milk
kendel (*kubak*) – a cup with a handle for taking water out of a bucket
kargeshir – a small pot, corrupted from the German "Kochgeshir", cooking utensils
reshete – a sieve with bigger openings, from Hebrew *reshet* (screen, net)
shtoisel – a small, brass barrel (mortar) with a pestle for crushing poppy seed, pepper, etc.
shtchirke – a dishtowel

[Page 199]

"Lubtch Pigs"

by H.K.

Translated from the Yiddish by Harvey Spitzer

Just as most of the Jews in the town, the Lubtch gentiles also had a nickname - "Lubtch pigs".

This came about from the fact that a few individual gentiles lived in the Jewish sections and their pigs used to creep about all day long in the Jewish streets. They especially liked the small, Jewish yards and it was a real delight for them to get into Jewish gardens and destroy everything.

In retrospect, the pigs were actually the predecessors of their owners- the gentiles.

[Pages 200-201]

Days of Activity and Hope

by Chaim Sonenzon

Translated from the Hebrew by Ann Belinsky

Lubtch maintained a traditional way of life, based on the heritage of its fathers, and a way of life which had taken root over generations.

The market was the center of the town: from there, the 4 main streets branched out; "Novogrudek", "Otshukevitch", *Hatira* (Castle) and "Delatitch". Also branching off from the centre of the market was the Bath-house Lane, where the *Tarbut* School stood, and the three synagogues, two of which were built of stone, and one of wood.

Chaim Sonenzon

There were no factories in Lubtch (except for a carpentry shop and a flour mill). Most of the residents made a living from commerce, peddling and crafts.

The commerce was seasonal, and was carried out mainly during the winter. Trade was in flax, grains, pig bristles and animal furs. Since we were far away from the large cities, many of the new fashions and innovations were not found here. The closest center, to which we were connected to for all governmental ministries and administration, was Novogrudek. But the youth found a means to change their way of life: Youth Movements were set up in the locality, although later than in the large centers, but with their creation, many were swept up with enthusiasm into their ranks.

In 1928 a group of young men, including Mordechai Kivilevitch, Hillel Shmuelevitch, Chaim Yankelevitch, Avraham Leibovitch, Yaacov Zaharvitch, and myself - founded the *HaShomer Hatza'ir* group. We joined up with the leadership of the Movement in Baronovitch, and with the close branch in Novogrudek, in order to request help, since we did not have a model of the way the branch should be managed. Help arrived - we were sent emissaries, especially for Shabbat. We eagerly drank their words and during their visits we solved problems and questions which bothered us; we were impatient and wanted to know everything as quickly as possible.

The local youth began organizing into groups and regiments. We had many discussions about current events, ideals and the history and heritage of our People. We went into the fields, to summer camps, on night hikes, we celebrated the Festivals together and together we wove our dreams.

On Lag B'Omer we went to an estate by Delatitch; we celebrated with song and dance, beside the flickering tongues of the flames of the bonfires. We managed to bring an atmosphere of festivity to the whole town.

We went to summer camps in Kromen, for 8 days. It was not easy to persuade the parents to permit their children to go to the camp for such a long time. We visited each house, begging and making promises. Also it was difficult to collect food for the camp. We finally succeeded, the camp took place and aided in bonding the members of the movement.

The Youth Group began started to acquire the character of a cultural center in the town. We arranged cultural evenings, lectures and trials. The youth found a challenge, there was something to fight for, and something to strive towards. It was a place where it was possible to give expression to ideals and ideas.

We set up a drama group, we organized parties where we acted, performed gymnastics, sang, and even traveled to Karelichi [Korelitz] and put on our program there.

Our main problem was where to conduct our activities, especially during the winter. In the summer we would meet mainly in the fields.

We were also active within the school - at first the teachers were opposed, claiming that we were damaging the pupils' handiwork. But since we had strong aspirations, they gave into us finally and the doors of the institution were opened to our activities.

The way of life changed - especially for the youth, many of whom went to training camps (*hachsharah*) and immigrated to Eretz-Israel. Thanks to the youth movements, they were saved from annihilation.

Lubtch was physically annihilated, destroyed and reduced to ruins by the Nazi soldiers, but the atmosphere that prevailed -and the memories of its inhabitants, will not be forgotten.

[Pages 202-205]

The Connection of the Family of President of Israel, Yitzchak Ben Tzvi, to Lubtch

Collated by: A. Aleph

Translated from the Hebrew by Harvey Spitzer

The book, "Pedigree Scrolls" (Jerusalem, 1957), written by Mr. Zvi Shimshi (Shimshelivitch), father of the late President Yitzchak Ben-Zvi, of blessed memory, tells of the relationship of the President's family to the *tzadik* (righteous man), Rabbi Moshe Ivyer.

In his preface to the above- mentioned "Pedigree Scrolls", Prof. Nahum Sloshetz (who is also related to the offspring of Rabbi Moishele Ivyer) writes *inter alia*: "A living tradition such as this was frequently mentioned by the descendants of Rabbi Moshe Ashkenazi Halperin, who was known as Rabbi Moshe Ivyer and, when claiming descent from this hidden *tzadik* [righteous man], always reminded one that he (Rabbi Ivyer) could trace his origin to Rabbi Shlomo Yitzchak (Rashi), one of the most important sages of France during the Middle Ages."

Everyone knows amongst other things that between Rashi and this Rabbi Moshe, there was a gap of 20 generations of dispersion and wanderings, but also during the travels of Rashi's offspring from one nation to another, they never stopped studying the Torah. The chain of Torah study was never halted. Rashi transmitted his Torah to his grandchildren, his daughters' children, and they to the "*Tosafists*" [annotators to the Talmud]. After the Diaspora in France, we find their descendants in the communities of Germany and Italy. More spread to the East, so that Poland and Lithuania eventually became the meeting place of Torah and the heritage of our Forefathers. Amongst these great names who taught the Torah of Rashi in that land we find the first rabbi of Brisk, Rabbi Moshe Ashkenazi, also known as Haylprin, taken from the name of the city of Heilbrun in Germany. Rabbi Moshe Ivyer was a descendant of that first Rabbi Ashkenazi. And my own grandfather, Rabbi Avraham was named after him. After his death, my younger brother Moshe was given his name, but Moshe's nickname was Carmon. (He died in Jerusalem on 24 *Adar* I, 5714 (1954).

According to the Hebrew Encyclopedia (Vol.9, pp. 173-177), the President's father was a sixth generation descendant of Rabbi Ashkenazi from the small town of Ivye, a pupil and associate of the Gra, the Gaon from Vilna.

**Yitzchak Ben-Zvi of blessed memory.
The second President of Israel**

The following are the biographical details of the family of the late president, Yitzchak Ben-Zvi, of blessed memory:

The grandfather of the late President Yitzchak Ben-Zvi, Rabbi Reuven-Yisrael Shimshi (Shimshelevitch), of blessed memory, was born in the year 5604 (1844) in the town of Lubtch (near Novogrodek), the region of Minsk. He married the daughter of Avraham Moshe from Smorgon- Esther. They had four sons and two daughters.

Their oldest son was R' Tzvi Shimshi (Shimshelevitch), who was born in the year 5623 (1863) in Smorgon. Then his parents moved to the town of Varnova, close to Lida. He received a traditional education at a *cheder*. He then traveled to Minsk and from there to Poltava. In the year 5644 (1844) he married Atara (Kraina), the daughter of R' Yisrael Kopilovitz. Three sons and two daughters were born in Poltava.

Their oldest son Yitzchak is **Yitzchak Ben-Tzvi**, second President of the State of Israel. He was born on 18 Kislev 5645 (1884) in the city of Poltava (Ukraine). There he learnt at the *cheder* and the gymnasia and afterwards at the University of Kiev. He visited Israel in 5664 (1904) and made *aliyah* to Eretz-Yisrael and settled there in 5667 (1907). From his earliest youth, he was one of the founders and activists of Zionism, devoted in heart and soul, dreaming and fighting for the Zionist idea first in Russia and afterwards in Eretz-Yisrael.

He was a great scholar, author and historian. He wrote very valuable books on the history of the Jewish settlement in Eretz-Yisrael and its antiquities, about the history of the communities of Israel and their leaders. He especially investigated the life of remote, forgotten Jewish sects and those that had distanced themselves from the general nation, such as the Karaites and Samaritans. He was beloved by all sectors in Eretz-Yisrael.

In the year 5679 (1919), he married Rachel Yanait, daughter of R' Yona Lishanski, one of the descendants of Rabbi Levi Yitzchak from Berdichev and one of the descendants of the Admor R' Nachum of Chernobyl, student of the Ba'al Shem Tov (on his mother's side). They had two sons, Amram and Eli. The older son, Amram, was born on 1 *Heshvan* 5683 (1922), and the second son, Eli, was born on 5 *Adar* I 5684 (1924).

Eli fell in battle during the War of Independence, while defending "Beit Keshet", on 5 *Adar* I, 5708 (1948). May the Lord avenge his blood!

At the first Assembly of Representatives in the year 5689 (1929), Yitzchak Ben-Zvi was elected Chairman of the National Committee, and afterwards as President of the National Committee, which he presided over until the establishment of the State. When the State was established, he was a member of the *Knesset* (Parliament) and one of the most active representatives on the Legislation and Justice Committee and on a number of other committees.

On 20 *Kislev* 5713 (8.12.52), he was chosen by the Knesset to be the second President of the State of Israel. In 1958 he was voted for a second term of office and in 1962 for a third round. Yet, he was neither haughty nor proud, carrying out his service to the people and to the state with modesty and humility. Despite his elevated role and his many state and public functions, he made time for Torah and scientific study, and devoted himself to studying the Bible and a daily page of the Talmud. We can say about the ways of the late President "The spirit of mankind and of God rested upon him".

President Yitzchak Ben-Zvi died on 29 *Nissan* 5723 (23.4.1963) at the age of 79 and was brought to eternal rest on Har HaMenuchot in Jerusalem.

May his memory never depart from the hearts and minds of the Jewish People!

[Page 205]

An Incident About an Informing Report

by Shalom Leibovitch

Translated from the Yiddish by Harvey Spitzer

A judgment based on strict Jewish law took place between Layzer Notkes and Yaakov-Berl. Since Yaakov-Berl lost the case when the judge decided in Layzer's favor, Yaakov-Berl became terribly angry and announced that he was going to report it to the authorities.

Hearing such words, the rabbi said in good humor: "You don't know yet how this informing report can end up for you."

As he was leaving the rabbi's house, Yaakov-Berl fell and broke a leg. Of course, he was no longer able to go and report the matter to the government, and the rabbi's decision was carried out.

[Pages 206-210]

The Righteous Rabbi R' Shmuel Bakshter
5543 (1783) - 5636 (1876)

by Moshe Tsinovitch

Translated from the Hebrew by Harvey Spitzer

R' Shmuel Bakshter was considered the "glory and magnificence" of Jewish Lubtch for all generations. The man did not hold a position as rabbi, nor did he earn a living from his knowledge of Torah. He was a landlord who managed big businesses with estate owners in the area. He was also a kind of private banker, according to the notion in those days. His name was famous near and far in the districts of Minsk, Vilna and Grodno. He was one of the first pupils of the Gaon R' Chaim of Volozhin, and his superb scholarship, fairness, good deeds and "good offices" on behalf of the public and the individual contributed greatly to R' Shmuel's fame, although he himself never stood out among the many because of his modest conduct.

R' Shmuel was worthy of reaching a very old age - his life span embraced three generations of his small town, Lubtch. He had the merit of seeing grandchildren and great grandchildren, among them famous personalities who made his name famous indirectly, as they glorified his name and that of Lubtch.

R' Shmuel came from distinguished lineage; he could trace his origin to the splendid Baksht family (whose is derived from the small town of Baksht which was in that area) as well as to the Bakshter, Bakshtansky and other families. His family connection with members of other well-known and prominent families constitutes a fine continuation to the biography of this great man. As to the special connection of R' Shmuel to Lubtch, he was related to a number of distinguished people in this small town. Members of the following families are branches of the great family tree: Shapira, Meizel, Tsunzer, Kivilevitch, Nochmovsky, Dayan and Shimshelevitch.

As the senior pupil of the Gaon R' Chaim of Volozhin, R' Shmuel gave considerable financial support to the *yeshiva* and would contribute money of his own and of others to the maintenance of the *yeshiva*. Sometimes, in an emergency, we would go personally to the little towns in the area, especially to Baksht family relatives and urge them to support the yeshiva.

It was he who proposed making a match between the young Gaon R' Raphael Shapira - son of a good friend of his youth from Lubtch, the Gaon R' Aryeh-Leib Shapira, head of the rabbinical court in Kovna - and the daughter of the Gaon R' Naftali- Tzvi-Yehuda Berlin, head of the rabbinical court and college in Volozhin. The Gaon R' Raphael inherited both positions of his father-in-law and served most of his days as head of the rabbinical court and college at that renowned yeshiva.

When R' Shmuel Baksht passed away in the year 5636 (1876), an article devoted to his memory appeared in the "Maggid" written by the distinguished Lubtch resident, R'Aryeh-Abba Bar Yosef Dayan. Because of the importance of this article in all fairness to the history of the Lubtch community, we are bringing it here nearly in its entirety, as it was published in the above-mentioned Hebrew weekly of the year 1878, issue #1, 13 *Kislev* 5736, week of the reading of the Torah portion "*Vayishlach*":

"Unhappy are the tidings I will now announce on the front page of the "*Maggid*". Woe! For stricken with illness and gathered to his people, [is] the glory of our town, our comrade, the rabbi, sage and erudite scholar, great in Torah and piety, old and full of years, our teacher and master, Shmuel Bakshter of blessed and saintly memory, May he abide in paradise! In his youth he was a disciple of the true genius, a "*gaon*" among the Jewish people, rabbi of all the children of the Exile, our teacher and master R' Chaim of blessed and saintly memory- May he abide in paradise!- in his great *yeshiva* in Volozhin. R' Shmuel studied there with outstanding geniuses of the Jewish nation and especially with the true genius, our rabbi and master, Aryeh - Leib of blessed and saintly memory, head of the rabbinical court of the holy community of Kovna.

He died at the age of 93, having produced five generations of progeny. And the whole town is brought down to the depths in relating the righteous acts and charitable deeds he performed. His coffin was brought to the old study hall of our town and the renowned Gaon, our master and teacher, Rabbi Tsvi Tiktin - May the Lord preserve him and keep him alive!- head of the rabbinical court of our town, ascended to the pulpit and raised his voice in lament over the coffin. Next in turn to deliver a eulogy was the Rabbi, Light of the Exile, our teacher, Ben Tsion of the town of Delatitch, who aroused the people to weeping".

Mr. Avraham-Abba Dayan concludes his article with these words: "Every eye shed tears unceasingly. The paths of the flow of tears left marks on every cheek and signs of weeping on every face, and afterwards they carried the coffin to the cemetery and the whole town accompanied him in the funeral procession. May he rest in peace! May God comfort us among the mourners of Zion and Jerusalem!"

On the basis of the aforementioned source, we noted above that R' Shmuel Baksht was born in 5543 (1783) and was one of the pupils of the Gaon R' Chaim of Volozhin. The *yeshiva*, in fact, was officially opened in 5563 (1803), when R' Shmuel was already 20 years old, quite an adult, according to the idea of age in those days. However, it may be said that R' Shmuel's period of learning at the Volozhin Yeshiva was earlier, right after the death of the Gaon, our Rabbi Eliyahu in 5558 (1798), within a special framework of a group of pupils which was the first experimental nucleus for the organization of a "*kibbutz*" [collection] of pupils studying Talmud within the framework of the upper division yeshiva, the first and newest of its kind, as the Volozhin Yeshiva seemed at that time. The young Aryeh-Leib Shapira also belonged to that group. He, too, was from Lubtch and a friend of R' Shmuel, who was a few years older.

R' Shmuel did not leave any written works behind. What he did leave were people, his descendants, many of whom were splendid men of spirit who glorified the face of Judaism in Lithuania and beyond. When the writer of the above article informs us that the man had the merit of seeing a "fifth generation of descendants", these included renowned rabbis, well-known Torah scholars and community leaders who were faithfully involved with needs of the public of the town whose name reached all the other small towns in these provinces. Their common point of departure was the small Jewish town of Lubtch, where their cradle stood and in whose religious atmosphere they soaked up inspiration.

In a book of reminiscences in Yiddish by Mr Pisuk (a native of Lubtch), R' Shmuel Baksht is recalled as one of the outstanding personalities of Jewish Lubtch, and episodes of his liberality in giving charity and his good deeds are brought down in this book. R' Shmuel had a brother whose name was R' Ben-Tsion Shapira-Bakshter, who was also one of the distinguished people of the town and who left a blessed generation after him. It should also be noted that Bakshter was related to the leader, R' Yosef Chishin (originally from Novogrudek) in Moscow, R' Pinches Rozovsky, head of the rabbinical court in Sontsian, R' Avraham Hirshovitz, head of the rabbinical court in Skidel and others and other like these.

1. Several grains of information about R' Shmuel in matters of Torah were reported indirectly by a number of Torah scholars in other sources - from hearsay. One of these words of Torah is conveyed by the Torah intellectual, R' Shlomo Levinson in the columns of "*HaLevanon*" 5627-28 (1867) where he calls him "My close friend and acquaintance".
2. In the book, "*Zekher L'yisrael*", on Pirkei Avot (Vilna), a number of endorsers- including several from Lubtch- appear out of order within the framework of a general listing. They are: R' Shmuel Bakshter, R' Nahum (of the Meizel family) and also R' Ben-Tsion Bar Eliyahu, his son, R' Shlomo-Shmuel and R' Tsvi. These three belong to the Shimshelevitch-Dayan family.

Descendants of R' Shmuel Bakshter

Rabbi Avraham-Dov Margaliot

R' Avraham-Dov became R' Shmuel Bakshter's second son-in-law (His first son-in-law was the righteous rabbi R' Yehonatan.) by taking his daughter, Rashke-Golda for a wife, and sat beside his father-in-law in Lubtch, studying diligently over his Talmud in the study hall and also set a fixed time for a lesson in Torah with his brother-in-law, the righteous rabbi, R' Yehonatan.

A few years later, R' Avraham-Dov moved to Minsk, capital of White Russia, where he owned a large drug manufacturing company and became an expert in the art of pharmacy. At the same time he was the head of a *yeshiva* in the Shoavei Mayim Study Hall but worked there without taking a salary. He also served for a certain time as a private tutor in Gemara at the home of the wealthy R' Shmuel Tsukerman in a city in the Mohilov district. R' Shmuel's son-in-law, R' Ben-Tsion, studied with him. He was the son of the Gaon R' Yaakov Ettinger, head of the rabbinical court in Altona, Germany.

Several years later, when the Russian government placed restrictions on the ownership of private pharmacies, R' Avraham-Dov became head of the rabbinical court in the following communities: Radoshkovitch, Zhilodok and Vasilkova (near Bialystok), where he performed blessed work for some 20 years, and where he was laid to rest in the year 5643 (1883).

Mr. Tsvi Shimshi, my late wife Batya's uncle, who knew R' Avraham-Dov personally, heard some details about his brother-in-law, Rabbi Yehonatan, directly from him:

"R' Yehonatan would sleep only 4 hours a day and ate very quickly. People often told about the sweet melodies he hummed or sang while studying and praying. Before his death, he informed those close to him of the time of the final redemption. He told them that he - just as the *Gra* [the Gaon from Vilna] - had never experienced a seminal emission, and so it was possible for him to know and reveal the day of the coming of the Messiah. A special place was set aside for his burial and no one was allowed to dig a grave near his plot. Many stories are going around the small towns of Lithuania about the miracles and righteous acts of this man. R' Yehonatan died childless in the prime of life. I have been unable to determine the year of his death."

R' Avraham-Dov had two sons, great and famous Torah scholars: R' Aharon, head of the rabbinical court in Globoki (Vilna district) and R' Yaakov-Moshe, who replaced his father in the rabbinate in Vasilkova. Both were born in Lubtch while their father, R' Avraham-Dov was dependent on his father-in-law, R' Shmuel.

R' Aharon was one of the Torah giants of his time. He was a child prodigy and, already then, the Gaon R' Yaakov from Karlin predicted a great future for him. R' Aharon climbed higher and higher up the ladder of Talmudic greatness. He succeeded in replacing the Gaon R' Shmuel Mohilever in the rabbinate in Globoki and served there as rabbi and head of the rabbinical court for 47 years. He died in 5662 (1902) at the age of 66. He left behind writings including questions and responses on matters of practical *Halacha*, new interpretations on the Talmud and its commentators, sermons as well as explanations and decisions on traditional laws regarding forbidden foods and vessels and laws regarding the reading of the *Shema Yisrael* based on the *Shulchan Arukh* (section *Yoreh De'ah*). An article about his death appeared in "*HaTsfira*" for the year 1902, issue #192.

Rabbi Avraham-Dov Margaliot's second son was Rabbi Yaakov-Moshe, rabbi of Vasilkova. Owing to dissention and sectarian fighting in that town, he retired from the rabbinate there, although the Gaon R' Shmuel Mohilever, head of the rabbinical court in Bialystok, supported his position and warned the faction of grumblers not to stir up trouble against him. He agreed to settle in Bialystok as a private person and passed away there at the age of 70 in 5680 (1920) and was buried there in the finest grave. Articles about him appeared in the daily newspaper "*Der Moment*" in Warsaw and in the local paper "*Dos Neiye Leben*". His book "*Margaliot HaYam*" (Part I on *Halacha* and Part II on *Aggada*), published in Warsaw in 1933 by his son, R' Haim-Yehonatan Margolin, a scholar in Warsaw and teacher at the Hevra Shas Study Hall on 8 Tvarda Street, Warsaw - testifies to R' Yaakov-Moshe's greatness in Talmud.

Many great authorities of the previous generation gave their approval to this book. R' Yaakov-Moshe possessed comprehensive knowledge of all Torah subjects and also stood out as a great expert in Bible, grammar and language usage.

In Bialystok, R' Yaakov-Moshe kept well in the background. There was a time when he received an offer to take a position in the rabbinate in Sokolka (to replace his father-in-law, the Gaon Zev-Volf Visoker) and was also offered a position in the rabbinate of the Lubtch community, but he didn't want to start over in the rabbinate and withdrew himself from consideration for these positions. Instead, R' Yaakov-Moshe secluded himself in the corner of one of the study halls for scholars in Bialystok and studied very diligently without allowing himself to stand out in his greatness in Talmud. Only exceptional individuals in that city knew, however, that a great man was indeed among them.

Among these exceptional individuals in Bialystok, those who took an interest in R' Yaakov-Moshe, was also the scholar, R' Eliyahu from Lubtch, a member of the Dayan family. He knew R' Shmuel Bakshter's family very well, the crown and glory of Lubtch and of the entire Novogrudek district.

[Pages 211-213]

Minikes, Chanan Yaakov

by Mordechai Jaffe

Translated from the Yiddish by Harvey Spitzer

Chanan-Yaakov Minikes was born in Vilna (Vilnius, Lithuania) in 1867. When he was 4 years old, he started going to *cheder*. By the age of 7, he was already learning *Gemara* (Talmud) and later studied with his father, Rabbi Hirsch- Nachum Minikes, presiding judge of the Jewish court of law in Lubtch. At the same time, he taught himself Russian. At the age of 14, he was accepted as a rabbinic student at the *yeshiva* in Volozhin [Wolozyn], where he became a *maskil*, an adherent of the "Enlightenment" movement. He subsequently went to Germany and through the recommendations of Rabbi Israel Salanter, Dr. Y. Rilf (from Memel) and the "*Malbim*" (in Koenigsburg), he became a close friend and regular house guest of Dr. Azriel Hildesheimer in Berlin.

Together with Shlomo-Zalman Fuks and Yitzchak Kaminer, he founded the Hebrew association "*Ahavat Zion*", corresponded with Peretz Smolensky and made his debut with an article in "*HaShachar*" (1881) .At the same time he took an active part in finding refuge for the survivors of the pogroms in Russia.

In 1888, he came to America, where he worked first as a teacher for Yiddish actors and later checked tickets in the Yiddish theaters. He was very helpful in building up Jewish unions and was one of the first delegates to the "United Jewish Labor Organization". He was active in various philanthropic and cultural institutions, mainly in the Y.L Peretz Writers' Association, serving for many years as a member of the board of directors. He was also very active in "Peoples' Relief" and later in "Peoples' Tool Campaign" during and after the First World War. He died in New York on March 27, 1932.

His literary activity was concentrated especially in the publication, "*Minikes' Yom-tov Bletter*" ("Holiday Pages"), which he brought out for 35 years starting in 1897. They were rich and diverse, although most of the articles were reprinted material. Here readers met Isaac-Meir Dick and Mendele at one table with the youngest of the young. This is how Minikes would, in fact, announce his "*Yom- Tov Bletter*": fifty Yiddish writers sitting at a Passover *seder* or in a *sukkah*. Among the writers was a mixture of Hebraicists, Yiddishists, anarchists, Zionists, atheists and Orthodox Jews. For Minikes, parties, trends or movements were non-existent in literature. In later years, Minikes began to include more and more material of younger writers in his "*Yom-Tov Bletter*".

In 1895 his musical play, "Among Indians or the Country Peddler" opened for the first time in New York. This was a "comic vaudeville piece in one act with singing and dancing adapted for the Yiddish theater by Ch. Y. Minikes of Vilna", which was performed successfully at the Windsor Theater on April 17, 1895.

In 1897, "The Yiddish Stage" edited by Minikes appeared in New York. This book contained articles, poems, one-act plays, treatises and stories from the Yiddish theater by Y. Katzenelbogen, Ch.Y.Minkes, Alexander Harkavy, M. Seifert, A. M. Sharkansky, Maurice Rosenfeld, Yaakov Gordon, B. Feigenboim, Dr. M. Siegel, Philip Krantz, V. Keizer, "Zaqef Gadol" (Leon Zalatkoff), Sambatyon, Reuven Weissman, Johann Paley, D. M. Hermolin, B. Gorin, A. Shamer, Y. Ter and others. It was also announced in the same book that a work, "*Ne'ilah*, or the Vilna Gaon and the Hassidim" would shortly appear- "a great Yiddish historical opera by Chanan Y. Minikes (of Vilna) containing folksongs, couplets and patriotic songs by William Keyser". This piece never appeared and was never performed.

Minikes also wrote articles, feuilletons, short stories, etc. and published most of them in his "*Yom- Tov Bletter*".

"Minikes was a worthy colleague and writer ... He would search out a story or article by every author from his already published things and introduce it with a few charming lines about the holiday... He would search out these works precisely from the most unfamiliar things which are easily forgotten and resurrected this material in his own publication....." (Shalom Asch)

Lexicon of New Yiddish Literature, Volume V., pp. 644-45

Guests from South Africa with former Lubtch residents in Israel

Sitting (right to left): Hillel Shmulevitch, Shmuel Baksht, Isaac (Itche) Jankelowitz, Chaim Yankelevitch, Beryl Jankelowitz, ----, Zalman Baksht (kneeling), Chemda Simchoni, Yosef Simchoni
Standing (right to left): Shmuel Yankel Kivlevitch, Meir Kalmanovitch, Yaacov Zacharavitch, Avraham Bruk, Reuven Simchoni, ----, ----, Moshe Yankelevitch (Elka and Chaim's son), Rivka Shimshoni, Elka Yankelevitch, Dov Cohen, ----, Yisrol Gershon Yankelevitch, ----
[Caption provided by Moshe Yankelevitch]

[Pages 214-215]

The Actor Matityahu (Matus) Kowalsky

Brought for publication: Moshe Tsinovitch

Translated from the Yiddish by Harvey Spitzer

Matityahu Kowalsky (Kowal) was born on January 13, 1880 in the small town of Lubtch on the Neiman River in the former governmental district of Grodno, White Russia. His parents were flax merchants. In his childhood years, he attended a *cheder* and then studied at the *yeshiva* in Vasilishok. At the same time, he sang with cantors and once secretly took part in a presentation of "Shulamit" in Vasilishok.

When the principal of the Yeshiva, Rabbi Leib, found out about it, Matityahu was expelled from school. He went to Radon and attended the yeshiva of the "Chofetz Chaim". From there, he moved to Ivya, where he studied by himself and at the same time took part in amateur performances.

In 1899 he was called up for military service, and when he came back the following year to Lida, he met and performed in Becker's troupe, making his debut singing "Hot Little Butter Cakes" in Goldfaden's *"Baba Yachne"*.

He traveled around with the troupe for a year, playing in various small towns and then joined Bernstein's troupe. He subsequently made his way to performing in companies under the direction of Kompanietz, Fizshon, Zshitomersky, Bernstein and Becker again, Genfer and back to Bernstein. He traveled with a company of actor friends through the Crimean Peninsula and then returned to Zshitomersky's troupe. He went from company to company: Genfer, Sabsai, Zandberg, Kaminski, Adler, various small troupes, again Genfer and Lipovsky.

In 1911, he performed in Hebrew, together with the actor Shumsky, in Shalom Asch's *"Yatsa v'Chazar"*. At the beginning of the First World War, when performing in the Yiddish theatre was prohibited, he played the leading role in a Hebrew production of *"Uriel Acosta"*.

When the Germans occupied Vilna during the First World War, Kowalsky, as a professional actor, received permission to perform in the Yiddish theater. He put together a group of actors and amateurs who began to perform under the name of "FADA" –Association of Yiddish Dramatic Artists- (later known as the "Vilna Troupe") with which he traveled through Poland, Lithuania, and later through Western Europe as well.

He was outstanding in the "Vilna Troupe" as an ensemble actor. In the first year alone, Kowalsky performed nearly all the leading roles in plays such as *"Der Landsman"* by Shalom Asch, *"Dos Farvorfene Vinkel"* by Peretz Hirshbein, and Yankel Boila in Kabrin's *"Der Dorfs-yung"*. Later, too, he was well suited and even brilliant as an actor in many roles, especially as Sender in Ansky's *"Dybbuk"* He was also very successful in the leading role of Ornstein's *"Der Vilner Ba'al Habayis'l"*.

In 1924, Kowalsky came to America with the "Vilna Troupe" and he performed with it until 1929. In 1930, he traveled with Azra's troupe to Europe and when he returned to America, he appeared on stage from time to time until he settled in Los Angeles, where he died on October 7, 1936.

Kowalsky's wife was the Yiddish actress Paula Walter.

[Pages 216-223]

Expulsion From and Rebuilding of Lubtch

by Nachum Shulman (Shlimovitch)

Translated from the Yiddish by Harvey Spitzer

Expulsion:

Fall 1915. An autumn rain is coming down slowly in small drops without a stop. Grey clouds hang over our heads, hard as lead, casting a gloom over the town. The streets are muddy and people can't get through the mud where the streets are unpaved.

Refugees from different regions are arriving in canvas- covered wagons. They stop to rest in the town and look for a place to dry off and get warm. They tell us that the Germans are getting closer to our region and that they were advised to go to Lubtch because the war would not be fought there. The Neiman River and the mud around Lubtch are not suitable for conducting a war. Especially in such rainy weather, it is almost certain that the German army will avoid taking the city. Meanwhile, they can rest there, feed their horses and then move on to Minsk.

It didn't take long, and Russian divisions with retreating soldiers began marching through the town. They went along Delatitch Street without stopping, day and night, and cut across the Neiman River on three pontoon bridges at Lubtch, Delatitch and Kupitsk.

A few days later, we could already hear the thunder of the heavy guns which the German artillery was shooting at the retreating Russian army.

Many of the Jews in Lubtch had already prepared horses and wagons so that they could escape if fighting took place in the town. The refugees' assurances that the war would not come here did not calm the Jews in Lubtch, and whoever had just a few rubles to buy a horse and wagon did so. My father, too, purchased a covered wagon and a pair of horses. The townspeople packed their best belongings in the wagon and buried the rest in the ground.

The weather cleared up and it was a nice, sunny morning. The horses were standing in the stall, chewing their hay with relish. The wagon stood in the yard, all packed up, and meanwhile I was playing, sitting inside, cracking the whip in the air, as though I were driving the horses on.

Suddenly, there was a terrible, thunderous sound, and clouds of smoke appeared in the sky. My brothers quickly harnessed the horses and attached them to the wagon. We took along some biscuits and went away onto the *vorek* [meadow], behind the synagogues. People said that the brick walls of the synagogues would offer good protection. The heavy guns thundered louder and louder and the shells were falling, at times coming close to us. Nearly all the Jews in the town were then lying on the wet grass.

Evening was approaching. The artillery fire had let up and the women went away to light and bless the Sabbath candles. They were really putting their lives in danger, but Jewish tradition must be observed. We suddenly heard the rattling sound of machine guns, and the noise continued throughout the night. Rumors were circulating that the Germans were already in Delatitch, that the Cossacks were plundering the town and that girls were hiding in attics and cellars.

It was a cold Sabbath morning. The heavy guns again began to thunder, and we were able to see where the shells were falling, landing closer and closer to us. We saw people covered with blood being brought to the synagogues. They were seriously wounded or dead. The Cossacks had set fire to the town on all sides and then withdrew. Coils of smoke and tongues of fire were rising to the sky. The shells were carried right over our heads and exploding very close to us. Everyone was lying on the ground and a mass "*Shma Yisrael*" accompanied each burst.

My dad held my hand tightly so that I wouldn't get lost. My brothers and sister ran off as my father had ordered them to do, saying: "If we are destined to be killed, at least someone will stay alive." He divided the family into three parts and each part was sent away to a different place.

The hours passed by slowly as though time were endless. The number of wounded placed along the wall of the white study hall kept on growing. People told of seeing many victims without heads, hands and feet.

A German airplane circled above our heads several times, an iron bird which we had never before seen. It would probably soon drop bombs right on us and no one would remain alive. Terrified, we wished we could crawl deeper into the ground for safety. Apparently, however, when the pilot noticed that civilians were lying below, he did not bomb us.

Between two and three o'clock in the afternoon, when the town was still burning, the Germans showed up. The Jews thanked God that they got through the fire safely. The Germans ordered us to leave the *vorek* and return to the few houses that stood standing after the fire. Only Castle Street remained intact.

Hardly a few days passed when an order came from the German army to leave the town in the direction of Novogrudek and Shelov because a great battle was going to take place and all the civilians could be killed if they stayed there. We would return home in a few days when the fighting was over.

We had no choice in the matter: the townspeople left, some with horse and wagon, some on foot, carrying a bag of things on their shoulders or with empty hands because everything had been burned and people had nothing left except their lives. People turned in wherever they could just find a place to rest their head and a piece of bread to alleviate their hunger.

The couple of days became years of wandering through towns, villages and refugee camps. Many died from hunger and epidemics. Graves of Jews from Lubtch were sown throughout the whole region. The children did not receive any Jewish education during those four or five years. They did not see a single letter of the Hebrew alphabet, lived in constant fear for the morrow and coped with the horrors of war. Only the longing for their town, the dream of returning home gave them support and the strength to endure the fate of a refugee.

Our family settled in Trischanke, a village near Shelub. But having lost the prospect of soon returning home, my father no longer wanted to remain living among the gentiles, and so we went to Iviya and from there to Lipnishok.

When we were finally allowed to go back home, the troubles and calamities were not yet over. The fighting between the Bolsheviks and the Polish legions also affected us. Several times the Polish legions withdrew and then retook the area. The Jewish community was always the sacrificial lamb. When the town was left without authority for even a short time, pogroms and robberies were perpetrated by the gentiles. Jewish blood and property are considered ownerless by every gentile in normal times. How much more so in times of unbridled lawlessness!

Rebuilding:

It is the year 1919. The war is over and people have decided to return home. They've been refugees long enough.

We were then living in Lipnishok, a small town 42 kilometers from Lubtch.

I also received my elementary education there. I remember that my father and older brothers walked all the way to Lubtch with the thought of rebuilding our house which was burned down in the war.

When I came to Lubtch in 1920 already a "bar mitzvah" boy, the town looked like a forest. Big trees were growing in the market place and in places where houses had previously stood. It was impossible to know where there was once a street or a square. Only the church and a few brick houses on Castle Street could be seen.

The town was completely dug up by a network of zigzag tunnels, bunkers with openings for guns, and little huts made of earth for which the Germans used a part of the houses that remained intact after the fire. All along both sides of the Neiman River were barbed wire fences and fortified trenches. Ammunition, hand grenades as well as not a few human bones lay all about.

Little by little, entire families came back. They began to chop down the trees, smooth over the plots of land and rebuild bigger and more comfortable houses. I remember that our house was already built up but not yet finished and winter was on the way. The kitchen was completed and we spent the winter there. The first Rosh Hashana and Yom Kippur, all the Jews gathered together and they made a *minyan* [prayer quorum] in our kitchen. Tuvia the Sexton was the prayer leader for the *Mussaf* [Additional prayers] service. He put his whole heart and soul into the prayers and the congregation wept exceedingly.

In 1921, with the considerable increase in the Jewish population, the question of building a synagogue and an elementary school arose. This was a time of modernization in Jewish life. The *cheder* had already played its role and the townspeople demanded a modern school for their children where they would be taught the official language, Yiddish, Hebrew, mathematics, history and natural science. Meetings of important townspeople, at which various social problems were discussed, regularly took place at our house. I can see before my eyes: Chaim-Issar Kabak, Yehoshua Shimshelevitch, Rabbi Yitzchak Aronovsky, the ritual slaughterer, Avraham-Aharons and others. A committee was chosen. It was made up of Yoshua Shimshelevitch, my father (Aaron-David Shlimovitch), Tuvia the Sexton, Baynish Rabinovitch, Yitzchak, Avraham Aharons and others. The townspeople raised money for the projects and also wrote to their compatriots in America for their support.

The red synagogue was rebuilt first and a little while later the elementary school was rebuilt.

A new, younger and more active generation of "doers" arose. They contributed a lot to the town's social life. A very special personality was Chaim Bruk, (Gute Chiene's son). He did a lot for the local school and was the acknowledged leader of the Lubtch community until its last day.

However, there were also disputes. Just as in the previous generation, a controversy erupted over the choice of a new rabbi. After long negotiations, Rabbi Yitzchak Weiss was finally accepted. He was the son-in-law of the old rabbi of Lubtch, who then served as chief rabbi of Novogrudek. Unfortunately, Rabbi Yitzchak Weiss was the last rabbi of Lubtch and was murdered together with his community.

Young people organized. Various groups sprung up including political parties, youth movements, philanthropic institutions, the library and the dramatics club which gave good presentations without filth and pornography. This club also supported many social activities in the town from its proceeds.

When I came from Vilna on my summer vacation, I helped the dramatics club with its activities and I was also the prompter in a performance of the play, "Song of Songs" ("*Shir Hashirim*").

A voluntary fire fighters brigade was also established. The men at the head were the "chiefs", Yidel Kasmayevitch and Reuvke Avraham-Aharons.

Farewell party for Kusha Shlimovitch. June 15, 1930

The town lived its normal life, had its joys and sorrows, accomplishments and disappointments, troubles and worries, hoped and dreamed of better times, of a better future for their children, hoped for the final redemption and the coming of the Messiah, kept the tradition and faith and was confident in the belief of a reward in the world-to-come for one's good deeds in this world.

And the reward was not long in coming.

It came with fire, death and destruction... Only ruins remained of Lubtch. Of its Jews, only a few individuals survived the Holocaust and bear in their hearts everlasting sorrow and unrelieved pain.

[Pages 223-224]

Mutual Support in Lubtch

by Mina Tzur

Translated from the Hebrew by Ann Belinsky

Lubtch was a poor town, and the number of those needing help was great. Although there were no organized institutions for the needy, there was a general feeling that one must help people in distress.

The help given to the needy was given modestly and discreetly, in order not to bring shame to the person; people tried indirectly to find out who was in need and they often gave help without even directly meeting the individuals.

Especially involved were a group of warmhearted open ladies who wished to help people in distress, including Shifra Rabinovitch (Payes) and Beila Brezinsky, who worked incessantly to find ways to assist. When they heard that a family had no firewood in the cold winter days, they would get up early in the mornings and lay firewood on the threshold of the needy family, and leave discreetly so that they would not meet the head of the household and put him into an embarrassing situation.

At dawn Shifra and Beila would hasten to the synagogue, where they would be told who was in need: this one's horse "fell" and thus he had lost his livelihood; another one needed goods for his wedding; others after they themselves had donated necessities. They would start knocking on the doors of all the houses to request donations; they went to houses where they knew that the people would not let them leave empty-handed for the needy. Sometimes, thanks to them, a bride would be able to stand under the *chuppah* [wedding canopy]. A pauper received a blanket and an unemployed person got help for his family.

After it was decided to build the synagogue, the women started organizing donations: at first they collected for the foundations, then the walls, the windows and even the roof. The venture was finished and their happiness was complete only when the building stood and the Holy Ark was put inside.

Despite being poor, the inhabitants of the town donated generously. They often donated above their own capabilities, and even needy families themselves donated.

There was a story about the rabbi - Rabbi Chaim Meizel (later on he became rabbi of Lodz). One Shabbat evening when his wife was about to bless the candles in their shining silver candlesticks, she saw that they had disappeared. The Rabbi urged her to bless the candles before Shabbat came in, and did not reveal to his wife, who thought that they had been stolen, where they had actually gone. On Saturday evening, when the congregants visited the Rabbi's house in order to request help for a bride to stand under the *chuppah*, the rabbanit said "What a pity that our candlesticks have been stolen, we could have donated them to help the bride". Here, the Rabbi revealed to his wife that they had been indeed donated and that was the reason for their disappearance.

Not only the Rabbi behaved in this way, but also most of the town's inhabitants. With faithfulness and with a feeling of responsibility, they helped each other.

[Pages 225-226]

Cultural Life in Lubtch

by Elka Levanon

Translated from the Hebrew by Ann Belinsky

Lubtch was a small town, and the number of inhabitants during the years that I am writing about (1928-1932) was small. But despite this, there was diversity of culture in the town.

In the town there was only one primary school, established several years after the First World War. Some of its graduates that were thirsty for knowledge and education, traveled to Novogrudek to continue their studies, others went to Vilna, to study in the Teachers' Seminary there. Others learnt in yeshivot, in towns in the surrounding countryside.

Those boys and girls who left the town to study returned during their holidays and at the end of their studies, and contributed much to development of the cultural life in our town.

I would like to mention in a few lines about the Dramatics Club of Lubtch. All its members were, naturally, amateurs who were usually employed in various occupations. All the theatrical work - staging, backdrops, music, songs, dancing and acting, was done voluntarily. The plays took place in the Firemen's Building; since it was built from wood, many who had not obtained tickets stood outside and listened to the songs and music, some of them even succeeded in seeing the play by peeking through the cracks in the walls.

Amongst those who took part in the Club and its productions were the "prima donna" – Zeltka Feivoshevitz, Shmuel Shapira, Alter Shmulevitch and others.

Public Trials: The trials were held in the evenings and the topics that were put on trial were generally current events. The trials were held seriously and honorably, with the participation of attorneys for the defense and prosecution, witnesses and the accused.

Amongst the judicial activists were: Eliezer Aronovsky, Alter Shmulevitch, Shaul Shmulevitch, Reuven Leibovitch, Eliezer Levin, May their memory be blessed, Nahum Slimovitz (May he live long), and others.

When the Fifth Aliyah began, there was much Zionist and pioneering activity; many of the members of the youth group *HeChalutz* left to go to a training farm (*Hachshara*) and some of them even managed to make aliyah to Eretz Israel.

A group of the *Hashomer Hatza'ir* was set up for all ages. The job of leadership was done by the oldest age group, whose members were very young and inexperienced. However they worked with much dedication and ardent belief in the Zionist idea. Many of the older ones managed to make *aliyah* to Eretz Israel before the Holocaust struck European Jewry.

[Pages 226-228]

The Town is Engraved in My Heart

by Baruch Spotnitzky

Translated from the Hebrew by Ann Belinsky

I am not a native of Lubtch, but the town is engraved deeply into my heart. From my earliest childhood I heard stories about the town and its inhabitants, from my mother Chana, who was born and educated in the town.

The sentences: "With us in Lubtch"..., "in Lubtch they say"..., "In Lubtch there was"..., were often uttered in our house by my mother. Amongst the *maasiot* - tales and stories - a tale about a Jewish woman who wanted to return from Novogrudek to Lubtch; since she didn't have money for the journey by wagon, she went on her way by foot. This happened on a Friday and for fear that she would not arrive home before candle-lighting, she remembered to take candles and matches in her bags.

She was indeed obliged to receive the holy Sabbath on her way home. She lit the candles on one of the trees that stood on the side of the path, and blessed them loudly. There was no wind, the flames flickered happily and their light could be seen from a distance. The Gentiles of the neighboring village came to see the meaning of the fire that was flickering in the forest. They saw the candles and decided that a miracle had occurred. The story spread quickly through the area; the religious leaders came to ponder on the reason for the miracle and it was decided to establish a church on the spot, since it was obviously a holy place. That is the little church that stands on the way, at the entrance to Lubtch.

The visits of my grandfather, R' Moshe Mordechai Asherovsky, gave us much pleasure. Our neighbors came to visit us and to hear his wonderful stories. There is a tale about a man from the Lubtch community who strayed from his way, abandoned the religion of his fathers, and acted out of spite, until he fell into the hands of conversion. He married a gentile woman, and lived in the village among the gentiles, as if one of them. One day the apostate came to the town with his produce. It was exactly the Day of Atonement, which the apostate had forgotten about. And here - everything is closed and locked, it is the Sabbath of Sabbaths, accompanied by peace and quiet in the streets of the town; only at the synagogue, the voices of the worshippers are heard. The trills of the *chazan* [cantor] are carried in supplication and fill the heart with yearning. And suddenly, longings were aroused in the heart of the apostate, recollections of the far-off days stirred and flooded his memory.... He was drawn towards the synagogue as if by magical strings, without even knowing why...when he arrived, he fell on the threshold in tears and a bitter cry "Woe is me and my soul...merciful Jews, I have sinned! My iniquity is too heavy to bear...Forgive me...Take me back into the fold of the Children of Israel!"

Yehoshua Yaacov Shimshelevitch and his wife

Rachel Levine

are honored to request
your honor to come and
rejoice with us
on the wedding day of
our dear children

The bride Miss
Batya Miriam
Shimshelevitch

The groom Mr
Chaim Leib Levine

who will marry for Mazal Tov on Friday, Eve of the Holy Shabbat, Torah portion Naso, 11 Sivan 5681 (17th June 1921)

The chuppa will take place at 4 in the afternoon, in the town of Lubtch

An invitation to the wedding of a young Lubtch couple in 1921

I first visited the town at the age of six for a wedding. Towards evening the bride and groom, led by the klezmer band, were brought to the *Shulhoif* [backyard of the Synagogue]. Despite the fact that on the same day rain had fallen and the dirt road was muddy, the ceremony was not cancelled and the *chuppa* [marriage ceremony] took place in the open yard by the synagogues, as was the custom of the Jews of Lubtch. After the *chuppa* there was an entertainer brought from the town of Trab who led the ceremony in a voice with a melody and made an announcement about the presents - "a gift sermon". And I wondered why the women were wiping tears from their eyes...

The klezmer band started playing, trilling melodies in which are hidden feelings of the Jewish heart - yearning, supplication, and much sadness, about the Exile, about the troubles of life and making a livelihood. R' Ozer HaKaner, "Der Fiddler"; streaks of silver in his beard spread out over his violin, shining, his eyes closed and he plays with much devotion; standing around him are "connoisseurs" of violin playing, amongst them my uncle, bursting with pleasure and swaying to the sound of the joyful tunes.

In 1915, when the echoes of the shots from the front came close, many left their houses and found shelter in the *Bet Midrash* [Study Hall], built from bricks. But fate was cruel to the inhabitants, for a bomb fell on the *Bet Midrash*, killed thirteen people, and wounded others; depression and mourning prevailed everywhere. When the

Germany army entered, the area was declared to be on the front line and the inhabitants were expelled.

I was with my uncle among the first to return to the town. It was difficult to recognize it; destruction and neglect dominated everywhere; the houses had been dismantled or destroyed by the Germans. The streets and the marketplace were cut up by trenches and defense pits. Weeds grew everywhere.

Many of those who returned found shelter in the defense pits and began energetically and with much initiative to reconstruct the town from its ruins.

Two years later, I again came to visit Lubtch. The town had been rebuilt, the *Bet Midrash*, which had been burnt down in the war, was again standing. It was not easy for the poor townspeople, many of whom were still living in the defense pits, to worry about its rehabilitation, but they did it with a willing soul. Moreover, they made sure that there would be a teacher who would teach Torah to the children.

[Pages 229-233]

Days of Joy and Sorrow
by Chana Kagan-Sirlis

Translated from the Yiddish by Harvey Spitzer

After a period of 55 years, it is not easy to remember the town, but neither is it easy to forget our Lubtch, a small, poor town, two-thirds of whose residents were Jews.

In particular, I remember the special, deeply rooted *Yiddishkeit* [Judaism] and piety in the town, the synagogue with the two study halls and the wooden synagogue. Yeshiva boys from every corner of the country were always sitting and studying the Law in the Red *Bet Midrash* [Study Hall]. Boys with short jackets and long cloaks coming from Poland, Galicia, Russia and Lithuania. The rabbi was a religious fanatic, and some of the students who had already tasted fruit of the "tree of knowledge" allowed themselves to dress like the German Jews and act a little more freely.

When the *yeshiva* boys needed something such as shoes, a cloak, or an "appointment" for a meal at someone's house, they came to Yechiel the Teacher, my father of blessed memory, and he would take care of matters right away. Not, of course, with his own money, as he was more of a pauper than they, but he knew where and to whom to turn; or a few girls were sent from house to house with a white kerchief to collect alms for that purpose. The Jews of Lubtch gave charity without asking too many questions.

My father was generally a person who liked to help another in various ways: placing cups for bloodletting, measuring one's temperature, helping guests find a place to stay for the Sabbath. Friday nights, he would not leave the synagogue until he saw to it that all the guests had accommodations. He was also the permanent Torah reader in the Red *Bet Midrash*.

I recall the dispute which broke out in town over taking on a new rabbi. One side was in favor of Rabbi Yosef-Eliahu, and the other side was for Rabbi Hirsh. Every Sabbath before the Torah reading, (when the rabbis preached a sermon based on the weekly portion) it was very "merry". Finally, Lubtch had two rabbis.

Not far from the bathhouse was a well from which we used to draw water for making tea on the Sabbath. The "ice house" was near the Red *Bet Midrash*. In the winter, we used to cut ice from the river and put it in the "ice house" where it would last until the following winter for the town's needs.

A boat ride on the Neiman River

The *vorek* [meadow], where the town geese fed, extended from the synagogue to the river. Children used to go there to collect the feathers. On Fridays, we used to go to the river to scour the brass candlesticks and the copper fish pans.

Until this very day I can't forget the walks we took on the Sabbath along Castle Street and behind the castle, the walks in the neighboring woods and the boat rides on the river on moonlit nights, when we sang and harmonized various Yiddish songs and often, as well, illegal, strictly forbidden workers' songs.

These were the last years before the First World War. Everything was then primitive and unchanging; every new happening was greeted with joy and youthful enthusiasm. I remember how thrilling it was for the town when a few young people started a dramatics club and put on "theater" in the barn belonging to Esther Raizel's son, Baruch. They performed "The Selling of Joseph", and whoever had a penny went to the show and shed tears at each scene illustrating a "moral".

On the Sabbaths during the summer, we would joyfully run to look at the steamboats on the Neiman River, with the fancily decked out passengers. We envied them and our thoughts would carry us away to distant places and unfamiliar cities and countries.

How can I possibly recall that time without remembering my six brothers of blessed memory who were called "angels" by the townspeople on account of their kindness, politeness, and loyalty to one another.

Many people from Lubtch probably still remember my brother Baruch. He was a teacher and an unforgettable personality. He was the first to introduce the free thoughts of that time into our town. He was a good speaker and a talented lecturer. The young people considered him their spiritual leader and a few actually called him "rabbi". When an illegal meeting took place in the woods, to which he had to be taken in a wagon due to a sore foot, a few of the boys would keep watch and, at the slightest suspicion that the police were coming, they would hide Baruch first because the police kept their eye on him in particular.

We lived in Mashinke's small house, behind his big house. Opposite our house was the "tea house", where the police held up. It sometimes happened that when my five brothers and a few friends left the house together, the police would immediately pay us a visit to check whether, God forbid, there had not been an illegal meeting going on. My parents would simply become ill from fright.

Once, at eight o'clock in the morning on Passover, a few policemen came into our house to search for an illegal activist who was supposed to come to Lubtch to speak at a meeting. My brothers were still lying in bed except for Motke, who had gone to hear the cantor. When he heard in the synagogue that the police were conducting a search in our house - and there was, in fact, a lot of illegal literature in our house - he ran straight home. Instead of entering the house, he first looked in through the window. The police, certain that this was the guest they were looking for, ran outside and right to him. Motke was terribly frightened and ran off. They chased him through the streets and over to the cemetery until he managed to escape their pursuit. However, while running away, Motke lost his cap which the police found and brought the "trophy" to the sheriff. Burning with anger, the sheriff screamed: "Who needs the cap? The head is what you should have brought"!

For a few days Motke hid in the attic at the home of Asher-Zelig, the tailor. Then, all dressed up in ladies' clothes, he went away in the middle of the night to Kotlova, where my brother Zvi-Nachum was a teacher at the home of Benyamin Kotlover. From there Motke later, in fact, went away to America.

When the peasants, riled up by the pope and the Czar's agents, began to go on a rampage so that we could expect a pogrom, my brothers formed a self-defense group. They got guns which they concealed in a straw roof not far from our house. When the group met for a deliberation, my mother would keep watch and not leave the boys, who were standing on guard outside.

My brothers left the town. A couple went to America, a couple went to study at a yeshiva, and Baruch went to Baranovitch, where he became a Hebrew teacher.

Baruch got engaged to a lovely girl but, a week before the wedding, he suddenly died in Baranovitch. We were all broken up by this misfortune, but there is no limit to misfortunes and, just nineteen days later, my brother Motke also died, having come back from America to seek a cure in the woods around Lubtch for consumption, which mercilessly raged amid the poor people of the region.

After these misfortunes, my father could no longer remain in Lubtch. The pain and sorrow were too much for him to bear and we left for America.

- -

As I recall those days of joy and sorrow, youthful dreams, hopes and disappointments, I am overcome by an unrelieved longing for my hometown, and my eyes are swelling up with tears, flowing on their own.

What has become of you, my dear, old home - Lubtch?...

[Pages 234-237]

R' Shmuel Meizel and His Family
by Moshe Tzinovitch

Translated from the Hebrew by Harvey Spitzer

He was one of the notables of Lubtch, brother of the renowned Gaon R' Eliyahu-Chaim, head of the rabbinical court in Lodz and son-in-law of the distinguished R' Ben-Tsion Shapira (Bakshter), brother of the righteous R' Shmuel Bakshter.

R' Shmuel was a respected man, like his brothers who lived in Lubtch. His house was a meeting place for Torah for all the rabbis, emissaries of institutions of charity and preachers. They made the home of this important man an inn for themselves. R' Shmuel was one of the first members of the Talmud group in the local study hall. He had the merit of having as sons-in-law two great Torah scholars and *Gaonim* [geniuses, rabbinic title], who were at certain times dependent on him: R' Yaakov-Moshe Direktor, head of the rabbinical court in Mush and R' Matityahu Mednitsky, head of the rabbinical court in Sharshobi and Bitan (Grodno District).

Rabbi Yaakov-Moshe Direktor

Rabbi Yaakov-Moshe (5579 [1819] - 5639 [1879]), head of the rabbinical court in Stolovitz and Mush near Baronovitch, was a great Torah authority, one of the outstanding figures of his generation. Questions and responses of his are brought down in "*Be'er Yitzchak*", written by the Gaon R' Yitzchak-Elchanan, rabbi in Kovno and in "B'veit-David" by the Gaon R' David Tevli, rabbi in Minsk. R' Yaakov-Moshe is described by both of them as a great man in Torah learning and in his righteous ways. And with respect to his righteous ways, it is to be noted that many were those who came to him for a blessing from his mouth and considered him a performer of acts of salvation and "*a guter yid*" [a good Jew]. He passed away in 5639 [1879]. In a death notice that appeared in *HaTsfira*, Issue #16, 1879, R' Yaakov-Moshe is referred to as "the rabbi, the *gaon*, the exemplary person." However, whenever he would come to Lubtch, he would hide his prestige and didn't wish to be conspicuous save in exceptional cases.

Well- informed people used to say that when R'Yaakov-Moshe was a [married] yeshiva student in Lubtch, he learned *Kabbala* [mysticism], from the righteous Rabbi Yehonatan and also prayed with a prayer book composed by the Ari [Kabbalist rabbi Yitzchak Luria], but not while he would pass before the Holy Ark. His knowledge of *Kabbala* and his behavior as "a good Jew" stood R' Yaakov-Moshe in good stead and he was also admired by the Hassidim of Mush, who constituted a great central power. Likewise, the *Admor* [title of Hassidic rabbi] from Slonim, R' Avraham Veinberg, would also come to visit him when he was a guest of the Hassidim in Mush.

R' Yaakov-Moshe's son, the Gaon R' Yisrael-Yehoshua Yerushalimsky, attended yeshivot in Jerusalem and later the Volozhin Yeshiva. Afterwards, he became head of the rabbinical court in Orleh (Grodno District) and Ihoman (Minsk District), where he was buried in 5677 [1917]. R' Yisrael-Yehoshua also excelled in his knowledge in the field of Jewish studies and was a fine stylist in Hebrew. In his article, "Did the Babylonian Talmud see the Jerusalem Talmud?", which he published in Elazar Atlas' "*HaKerem*", he disagrees vehemently with the Sage, Rabbi Hirshenzon.

R' Yisrael-Yehoshua spent his childhood in Lubtch at the home of his grandfather, R' Shmuel Meizel in order to soak up the religious and Torah inspiration of the scholars in the small town.

Rabbi Yisrael-Yehoshua's son-in-law is the Gaon R' Yechezkel Avramsky - May his light shine! - who lives today in Jerusalem and was previously head of the rabbinical court in Smolian, Smolvitch, Slotsk and was senior head of the rabbinical court in London, England, chairman of the Ultra-Orthodox Independent Educational System in Israel and teacher of Talmud at the Slobodka Yeshiva in Bnei Brak. R' Yechezkel became famous in the Torah world with his comprehensive book "*Hazon Yehoshua Al Kol HaTosefta*". In 5716 [1956] he was awarded the Rabbi Kook prize for this book by the city of Tel Aviv.

Rabbi Matityahu Mednitsky

R' Matityahu Mednitzky, R' Shmuel Meizel's second son-in-law, was also one of the great rabbis. His scholarly work, "*Matat Yado*", gained wide popularity in the rabbinical world. He was head of the rabbinical court in two communities- Sharshovi and Bitan (Grodno District). He went on *aliya* to Eretz Yisrael toward the end of his life and died in 5676 [1916].

Before becoming a rabbi, R' Matityahu lived in Lubtch for a number of years while he was still able to be well acquainted with R' Shmuel Bakshter. R' Bakshter transmitted to him personally and orally the ways of his own teacher and rabbi, the Gaon R' Chaim of Volozhin in matters pertaining to the rabbinate and in maintaining good relations with the members of one's congregation in the spirit of Torah. All of this served as a guiding principle for R' Matityahu in the manner in which he conducted himself with his flock in the synagogue.

R' Matityahu Mednitsky's connection to Lubtch is also expressed in his suggestion to R' Yosef Yozel of the Horovitz family- a follower of Rabbi Salant's *Musar* [ethics] movement - to establish a branch of a *kolel* [yeshiva for married men] in Lubtch having the character of a *Musar* type yeshiva similar to the one he had set up in Novogrudek. R' Matityahu was close to this movement as he had studied in Kovno as part of a group of scholars and was close to R' Yisrael Salant, the spiritual mentor of the group.

While at the *kolel* in Lubtch, R' Matityahu became acquainted with the scholarly and famous student, R' Malkiel HaLevi Tennenbaum, who was living at that time on his father-in-law's estate near Yarmitch adjacent to Lubtch and Karelitch and would come to Lubtch to converse with the local head of the rabbinical court and with the scholars at the study hall and to exchange words of Torah with them. Subsequently, R' Malkiel became famous as a *gaon* and responder to questions dealing with rendering Halachic decisions, having already been head of the rabbinical court in Lomzhe and having gained fame with the publication of his well-known book, "*Divrei Malkiel*". R' Malkiel married off his daughter to Rabbi Matityahu's son, R' Shmuel-Moshe Mednitsky, who was also a great scholar and who later settled in Tel Aviv.

In 5608 [1848] the book "*Galia Masechet*" by the Gaon R' David Bar Moshe, head of the rabbinical court in Novogrudek, was published. In the front of the book, in the list of endorsers of this book, the names of a group of endorsers from Lubtch also appear. They include the head of the town's rabbinical court (not mentioned by name), R' Eliezer Lipman, R' Yeshayahu-Zalman, R' Nahum Meizel (brother and father-in-law of the Gaon R' Eliyahu-Chaim Meizel) and also R' Chaim-Shlomo Bar Yosef, R' Moshe Segal and R' Binyamin Bar Dov.

Additions to the List of Descendants of R' Shmuel Meizel

Rabbi Yaakov-Moshe Direktor's son-in-law, head of the rabbinical court in Stolovitz and Mush, was the Gaon Yaakov-Yitzchak Varnovsky, native of Babroisk (b. 5603) [1843]. He was the son of Rabbi Aharon-Dov of the Hassidim from Lechivitch and Koidanov and was a student at the Volozhin Yeshiva during the tenure of the *"Netziv"* (Naftali Zvi Berlin) and the Gaon R' Yosef-David Soloveitchik. Rabbi Varnovsky was the head of the yeshiva in Lida for a certain period of time and in 5639 [1879] was appointed to replace his father-in-law in the new rabbinate of Mush. There he worked successfully until the day of his death on 23 Tevet 5663 [1903].

Rabbi Varnovsky was renowned as a great authority in Torah, diligent student and exemplary religious and public leader. He went over the six *Orders of the Mishna* 40 times during his life! He was a great innovator of ideas and was also attached to the study of the *Zohar* and other books of *Kabbalah*. He was an expert in both the Babylonian and Jerusalem Talmud as well as in any subject of *Halacha* and *Aggada* [non-legal portions of the Talmud] and in *Midrash* [homiletic interpretation of Scripture]. He would rise early for morning prayers and could be found in the study hall - studying while wrapped in his prayer shawl and phylacteries - until noon. He was respectful to everyone and his conversation always reflected the purity of the holy place. He never became angry with anyone.

He founded a "*kibbutz*" [group] of young people, and a "Supporters of Torah" society was established to support them. He had a profound love for his pupils, to whom he was devoted with all his might. When he left this world, the Gaon R' Tsvi-Hirsh Lampert (author of "*Piskei HaGra*") eulogized him and, in the presence of a large audience from the town and the surroundings, said that with his death, the three pillars on which the world is sustained - Torah, Worship and Charity - fell.

Rabbi Yaakov-Yitzchak Varnovsky was recommended for a position in the rabbinate in Lubtch. However, he turned down the offer because he was unwilling to give up his regular visits to the *Admor* [Hassidic rabbi], R' Aharon from Koidanov. This was very upsetting to the *mitnagdim* [opponents of Hassidism] officials in Lubtch and his appointment never became effective.

His son, Aharon-Dov Varnovsky, was secretary of the Board of Yeshivot in Vilna. While still a young man, he published his father's book "*Halek Yaakov*", which also contains the biography of his father, of saintly and blessed memory.

- -

R' Shmuel Meizel from Lubtch had a third daughter whom he married off to Mr. Avraham Harkavy from Novogrudek. He lived in Lubtch and was dependent on his father-in-law for a number of years. He later moved to Yekatarinaslav (Ukraine), where he was well know as someone always involved in public affairs. He published articles in the Hebrew newspaper "*HaMelitz*" dealing with the life of the Jewish community in this large city, its leaders, institutions, societies and organizations. He encouraged public figures in their activities in the field of education and original Hebrew culture as well as in organizing charity and benevolent organizations.

[Pages 238-240]

Lubtch in the 1930's
by Elka Yankelevitch

Translated from the Hebrew by Shirley Horwitz

Elka Yankelevitch

Polish anti-Semitism raised its ugly head before the rise to power of the Nazis in Germany. Our area, called "The Eastern Kresy of Poland" (Western White Russia) began to suffer from anti-Semitism, which spread like an infectious disease.

We - the older youth - felt that the atmosphere around us was filling up with a spreading poison, and that there was no other way but to get away before disturbances would strike us. At the same time, a mighty wave of Zionism engulfed Polish Jewry: the Jewish press preached *aliya* to Eretz-Israel, by all ways and means. We began to think of aliya as an opening for being saved.

In the 1920's a group of *chalutzim* [pioneers] from our time made *aliya*. In 1927, however, due to the crisis in Eretz-Yisrael (lack of work and famine), some of them returned to Lubtch. And we, what would we do there? We lacked life experience and had not yet acquired a trade or profession. We were all dependent on our parents. How could we go out into the wide world?

One day is engraved upon my memory (during the days of the riots in Eretz-Israel) in 1929. It was a cold winter's day, with a snowstorm raging outside, covering the sun. On that same day, we bid farewell to Itka Shmuelevitz, who was making *aliya*, prepared for all the hardships and experiences that lay in front of her.

In 1931 better news began to arrive from Eretz Israel. The riots had ceased. Large-scale building had begun and preparations were beginning for the 1932 *Maccabia* games [sports event for Jewish athletes]. A group of young people began to organize to make *aliya* to Eretz Israel, under the guise of tourists visiting the *Maccabia* games. The problem was how to stay in the country. It was pretty hard for the men who had to disappear and stay there anonymously. On the other hand, a solution was found for the girls: fictitious marriages to citizens of the country.

I began to think of making aliya this way. The decision was not easy, but in my imagination I already saw myself packing my bags and going. I spent many sleepless nights in which I pondered how to tell my parents, my brothers and sisters of my decision. Although we were a large family, there was not a "spare" person in the house. As I expected, my decision created a furor and met with heavy opposition. My decision was received with shock and there was great opposition. The first person I told was a close friend of the family, Shmuel Shapiro, of blessed memory. He was furious. "Really? Where will she go? A young girl with no experience? To the *halputzim* [derogatory term for *chalutzim* - pioneers]?! Everyone is fleeing from there! If it were up to me, I would not let her go."

He turned my parents against me. Everyone was against me. "Have you gone crazy? What will you do there? You will starve. At least if you had a profession, all right! But thus, you will just waste money and will flee from there in disgrace." The arguments with my parents did not stop; threats and pleas also did not help. Because I didn't give up and fought back, my parents came to terms with my decision and preparations began. On a snowy winter's day in March 1932, I parted from my parents, my grandmother, my sisters, my brother, from relatives, girlfriends, boyfriends, neighbors and from my home, Lubtch. It was a difficult farewell, laden with tears and sorrow, as if we sensed it was an eternal departure.

*

My beloved family! How dear you are to me. As the years pass, I value your special and dear qualities even more.

My father[1] of blessed memory, for whom no effort was too much to provide a livelihood for his family, worked in a trade and in a bakery. He worked all week, but when the Sabbath came, he would radiate happiness. On Friday night, he would bring home a Sabbath guest from the synagogue, bless the wine and sing Sabbath table hymns.

My mother[2] of blessed memory raised her children and cherished the family. She would get up before dawn for her daily chores and found time and strength to help my father in the bakery.

My grandmother[3] of blessed memory, the typical Jewish mother for whom the good of her children and grandchildren was her main concern. In spite of being weak and sickly, she was full of energy and initiative in all that concerned her grandchildren. On the cold wintry days, she would travel to the school to bring hot food to the children.

On Fridays she would collect *challot* [Sabbath bread] for the Sabbath from homes and put them in a basket near the doors of the needy in order not to embarrass the receiver. She worked hard for needy brides to get them a wedding dress and gave much anonymously.

My dear sisters, Shayna and Ashkala (Esther), my beloved brother -Yosef. You have remained in my memory as at the hour of our farewell - young, beautiful and filled with dreams of the future, which you were unable to fulfill.

Translator's Footnotes

1. Father - Reuven Movshovitch.
2. Mother - Mina Raisel Movshovitch. They appear in the photo on page 388, upper right hand side (the photo legend is reversed). The family also appears in a photo on page 379. Reuven and Mina Raisel Movshovitch are seated on the left. Sitting on the ground from left to right are Yosef and Ashkala. Standing, second from the left, is Shayna. Third from the left, is Chaim Yankelevitch, Elka's future husband. Fourth from the left is Batya, one of Elka's sisters, who also made aliya to Eretz Yisrael.
3. Elka's grandmother was Rivka Levin. See the separate paragraph written about her on Page 267 by Elka's sister, Chemda Simchoni (Movshovitch).

[Pages 240-243]

The Amateur Club
by T. Shimshoni

Translated from the Hebrew by Ann Belinsky

In Lubtch there was an amateur dramatics club, which put on plays; this club was called in Yiddish "*Amataran Farayn*", and talented people of all ages belonged to it, not only the youth. Among the members were: Shmuel Shapira, Nachum Shlimovitch, Kusha Shlimovitch, Berel Kabak, Alter Shmulevitch, Zeltka Feivoshevitch, and others. The club was headed by a committee made up of several members (not only actors). Their role was to choose the plays to be presented - mainly those of Golfaden. The committee was divided into 2 subcommittees - artistic and administrative.

The job of the artistic committee was to choose the roles, to suit them to the actors and to produce the play.

The job of the administrative committee was to organize the technical side of the play; to find a hall, to get a license from the authorities, to organize the backdrops, to advertise the play and to sell the tickets.

Most of the plays were directed by Shmuel Shapira, who was at one stage an aid to one of the directors in Moscow and had an inborn talent for directing and acting. He himself took part as an actor (usually as a matchmaker or a *shlumiel* [good-for-nothing] Jew). When he stopped participating in the plays, other members of the troupe began to direct.

Because there was no suitable hall for plays, a stage was set up in one of the rooms of the elementary school. Afterwards, when a permanent structure was built for the voluntary firemen, a permanent stage was set up on the side of the building, where the plays were performed. The "Fire Brigade Building" was in the middle of the Market Square, and various items of equipment such as pumps, barrels of water on two wheels, ladders and sledge-hammers were kept there. On the day of a performance, the equipment was taken out of the hall and instead, benches for the audience were placed there.

Usually the performances took place on Saturday nights. The play would begin at a very late hour, almost midnight, because it would start only when the hall had filled up.

One of the important tasks was that of the "prompter" (the author filled this role several times). The prompter had to follow the speech of the actors, making sure they were familiar with the text, or, God forbid, deviating from the script and then it was necessary to help them get back on the right track by whispering the forgotten words. The hall was not built for such acoustics, sometimes the words of the actors did not reach the ears of the audience sitting on the back benches, but the prompter's voice certainly did! The prompter caused embarrassment to the actors, because his place was under the floor of the stage and his head bobbed up above the boards, hidden by a little roof opening to the inside of the stage, so that the audience would not see him. The actresses - modest daughters of Israel, were shy to walk by the prompter's box, lest his detective eyes...

Sometimes a professional troupe of actors would come to the town, presenting themselves as an offshoot of the "*Vilna-Troupa*" (the Vilna group). When they didn't have enough actors, they would be helped by the members of the Lubtch dramatics club, especially for secondary characters. We willingly helped them also in organizing the play, for we learnt from them the art of acting and when our fate improved, they guided us in directing the play on which our club was presently working.

The presentation of a theatrical production required a license from the government. In order to get it, it was necessary to translate the play into the Polish language and send the translation to the government offices of the Novogrudek District. Generally, we didn't come across any difficulties in getting the license, since we presented productions from the life of the Jews, and these had nothing which could be interpreted as criticism of the government. I remember one case when the license did not arrive in time because of a mistake, which caused us a lot of bother and sorrow.

This happened on Shabbat when the play was to be presented on Saturday evening. Advertisements had been placed in the streets, all the tickets had been sold, all the preparations had been done and for some reason the license didn't arrive. We phoned the licensing clerk and asked him about the delay. He answered that the license was ready, but by mistake had not been sent to us on Friday, and promised that he would send it on the train due to arrive in the town in the evening.

On the same Shabbat, in the morning, a policeman came to our house and asked me to come to the police station. I didn't know why I had been summoned, but was not worried, as all the policemen were my friends thanks to my father, who in his daily work was close to the authorities, as he was director of the local bank and a well to do merchant.

When I came to the police station, I was told that they were forbidding us to put on the play that evening, as we did not have the license and I, as responsible for the organization, must be judged because we had advertised the time of the play without having the license in our hands. I said to the policemen that we had contacted the

District authorities and they had promised that the license would be sent the same evening, before the play started. The policemen didn't even want to listen. I thought that nothing bad would happen to me, since each of the policemen received "presents" from my father every Jewish holiday, and I allowed myself to raise my voice; I berated them about the difficulties they were causing us, for which we were not to blame. To my amazement, they immediately threw me into a cell, where I was imprisoned for more that two hours. My friends knew that I had gone to the police station, and when I didn't return, they came to see what had happened to me. When they found out that I had been arrested, they called my father, who extricated me from the imprisonment, while promising that he would punish me for my cheek. The license arrived in the evening, as promised, and the play was put on at the right time.

The profits from these plays were dedicated to purchasing books for the library, and for helping needy friends who were about to immigrate to Eretz-Israel and who lacked money for the journey. More than one of the people from Lubtch living in Israel made aliyah with the help of this amateur club.

Thus the dramatics club contributed to the inhabitants of the town, serving as a source of pleasure and from which they also derived knowledge about the sources of culture of our people. Indirectly, the club also contributed to the important building of Eretz-Israel.

[Pages 243-246]

My Town Delyatichi (Delatitch)
by Avigdor Shmukler

Translated from the Hebrew by Harvey Spitzer

> "A small town there
> A few houses
> As for amusement
> The children built it."

I am quickly inundated by memories of my town, and the words of the poem, which are so suited to my small town, echo in my ears.

Here is the lovely study hall, from which the voices of those learning *Gemara* and *Mishnayot* break through and are carried aloft. In its shadow, the "ignorant" often visit, intently reading psalms with much devotion. Between its walls, the Jews poured out their hearts in conversation before their Father Who is in Heaven, asking that He open the gates of His mercy. Inside the study hall, the worshippers danced with ever-growing enthusiasm on Simchat Torah, carrying the Torah scrolls and joyfully striking Haman the Wicked with their noisemakers on the Purim holiday.

Sabbath Eve: The town is already at rest while it is still day. Jews are returning from the bathhouse, clean and purified from the vexations of the weekdays and directing their hearts to receive the holy day.

The town is dressed up for the festive day: wearing their finest Sabbath apparel, they go to the synagogue with measured steps, each person greeting the other with "*Shabbat Shalom*". The sound of prayers rises and is carried aloft from the study hall - the Jews are welcoming the Sabbath Queen.

At home, there is a glistening white tablecloth on the table. The candles are burning with a holy flame. We sing table hymns and welcome the Sabbath angels, angels of peace, and make a blessing over a cup of red wine and over the braided *challot* [Sabbath bread] on the table. We eat the Sabbath meal: peppery *gefilte fish* dipped in horseradish, the delicious smell of which is carried far and wide, noodle soup and carrot *tzimmes* [stew].

Fatigue gains mastery over us and we begin to get drowsy. We say the grace after meals and retire for a restful night.

Sabbath day: Jews go to the synagogue for the prayer service. He who is lucky gets called up to the podium to recite blessings at the reading of the Torah, or purchases the opportunity "at a cheap price" to chant the *Haftarah* [excerpt from the Prophets].

The *tcholent* [Sabbath meat stew kept warm from Friday], which the housewife troubled to prepare from the day before, awaits the husband. Its fragrance rises from the homes. We sit down at the table to have our meal. We sing Sabbath table hymns, say grace and we then "grab" some sleep. Families take a walk through the streets of the town to get some fresh air and to digest the heavy Sabbath meal.

The "house owners" sit at the entrance to their homes and make idle talk about secular matters. Young people, walking arm-in- arm, prattle cheerfully.

Horses graze in the meadow outside the town and also enjoy their Sabbath rest, instead of having to carry heavy loads over the dirt roads between the towns.

Evening is approaching. The study hall again fills up completely with worshippers asking for a good week of health and livelihood. They greet each other with "Have a good week!" and return to their homes where they recite blessings over wine, spices and fire, thanking God for making a separation between the holy and profane, for making a distinction between a day when everything is good (Sabbath) and the six days of worrying and trouble due to making a living.

I remember my mother singing in a pleasant voice with the departure of the Sabbath: "The God of Abraham, Isaac and Jacob, behold the Sabbath that You have given us in your great kindness is now ending, the week- day is approaching. May it be Your will that the coming week also be a week of blessing, health and good livelihood".

A wedding in the town: The whole town dresses up festively. Everyone is invited, rich and poor, young and old. They wear holiday clothes and come to rejoice over the happiness of the young couple. The musicians sing and play their instruments. There is also someone who composes songs and rhymes in honor of the occasion. Others go out to dance.

The *cheder* [elementary school]: a small, narrow room and in the corner was a chamber pot. The tumult of little children playing pranks fills the room despite the punishments the "*rebbi*" would mete out to us without ever checking to see who was to blame. Whenever the "*rebbi*" would spank us, he didn't distinguish between the "righteous" and the "wicked"- all the children were guilty before him. And here is a true incident: Once, the "*rebbi*" dozed off during the lesson, and the children in the room stuck his beard to the table with wax, and when he woke up, he couldn't free his beard from the table. Of course, there was a collective punishment, and each of us was given a spanking.

On summer days we ran to the river. On the way, we impatiently removed our clothes. Naked, we made a lot of noise between the cool ripples and forgot the world and its fullness.

Sometimes we engaged in "wars" with the children of the Gentiles. The war was fought mainly with stones. Although "Esau" nearly always had the upper hand, we didn't stop our mischief.

Only a handful of Jews lived in Delatitch among a foreign environment. Although relations between Gentiles and Jews were normal, both with regard to trading and craftwork, quarrels and scuffles sometimes broke out. An incident occurred with our neighbor, Chaim-Leib the Fisherman and his wife when drunken Gentiles came to smash the windowpanes of their house. Chaim-Leib grabbed a rake, and his wife didn't lose her presence of mind either and grabbed a hoe. They both hit the Gentiles with strong blows until they chased them away - they didn't come back again.

The road to Lubtch passed through our town. When the Gentiles went to Lubtch on their holidays and to fairs, it was possible to do business with them. However, the squire suddenly decided that the road annoyed him, as it passed by his estate and that it should be moved outside the town. When his servants began demolishing the bridge near the flour mill on the road leading to Lubtch, all the town's residents came out in opposition to the project. The demonstration turned violent. Some people were seriously injured, but it was to no avail. Even after they set fire to the squire's barn, he refused to back off. The conflict reached the courts, and the town won the case. The road remained in its place to the great sorrow of the squire and to the delight of the Jews.

I remember the Neiman, on whose clear waters we spent time boating and fishing. An elevated plain covered with grass and old trees with thick tops and branches spreads out near the river. I liked to be by myself in the shade of these trees and weave dreams for the days that would come. The place served as a meeting place for teenagers. In the shade of the tree tops, they could even hug and kiss without having to worry that they might be seen.

Refreshingly cool forests surrounded the town. On hot days, we spent our time resting among the trees or gathering mushrooms or picking berries and nuts. In the grove half way between Lubtch and Delatitch, joint meeting took place between the youth of both towns. Every meeting was an unforgettable experience for us, and the time passed in song and games. I still remember that I lost a game of forfeits and had to recite some of Bialik's poems.

*

I went back to Delatitch after the First World War as refugee who had wandered numerous times. The town was totally destroyed, only a few houses suitable for occupancy. There was ruin and destruction everywhere. Pits and foxholes and deserted places. Even the Neiman - Heaven's gift to the town - was blocked by an electric security bridge in the Biblical sense of: "From far off you will see it, but you won't approach it." I stayed at home about two months and again took my wandering stick in hand.

I never saw my town - the cradle of my childhood- again. I didn't manage to see the good Jews again, God-fearing people who served their Creator with perfect faith, as the German destroyer also fell upon them. They were annihilated, together with all of European Jewry, in the terrible Holocaust that decimated our people. May they rest in peace!

[Pages 247-250]

Remember and Do Not Forget!
by Yona Degani (Litchitzky)

Translated from the Hebrew by Ann Belinsky

Yona Degani (Litchitzky)

Every year we celebrate the victory over Nazi Germany, the monster that exterminated six million Jews, burnt and destroyed cities and towns.

Notwithstanding the happiness of the victory, sadness and sorrow overwhelm it, since the cradle of my childhood was destroyed, my little town with its ties to my childhood memories.

Lubtch was located in East Poland, a typical Jewish town, like those found in the stories of Mendeleh Mocher Sfarim, Shalom Aleichem and other writers. But the bells of change were also heard there. The Hebrew school and the Youth Movements filled young hearts with a longing to return to Zion, the desire to come to Eretz Israel and to conquer the wilderness with hard work.

Any family who had a relation in Eretz Israel, saw itself as a source of pride for this reason. When I was already in Eretz Israel, I received a letter from my 15 year old sister where she wrote how happy she is because her sister is in Eretz Israel, and sad that she herself is not with me here. My brother too, a child aged 12, asks me to write "very very much" about Eretz Israel.

When I lived in the town, two women would pass every day by my house, several months before I made *aliyah*, and sometimes we would talk; one talked about her three daughters who were in Eretz Israel and her deep longings for them; the other - she had been left with her small children without support or help, as her four older children had also already gone there; but no word of complaint was heard from her, despite her bitter fate. Every morning she would get up early to go to work - to sieve flaxseed - in order to make a livelihood and not need to accept presents; on the contrary, in her eyes one saw the pride from the merit that had fallen on her, that children from her loins were now in Eretz Israel, where they would hear the bells of redemption. This thought straightened her back and helped her bear the burden of the difficulties in making a living.

In front of my eyes pass a long row of personalities from the town, Jews busy with different crafts, small merchants, artisans, working hard to make a livelihood, but even the poorest, those who did not know to read or write, their hearts were open to what was going on in the world and in Eretz Israel in particular.

I cannot forget Avraham-Itshe Shkallot, the shoemaker, bent over his work, using his awl, putting a patch on the shoe, his hammer jumping in his hands and he is praying to his Father in Heaven, that his income will be sufficient, but in his heart he is yearning to know what is happening in the wide world. Since his knowledge of reading is not enough to understand the small letters, and he doesn't have money to buy a newspaper, he runs every day to Luba the tailor, to hear the news that was read out aloud from the daily newspaper.

Yaakov the cart-owner - in the summer he would drive in a large cart and in the winter, he drove a wide sled. When it was still dark outside he would get up to work, in drizzling rain, in heavy snow and in the cold of 30 degrees below zero, in order to support his family with honor. His exhausting work did not take away his sense of humor, quite the opposite, an additional side of his personality was his sharp wit, added to sarcasm, which was aimed at laughing at the high society. Young and old alike loved to spend time with him, in the long evenings of the winter, to hear his stories, spiced with juicy sayings, about his adventures along the way he had traveled, about the First World War and what was going on in the outside world.

Sometimes, when the shoemaker and the cart-owner were together, they would stand and argue with each other over *politika*, about the events in both general and Jewish history. They would express their opinions and prophesized the future with great respect and enthusiasm.

Itshe Tobias - my dear good uncle, who would always help us when we needed it, took it upon himself to act as father to his family after his father died, and thanks to him they did not feel the sorrows of orphans.

Sarah Atshe - my modest and devout mother, whose God-fearing and good hearted qualities, her simple and modest ways, had a healthy outlook on life. With common sense, talent and natural intelligence she was able to overcome the tribulations of life, to raise her children and teach them Torah and knowledge, to promote in their hearts love for one's fellow-man, to create an atmosphere of happiness the whole year around and especially on Holy Days. Many of the townspeople considered her as a support, because despite all her troubles, she found time to help others.

Rivkah - all the people of the town knew her and honored her; her back bent over from old age, yet despite the burden of the years, she would go around the town collecting penny by penny for the needy; she knew who needed her and her work, and did not stop until she managed to gather an amount which could be used to help others.

Dear townspeople - who, in a town surrounded by *goyim* [gentiles], had the sense to build a Hebrew school, which taught Torah, knowledge and Hebrew and National culture. Poor Jews, who worked together to build the school, with enthusiasm, with their very own hands, saving from their meager earnings in order to pay for tuition for their children and doing this with happiness and willingness.

The school teachers - who educated many generations of pupils: Chaim Persky - who was never daunted by any difficulties and continued to work diligently, the teachers Shalom Sonenzon, Yaakov Shmulevitch and others.

The amateur drama club - Shmuel Shapiro, Kalman (Shimshons) and Zeltka Feivoshevitz, who, with talent and charm, knew how to bring to the public what was going on in the Jewish society, in the *Bet Midrash*, in various committees, but did not fear to expose in public the failings of the life of the people. The drama club added an important contribution to the experience of the culture lovers of the town.

Alter Leibovitch - was 3 years on *Hachsharah* [at the training farm], but he was asked to be a leader in the group and thus was not allowed to make *aliyah*. Kayleh Shmulevitch - with her personal charm and ways, knew how to educate, to lead and to discipline. I remember the summer camp where she invested much personal initiative in setting it up and making it a success:

Summer camp: members of the group, young and old, would go back to nature, to be together and get used to being on the training farm in preparation for the kibbutz in Eretz Israel.

The departure back to nature and the cooperative life, gave an atmosphere of unity and closeness. The days went by with happiness and joy, until the late hours of the night, we would spend time around the flames of the burning bonfire, with dances and songs.

The camp was a really special event. Many of the townspeople came to see it, how the youth were living outside their parents' houses.

Avremeleh Kalmanovitch - a prominent and respected figure, despite being in the young age group, was one of the pillars of the group. He was very talented, quick to understand, sharp-witted and well versed in the Torah. Many of the elders of the town were very sad that Avrameleh did not turn to Torah studies at the *yeshiva*. They tried to entice him to continue with the heritage of his Fathers and made him many promises, but Avremeleh was stuck on Zionism and believed in it. He worked towards revival of the Jewish culture; in the newspaper that he put out for the group, he wrote articles full of youthful enthusiasm, wisdom and ideas about the world, Judaism, Zionism and Eretz Israel.

It is difficult for me to think that that the spirited Avrameleh, full of energy and so jolly, is no longer. His wick of life was cut off because of the cruelty of the Nazi monster.

Many years have passed since the victory over the Nazi beast, but the wounds have still not healed. The memory of our dear ones and the pure blood that was spilt, cry out to us and command: Remember and do not forget!!!

[Pages 250-252]

Two Religious Undertakings in Lubtch
by Shalom Rabinovitch

Brought for printing: Moshe Tsinovitch

Translated from the Yiddish by Harvey Spitzer

"*Dos Vort*" No. 211, Vilna,
28 *Tishrei*, 5688 (1928)

Storage in the Synagogue of Torn and Abused Torah Scrolls and Other Holy Books in Lubtch

A few weeks ago our town performed a remarkable eulogy. Many Torah scrolls and books were torn and otherwise abused during the war. Concerned citizens of the town, however, under fire of guns and artillery, risked their lives and ran and saved the holy articles where they have been lying until now, gathered together in one place. They have finally been eulogized and given a proper burial.

The eulogy which the rabbi gave was very moving. Particularly heart-rending was when the rabbi mentioned the 13 martyrs of Lubtch who fell in those terrible days. With heads bowed, the townspeople followed the bier to its final resting place. Everyone felt crushed by the effect of the eulogy.

A Celebration of a Torah Scroll

A week later we already celebrated a happy event. A Torah scroll and two sets of the Talmud were carried into the study hall of the synagogue. The Torah scroll was donated by Mrs. Shifra Rabinovitch. The celebration took place with much pomp. A band played. The canopy under which the Torah scroll was carried was decorated with a golden crown. Step by step, the townspeople took turns holding the Torah scroll under the canopy. Each person was thus honored until they reached the door of the synagogue. And then the real celebration first began. Our rabbi gave a solemn sermon in which he explained the significance of the day, lacing his talk with sayings of our sages of blessed memory. He connected that sad day when the damaged scrolls and books were buried with the day when the community was cheerfully bringing in and dedicating a Torah scroll and holy books.

The community then went directly from the synagogue, accompanied by the band, to get the sets of the Talmud. It was a joyful day. The band played till late at night in the presence of all the townspeople.

In a few days, another celebration will take place here with the bringing in and dedication of an additional Torah scroll presented by the Society of Psalm Reciters.

Shalom Rabinovitch

[Page 252]

A Remark Regarding the Above-mentioned Correspondent's Report

The author of the abovementioned correspondent's report, Shalom Rabinovitch, was a good friend of mine from the time we studied together at the famous "Mir Yeshiva". He was called "Shalom Zhetler" at the *yeshiva* because he came from the town of "Zhetel", where his parents lived during the First World War and for a certain time after the war. We became friends and shared a subscription to the Warsaw "Moment".

He was a good-looking, charming, young man, blond, with good manners, well educated, with a lovely smile on his bright face. I think he was musically gifted as well. His father had already passed away, but his mother was a true "woman of valor" and she is apparently the Shifra Rabinovitch who donated the Torah scroll for the synagogue in Lubtch.

As I recall, Shalom Rabinovitch was well-read as a youth and had a fairly good knowledge of Hebrew and Yiddish literature. He was strictly religious but not after the fashion of the followers of the *Musar* (strict ethical behavior) movement whose philosophy then dominated the Mir Yeshiva. Rather, he considered himself part of the smaller, that is to say, more liberal group at the *yeshiva*.

Shalom had a weakness for writing. He used this talent in later years, already being in Lubtch, as a correspondent, writing local news reports for the Orthodox weekly, "*Dos Vort*", which was published in Vilna. This periodical was the organ of the "Board of Yeshivot" in Vilna, which was half influenced by the *Aguda* organization, but writers with leanings towards *Mizrachi* also contributed to it.

Bringing a couple of Shalom Rabinovitch's reports about Lubtch to the press, I remembered this fine, quietly noble "Shalom Zhetler" and I considered it my duty to add a couple of lines of my own about him, May God avenge his blood!

Moshe Tsinovitch

[Page 253]

Activity of the Branch of the "Board of Yeshivot" in Lubtch

by Shalom Rabinovitch

Brought for printing: Moshe Tsinovitch

Translated from the Yiddish by Harvey Spitzer

"*Dos Vort*", No. 178, Vilna
Friday, weekly portion, *Ki Tissa*,
5688 (1928)

On the Sabbath of the weekly Torah portion, "*Terumah*", the esteemed rabbi, Rabbi Shmuel Markovitch from Turetz, paid our town a visit. He preached a brilliant sermon in the synagogue. All the congregants, both old and young, were deeply moved by the inspiring words of this talented orator. In his speech, the rabbi explained the obligation of contributing a *terumat hashekel* [monetary donation] to the yeshivot at all times and especially now. All those present warmly responded to the rabbi's appeal and a large gathering took place on Saturday night after the Sabbath.

New strength was co-opted for the existing board and the following morning the new board, together with the Rabbi from Turetz, came to collect the donations. According to the figures from the last collections, we will see to what extent the financial situation of the "Board of Yeshivot" has improved thanks to the efforts undertaken in our town.

As for the future, it has been decided to divide the town into four sections which the board members have solemnly obligated to carry out the raising and collection of money, and the local rabbi, Rabbi Yitzchak Weiss - May no harm befall him! - has volunteered to make a monthly appeal in the synagogue for this purpose.

Serving on the Lubtch branch of the "Board of Yeshivot": Town Rabbi, Chairman, Rabbi Zvi Ziversky, Treasurer, Shalom Rabinovitch, Secretary, Yitzchak Aronosky, Ritual Slaughterer and Kashrut Inspector, Leib Sokolovsky, Yitzchak Baksht, Avraham Rabinovitch, Yisrael-Yosef Levin, Avraham -Yosef Navamishsky, Avraham-Yisrael Mishkin, Yisrael Cohen and Reuven Kantorovitch.

Pages 254-264]

Rabbis Born in Lubtch

by Moshe Tzinovitch

Translated from the Hebrew by Harvey Spitzer

The Gaon Rabbi Eliyakum Shapira

Born in Lubtch in the year 5586 (1826), he was the son of Rabbi Chaim Shapira, who was later head of the rabbinic court in Solchnik (Vilna District). He was part of the family of the Gaon Rabbi Eliezer Shapira, head of the rabbinic court in Lubtch and was also related to the Gaon Rabbi Aryeh-Leib Shapira, head of the rabbinic court in Kovna. The young Eliyakum was a favorite of Rabbi Aryeh-Leib Shapira, from whom he learned the ways of conduct in the rabbinate, serving before him and before the Gaon Rabbi Reuven HaLevi, learning how to put rabbinic directives into practice.

Rabbi Eliyakum was rabbi and head of the rabbinic court in Horodok, (Vilna District), Ibnitz, Eishishok and Grodno. He was considered one of the most prominent rabbis in these places. R' Eliyakum was great in Torah learning, an expert teacher and a wise man, who was familiar with the problems of the world. He also had a good command of spoken and written Russian and was well known even in the circles of the authorities and senior officials in the Grodno District. He was invited to rabbinic assemblies at which his advice in matters pertaining to the general public was taken into consideration. He initiated an assembly of rabbis in Grodno, receiving special permission from the minister of the Grodno district for this purpose but, because of various reasons, the convention did not meet.

In his book, "*Dor v'dorshav*" ("A Generation and its Preachers") by Eliezer Efrati, Rabbi Eliyakum is described as "a great genius, wise and magnanimous, knows the language of the state and is very capable in arithmetic." In another book, "*Dor Rabbanav visofrav*" ("A Generation of Rabbis and Writers") by Ben-Zion Eisenstadt, it is brought down that in his youth, Rabbi Eliyakum was famous as a prodigy, having an exceptional memory.

His innovations are found in books and essays dealing with questions and responses. More of his essays dealing with questions and responses relating to the Talmud and deciders of matters of Jewish law are found in manuscript. One of Eliyakum's responses is found in the book, "*Tshuvat Shmuel*" ("Shmuel's Response") [Laws of Divorce, Law #2] and, in "*Beit Vad leChachamim*") ("Meeting Place for Scholars"), [Weekly collection for Torah and Jewish Wisdom by Rabbi Yisrael-Haim Deiches], Rabbi Deiches bases himself on one of Rabbi Eliyakum's questions and answers and writes that he is "the father of instruction, the sage of the rabbis of Grodno, a great genius."

Around the year 5664 or 5665 (1905), Rabbi Eliyakum Shapira emigrated to Eretz-Yisrael and settled in Jerusalem, where he was honored to be the president of the "Grodno Community". He died in the year 5668 (1908) and had the honor of being laid to rest on the Mount of Olives. A list of appreciation to his memory appeared in one of the issues of "*Havatzelet*" for 5668.

The Gaon Rabbi Raphael-Alter Shmuelevitch

He was born in Lubtch around 5635 (1875) and received an intensive Talmudic education. He studied at *yeshivot* in Lithuania and in the *yeshivot* in Slutzk and Novogrudek where ethical conduct was emphasized. He was famous as having wonderful talents and for his diligence. He abounded in innovations according to the school system of the Lithuanian yeshivot and he became famous in Lithuania and Zhamot.

He was the son-in-law of the righteous, wise and devoted rabbi, Rabbi Yosef-Yozel Horvitch. Afterwards, he was appointed to fill the role of head of the rabbinical college in the *yeshiva* at Novogrudek. He also spent some time as deputy head of the rabbinical college in Slotzk.

When the upper division *yeshiva* was established in Grodno in 5676 [1916], Rabbi Raphael was appointed head of the college of the *yeshiva*. However, he was active for only a short time and died the following year, 5677 (1917). His lessons are passed around until this very day in all the *yeshivot*, and copied from hand to hand.

His son is the prodigy, the Gaon Rabbi Chaim Shmuelevitch, head of the rabbinical college at the Mir Yeshiva in Jerusalem.

Rabbi Yosef Yossilevitch (5639-5695)

He was born in Lubtch in the year 5639 (1879) and received a Torah education in his hometown and in *yeshivot* in the area. Afterwards, he studied at the *yeshiva* "Knesset Yisrael" in Slobodka-Kovna (5654-62) (1894-1902) in the period when the Gaonim R' Issar-Zalman Meltzer and R' Moshe-Mordechai Epshtein served as heads of the rabbinical college. He was also among those who came to the house of the Gaon R' Yitzchak Blazer, one of the fathers of *Musar* movement who was then living in Kovna and whose spirit influenced those studying in the Slobodka yeshiva and in the *kolel* [*yeshiva* for married students, some of whom left their wives to study] in Kovna.

Rabbi Yossilevitch's first position as rabbi was in the town of Silev [Vyselyub] (5667-72) (1907-1912) and after that he served as rabbi and head of the rabbinic court in Terrestina (Bialystok District), Samiatich (5681-86) (1921-1926) and in Sovalk, a district town.

In every place where he served, Rabbi Yossilevitch was active in the area of education and strengthening religion. In Sovalk he supervised the Talmud-Torah and the local *yeshiva* attached to it, until it was considered to be the official educational institute for Jews of Sovalk and the whole area.

He was known amongst the rabbis of Lithuania and Poland as a genius, a great innovator (discoverer of new interpretations) and as a research scholar in the sea of Talmud and its commentators. He left behind manuscripts on *halacha* [Jewish law], some of them relating to martyrs based on the way of understanding in the Lithuanian style of learning. He did not live, however, to see these manuscripts in print. A few of his Talmudic innovations were published in his lifetime in the Torah compilations "*Sha'arei Tzion*" in Jerusalem and "*Knesset Yisrael*" in Vilna.

Although Rabbi Yossilevitch's growth and education in Talmud were at the *yeshiva* in Slobodka, where they were opposed to Zionism, he himself joined the *Mizrachi* movement and was loyal to it all his life. His sermons were always about the ideas of revival of the Jewish homeland: he signed declarations calling on Jews to join the *Mizrachi* movement and acted in support of the Jewish National Fund, the Jewish Foundation Fund and other Zionist settlement and pioneering fundraising drives.

In the year 5683 (1923), he participated in the conference of *Mizrachi* rabbis, which took place in Warsaw. He was a candidate from the national center of *Mizrachi* in Poland as a delegate to the 13th Zionist Congress which took place that same year.

All this did not detract from his worth and status as a great rabbi and brilliant scholar in the general rabbinical circles in Poland and Lithuania. He was also accepted in the circle of the Gaon Rabbi Chaim-Ozer in Vilna and among the people of the *Musar* Movement in the *yeshivot* of the Polish part of Lithuania. He took part in a conference of pupils of the Slobodka Yeshiva which took place in Baranovitch in the year 5688 (1928), marking the first anniversary (*yahrzeit*) of the death of the grandfather from Slobodka. He was among the heads speaking at this convention in which the scholar of the *Musar* Movement, R' Yerucham Leibovitch, a leading figure from Mir, also participated.

Rabbi Eliyahu-Dov Berkovsky

Born in the year 5625 (1865), he was the son of R' Netta Mordechai, one of the town honorables and scholars. At the age of 12, he already started learning at the great Mir Yeshiva and was one of the most brilliant pupils of the head of the college, the Gaon R' Chaim-Leib Tiktinsky. Afterwards, he moved on to the Volozhin Yeshiva where he studied Torah from the head of the college, the Gaon R' Naftali-Tzvi Yehuda Berlin (the *Netzi"v*). From Volozhin he went to Slobodka, where the famous upper-level *yeshiva* had begun taking shape out of a group of young people who were part of a Torah group. R' Eliyahu-Dov was among the first ten students that learnt in the above group in the synagogue, "*Halivyat HaMet*". This was the nucleus of the *Musar* movement's *yeshiva*, "*Knesset Yisrael*" in Slobodka, at the head of which stood the *Musar* rabbi, Rabbi Netta-Hirsh Finkel. There R' Eliyahu-Dov was close to the Gaon R' Yitzchak Blazer, who was counted among the brightest of the students of the Gaon Rabbi Yisrael Salanter, who inspired him with the spirit of ethical conduct and to whom he was connected with bonds of love.

When he was 22 years old, he married the daughter of one of the honorables of Novogrudek. He then made the acquaintance of the head of the rabbinic court, the Gaon Rabbi Yechiel-Michal Epshtein, author of "Aruch HaShulchan". After the marriage, he returned to Volozhin and studied at the *yeshiva* for young married men founded by Brodsky. In the year 5651 (1891) he was ordained by the *Netzi"v* and by Rabbi Yehiel-Michal Epshtein and Rabbi Yitzchak Bonimovitch, head of the rabbinic court of Lubtch, who pointed out his greatness in Torah and his wonderful qualities.

Several years later Rabbi Berkovsky became active in the *Musar* movement and filled an important role in this movement. Those were the days when *kolels* and *yeshivot* were beginning to be established in different cities in the manner prescribed by Rabbi Yosef Yozel. With the approval of R' Yosef Blazer, the town of Lubtch served as the founding place for the first *kolel* for young married students. At the same time, a *kolel* was founded in Novogrudek. Some time later, the *kolel* in Lubtch was dispersed and the one in Novogrudek became the central yeshiva for all the *Musar* movement *yeshivot* of the type of R' Yozel Horvitch.

In the year 5657 (1897) when a controversy of opposition to the *Musar* method was disclosed, R' Eliyahu-Dov went, as an emissary of R' Yitzchak Blazer, to a number of towns where famous rabbis who were sympathetic to the *Musar* movement were then serving, and obtained their signatures on the declaration, "For the Truth", which was published on the pages of the "*Hamelitz*" newspaper in the year 5657. He stood for 10 years at the head of the board of directors of the *yeshiva* in Novogrudek and bore the difficult yoke and heavy responsibility of both the spiritual and financial administration.

When an extreme *Musar* rule took over the leadership of the *yeshiva* in Novogrudek, something that was not to the liking of Rabbi Berkovsky, he withdrew from the above- mentioned *yeshiva* and moved to Lida to sit beside the Gaon Rabbi Yitzchak-Yaakov Reines, to help him in administering his new *yeshiva*. The whole burden of administration lay on his shoulders in the years during the First World War, when Rabbi Reines died and the *yeshiva* was uprooted to Yelisotograd in Ukraine. It continued to exist there for four years with the great effort and extraordinary devotion of Rabbis Berkovsky, together with the prodigy from Maytchat, R' Shlomo Polachek. This continued until after the days of the pogroms in Ukraine, and when the *yeshiva* was closed, it moved to independent Poland. For 10 years he served in office in the *yeshiva* in Lida, spent a few more years in Rovna and then served half a year as head of the college and spiritual monitor at the Techachamoni Yeshiva in Bialystok. He made *aliyah* to Eretz-Israel in the year 5684 (1924) and made his home in Tel Aviv, the final station of his life.

Rabbi Shlomo HaCohen Aronson, Chief Rabbi of Tel Aviv, held Rabbi Berkovsky in high esteem and appointed him head of the rabbinic college and spiritual monitor in the *yeshiva* for young people, "Yeshivat Tel Aviv", which was founded on his initiative. Thanks to his hard work and great experience, the *yeshiva* developed and its prestige spread about in the new Jewish community of Mandatory Palestine. In the year 5695 (1935) he retired from work due to age, but remained connected to the work of the *yeshiva*, tested students and even set their manners and way of life.

He was also a speedy writer and had a well-developed sense to comment, enlighten and conceive ideas. He published his works in "*HaTzofeh*", "*HaYesod*", "*Bamishor*" and "*HaHed*". He left behind various manuscripts on *halacha* and *agada*.

He was a man of noble character. He walked modestly with every person, shared in the fate of his fellow man and was always willing to help the suffering and the needy with spiritual and financial support. He took a special interest in helping young scholars who lacked material means, and looked after them constantly without taking his mind off their needs, not even for a short time.

As much as he belonged to the rabbinical, patriarchal world, Rabbi Berkovsky was a clear "Lover of Zion", a loyal member of the "*Mizrachi*" movement in Eretz-Yisrael. He believed in the redemption of the Jewish People. Therefore, he was enthusiastically engaged with studying the traditional laws and commandments dependent on living in Eretz-Israel. He served as rabbi at the *Beit Midrash "Yerushalayim"* on Gruzenberg Street in Tel Aviv, where there was a large concentration of students from Lithuania. Every day he gave a lesson on a page of *Talmud* before well-known people.

Rabbi Eliyahu-Dov Berkovsky died in Tel Aviv on 25 Adar I, 5703 (1943) at the age of 78. Editorials devoted to his memory appeared in the daily newspaper "*HaTzofeh*" and also in "*HaYesod*" with details about his life.

Rabbi Yisrael-Yehuda Halevy Kapuchevsky

Born in the village of Ratchmilla, which is between Lubtch, Silev [present day Vyselyub] and Novogrudek, R' Yisrael-Yehuda was the son of R' Yaakov and Feyga, whose ancestors had lived in this village for generations upon generations. Although they were "country folk" from birth, they took pains and saw to it that their children were educated to be Torah scholars. Their efforts bore excellent fruit and from the village home of the "farmers", two sons went out to the region in search of Torah and knowledge. One of them, the firstborn, Rabbi Yosef HaLevy Kapuchevsky, settled with his wife, Hinda, in the town of Lubtch where he was accepted as a teacher of *Talmud* for the local youth, and his fame spread as a great expert in the teaching of *Talmud*.

The second son, Rabbi Yisrael-Yehuda, studied at the Mir Yeshiva, where he attended the lessons of the head of the college, R' Chaim Leib Tiktinsky. At the age of 21, after filling his stomach with Talmud and deciders of Jewish law, he came to Minsk. There he was introduced to a Hebrew and general education and perfected his knowledge of Hebrew and Russian. He excelled as a master of style, a brilliant scholar in Bible and general literature. Upon his return from Minsk, he married the young Mina, daughter of R' Itche Meir and Riva-Nacha from Lubtch.

Influenced by his father-in-law, who owned a bakery and flour shop, R' Yisrael-Yehuda also opened a store, selling flour and grains. After a short time, however, he left the business in the hands of his wife and devoted himself to his pioneering work in the field of education in Lubtch. His aim was to insert an addition of the achievements brought about by time: the study of Hebrew and secular subjects into the framework of the traditional *cheder* (religious elementary school). And, indeed, the *cheder* that he founded in the town was a fine example to all the environs. In the *cheder*, children learnt Hebrew, Russian, arithmetic, grammar, history and other subjects, - a revolutionary idea in those days. The results were positive and justified his experiment. Most of the pupils were equipped with much knowledge in the above subjects, and together with this, they also deepened and strengthened their religious knowledge in the spirit of the heritage of their forefathers.

R' Yisrael-Yehuda's *cheder* also served as a corridor for streaming pupils to the yeshivot. He himself was one who "practices what he preaches" and sent three of his sons to the *yeshivot* in Baronovitch, Radon and Mir. This Lubtch educator also recognized the importance of the Zionist movement and was wise enough to introduce a Zionist atmosphere in the spirit of traditional Israel into the framework of his *cheder*.

R' Yisrael-Yehuda HaLevy was uprooted towards the end of the year 5675 (1915) from Lubtch, his town which was reduced to ruins in the fire of the war between Russia and Germany. He moved to the town of Dervna, where he set up a perfect *cheder* modeled after the one in Lubtch and saw blessing in the area of education in continuing his method of education.

His name as an educator became famous throughout the villages close and far. The rabbi, the Gaon R' Yehoshua Liberman, head of the rabbinical court in Stoybtch, invited him to stand at the head of the "Talmud Torah" which he had founded in his city, and R' Yisrael-Yehuda accepted his offer. In this new place as well, he conquered the hearts of the parents and the pupils with his modesty, his devotion to his work and with his knowledge. He succeeded in raising hundreds of pupils to Torah and good deeds. Many are his pupils spread around the world and in the independent State of Israel who suckled from his Torah, wisdom and piety.

Mr. Zvi Stolovitsky, in his article "Religious Schools in Stoibtch" (in his book "Stoibtch- Sverzhina", Tel Aviv, 5725 (1965)) reports the following about R' Yisrael-Yehuda's activities:

"With the arrival of R' Yehuda Kaputchevsky, a native of Lubtch and resident of Dervna, to be a teacher at the "Chorev" Talmud Torah school, the school flourished. He taught Bible and *Gemara* (*Talmud*). Teaching of *Gemara* was accompanied by a captivating melody, when the eyes of the teacher are closed from emotion and the pupils are reading the verses. In the *Gemara* lessons, he was used to emphasizing the difference between the *Talmud* and Bible studies. While it is possible to sometimes continue studying a verse in the Bible even with deficient listening to the previous verses, it is not the case in studying the *Gemara*, where continuous and complete listening is required, for otherwise the internal connection of the topic under discussion will be cut off."

R' Yisrael-Yehuda Halevy, a man from Lubtch, perished in the Holocaust in Stoybtch together with his wife Mina, also born in Lubtch, along with their daughter Sarah-Devorah and her husband, R' Avraham Moallin and their children and also their unmarried daughter, Nechama. His son, Rabbi Avraham, who was called "Avrahmel Derevener" was exiled with his *yeshiva* to Russia and nothing is known of his fate.

The following are members of the R' Yisrael-Yehuda's family who are still alive according to the aforementioned document: His eldest daughter, married to Mr Dov Berger in New York, an intellectual and linguist who serves as a language and literary translator. His daughter, Batya, who lives in Poland, his son, Rabbi Yosef Kapi, living in the city of Providence [Rhode Island], in the United States, and his son, the Gaon Rabbi Moshe Levin, may his light shine!, a former pupil at the Mir and Radon *yeshivot*, and now the chief rabbi of Netanya.

Rabbi Avraham-Yitzchak Nochimovsky

The Nochimovsky family was one of the most distinguished families in Lubtch. Their parents and forefathers were relatives of the well-established families of the town: Bakst, Bakster, Meizel, Shapira and others.

Avraham-Yitzchak was born in Lubtch, where he received a Torah education. He studied at the *Musar* movement *yeshiva* in Novogrudek, in Radon and at the *Kolel* in Kovna. He was a rabbi and judge in Shably (Lithuania), where he had influence of wide circles, bringing them closer to authentic Judaism and in keeping the Torah and the commandments.

He belonged to the "*Mizrachi*" movement. He was a signatory on its funds and preached on behalf of the *Keren Hayesod, Keren Kayment Leyisrael* (JNF) and all types of fund raising appeals for the new activities of settlement in Eretz Yisrael. In the year 5698 (1938), his signature appeared on a special petition of a group of "*Mizrachi*" rabbis concerning the holy obligation to donate towards a department of ultra-orthodox Jews that was founded then close to the main bureau of the Keren Kayemet Leyisrael, a thing that allowed any Jew, even the most orthodox, to give his share.

Rabbi Avraham-Yitzchak Nochimovsky was murdered by the Nazis - may their name be erased!- on 15 Tammuz 5701 (1941) together with the head of the rabbinical court, the Gaon Rabbi Aharon Baksht, may the Lord avenge their death!

Rabbi Shabtai Varnikovsky

Rabbi Shabtai Varnikovsky was known in the *yeshivot* of Lomzha, Slobodka and Novogrudek by the name of "R' Shabtai HaLubtchai". He was admired by all the great rabbis of the generation in Lithuania.

In line with the recommendation of his teacher and guide, the Righteous Rabbi Netta-Tzvi Finkel (the grandfather from Slobodka), he married the daughter of the saintly Rabbi Tzvi-Dov Heller, spiritual monitor of the Slobodka Yeshiva.

After having been a member of the "Beit Yosef" Kolel in Slobodka for a several years, he was invited to the Lomzha Yeshiva to assume the position of head of the college, a mission which he accomplished with success, raising hundreds of pupils to the Torah and to certification as rabbis. He perished in the Holocaust, May the Lord avenge his blood!

Rabbi Eliezer Bar Baruch

In his book "*Bnei Minsk v'chachameiha*" (Vilna, 5659- 1899-) Part 2, Section "*Avnei Tzion*", the author, Ben Tzion Eizenshtadt, brings inscriptions on tombstones on the graves of personalities who are buried in the Jewish cemetery in Minsk. Among these inscriptions is also that of a famous Lubtch resident who was active in Minsk and was brought to eternal rest there in great honor.

The name of this person is R' Eliezer Bar Baruch, who came from Lubtch, his place of birth, to Minsk, where he held the office of head of the yeshiva and rabbinical court judge.

This is the text of the inscription on the tombstone as written in the aforementioned book:

Here lies the rabbi, a genius in Torah and outstanding in piety and good qualities.
Rabbi Eliezer bar Baruch, who was called R' Eliezer Lubtcher, may he rest in peace!
Eliezer, like Aharon, always seeking peace, and caring for the
sacred furnishings was the charge of Elazar [son of Aharon the Priest].
In the synagogue and in the study hall, many heard his lesson.
Judge and yeshiva head he was
He longed to frequent the beloved tent of Torah
Many stood before Eliezer; he issued a law in its light.
And Eliezer said: This is a decree of the Torah. Who knows the explanation of this matter?
He scorned the cunning craftsmen. He will justify the humble person who is pleasing and a friend to God and to men.
His soul departed in purity on Tuesday, 26 Sivan, and Eliezer died in the year 5647 (1887).

Rabbi Ben-Tzion Eizenshtadt, author of the book, adds:

"Rabbi Eliezer Lubtcher, native of Lubtch, was judge and head of the yeshiva in Minsk. He disseminated Torah and knowledge to many and was magnanimous in his actions and one of the great personalities of the city, both its scholars and rabbis."

According to Rabbi Ben-Tzion Eizenshtadt, the son of R' Eliezer Lubtcher was the leader, our master and teacher, The *Admor* Antzelevitch.

The Gaon Rabbi Avraham-Baruch Kliatchky

"Hayom", Volume No.264, from the year 1887

8 Tevet 5648. Reporter: "Ben Shalom"

"The Gaon Rabbi Avraham-Baruch Kliatchky, was son of Rabbi Aryeh-Leib from Lubtch, son of the wealthy R' Yaakov-Peretz Kliatchky, (mentioned in the book, "*Kiriyah Ne'manah*", p. 212) one of the leading members of the distinguished families in Vilna.

Rabbi Avraham-Baruch Kliatchky became orphaned from his father as a child of six (his father died on 4 Tishrei, 5576-1816) and was brought from Lubtch to Vilna where he grew up in the home of his eminent uncles.

As a youth he excelled in Torah and philosophy and was taken for a bridegroom by a wealthy man who gave him a dowry and gifts, a Code of Jewish Law and a good and highly praised bride. In his father-in law's home, he became great in Torah, learning by expanding his heart and mind and by dint of sheer perseverance. In the year 5594 (1834) he eagerly wished to pray in the *Beit Midrash* [study hall, synagogue] of the great Rabbi Haim "Gitke-Toyvas" of blessed memory, who was the director of an upper-division *yeshiva* there. The head of the *yeshiva* chose the young Avraham-Baruch to test the pupils in their studies. At that time, Rabbi Yaakov Horander, author of the commentary "*Yagel Yaakov*" on the "*Tzohar Hateva*", was head of the grammarians, and he too took great pleasure in the young Avraham-Baruch's knowledge of grammar. In general, nearly all the Torah leaders of the generation held him in high regard.

When he was still a young man, he began to give a lesson in the *Talmud* with its commentators to a group of friends who excelled in learning, and he was the teacher of this lesson for several years. In addition, he was very capable in algebra and geometry. He also read many books on science and education. Nature favored him with good looks, and when he walked through the streets of the city, wisdom shone upon his face. Everyone saw this and gave him honor befitting a king.

Thus did this man live with honor and satisfaction all his life until last year, when his beloved son, Rabbi Binyamin Kliatchky, of blessed memory, died during his father's life (on the holy Sabbath, 25 Kislev). From that time on, his strength abandoned him and the sun of the spirit of his life begun to set until he himself went down in sorrow to his son's grave, a full year and a week after his son's death. He was buried with great honor and the local acting rabbi eulogized him in the above-mentioned *Beit Midrash* and also at the cemetery."

Printed in the book, "*Erech Tefillah*" (Vilna 5629-1869) by Rabbi Levi-Yerachmiel Kliatchky (the only son of the aforementioned deceased) is a letter replete with knowledge of Talmud and deciders of Jewish law written in good taste and knowledge by the deceased.

Rabbi Eliezer Bakshtansky

Rabbi Eliezer Bakshtanksy was the son of Rabbi Nahum of Lubtch. R' Eliezer moved to Pinsk and became one of the town's notables: a scholar, righteous in conduct and possessing good qualities and good deeds. His name, "R' Eliezer Lubtcher" preceded him in the surrounding towns, close and far.

His father, R' Nahum, was the brother and also father-in-law of the Gaon, R' Eliyahu-Chaim Meizel, head of the rabbinical court in Lodz. He was the pupil of the "*tzaddik*" (righteous man), Rabbi Yehonatan Stanover, in Lubtch, his place of birth.

At the age of 14, he married the daughter of the wealthy and generous Rabbi Meyer Soltz from Vilna (father-in-law of the Gaon R' Hirsh Rabinovitch, head of the rabbinical court in Kovno, son of the great and famous Gaon Rabbi Yitzchak-Elchanan Spector, head of the rabbinical court in Kovno) and became a merchant. However, he devoted most of his time to studying Torah, praying and giving charity. In Pinsk, where he lived, he carried on ramified business dealings.

He was a close friend of R' David Friedman, head of the rabbinical court in Karlin and R' Eliezer-Moshe Horovitch, head of the rabbinical court in Pinsk and likewise of R' Eliyahu-Chaim Meizel, head of the rabbinical court in Lodz.

He passed away at the age of 73, 21 Shvat 5669 (1909) and was buried with great honor.

He left behind many sons who were rabbis, giants in Torah and highly educated: R' Moshe-Aharon, R' Assir, R' Leib-Yehuda, R' Ben Tzion, R' Yehonatan and R' Yitzchak. His sons-in-law are the Gaon R' Eliezer-Yitzchak, son of R' Chaim-Hillel Fried, head of the rabbinical college in Volozhin, and the Gaon R' Yaakov Tiktinsky (grandson of the Gaon, R' Chaim-Leib Tiktinsky, head of the college and director of the Mir Yeshiva).

"*Dorot Rishonim*", Book One, א-ו
New York, 5673 (1913) by Ben-Tzion Eizenshtadt

[Pages 265-270]

Rabbi R' Chaim Krasilov z"l
[And three other Rabbis]

by Avraham HaCohen Eliyav

Translated from the Hebrew by Ann Belinsky and Harvey Spitzer

R' Chaim was born around the year 5617 (1857) in a small town near Minsk (White Russia). As a child, he was educated by his father. Still in his youth, he went to study Torah at the Minsk Yeshiva with Rabbi Binyamin HaCohen Shikovitzky of blessed memory, known as "The *Maggid* from Minsk". He was considered to be amongst the finest of the *yeshiva* students with a sharp mind capable of grasping ideas quickly.

He learnt diligently and at a young age was ordained but did not want to serve as a rabbi, preferring a ritual occupation. He said: "Our wise ones said: Love work and hate the rabbinate." Therefore, R' Chaim studied the laws of slaughtering animals and received the authorization to be a ritual slaughterer and inspector.

About the year 5642 (1882), he married Feygeh, daughter of a Torah scholar from Lubtch, from a family of distinguished rabbis, the older sister of my aunt, Slova Kashtzer, from Ivyeh. After the wedding, R' Chaim was accepted to be the ritual slaughterer and inspector in Lubtch.

R' Chaim and his wife had two sons: I don't know the name of the firstborn, and the second one was named Avraham. They received their education in the parents' home in the spirit of Torah and Good Manners. Aunt Feygeh was a modest woman, pleasant in her ways, especially outstanding in her welcoming of guests. Her house was always open and she received each and everyone with cordiality.

Their firstborn son was one of the participants in the failed revolution of 1905. For fear of being arrested, he secretly emigrated to America.

In the year 5674 (1914), during the First World War, when Lubtch was completely burned down, all its inhabitants remained without a roof over their heads and were forced to disperse to the neighboring cities and towns. Many went to Ivyeh, including R' Chaim and his family; they lived there in the house of my aunt Slova Kashtzer, Feygeh's sister.

During the war years, the residents of Ivyeh, which was close to the front and under German control, suffered from a lack of basic foodstuffs. Feygeh was a sickly woman, her health deteriorated and, with no suitable medical treatment, she died in the year 5676 (1916) on the eve of Shavuot, may her soul rest in Paradise!

In the year 5679 (1919), with the end of the First World War, Avraham married his cousin, Chaya-Feygel, daughter of Aharon-Eidel and Slova (Kashtzer). When the Bolsheviks retreated and the Poles set up government, most of the Jews of Lubtch returned to their town and renewed their life there; R' Chaim and his son also returned to Lubtch.

In the year 5686 (1926), R' Chaim, the ritual slaughterer and inspector died. He was about 70 years old.

His son Avraham was the owner of a bakery in Lubtch. He and his wife Chaya-Feygel were blessed with five daughters: Asna-Eideleh, Chassia, Slova, Miriam and Liba. Chaya-Feygel was a "Woman of Valor", who built her house in the spirit of the tradition of Israel. And even though she had to look after her small daughter, she also worked in the bakery in order to help her husband bear the yoke of earning a living. Their house stood on Market Street and was wide open to all. They gave charity generously to all the needy. Chaya-Feygel was a good-hearted woman, delicate and modest in her ways. She would receive all those who came to her house with a smile and radiant face. The words of King Solomon, the Wisest of All Men, apply to this lovely woman: "She anticipates the needs of her household, and does not partake of the bread of laziness."

In the year 5702 (1942), on that bitter and violent day, Avraham, his wife Chaya Feygel, and their five daughters were killed by the murderous Nazis, together with all the martyrs of the Lubtch community.

[Pages 266-267]

Rabbi Yaakov-Shlomo Kivelevitch z"l

Rabbi Yaakov-Shlomo was born in the year 5655 (1895) in Lubtch. In his youth, he studied in the *cheder* in his hometown and then traveled to study Torah in the Novogrudek and Stutchin *yeshivot*. He was a disciple of Rabbi Alter Shmuelevitch of blessed memory, who looked after him as a son. He was very gifted and learnt diligently. Rabbi Yaakov-Shlomo was close to Rabbi Chaim-Zev Finkel, head of the Mir Yeshiva in Jerusalem.

At the end of the First World War in the year 5681 (1921), he married Gittel, daughter of Haim-Leib and Malka Gnissin from Ivyeh and settled there. Rabbi Shlomo and his wife were blessed with two sons and a daughter. In those days after the war, Rabbi Shlomo-Yaakov could not find work to support his family, who lived in a small house with poor accommodations.

Rabbi Yaakov-Shlomo was a quiet and modest man, making do with little and happy with his share. Once, when I asked him about his situation, he answered, "Thank G-d, all right. I can't complain. After all, our Sages of blessed memory said, A person's food is as difficult to come by as the pangs of redemption and the dividing of the Red Sea."

Because of his difficult financial condition, he decided to try his luck overseas. In the year 5685 (1925), he emigrated with his wife and children to South Africa, where different communities offered him a position as rabbi, but he chose an occupation as a ritual slaughterer and inspector in the city of Bulawayo in Rhodesia. In the last years of his life, although unofficially, he also fulfilled the role of rabbi.

During the Second World War, he was very active in extending help to the Jewish refugees who arrived in South Africa. Day and night his house was full of people requesting aid and support.

Rabbi Yaakov-Shlomo was an ardent Zionist all his life. His ambition and dream was to make *aliyah* to Eretz-Yisrael, but he did not achieve this ambition in his lifetime.

Rabbi Yaakov-Shlomo died in South Africa on 1 Kislev 5722 (1961). He was brought to rest in the sacred earth of Jerusalem, the Holy City.

[Pages 267-269]

Rabbi Avraham-David Bloch

Rabbi Avraham-David Bloch was born in Lubtch in the year 5662 (1902). He married Feygeh, daughter of Rabbi Eliyahu HaDayan and was known by the name "Rabbi Eli's Son-in-law". In his youth, he studied Torah at Rabbi Yosef-Yozel's *yeshiva* in Novogrudek and was a passionate "*Musar'nik*", follower of the ethics movement. They had three sons: Mordechai, Yitzchak and Eliyahu and a daughter Malka. They were educated in Torah and in the performance of *mitzvoth* and good deeds.

The sons studied at the *yeshiva* in Ivyeh and afterwards went to study in *yeshivot* in other towns. Mordechai, the oldest, who had a natural bent for fine craft, went to Vilna where he learned Torah and crafts together at a technical-occupational school. Their son Yitzchak studied at the Mir and Kletsk *yeshivot*. He was very gifted and was numbered amongst the best students at the *yeshiva*. Eliyahu, who also studied at the Kletsk *yeshiva*, was a diligent student with a sharp mind capable of grasping ideas quickly.

Their daughter Malka married Rabbi Yehoshua Lev, one of the best students at the "Bet Yosef" Yeshiva, which was founded by Rabbi Shmuel Veintroyb in Ivyeh. With time, he became head of the "Beit Yosef" lower division *yeshiva*. In Ivyeh he was called "*Der Mashgiach*" because he was the spiritual overseer of the *yeshiva*.

Like his father-in-law Rabbi Eliyahu, Rabbi Avraham-David also lived a life of poverty and perpetual need with his family, but they were different in their character. His father-in-law was a quiet and slow man in his manners and actions, while he, Rabbi Avraham-David, was fast and energetic in all his ways. He would rush on his way to the *Beit Midrash* and not even look at the people whom he met on the street in order to do as is written: Be as fleet as a deer to do the wishes of thy Father in Heaven.

In the year 5686 (1926), he moved to Vilna where he entered the *Beit Midrash* of the "*Gra*", the Vilner Gaon, and founded a group called the "Ten Abstainers" [*Aseret Prushim*], who sat in the Gaon's *Kloiz* [synagogue], wrapped in their prayer shawls day and night, studying the doctrine of ethics according to the *Gra*.

Rabbi Avraham-David also wrote a few books on Jewish law and ethics: *Keter Tefilin-vetzitzit hakanaf* about laws brought down in the Shulhan Arukh - *Orah Haim*, *Heshbon Olam* about matters pertaining to Torah and ethics, *Divrei Eliyahu*, selections of Torah remarks by the Gra (together with Rabbi Farfel, "HaMaggid from Oshmina" and afterwards *maggid* [preacher] in Vilna.

His son Eliyahu was lucky to be saved from the claws of the Nazi murderers and after years of wandering arrived in America where he studied in the *yeshiva* of Rabbi Aharon Kotler, in Lakewood, New Jersey and was considered to be among his outstanding students. Rabbi Eliyahu wrote two books on *Halacha* [Jewish law]: "*Ruach Eliyahu*" ["The Spirit of Eliyahu"] and "*Mida Kaneged Mida*" ["Measure for Measure"].

All the other family members perished in the Holocaust in the great massacre in Ivyeh on 25 Iyar 5702 (May 12, 1942), and the father of the family, Rabbi Avraham-David, "*Haparush*" ["The Abstainer"], was slain by the defiled murderers in Vilna.

[Pages 269-270]

Rabbi Moshe Meyerovitz

Rabbi Moshe was born in the year 5651 (1890), son of Rabbi Reuven Meyerovitz, in Novogrudek. He received a traditional education from the teachers in his town. He studied for a few years at the Lubtch Yeshiva and continued to study at the famous *yeshiva* of Rabbi Yosef-Yozel Horvitz. Rabbi Moshe was among the outstanding *yeshiva* students. In the year 5672 (1912), he married the daughter of Rabbi Shmuel of Delatitch, who was a Torah scholar and property owner but also did not disparage the profession he learned in his youthful years, that of a cobbler, and in this way carried out the words of our Sages of blessed memory: "Love work and hate the rabbinate!" When his only daughter reached marriageable age, Rabbi Shmuel turned to the head of the *yeshiva* in Novogrudek, Rabbi Yosef-Yozel, requesting him to choose a *yeshiva* student and scholar as a bridegroom for his daughter. According to the *yeshiva* head's suggestion, the lot fell on Rabbi Moshe Meyerovitz, one of his finest and brightest students.

In the year 5674 (1914), when the Russian soldiers were retreating during the First World War, they looted property and burned the houses of the inhabitants of the towns of Lubtch and Delatitch. Rabbi Shmuel and his family moved to Ivyeh and settled there. Rabbi Moshe and his wife were blessed with a son whom they called Meir.

The town of Ivyeh remained as a flock without a shepherd when the local rabbi, Rabbi Yitzchak Kosovsky, left for the depths of Russia. Rabbi "Moshe from Deliatich" (as he was nicknamed) was chosen to be the rabbi and rabbinic judge in Ivyeh. He was a great scholar, well versed in Talmud and in the decisions of the authorities of Jewish law. He used to arise after midnight and study Torah. He was diligent and tireless and was blessed with the good attributes of Aharon the High Priest, "a lover of peace and a pursuer of peace, loving people and bringing them close to Torah". He was a brother and friend to all, made do with little and led a modest life. He was humble and simple in his ways, did not know what it meant to be angry, was always cheerful and smiling and was thus loved and admired by all the residents of the town.

Also Rabbi Moshe Shatzkes, the local rabbi and his successor, Rabbi Ze'ev Perlman, respected him, considered his opinions and valued his deep knowledge of Talmud and the decisions of the authorities of Jewish law. They also joined him in discussions and decisions regarding matters of Jewish law, arbitration and public-religious questions. His only son Meir, who was educated by his father and studied at the *yeshivot* in Ivyeh, Radon and Mir, was one of the outstanding students. During the Second World War, he fled with the Mir Yeshiva to Russia where, according to rumors, he died from torments and hunger.

Rabbi Moshe Meyerovitz and his wife were among the first to be killed by the Nazi murderers in the Massacre of the Intelligentsia, on Shabbat, *Tisha b'Av* 5701. (2nd August, 1941.) May their memory be for a blessing!

[Page 270]

No More Wars...

by Chaim Yankelevitch

Translated from the Yiddish by Harvey Spitzer

"A pleasure", my grandfather used to say. "Today there's a train and a bus. You can go to Novogrudek like a rich Polish squire. You get there very early and can take care of everything in one day and come back home in time for supper, just like a nobleman. In the old days, however, traveling to Novogrudek was another matter, and there were not even any wagon drivers."

People would get up before dawn, take their *tallit* and *tefillin*, a little food for the trip and leave on foot. When you came to a town exhausted, you had to rest up. Staying at an inn costs money, so where do people go if not to relatives…?

And the relatives: Oh relatives! What cordial relatives! One sends guests to the other. It simply becomes a war. They fight one another over a relative. But today there's no more getting up at the crack of dawn, no more walking, no more going to relatives, and most important, no more war. Just look at what a car has been able to achieve! "We're really living in Messianic times"!

[Page 271]

Chaim Bruk, May The Lord Avenge His Blood!

From the book of records: "Out of the Ruins of Wars and Tumult",
edited by Moshe Shalit, Vilna 5691 (1931)

Translated from the Yiddish by Harvey Spitzer

Chaim Bruk

Born in Lubtch in 1893, Chaim Bruk studied in traditional elementary schools and yeshivot and received rabbinic ordination. In 1913 he pursued a general education and went to Frankfurt where he prepared for a degree as a high school administrator.

With the outbreak of the First World War, he was forced to leave Germany and returned to Russia where he became active in the committee for aiding war victims in Minsk. When the Germans captured the Lubtch area in 1915, he worked in the aid committee in Vaseliov.

In 1917, when the Lubtch residents returned to their war-devastated little town, he organized the aid committee in Lubtch and took charge of other social services such as the public bank, public school, etc.

In the years 1928-30, he served as elected chairman of the Lubtch community which included the towns of Lubtch, Karelitch, Delatitch, Negnievitch and was also one of the only Jewish representatives on the community council. He was likewise a delegate at the *Yekopo* conference and a member of the plenum.

[Pages 272-274]

The *Chevra Kaddisha* in Lubtch

by T. Shimshoni

Translated from the Hebrew by Ann Belinsky

Among the important institutions that Lubtch was blessed with, it is important to mention especially the *Chevra Kaddisha* [Burial Society]. Its distinguishing feature was that it was not party-orientated. The Jews of Lubtch were divided amongst themselves over many matters, such as appointing rabbis and ritual slaughterers, education, etc. This was expressed in arguments and stormy disputes in the synagogue or at various meetings. But in the *Chevra Kaddisha*, dissention was absent. Even people who were at odds with one another, forgot their squabbles, rows, spats, disagreements, fights and hostility when they came to deal with matters of the society group association. There was no restriction on joining the *Chevra Kaddisha*, and anyone could join it regardless of one's outlook. You only had to be ready, at any time, to deal with the affairs of the "Chevra", mainly to take care of the "*tahara*" [ritual cleansing] of the dead person, to recite psalms and to be involved with the actual burial of the deceased.

Once a year, the people who belonged to the *Chevra Kaddisha* came together for a general meeting where the *gabbays* [ducs collector] and the *gizbar* [treasurer] were elected. The *gabbays* chose among themselves the chief *gabbay*, who was the chairman of the *Chevra*.

Amongst those active in the *Chevra Kaddisha*, it is worthy to note my uncle, R' Tuvia Shimshilevitz, the chief *gabbay* for dozens of years, who was re-elected every year. Actually, he was the controller, without whose authorization, nothing was done. He knew all the residents of the town, remembered by heart when they were born, when they died and the place of their burial. Often the district authorities would turn to him in order to confirm a birth date or a burial date of a person (who, for some reason, was not listed in the district administration records), and they always accepted his word as final.

The treasurer of the *Chevra* was one of those chosen by the general assembly. His duty was to manage the accounts of the *Chevra*. Income and expenses were listed in his notebooks. The treasurer was not a certified accountant but was chosen as an honest Jew, clean handed and good in arithmetic, to whom everyone gave their trust. For many years the treasurer of the *Chevra* was my father-in- law, R' Itzil Der Shochet (the ritual slaughterer and meat examiner, Rabbi Yitzchak, son of Rabbi Feivel Aharonovsky), a person of majestic appearance, of honest ways, good-hearted and accepted by all.

The task of burying those who died in the town was imposed on the *Chevra Kaddisha*. The *gabbays* decided on the amount of money to be received from the family for the burial expenses of the deceased. The fees were progressive, not according to the value of the plot in the cemetery, but according to the property that the dead person had left to his heirs. No payment was requested from a poor family, but since the honor of a family was diminished if they had not paid for a burial plot, the family members tried to pay even a minimal sum so that people would not say that the dead person received a plot for free.

The *gabbays* evaluated the property that the deceased left to his heirs but took into account his personality and behavior during his lifetime. If he had taken part in the activities of the community and donated money to public causes, they settled on a reasonable sum for his burial expenses, allotted him a place in the cemetery, according to his worth, and the family accepted this without complaining. However, woe to the family of a man who had been a miser all his life, not involved in the community and had not donated anything towards its needs according to his ability to do so; for then the *gabbays* would firmly demand a high amount of money for his burial in order to somehow compensate the community for all the years that the deceased had been close-fisted while still alive. Naturally, the family would bargain so that the *Chevra Kaddisha* would lower its price, and the *gabbays* would enter into negotiations. However, it was difficult to argue, and the funeral would often be delayed-sometimes even for several days- until they reached an agreement on the amount to be paid for burial expenses. The *gabbays* stood very firmly on this principle. There were Jews in the town who were so anxious that when their time arrived to be gathered to their forefathers, the *gabbays* would "skin" their heirs, that they sometimes moved to another town when they felt that their time was close in order not to fall into the hands of the *gabbays* of their hometown!

The *Chevra Kaddisha* was a sort of independent institution, with permanent sources of income that never disappointed. They never lacked for funds.

The *gabbays* were mainly from the important landowners in the town and also held important positions in the life of the community in other institutions. They allotted funds from the income of the Burial Society to public needs such as financial support to the schools.

Once a year [7 *Adar*- the traditional *yahrzeit* of Moses], a festive dinner was held for all members of the *Chevra Kaddisha*. The meal was held in the house of one of the *gabbays* and for several weeks before it took place, the women began preparations. The participants came together with their children, who enjoyed the good things to eat, while the men ate and drank somewhat excessively, but did not lose the "image of God" even when drunk - their drunkenness was expressed in dance, song and a rise in spirit.

[Pages 274-276]

Remember!

by Yehoshua Shragai

Translated from the Hebrew by Ann Belinsky

Yehoshua Shragai

From my earliest childhood I was told about the pogroms that took place in the Jewish communities of Tzarist Russia, - the riots in Odessa, Bialystok, Kishinov, and other cities. The slogan in Russian was: "*Bay Dzhidov Spasai Rossiu*!" ("Hit the Jews and save Russia!"); the Jewish youth organized together for defense but did not have the strength to overcome the fierce stream of hatred of the rioters who were supported by the government.

We grew up in an atmosphere of hate and fear, and it is not surprising that we did not feel a friendly connection to the place of our birth. Tzarist Russia was not the homeland for us, and our only wish was to leave it. Although our civil rights were negated, we were obligated "with the great privilege" to serve in the Russian army, where Jewish soldiers were satiated with bitterness and torments.

It is no wonder that the young Jewish youth would deform their bodies, just so they would not be drafted into the army; but that didn't always help. I remember some of my peers who went to the army: Eliyakum Halperin, Reuven Moshkes - the *klezmer* [Jewish folk musicians and their music], who managed later to emigrate to America, my brother Shabtiel and Shabtiel's son Kavak.

When the First World War broke out, there was much worry and lamenting in the town as to the fate of the enlisted soldiers who were called to defend the Russian "homeland", under the flag of the Tzar "*Batoshka*", Nikolai. With twice as much vigor, fathers had recourse to the Jewish means - tested through generations - reciting psalms; mothers lay on the graves of the dead ("greeting graves"), pleading that the deceased would be advocates in Heaven for their dear ones in the army. They fasted every Monday and Thursday, prayed intently that God would have mercy on them and that the war would end. But nothing helped; the situation continued for a year and half, until the Germans conquered the town.

At *Succot*, on *Shmini Atzeret* [Eighth Day of Assembly], the Cossacks passed from house to house, poured kerosene and ignited them; the Russians made their retreat, as always, by the method of scorched earth. In a number of hours the whole town went up in flames. On the piles of ash, under the gloomy autumn skies, hundreds of families who had lost all their property, sat and lamented.

The Germans entered the town and ordered it to be evacuated, while making false promises, that "in a few days you will be able to return and rehabilitate and build your houses". We left the town, but as to returning, we were able to do so only at the end of the war, several years later. We became refugees (*biezhentzes*) and wandered from place to place. Whole families were wiped out by plagues, hunger and disease, and never returned to their homes.

We returned to the town at the end of a few years. With great toil, we built our houses, but we continued to suffer from anti-Semitic persecution. The Polish government placed a heavier yoke on us mercilessly, by imposing such heavy taxes, that bread was taken out of our mouths....

The desire to leave the town did not give us rest. Everyone who had the possibility emigrated to America, South Africa, Argentina and other places, and even to Eretz-Israel - as long there was free aliyah.

In 1924, a branch of *Hechalutz Haklali* [General Pioneers] was established. Part of the youth joined the movement because of the ideological thrust while other joined its ranks because of the chance that they would receive an entry permit (*certifikat*) to Eretz-Israel. We received four *certifikats* which we gave out to the members: Avraham Bruk, Yehoshua Faivoshovitch (Shragai), Moshe (Moshka) and Hadassah Solodocha; the last two returned over the years to the town and were murdered in the Holocaust.

Despite the many years that have passed, I cannot forget my town. I remember all my relatives and friends whom I left behind and will never see again, for the enemy cut them down, fountains of tears pour from my eyes and my heart is sad and bleeds.

I remember the *melamdim* [teachers] from whom I absorbed my Jewish consciousness and my childhood education. By the poor light of the kerosene lamp, they would teach and review with us until the late hours of the evening.; R' Yisrael Yeshayahu, R' Reuven, R' Yehoshua-Yaakov, R' Avraham and R' Yaakov; they succeeded in implanting in us love of the Jewish people and tradition, aroused our hearts to the divine-ethical mission of the Jewish people, thanks to which the Jewish people continues to exist.

I remember the joy and happiness on Sabbath and Festival nights; I loved to go to the synagogues, to see my Jewish brothers praying, pouring out their hearts in conversation with the Creator with happiness, reverence and intense devotion.

Although the town was not Chassidic, the prayers were rich in songs, happiness and devoutness.

I remember my taking leave, before going on aliyah, from the rabbi of the town - Rabbi Meir Abovitz, of blessed memory, a Jew with a majestic appearance, with a white beard flowing down his chest, dressed in a black coat and black hat with wide rims from under which peeped his eyes with a look full of good-heartedness and mercy.

I cannot forget my father, R' Zalman-Nachum, of blessed memory, and my mother Itka of blessed memory, or my brothers: Shabtiel, Moshe-Faivel, Zalman-Nachum amd Kalman and their children, may the Lord avenge their deaths!, - the family was slaughtered, till no remnant was left. In my heart I always nurtured hope that I would bring them to Eretz-Israel and would be worthy of having the gratification and happiness which a person attains when he is close to his dear ones.

Sadness envelopes my being...sorrow gnaws and squeezes my heart.... Tears choke my throat....

Can I forget them? Is one permitted at all to forget them? In letters of fire was inscribed the command "Remember"!!!

I will remember until my last day. I will remember and I will not forgive the enemies!!!

[Pages 277-279]

The Memory of My Town is Kept Safe in My Heart

by Chaya Solominsky

Translated from the Hebrew by Ann Belinsky

Chaya Solominsky

I went through difficult years during the Second World War. Years of hunger, hardship and bereavement of sons, but the memory of my town Lubtch is inscribed and carried in the depths of my heart.

Lubtch - a small town on the banks of the Neiman, peaceful and quiet. Most of the inhabitants were God-fearing Jews, who kept the tradition and religion scrupulously, mainly expressed on the Sabbaths and Holy Days.

Sabbath evening in the town: - the women are busy and active, cleaning and cooking, so as not to shame the Sabbath Queen, to receive her in time and with honor. The men - hurrying to finish their daily work and turning to the bathhouse for purification in honor of the Shabbat.

As evening came, the streets became deserted, in the houses there was an atmosphere of festivity and happiness; the white tablecloth was spread on the table and the candles were burning with a gay flame. Braided *challah* breads are waiting for the head of the household who will return from the synagogue and will bless them.

Rosh Hashana: - the inhabitants went to the synagogue to do their moral stocktaking, to be reconciled with their God in heaven, who will open the gates of His mercy and that the new year will be a blessed year.

Yom-HaKippurim: - the Jews of the town rose early to go to the synagogue, and with great devotion poured out their hearts in conversation before their Father in heaven. The children were equipped, earlier on, with parcels of food, but they finished their meals in secret and ran to the synagogue to stand by their parents during the prayers, to absorb something of the holy atmosphere.

Passover: - several weeks before the festival, the household members, mainly the women, would begin the preparations. It was a very thorough cleaning and scrubbing. The tables and chairs were taken out of the house and washed down with boiling water, the floor was scrubbed, and straw was spread out on the floor from fear that it might became defiled, God forbid, with leaven. For the children this was a great festival, there was much going on in the house, they would sleep on the straw and eat in a small corner of the kitchen, causing them endless pleasure that cannot be described in words. It seemed to us children that Passover was winking to us from the corners and promising us that it was not for nothing we were full of expectations. We waited for the Seder night with impatience, and to the "coming" of Elijah the Prophet with happiness mixed with anxiety. The festival was full of pleasantry: new clothes, delicious foods, games with nuts and a festive air, special in its own way. Even the renewal of nature, the warm sun, the chirping of birds, sprouting and blossoming, fragrance of the flowers, filled our hearts with much joy.

Most of the inhabitants were merchants, some of them owned shops in the marketplace, whilst others went out to trade in the villages in the countryside, bought mainly flax fibres and seeds and sold all sorts of fancy goods, soap and matches. On Tuesdays it was market day, when the farmers from all the environs brought their vegetable and animal produce.

On Sunday the Jews had to close their shops. There were shop-owners who looked for revenue, even on the day of rest which was forced upon them. What did they do? They stood next to the closed shop and if a customer came, they smuggled him inside, while one of the family members stood "on guard" outside; sometimes when a policeman passed by, they would lock the shop and imprison the people inside, until "the wrath passed".

There was much concern to educate the young generation and even the poor people scraped and saved in order to send their children to study. The heart's desire of the parents was that their children would attend the large *yeshivot* in the area, the Mir Yeshiva and the Volozhyn Yeshiva. There were youth who travelled to Vilna to attend colleges for teachers.

Active social life was carried on in the youth movements, in evenings of readings and in the drama society which mainly put on Jewish plays (I remember "The Jewish King Lear" and "The Orphan Chassia"). Many young people went to the training farm and from there made *aliyah* to Eretz Israel.

Mutual help and willingness to help others in their troubles were foundation stones of the Jewish community in Lubtch. The houses were open to receive guests, and all the poor people who arrived at the *Beit Midrash* were invited by the heads of the households to dine at their table.

When a poor family needed money, volunteers from the townspeople would go from door to door to request a donation for the needy family.

- -

Lubtch - my little town, in you there lived Jews according to a tradition going back generations, in you they fostered hopes for the future, in you they loved and were active, until the grim reaper fell on them and they were annihilated.

My Jewish town Lubtch is no more, it has disappeared for ever and has been deleted from our life.

Itche Jankelowitz from South Africa with former Lubtch residents in Israel

Left to right: Yosef Simchoni, Hemda Simchoni, Itche Jankelowitz, Yisrol Gershon Yankelevitch, ----, ----, Chaim Yankelevitch

[Caption provided by Moshe Yankelevitch]

[Pages 280-283]

The Gaon Rabbi Eliyahu-Chaim Meizel, Head of Court of Lodz and His Relationship to Lubtch

by Moshe Tzinovitch

Translated from the Hebrew by Ann Belinsky and Harvey Spitzer

The Gaon R' Eliyahu-Chaim Meizel was one of the most well known among the rabbis of Russia and Poland in the 19th century, second only after the great Gaon R' Yitzchak- Elchanan. He was one of the most prominent of all the religious and public leaders, and legends were woven around him, even in his own lifetime.

He was born in Horodok (Vilna District) in the year 5581 [1821] and was named after two Lithuanian Gaonim: Eliyahu, after the Gr'a from Vilna and Chaim, after the Gaon Rabbi Chaim, founder of the Volozhin Yeshiva, who died that same year. His father, R' Moshe was a well-to-do religious scholar, 7th generation in line from the saintly R' Yisrael Marozino (put to death as a martyr on Rosh Hashana 5420 [1659]). His mother was a daughter of the R' Eliezer Greiver from Slonim, author of *"Mishnat D' Rabbi Eliezer"*.

In the spring of his life he married a woman from Pinsk. The Gaon R' Yaakov Bruchin, head of the rabbinic court in Karlin, (author of *"Mishkanot Yaakov"*), was amazed at the wise young man and gave him rabbinic ordination to teach and judge, prophesizing a bright future for him as a light in the heavens of Judaism. The coupling with Pinsk did not work out well, and he divorced his wife and arrived in Lubtch, to his brother, R' Nahum Meizel, and there he married his brother's daughter.

He remained some time in Lubtch, frequenting the "tent of Torah" in the local *Beit Midrash*, together with a group of newlywed *yeshiva* students. On the advice of a relative, the scholar and benefactor, Shmuel Bakshter, he traveled to Volozhin to grow there in Torah knowledge. He managed to get to know the Gaon R' Yitzchak, head of the rabbinic court and of the rabbinic college; he was also an aide to the new head of the rabbinic college, the Gaon R' Eliezer Yitzchak Fried (who inherited the chair of the rabbinate from his father-in-law, the Gaon R' Yitzchak), and the deputy head of the college, Naftali-Tzvi-Yehuda Berlin (the *Netzi"v*): from that time on and for the rest of his life, his soul was bound in strong friendship with this great *yeshiva*.

R' Eliyahu-Chaim Meizel served for some time in the rabbinate in Horodok, his birthplace: his name went before him as a genius in Torah, virtuous qualities and charity, and as unique amongst the rabbis in that he was fluent in the Russian language. He was also accepted as rabbi and head of the rabbinic court in the town of Dertshin (Grodno District, 5613-5621[1853-1861]), and Prozshney (Grodno District, 5621-5627[1861-1867]). During the time of the cholera epidemic, he was prominent there with his devotion to the community. He founded the hospital for the whole area and thanks to his efforts, the epidemic was stopped and the number of fatalities reduced.

In the years 5627-5634 [1867-1874], he sat on the chair of the rabbinate in Lomzha, a district town in NE Poland, whose boundaries were set by the Congress of Vienna in 1815. Here he was liked by all circles of the community. He was also liked and accepted by the authorities, as he knew the language of the country and would appear before the district minister and other high-ranking officials. When he came to this city, he checked and found out that too many Jews were being enlisted in the army, as they did not have enough money to redeem themselves with 400 rubles (according to the laws of the time); so he founded a fund for the "redemption of captives", which helped those boys called up for army duty to free themselves from the "king's service".

From the year 5634 [1874] until the day he passed away in the year 5672 (1912), the Gaon R' Eliyahu-Chaim Meizel served as head of the court (religious and official) in the city of Lodz, the second largest city in Poland, then under Russian control. The area of his activity encompassed all aspects of religious life, the Torah and charity institutions as well as lobbying to the authorities in this large industrial city and its environs. He was active also in bettering the economic condition of the hordes of Jews who swarmed to this city in search of work. When the Jewish workers were supplanted by others from their jobs in the factories in Lodz, he made many efforts, with his personal influence on the Jewish industrialists, to act on behalf of the ousted Jews, and even opened a special factory to employ Jewish workers in the textile industry.

He was dedicated to the public with heart and soul: all matters of the large community were under his control. An orphanage, an old age home, a Jewish hospital, and *Talmud Torah* [Religious school] were all built on his initiative. Even his household belongings were mortgaged in order to help the needy. He helped thousands, and Jews from all over Poland flowed into Lodz to get his help. He helped many of those who were injured or suffered loss in the fire in Lubtch (in 1899) and transferred two thousand rubles that were collected from an internal fund-raising drive for their benefit. The authorities showed favor to him, even though he bothered them with his lobbying. His house was the meeting place for the emissaries of the Lithuanian *yeshivot* [rabbinic seminaries]. He himself acted as the honorary representative of the Volozhin Yeshiva, and every year he sent a sizeable donation to ensure its continuation. He worked with great energy right up to his nineties and participated in all matters pertaining to the Jews. He was called to many assemblies of rabbis and lobbyists in the capital city, Petersburg, and his words were used as a guiding line for all the participants at the assemblies where the best of people gathered - highly learned rabbis, lobbyists and public officials - from the whole of Russian Jewry.

He was on guard for the protection of religious life and didn't let into Lodz any changes in religion deriving from imitating non-Jewish customs.

Thanks to his hate of greed, his love for poor people, his many acts of charity and his devotion to his ideas, he was honored in all circles. He was holy in the eyes of the Chassidim of Lodz and even by the *Admor* rabbis of Poland and was beloved and admired by the Jewish masses, who saw him as a symbol of truth, honesty and righteousness. He was honored by the Lithuanian Gaonim, who saw him as one of them: they consulted the Gaon from Lodz, R' Eliyahu-Chaim, on any public issue or any matter relating to strengthening their beliefs. Everyone, in every circle, listened attentively to his words, and his name was great as well outside the borders of Poland and Russia.

When the Gaon R' Eliyahu-Chaim Meizel died, the Jewish masses mourned him as orphans. A general day of rest was announced in Lodz on the day of his funeral. Even Christian shops were closed during the hour of the funeral. The number of those attending the funeral numbered some 100,000. Following the coffin in the funeral procession were Chassidic *Admor* rabbis and well-known rabbis, among them the rabbis of Warsaw and townships from all the surrounding area.

The Jewish newspapers printed long articles of appreciation in remembrance of this wonderful man, emphasizing that by his death, Russian Jewry had lost its pilot and that all of Judaism had lost one of the best of its children, a scholar who was strong as iron in his ideas, but tenderhearted and merciful at the same time. Many eulogies were made in hundreds of Jewish townships with his passing.

There was much mourning in Lubtch. The elders of the community knew him from the period of his life in their town: here he was found and here he was their glory. All the Jews of the town, from the youngest to the oldest, entered the old *Beit Midrash* to hear the eulogies delivered by the local head of the rabbinic court, the Gaon R' Meir Abovitz and also the Gaon Raphael-Alter Shmuelovitz, head of the *yeshiva* in Novogrudek (born in Lubtch). In their speeches they described the background and the Torah-based atmosphere of Lubtch in the day of R' Eliyahu-Chaim Meizel, R' Shmuel Bakshter, R' Yehonaton-from Volin and other famous personalities whose cradle or place of spiritual growth was in the town of Lubtch.

On the 30th day following his death, a ceremony of bitter mourning was organized at the great *yeshiva* in the town of Mir, close to Lubtch, by the Gaon R' Eliyahu-Baruch Kamai, head of the court and of the academy. About half of the Jews of Lubtch came especially to Mir to participate in this great event.

Right to left: Beryl Jankelowitz, Tuvia Shimshoni, Dov Cohen, Avraham Bruk, Yaacov Zacharavitch, Chaim Yankelevitch

[Caption provided by Moshe Yankelevitch]

[Pages 284-288]

Between Two World Wars

by Avraham Bruk

Translated from the Hebrew by Ann Belinsky

Avraham Bruk

In the First World War, the Germans advanced at enormous speed; already in 1915 they arrived in the environs of Lubtch. In the bombarding, a number of people were killed or badly hurt and a large part of the town was destroyed and burnt. The Germany army ordered the inhabitants to retreat at least 14 kilometers from the town. A number of families, among them my family and the family of Leibovitch the photographer, survived in a village near Silev called Gordovka. The inhabitants of Lubtch who had relatives in more distant places moved there; all the property remained ownerless, as there was no transport to move it and the horses were taken by the army (the army was still not mechanized as it is today). The men, even of very young age, were recruited for forced labor, for digging and for war-connected building in the area. Slowly there was a growing lack of basic necessities, starting with bread, salt, sugar and finally even clothing.

In 1917, with the ceasefire, there was a possibility of returning to the town; various missions, which went to see the place, found it destroyed to the foundation, and only a very few houses were worthwhile repairing. The inhabitants, who had a strong desire to return to their hometown, and to their poor possessions, mainly the plot where their house had stood, began to return and tried to begin their lives anew.

One of the buildings which remained in good condition was the *Gmina* [Local Council] building, into which moved the first 18 families that arrived. The other building which was not destroyed was our house, a building of 2 stories and a basement made of bricks. In this building the institutions such as a school, synagogue and the beginnings of public offices were concentrated. Help started to come from leading Jewish institutions in the United States.

The life of the returnees slowly entered a routine. Conditions were difficult, but the people who had spent several years wandering with no permanent house, in the war years, under terrible conditions, tried to come to terms with the situation and to overcome their distress by work and toil. Most of the inhabitants worked in their previous occupation, they opened shops, leased fruit gardens and dairies to make cheese, tradesmen opened up workshops. There were tailors, shoemakers, butchers, blacksmiths, seamstresses, tinsmiths and even a number of horse-traders. Many traveled to the villages in the area (the villages were less destroyed, even those which were closer to the front were less damaged than Lubtch). They sold the villagers various wares and bought their produce, especially rags and linen. A number of inhabitants made a livelihood by making ropes.

Forced labor in 1916, during the German occupation

Trade in lumber had not yet developed, because the bridge on the Neiman had not yet been opened and the roads had been mined, all along the Front. Danger was lurking on every side in the area.

Help began to arrive to the inhabitants of Lubtch from *Yakapa* [Institution for Aiding Injured for the 1st World War] and the "Joint". As well, help began to arrive from relatives in America. The *Yakapa* took upon itself to care for war orphans, and built orphanages in the cities, to which orphans from the surrounding towns were also sent. The Jewish communities including Lubtch began to reorganize. Institutions such as "*Gmilut Hassidim-Casa*" - a fund for mutual help, were established, which gave interest-free loans for building, reconstruction and demolishing, for building workshops etc. Most of the money in the bank came with the help of *Yakapa*.

The number of Jewish inhabitants increased, until in 1922 there were more than a thousand Jews in the town. During the building period, the people of the town were mainly concerned with their livelihood, which we called "the psychology of bread and potatoes". But despite the difficulties of the period there were a group of young people, who began to be concerned with the cultural life of the place. The active people in this group were Shmuel Shapira and Chana-Chaya, who were gifted in dramatic talent. The activists in that period, in all areas of public life, were: my brother Chaim, Dov Kavak, Yitzchak Shlimovitch, Yitzchak Berkovitch, Chaim-Leib and Batya Levin, Avraham-Chaim Ostshinsky, Haya Naganivitsky, Yoel and Kusha

Shlimovitch, Moshe Shlimovitch, Yitzhak Solodocha, Cyril Meyerson, Dov and Gittel Viner, and others.

Until the First World War, there were only a small number of immigrants to Eretz-Israel from Lubtch. Amongst them were the Zalovensky and Shaklot families; most of the immigration, however, was to America. The Balfour Declaration changed the relationship of the Lubtch Jews to immigration [aliyah] to Eretz-Israel. A wave of national awakening passed over all the Jewish communities in Europe, and didn't miss our town. News reached us of the *HeChalutz* (pioneering) movement, which was mainly established in the large cities of Russia; in Poland branches of *HeChalutz* were also established in small towns. In Vilna the regional council of *HeChalutz* was organized, a branch was established in Lubtch and connections were made with the center in Warsaw and the Regional Council in Vilna. As well, political parties such as *Poeley-Tzion*, *Tz'irey-Tzion*, and *HaMizrachi* were organized. The Jewish National Fund and *Kapai* [Palestine Workers Fund] started raising money. The young people, who during the Bolshevik period had been enchanted by the Communist party, began to distance themselves from it in order to reorganize in Zionist movements.

As well, the older citizens of the town were also sympathetic to the national revival movement; in the synagogues during the Holy Days, money was donated to the Jewish National Fund and to the *Kapai*. We too, who were younger than the youth in the above movements, were involved. Our group consisted of: Nachum Shlimovitch, Yaakov Chaimovitch, Moshkeh Solodocha, Chaim-Gimpel Faivoshevitch, Shmuel-Yaakov Faivoshevitch, Yehoshua Faivoshevitch, Avraham Faivoshevitch, Reuven Leibovitch, Chaim-Shmuel Kasemivitch, Hadassah, Bilha Shimshilevitch, Leibah Levine, Shmuel-Leibel Faivoshevitch, my sister Rachel, myself, and a few other youth.

The assemblies and meetings of *HeChalutz* took place in the women's area of the synagogue. We received organizational help from the branch of *HeChalutz* in Novogrudek, mainly from Kartzinski, one of its members. From the branch of *HeChalutz* in Karelitz, we received help from another member, Moshe-Eli Shuster, who was a university student, and the main activist in his branch. From the regional council of Vilna we had a visit from the member Yosef Bankover, who lectured about the movement and guided us in our activities. We began to think about going to training camps, as a first step for emigrating to Eretz-Israel. Instead of sending the members to faraway training camps, we decided to take on the challenge and organize local training groups. We found a suitable place close to Lubtch, on an estate called *Potrei Brody*, near Nikoleiva, and worked there in the industrial lumber division.

We didn't succeed in running the organization by ourselves, so we joined up with the branches of Iviya and Karelitz; each branch sent a number of members and the "*kibbutz*" was set up. From Lubtch the following members were sent: Yaakov Savernik, Hadassah, Zeltka Faivoshevitch, Dov Cohen and myself.

During this time, we started organizing our emigration to Eretz-Israel; the *Merkaz* [Center] allocated a number of Certificates to us and other branches in the area. The first to emigrate from Lubtch were: My sister Rachel, Bilha Shimshilevitch, Moshkeh

Solodocha, and Hadassah. At the second stage, the following people emigrated: Yaakov Savernik, Yehoshua Faivoshevitch and myself. Until our emigration, we worked at various places and our income was put into the branch fund. The work was done skillfully, as if we had been workers all our lives.

In the meanwhile, life improved in the town. Commerce flourished, craftsmen saw reward in their hard work. From Eretz Israel, news about a crisis started to arrive; Moshkeh Solodocha and Hadassah returned to Lubtch, and with them, disappointment came to the town. The candidates who had registered for emigration, did not hurry to emigrate, and waited for quieter and better days. The branch in the town was weakened and its influence on the youth decreased, although not for long.

A group of members of *HeChalutz* working on a loading job.
The income was put into the branch fund.
Right to left: **Yoskeh Yedidovitch, the contractor, Reuven Leibovitch, Sander Shitzgal, Avraham Bruk, Yaakov Savernik, Yaakov Shmulevitch, Chaim-Shmuel Kasemivitch.**

When I was in Eretz-Israel at Kibbutz Ein Harod, new immigrants again began to arrive after the temporary halt, including Tuvia Shimshoni, Rivka and Eliezer Aharonovsky, Rivkah Sonenzon and others.

It is sad that so few succeeded in emigrating from our town. In the meanwhile, the young people, who had been educated in the spirit of love of the People and of Eretz-Israel, grew up, but were prevented from making *aliya* to their Land, because of the restrictions on immigration imposed by the Mandate Government. They went to their deaths together with all of European Jewry, which was so rich in spirit and activity.

[Pages 289-290]

A Chazan (Cantor) in the Town

by T. Shimshoni

Translated from the Hebrew by Ann Belinsky

Lubtch was a small town, totaling over 300 Jewish families. Although there were three synagogues, which were filled with worshipers on the Sabbaths and Holydays, and also during the week, there was always a *minyan* [quorum], but the inhabitants didn't manage to employ a permanent *chazan* [cantor]. So they made do with local prayer leaders from amongst the congregants, who would stand and pray before the ark, but not for a salary. These prayer leaders were gifted with a pleasing voice, and their prayer was pleasant. Prominent amongst these were: my uncle, R' Tuvia Shimshilevitch, R' Shmuel Leib, R' Leib Sokolovsky, R' Moshe Sonenzon and R' Yitzchak Baksht. Sometimes they would bring Meir Samocha, a prayer leader from a neighboring town, for a wage, only so that the prayers would be varied, and also to distinguish between weekdays and festivals.

From time to time, a wandering cantor would arrive at the town, generally a man who had to marry off his daughter and lacked money for her dowry. He would receive an unpaid holiday from his place of work and journey from town to town, stand and pray before the ark and organize concerts in the synagogues in order to save penny upon penny. A cantor like this would turn to the synagogue and speak to the *gabbays* [sextons], who would arrange a place for him to eat and sleep amongst the home owners.

For such a cantor there was no payment for praying; he would pray during the *Kabbalat Shabbat* [Welcoming the Sabbath] and *Mussaf* [additional Sabbath or festival prayer], and on Sundays he would go to each of the households, accompanied by one of the important members of the congregation. Each of the inhabitants would donate as he wished. The cantor knew he was dependent on the goodwill of the worshipers, so he would try to make a good impression and hope they liked him. And woe to the cantor whom they did not like! They would make his life miserable.

I remember a case that happened on Passover, when the visiting cantor prayed the *Mussaf* prayer, (for which there is a special tune for each Holy Day). For some reason, the worshipers didn't like his way of praying. A group of youths organized themselves and decided to "drive him crazy." How did they do this? Very simply. When the congregation joins in the singing with the cantor, the cantor has time to relax his efforts, as the congregation continues the tune that he has begun. The group of young people then started singing the melody of the High Holy Days [Rosh Hashana and Yom Kippur]. At first, the cantor didn't realize what was happening and continued praying, according to the tune that the youths had sung. When he realized what was going on, it was too late. In the back benches, they began to pound on the book stands. Tears started flowing from the eyes of the cantor, for as well as the shame they had caused, he was also probably going to lose any money he had hoped to earn. The group saw that they had gone too far and had crossed the line of bad taste, causing him shame and embarrassment. So the next day, in order to compensate him for the damage they had caused, two of the most important members of the congregation went with him from house to house. Everyone increased their donation and from his loss he made a profit.

[Pages 290-291]

Farewell to the Town

by Shmuel-Yaakov Kivelevitch

Translated from the Hebrew by Ann Belinsky

Shmuel-Yaakov Kivelevitch

Memories of the parting from my town and its inhabitants live in my heart in bright, light and refreshing colors.

I remember a hot day, towards the end of summer 1939, where I worked near Kopetchik, measuring the wood rafts on the Neiman. I worked with a group of youth from the town, including Avrameleh Soltz - handsome and friendly, Mottel Kaplinsky, Yoskeh Shaklot and the brothers Yaakov and Yoskeh Yedidovitch.

My sister Sarah (who joined the partisans during the Holocaust, and now resides in the USA), arrived at the place with good tidings: my immigration to Eretz-Israel had been approved. Seized by the fever of travel and with much happiness, I returned to the town. Preparations began and the moment of leave-taking arrived.

Leave-taking is a word with a sad and sorrowful connotation, but I was young and the tragic significance of that very parting was hidden from me. I didn't know then that I would never again see my loved ones. For me, my life was decreed to be a builder of Eretz-Israel, while for those who remained, the decree was destruction - by burning, shooting at the edge of the pits, hunger and sickness.

A gallery of images passes through my memory: my mother, concerned with preparations for the journey; my sister Rivka with her four children, my brother-in-law Alter Boldo. The carpenter Itchke (the midwife's son) and his children, amongst them my good friend Moshe, the sisters - Taubeh, Pashke and Gittel, the brothers Meir and Shlomo, Rachel (Notkes) with her husband, the butcher, and their children. My aunt Bashkeh with her husband Hashil, expert in the intricacies of the Torah, the pauper

Perchik, the village gossip, whose son Asher, was my friend in the *yeshiva*, our neighbor Yitzhak Kivelevitch with his wife Shayna and their children: Mina, Chana, Benyamin and Ben-Tzion (named after his grandfather R' Ben Zion the Blacksmith) and many other of my acquaintances, friends, and neighbors stand before me in procession. I cannot understand or believe that they are no more. A terrible feeling accompanies me to this very day, for I didn't say goodbye to my father, who was absent from the town precisely on that day, because of business - and thus I left without his blessing.

The parting was difficult, also from the town itself. Views from my birthplace where I grew up and absorbed within me. Every corner, all of a sudden, seems to be so dear to me. Here, also, the Neiman is entwined with my youthful experiences - hours of swimming at dawn and sailing in the evenings and, in the winter when the countryside was clothed in white, the river served as a wonderful place for us to toboggan and sleigh ride.

Here - the Hebrew *Tarbut* school, the spiritual centre for the youth, which was full of schoolchildren reviewing passages in Hebrew. Between its walls the pupils were taught to love Eretz-Israel and to love the Hebrew culture. The yearning for Eretz-Israel and the Redemption of the People of Israel was the wish of the teachers, youth leaders and pupils as one.

I move in the lively streets and lanes of my town: boisterous children and mothers scolding them. Troubled men hurrying to their daily work, the sound of life is carried from every direction...

I immigrated to Eretz-Israel to build my house there, but the memories of my town and its people accompany me all the years of my life.

[Page 292]

Yehoshua Levinson, Bible Scholar

by Moshe Tzinovitch

Translated from the Hebrew by Harvey Spitzer

Yehoshua Levinson, son of Elchanan HaLevi Levinson, a resident of Lubtch, was a Bible scholar. He possessed a comprehensive knowledge of the Talmud and its commentators and was an expert in Jewish studies. He published Biblical and scientific articles in Hebrew journals in the 1860s when he was already living in Grodno.

In one of his articles which appeared in "*HaLevanon*", vol. 12 (5627-8, 1867-8), he relates that he studied at the Volozhin Yeshiva in his youth. Next to this article devoted to certain new interpretations of the Torah, he also brings a report of the

passing of Rabbi Aharon-David, head of the rabbinical court in Lubtch, in the winter of 5627 (1867). In volume 22 of the aforementioned journal of the same year, he laments the passing of the well-known researcher, Rabbi Shlomo Yehuda Rappaport of Prague.

Several articles written by Yehoshua Levinson are also found in "*HaMelitz*" of the year 1867-8, in which he shows himself to be a great scholar familiar with the paths of Jewish studies and those of books of scholars of Jewish studies dealing with both Torah and science. He sometimes argues with Hebrew scholars and researchers, and one can see his supremacy and vast knowledge of Talmudic literature which he acquired in his youth in Volozhin and in the local study hall in Lubtch.

This great Torah scholar moved from Grodno to London, but nothing is known about the remainder of his life and his later writings.

[Pages 292-293]

Alter Yosselevitch

by Moshe Tzinovitch

Translated from the Hebrew by Harvey Spitzer

Alter Yosselevtich was born in Lubtch. His brother was the Gaon Rabbi Yosef Yosselevtich, head of the rabbinical court in Silov, Terestina, Samiatitch and Sobalki. Both brothers studied together at the start of their careers at the Mir Yeshiva near Lubtch. His brother was destined to be a leading rabbi in well-known communities. Alter became a scholar and a Zionist and saw his future as a Hebrew teacher and as a Zionist educator.

He was active as a teacher and educator in the town of Stoibtch, where he raised two generations of fathers and sons. Alter arrived in Stoibtch at the beginning of the 20th century and founded the first modern Hebrew school. One of his innovations was that pupils of every origin and social class were accepted in his school, for "Torah will come out from the children of the poor."

Several important chapters in the development of the Zionist movement and communal activity in Stoibtch are connected with the name of the teacher, Alter Yosselevitch. He established the first youth movement called *Bnot Tsion* [Daughters of Zion]. Thanks to his influence, the *Pirchei Tsion* and [socialist] *Poalei Tsion* organizations branched out, despite the fact that he himself was a general Zionist all his life. He was also the first communal worker of the *Keren Kayemet* [Jewish National Fund] and saw to the distribution of the blue and white boxes in every home and to the collection of monies for the redemption of the land in Eretz Yisrael.

He was active in his educational work with other teachers in creating a suitable atmosphere for the acceptance of the idea of the revival of the Jewish nation and the implementation of this idea through the efforts of pioneers.

After the First World War, a *Tarbut* Hebrew school was founded in Stoibtch in the year 5681 (1921) and Alter, the senior teacher, again worked as an administrator in this school.

Alter was the living spirit in all the Zionist activity in his city including the Jewish National Fund, *Keren HaYesod*, Channuka and Purim parties, memorial services for Dr. Theodore Herzl, special fund-raising drives for the benefit of Eretz Yisrael, cultural affairs and other activities. He had a great influence on all the youth movements in the city: *Freiheit, HaShomer HaTsa'ir, Hitachdut, Gordonia, HeChalutz, Wizo* and, of course, *HaNoar HaTsioni* of his movement. Thanks to his influence and activity, Stoibtch became an outstanding Zionist town. In the elections of the Zionist congresses, this town surpassed all the cities of the region, relatively speaking, in the sale of *shekels*. The term "Zionist", was for him Zionism "with all one's soul and might". It was constructive Zionism, love of Israel going beyond and rising above political factionalism.

He did not succeed in going on *aliya* to Eretz Yisrael, his ideal and vision; he perished in the Holocaust together with all the Jews of Stoibtch. The immigrants from Stoibtch who live in Eretz Yisrael memorialized the name of "Alter the Teacher" by setting up a library in his name in Tel Aviv.

From an article by D. Ben-Yerucham:
"The Exemplary Teacher" in the memorial book of Stoibtch and Sverzhna.

[Page 294]

A Panoramic Gem

by Meyerim (Meir) Kalmanovitch

Translated from the Hebrew by Allen Katz

The village of Lubtch was small and far away from the larger towns. Between it and the other towns there was no easy access, because the Neiman River and a thick forest surrounded it. Despite this, there were strong connections with the Gentile villages, especially on market days that were held on Tuesdays and Sundays, at the hour when the villagers came to pray at the Russian Orthodox church in the town. The market days provided an income for many Jews.

Since access to the town was difficult, as said, no industry developed there. People earned a livelihood with difficulty, and for the youth there was no indication of a future with expectations of change and progress.

A major turning-point came about when youth movements were established: *HeChalutz* [The Pioneers], *HaShomer HaTza'ir* [The Young Guard], *HeChalutz HaTza'ir* [The Young Pioneers], and *Beitar* [The Revisionists]. The vision of the Revival of the People of Israel had been ignited in the hearts of the young and, with all their might and in the flame of youth, they endeavored to realize the ideals that they were taught. The youth movements were instrumental as a place for recreation and for meeting in leisure time.

Next to the Neiman stood a castle, surrounded by gardens. Its presence added beauty and grandeur to the area. The small houses of the town's population, the green forests, the river with its strongly flowing waters, and the majestically elevated castle gave the place a legendary mystery and beauty. A very beautiful panoramic gem, asleep within itself.

[Page 295]

The President of the State of Israel, Mr Zalman Shazar,
blessing the initiative to publish the book on Lubtch and Delatitch
[On the left: Haim and Elka Yankelevitch – AB]

[Page 295]

The History of the Town
(From the Encyclopedia Judaica)

From the "Encylopedia Judaica" Volume 10, in German, (1934) published by "Eshkol" and edited by Dr Yaacov Klatchkin and Dr Nahum Goldman

Translated from the Hebrew by Ann Belinsky

Lubtch: Novogrudek District (Veebodstabo during the days of Polish rule - 1921-1939). The first time names of Jews are mentioned is in the second quarter of the 17th century in the Committee of the State of Lithuania. This community was autonomic in matters of tax paying and not dependent on any of the cities in the aforementioned state.

In the year 1720 (5480) the tax per head amounted to 300 pieces of gold and in the year 1761 (5521), it amounted to 450 pieces of gold. In the year 1705 (5465) 369 Jews in Lubtch and the environs paid poll tax. In the year 1847, 973 Jews lived there. In 1897 - there were 2,463 Jews (73% of all the town's inhabitants). In 1921 - 496 Jews, 52% of all the town's inhabitants. The decrease in the number came about following the First World War, when Lubtch was a town on the war front from 1915-1918. Jews of the town fled and moved to other places, especially to nearby Novogrudek, and many of the refugees did not return to Lubtch.

[Page 296]

My Town
(Unrhymed Translation)

by Chaim Yankelevitch

Translated from the Hebrew by Ann Belinsky and Harvey Spitzer

I will try and arouse forgotten memories
About my town
Where I spent my youth.

Lubtch - a small town
Dipped in green, trees and light;
A strong-flowing river passes you,
Your markets are full of hustle and bustle.

You had public institutions - for the enjoyment of all,
For aid to the needy and the bestowal of loving- kindness.
Various societies for studying Talmud, for reciting psalms,
For Shabbat, Festivals and the Holy Days.

Theatre, bank and firemen
And a Jewish commander at the head of the brigade.
Keren Kayemet - headed by our teacher Persky of blessed memory,
Who volunteered himself for the good of all.

Disputes between Jews
And wars between Jews and Gentiles,

For acquittal openly and publicly
In the trial of a "Jewish civic head".

And when the beloved *chazan* was boycotted - the Rabbi was angry,
The argument rose, arrogant words were heard,
A second rabbi was about to be brought - the rabbi's wife Soshka cried out:
"What about my livelihood from all the taxes?!"

In the theatre - Shmuel Shapira produces
"*The Pintaleh Yid*" - and a condition,
That it will not be shown until his request is met
That they bring Tzeitlin and his orchestra.

In the *cheder* we studied and gained knowledge
There we absorbed holy values
Love of Zion and a longing for redemption,
Thanks to the *cheder* many raised the banner of Zion.

R' Avraham and Eliezer-Yankel - may their memory be blessed
Strove hard to instill the Torah
R' Reuvka, R' Layzer-Eli and R' Leib
Worked with all their hearts on our education.

In our town was established by order of the "*Saltis*" and the State
An institution where we received knowledge and wisdom,
This was the "*Tarbut*" - our school
Which became our pride and glory.

Three Synagogues towered proudly
Which the people come to with reverence.
Where there were sextons [gabbays] and notables of the congregation
Who wholeheartedly took care of the needs of all.

There were many Youth Movements in our town,
"*Poeley Tzion*" "*Beitar*" "*Hechalutz*" and "*Hashomer Hatza'ir*";
Where the youth spent much time and wove dreams
About making *aliyah* and the pleasant Land of their Forefathers.

*

I will mention Yankel-Chaim the Blacksmith
In my heart I remember Shizgal the Tinsmith,
And Itzche "the midwife's" son, my craft teacher

And Itzchele Baksht, My *Gemorah* teacher.

And Gershon - Sarah-Chana's son
And Chaim-David - Sara Feyga's son
And R' Tuvia, the prayer leader for *Mussaf*
And members of the burial society.

And Mordechai Sheykas, member of *Hashomer HaTza'ir*,
And Moshe Persky, the "intelligent one" of the town,
And Hershel "The Maid", the sinless "*shamesh*".
Who could easily recite Psalms by heart;

R' Layzer the bootmaker,
Herschel Zalikovsky, the carpenter,
Shmuel Leib, the prayer leader
and Eli-Avrameleh Shapira, the *Megillah* reader…

It is hard to believe that our dear ones were murdered,
Led as sheep to the slaughter,
It seems as if this is a terrible nightmare
But this is the awful reality which cannot be changed…

We will hold their memories in our hearts forever !!!

***

In our little house in the town
Every Shabbat and Festival evening - there was much rejoicing,
Father would bless the Kiddush wine,
Mother would bless the candles.

There was much delight when a guest came
Mother was happy even though she worked hard,
Receiving the Sabbath Queen, with the Angels of the Exalted One
And sweet table hymns like "Creator of the World" were sung.

All present recited Grace after Meals
And finished with "May it be His Will…"
Grandfather was busy studying "Ethics of Fathers"
And Grandmother prayed "To The Great God".

The women look at their special Yiddish prayer book in awe
And all carry a heartfelt prayer

To the God of Abraham, Isaac and Jacob
That the troubles will cease and the Exile will come to an end.

[Pages 299-300]

(Poem)
(Unrhymed Translation)

by Ayala Amitai (Faivoshevitch)

Translated from the Hebrew by Ann Belinsky

Ayala Amitai (Faivoshevitch)

Lubtch my small and beautiful town
I will remember you with sadness and gloom
Forever I will carry memories of you in my heart
I see my father and mother in front of my eyes;

Honest and innocent and God-fearing
At peace with their Creator and with people;
I see the yards of our little houses,
Where we played hide and seek.

I remember the Neiman - the river
And the murmur of its waters flowing majestically;
Within its waves, during the hot summer days,
We would swim and play mischievously.

Days passed and become years,
We grew up and became adults,
We studied and we established youth movements
Where we were active and wove dreams.

Amongst the rows of *Hashomer Hatza'ir* many united;
We read "*Das Kapital*", we were proud of the poor people,
We debated day and night
About equality, with the fire of youth.

We fought for fair work conditions
And we succeeded and triumphed over the employers;
We drew up plans of aliyah and self-realization
To Eretz-Israel - the Chosen Land.

In front of my eyes I see the last days
Before I left my town, forever;
I will remember the faces of my friends and family,
When they made their farewells from me forever.

I remember the dear ones whose hearts never guessed,
That they would be prey to the foe and the oppressor,
I remember my town and all the past
That was burnt and ground to dust and ashes;

I cry, for my unfortunate dear ones never had the privilege
To see the establishment of the Land of the Jews,

About which so many generations dreamed,
On the ways of Exile, on the paths of sufferings.

*

Lubtch my town - how you stood aside!
Why did you not defend your Jews?
You saw how old men and women were led,
For no guilt of their own, to the crematoria.

Even though my town was destroyed,
Ruined, burnt and exterminated.
(May your blood be infinitely avenged!)
We swore that we will never forget you!!!

[Pages 301-302]

Memories

by Yona Degani

Translated from the Hebrew by Ann Belinsky

The first years of my life are entwined with depressing events: The First World War was in full force, its front arrived at our town, inhabitants of the town were exiled to other places. We went through three difficult years, suffering hardships and hunger. People's bodies were crushed under the burden of work, but there was still no livelihood.

My father served in the Russian army and fought against the Germans; my mother, on whom our livelihood was dependent, toiled from morning to night and I was left with my grandmother.

I remember the visits to my grandmother's sister. She was a pale woman who lay in bed alone in her house because all her sons were fighting at the front, and her daughters had gone out to work. My grandmother, therefore, was the person who cared for her during her sickness, until one day, when I arrived with my grandmother at the aunt's house, she was no longer among the living.

My grandfather, on my father's side, often came to our house and each time my mother would give him bread and potatoes. There was no other food in our house at that time. One day they were conferring secretly in our house. I was dressed hurriedly and indifferently - our grandfather, too, was taken from us, and an atmosphere of sadness and depression dominated our family.

We returned to the town. The street where we had lived before our expulsion was completely destroyed, except for my uncle's house, but he himself had died in exile and didn't live to see the day of return. When we stood over the ruins of our house, my mother tried to explain to me that the heap of ashes was once a dwelling where our family had lived.

Four families were crowded together in my uncle's house, among them the Leibovitch family. I heard much about their son Alter. I was told many times, maybe seriously, maybe as a joke, that he was destined to be my bridegroom. With our return from the expulsion, we got to know each other. The "groom" and the "bride" ran around the neighborhood all day, jumping in the potholes and pits that had been caused by the falling of bombs. Spring, with it masses of flowers and fragrances, had begun, and we felt ourselves - four-year old children - extremely happy.

My mother harnessed herself to the yoke of earning a livelihood, and I again was left with my aunt at home. Sometimes my mother would bring me to our family who lived in Delatitch, in an area completely surrounded by gentiles.

Once, on New Year's Eve, the gentiles appeared in their traditional costumes, entered the rooms of the house, checked out every corner, while shouting and yelling, and then left. My grandmother locked and bolted the doors of the house, the windows and the shutters, feeling that something might happen during the night.

At midnight, we were awoken by strong knocks on the door, with loud shouts to open up. My grandmother began to call the names of her sons -who were not at home that night - "Itche! Chaim! David! Moshe! Get up!", she shouted. After knocking and shouting for a long time, the gentiles, whose aim had been to loot Jewish property, left.

One evening, my mother woke me up from my sleep and with great emotion told me that my father had returned from the war. Father?!! I had not known my father since my birth; he was further to me than a dream. I entered the room where many of the townspeople had crowded together. I knew them all except for one man; precisely this man, unrecognizable and unknown, stretches our his arms towards me and his face lights up - this is Father, the idea flashes through my mind, and immediately I am in his embracing arms, which hug me with tenderness and love. Until the light of the morning, my father did not stop telling our neighbors about what he had gone through in the war.

[Pages 302-303]

My Sister Itka, of Blessed Memory

by Elka Levanon

Translated from the Hebrew by Ann Belinsky

1929: Days of the riots in Eretz Israel, the land was still recovering from the crisis of the Fourth Aliyah, news was received about a lack of work, about many who wanted to leave Eretz Israel, there were also those who left and spread seeds of despair and disappointment.

But after some time, the awakening towards the Fifth Aliya began. From our town of Lubtch a few made *aliya*; among them was my sister Itka Shmulevitch, a young healthy girl, who knew how to work and with all her heart she adhered to the pioneering ideals. While still a young girl, she was amongst those who started up the branch of *HeChalutz Hatzair* in Novogrudek, whose members went to *Hachshara* [training farm] on *Kibbutz "Tel Hai"*, in the environs of Vilna. Itka was one of the strong and industrious workers on the *Hachshara*; when she returned home - she began to prepare for *aliyah* to Eretz Israel.

Time pressed and she did not have money for her travel expenses. But Itka succeeded in attaining her desire with the help of various people; mainly members of *HeChalutz Hatzair* in Novogrudek helped her.

She made *aliyah* to Eretz Israel during the days of the 1929 riots there. When she got off the boat at the Jaffa Port, there was a curfew in the city. Together with a group of other young immigrant girls, she was transferred in an armored police vehicle to the workers farmstead in Petach Tikva, where she spent the first two years of her life in Eretz Israel. Also here she excelled as a diligent worker.

Itka started a family in Tel Aviv. But fate was cruel to her and at a young age she became sick with a malignant disease. After several years of suffering, she died in 1953, aged only forty-two.

May she rest in peace

[Pages 303-304]

To the Memory of My Family
by Chaya Slominsky

Translated from the Hebrew by Ann Belinsky

My grandfather, Faybeh Aharonovsky, "*Der Shochet*" [the slaughterer], son of a family of slaughterers, was an honest and modest man; his time was divided between involvement with the Torah, and slaughtering - for his livelihood. He would rise at dawn to do the work of the Creator, and to the light of kerosene lamps, he would sit and learn Torah. After he returned from the synagogue, from his prayers in the first minyan he would go out to his work, but not before he passed by the beds of his grandchildren, covered them with love and softness and put a slice of cake and a sugar cube next to every bed.

My grandmother, Mina Henia, was a modest housekeeper, as well as being a midwife with no salary. She would come to the houses of the birthing mothers and brought them pots of chicken soup, she looked after the babies and washed the nappies, all for the sake of doing a *mitzvah* [good deed].

Their house - a spacious stone house, was surrounded by a park, and stood not far from the *Beit Midrash* and the market square. In the cowshed was a cow that provided milk for the family. In the courtyard stood a small slaughterhouse where my grandfather worked. My grandparents had three children - two daughters and a son - my father Yitzchak.

My father followed his forefathers, and was both a slaughterer and a *mohel* [circumcisor]. But his livelihood was only from slaughtering. His activities as a *mohel* were for the sake of a *mitzvah*. He would also go around to the settlements in the area to perform a circumcision. He brought wine to the poor people, and always left some sum of money for the needs of the new baby that had been added to the family.

My father had five children, four daughters and a son - Eliezer. My brother excelled in his studies and was sent to learn in the Mir and Radon Yeshivot. In the heart of my father beat the hope that his son would receive ordination from the Rabbinic authorities. But the winds of *haskalah* [enlightenment] also influenced Eliezer. He did not want to go in the way of his forefathers, but headed for Vilna. He passed the matriculation exams and studied law at the University. After he made *aliyah* to Eretz Israel, he continued his studies and was certified as a lawyer. Eliezer died at an early age in 1964.

I was the oldest daughter. I got married in Vilna to a lumber merchant and we had three sons. In the 2nd World War we were in a Nazi concentration camp. After many sorrows, during which we lost two sons, we were liberated in 1945. In 1950 we arrived in the United States. My sisters Mina and Mirka were murdered in the Holocaust.

From my wide-branching family only a few remained after the Holocaust. The heart refuses to believe the tragedy that struck us, but reality is very cruel. Life continues nevertheless, we continue to strive and hope, but the memory of our murdered ones is forever carried in our hearts.

[Pages 304-305]

My Father, Avraham-Aharon, of Blessed Memory

by Eliyahu Berkovitch

Translated from the Yiddish by Harvey Spitzer

My father, Avraham-Aharon Berkovitch, of blessed memory, was totally involved in community affairs all his life. He used to travel to Minsk and bring back glass lamps for the study hall in the synagogue. He would also worry about getting wood for the bathhouse and for heating the study hall in the winter. On the holidays, he was the permanent prayer leader at the altar.

When a dispute broke out in 1913 between the town's Jews and the gentiles, who had seized possession of the Jews' pasture lands, and there was a real possibility of bloodshed, my father, who was very ill, came to me in Vilna and asked me to find a good lawyer to defend Jewish rights of ownership of the pasture lands near the Neiman River.

After receiving a decision from the Vilna district court in favor of the Jews, my father brought the court representative to Lubtch and he carried out the decision, returning the pasture lands to the ownership of the Jews. The rejoicing was unimaginable; it was simply a holiday, another Purim. People drank fiery brandy and ate honey cake and wished that they would live to see our enemies suffer more defeats. It must be known, that nearly every Jewish family in Lubtch had a cow, which was an important part of their livelihood.

When Lubtch was destroyed in the First World War, my father moved to Novogrudek, but he was always drawn back to his beloved hometown. He built a new house and moved back to Lubtch.

My father passed away in 1925 and went straight to heaven. A year later, my mother, Sarah, also died. May she rest in peace!

[Pages 306-307]

Memories from My Father's House

by Aryeh Sivitzky

Translated from the Hebrew by Ann Belinsky

Aryeh Sivitzky

The family of my father, Chaim-Tzvi, had lived in Lubtch for several generations. Our family was rooted there, but during the First World War, we left our house and the town. Since my mother's family was in Lipnishuk, they went there for several years. We saw ourselves as refugees and were happy to return to Lubtch at the first possible opportunity.

Since our house had been destroyed during the battles, we found a temporary dwelling until we built a new large comfortable house. There my sister Miriam and my brother Yitzhak were born.

Despite the fact that my parents had a shop in the market, their financial situation was not easy, as they had heavy debts and many worries. My father was forced to travel with a horse and cart to buy merchandise in Lida and in Novogrudek, which took a lot of time, and he would return from these journeys tired and exhausted.

In the township, the financial situation improved, especially due to the trade in logs, which were plentiful in the surroundings. With the economic developments, social life became more alive, and public buildings and the Hebrew school "*Tarbut*" was established. The Zionist youth movements became organized, and from these we absorbed the love for Eretz-Yisrael and the faith in the Resurrection of the People of Israel [*Tekumat Am-Yisrael*].

In 1935, a fire broke out in Lubtch and many houses were burnt down, including my parents' house. At this time I was on *Hachsharah* [Training Farm] at *Kibbutz "Shechariya"* in Baronovitch. When I heard of the catastrophe, I immediately returned to Lubtch.

The sight of the town was depressing, as most of the houses were smoking embers. When I arrived, the family sat as if in mourning by the remnants of the house, next to the possessions that they had managed to save from the flames.

In our house there was a concrete cellar and it had not been damaged; we put the possessions and the merchandise that remained into the cellar, and there, by the light of kerosene lamps, my father continued with his trade. Luckily the house was insured, and from the insurance money received, my father built a new house, and even had enough money to increase the amount of merchandise. When our economic situation improved, I returned to the *Hachsharah* at Baronovitch, and made *aliyah* to Israel before the war broke out.

During the 2nd World War, when Lubtch was conquered by the Soviet army, my father and my brother worked as simple laborers and my sister worked as a clerk. During this stage there was a close exchange of many letters between me and my family.

During the German occupation, my family was imprisoned at Vorobievitch, and there they were burnt alive by the Nazis and their helpers, inside a grain barn together with all the Jews of Lubtch that were at this camp.

I have remained only with my memories, alone and in pain by the bitter fate of my dear family and the Jews of my town Lubtch.

[Pages 307-308]

Only Letters Remain...

by Haim Sonenzon

Translated from the Hebrew by Ann Belinsky

My mother Taibeh, was a daughter of the Maslovety family - a well known Lubtch family. My father, Moshe, was born in the town of Karelitch. After their wedding, they built their home in Lubtch.

In 1915, after the expulsion during the First World War, we arrived in Ayshishuk where my uncle Shaul Sonenzon, a well-off and established Jew, lived with his large family. In Ayshishuk we grew up and were educated. My grandmother Dvorah also lived with us.

In the summer of 1925 we returned to Lubtch. My father was a tradesman. He was a diligent and sensible man; he was one of the Torah readers and used to stand in front of the Ark, especially during the Ten Days of Penitence and the Holy Days. He was well versed in "the small letters", in the Jewish customs and in the *Shulchan Aruch* and the Bible. He was also very well versed in Hebrew. Because he was busy making a livelihood, he did not learn *Mishna* and *Talmud*.

My mother knew how to run the household and her life calmly, patiently and with forbearance, without anger or irritability. She took good care of us and we were attached to her and loved her very much.

My brother, Shalom, finished his studies at the Teachers Seminary "Tscherno" in Vilna, in 1925. He taught at the *Tarbut* School in Lubtch. During that period he was very active in the social life, organizing shows at the school on Channuka and Purim; he ran the school choir; for a short time he was head of the *Hashomer HaTza'ir* movement; he was active in the Jewish National Fund and in the League for *Eretz Yisrael Haovedet* [Workers in Eretz Israel]. He was a talented influential speaker.

My sister, Shlomit, studied at the *Tarbut* seminar in Vilna; she made a living there giving private lessons and was helped by the food parcels which were sent from home.

My sister Golda, married Alter Shmuelevitch and they had a son. She was active with many pursuits, she helped her family with much devotion

I left Lubtch in 1934. From my father's letters, which were written in Hebrew, I knew about what was happening there. To this day I have kept those wonderful letters, from which arise the dear images of my family and the Jews of the town, with their hopes and desires.

My dear family is no more. Only the letters remain, written by a loving father, brother and sister, a memory of a Jewish family in my birthplace, the town of Lubtch.

[Pages 308-309]

My Grandmother Chaya

by Puah Nashkes

Translated from the Hebrew by Ann Belinsky

Memories of my childhood are enmeshed and embroidered with adventures connected to my father, mother, brothers and sisters; the Jewish mother, "*Di Yiddishe Mama*", became a symbol of love, good heartedness and boundless self-sacrifice for her children.

From all the experiences of my childhood, many longings and pleasant memories are connected to my grandmother, Chaya, may her memory be blessed! In my heart is engraved the fondness to my grandmother, despite the many years that have passed since then, years of youthful dreams and hopes, years of the struggle to make aliya and settle in Eretz-Yisrael, wars, troubles, hard work and toil; but the image of my grandmother lives in my heart and lights my way to this day.

She was a likeable woman, God-fearing, at peace with God and with man, always trying to make the most of every situation, wisely, with charm and cleverness, with a good-hearted smile on her face. She never knew what tiredness was, and helped my mother who always had small children to look after.

She was a simple woman "from the old generation" who certainly had never read psychology books or those with the latest methods, but despite this, her attitude to a child was full of understanding. With her good-heartedness and well-developed intuition, she knew how to educate and to amuse her small grandchildren, to look after them with endless devotion and love. And we, her grandchildren, returned her love. We were very bound to her.

She had much personal charm. She related with honor to her fellow man, tried to help people with troubles, more than once she brought comfort to a troubled soul, with a good word - thanks to her wisdom of life.

My grandmother is a symbol to me. I try to go in her ways in my relationships to my children. And my wish is that they too will one day understand that the dynasty of generations is intertwined, generation after generation and must not be cut off, because we too, today, are deriving spiritual strength from generations of Jewish mothers and grandmothers.

[Pages 309-311]

My Rebbe, Rabbi Chaim

by Yitzchak Shlimovitch

Translated from the Yiddish by Harvey Spitzer

I was probably seven or eight years old when I was placed in Rabbi Chaim Avraham'che's *cheder*. He was the best Bible and *Talmud* teacher.

As a Jew, Rabbi Chaim was an exception on account of his height and unusual heaviness. He was highly respected in the town for his piety and good teaching ability. In addition, he read the Torah very well, better than anyone in the town.

He was a very strict teacher. He would hit the pupils if they made the slightest mistake in reciting a verse from the Bible or a passage in the *Talmud*. The children were deathly afraid of him and would beg their fathers to send them to a different *cheder* the following term. The pupils would come to school every day with a heavy heart. A day seldom went by when a few children did not cry from the rabbi's slaps.

It was a little easier for us in the hot summer months. Due to his excessive weight, Rabbi Chaim suffered greatly from the heat. He would then send the pupils to clean out the hall and we would set up the classroom there. The change had an evident effect for the good on his mood and he was, in fact, less strict. As a matter of fact, he would often dismiss us early so that we could go bathing in the Neiman. He himself also liked to swim in the river, but he did so later before it got dark and a little further from everyone where no one bathes, evidently on account of the fact that he was ashamed of his heavy weight. It was said that he was a very good swimmer.

Once, on a summer evening when it was already beginning to get dark, he went out for a swim. This time he was late in coming home. His family was getting nervous. His son, Shlomo, went out to look for him in the study halls of the synagogues, but no one had seen him. There was a commotion in the town. Young and old ran to the river.

People lit lanterns and began looking for Rabbi Chaim at the river's edge and also in the water. Late that night, they found him by the river in his underwear, holding a sock. The doctor who was called to the scene could do nothing more than certify his death, which came about from his being overweight.

Although we no longer had to be afraid of the rabbi's slaps, and besides we were free from going to school for over a month until the new term, his death made a very strong impression on us. We recited psalms with great devotion over his dead body, until the burial, and we spoke about him with great respect.

[Pages 311-312]

Tuvya the Sexton

by Nachum Shulman (Shlimovitch)

Translated from the Yiddish by Harvey Spitzer

I remember Tuvia the Sexton [shamesh] a lot better than I do the other Jews in the town. Tuvia was my father's partner in building the synagogue and was often a guest in our house. Every Saturday night, he would come over to make an account and record in a book the amount of money pledged when one is called up for the reading of the Torah. I also know that at that time he no longer needed to serve as the sexton to make a living. The name sexton remained with him from earlier times because he was a sexton before the First World War.

He was also called "the blind man". It was told that on the Fast of the 9th of *Av*, some children - rascals - threw pinecones at him and hit him in the eye, causing the loss of sight in one eye. How much truth there is to that story, I really don't know.

Thanks to the support of his children in America, he began to deal in flax and made a nice living.

Nevertheless, his sole purpose in life was to pray at the altar. He was, in fact, a very good prayer leader for the additional service on the Sabbath and holidays, and to this very day his rendition of "And rebuke the Accuser lest he accuse me" still rings in my ears.

Tuvia paid additional taxes for the re-building of the synagogue after the First World War.

May his name be remembered for good!

[Page 312]

My Grandmother Rivka

by Chemda Simchoni (Movshovitz)

Translated from the Hebrew by Shirley Horwitz

The elders of the town knew my grandmother Rivka as an active woman, tall and erect. But while giving birth to her fourth child*, she became paralyzed and lay immobile for many years, unable to move, until a miracle occurred. At the wedding of her eldest daughter Raizel, she got off the bed and began to walk! Thus, although very bent over, she was able to lead her daughter to the *chuppa* [wedding canopy], on her own two feet. She then made a vow that her life would be devoted to helping the needy.

My grandmother knew all the needy of the town. She would go to homes of the well-to-do and gather penny by penny. At dawn, she would lay food, clothing or firewood at the door of the poor according to their needs. She would leave stealthily in order not to embarrass them.

The townspeople held her in esteem and thanked her for her deeds. She knew how to convince small and big to donate and gave the donor the feeling that he or she had done a good deed. I remember that she convinced me to give charity with the explanation that for every exam I did well in, I had to donate a *zloty*. And that the more I would give, I would get better marks. So when my grandmother asked for a donation, people would respond. Even Gittel, the owner of the hotel who had rich guests and would not allow others to bother them, would herself tell my grandmother when a rich guest was coming in order to get a few *zlotys* from him.

An old woman, bent and weak who, with the willpower and the desire to help the needy, planted in our hearts the idea of mutual help.

* [Pasha Malka Lewin, who later migrated to South Africa - S.H.]

[Pages 313-316]

My Father Eliezer, of Blessed Memory

by Danny Aharonovsky

Translated from the Hebrew by Ann Belinsky

The family of the ritual slaughterer and the ritual circumciser, Yitzchak HaCohen Aharonovsky, was one of the well-known established families in Lubtch: even in the days of pogroms and war, they did not leave the town. Only during the German occupation, in the First World War, were they forced to move, but returned to the town at the first opportunity.

Yitzchak, slaughterer and examiner, had four daughters: Chaya, Mina, Rivka and Mirka, and one son - Eliezer Layzer.

The only son is a sign of a strange coincidence in the family. In every generation, several daughters were born, but an heir - a son who would continue the family's name - only one. (Yitzchak also was the only son of his father, Reb Faivel, who lived more than 100 years, and had many daughters. Faivel, too, was a single son to his father, R' Eliezer). It is not surprising, therefore, that after two daughters were born Yitzchak very anxiously awaited an heir. When he was born - the house was filled with light and happiness, and Yitzchak knew that when the day came for him to be gathered to his forefathers, there would be someone to say *Kaddish* at his grave and that the family name would not disappear. The newborn was called Eliezer Layzer after the name of the grandfather, and from childhood, his father destined him to be a rabbi. The child was very spoilt, but already in his childhood, he was good-hearted, sharing his presents with his sisters.

The atmosphere in the house was suitable for his destination; the house was large and spacious, the door was always open to anyone and many came there happily. In the house, the traditions and the religious commandments were kept, but there was no fossilized orthodoxy, rather a deep belief in G-d, good heartedness, humanity and love for others.

In the small town, the way of life was simple - a person was close to nature, honest life and thoughts, his heart close to G-d. The Jews were hard-working and honest, full of joy, slightly innocent, many of the worldly innovations arrived with much delay.

The young Layzer - a real country bumpkin - is strong and powerful, broad-shouldered, unafraid of the river, swimming from shore to shore, even in places where the riverbed is wide and deep. He runs in the forest, which is cushioned with green pine needles, fills his mouth with *yagdas* (wild berries), and rolls in the flower-covered meadows. His loving father gives him a horse as a present, and he gallops on it with unmistakable pride. His face is sunburnt, his hair short. In his strength and mischievousness, he looks like the child of a gentile, Heaven forbid!

During the winter, when the country is chilly and large snowflakes fall, dressing the earth with a white, shining robe, when it bows to the Lord of the Winter, the house is warm. There is a smell of tasty cooking, but the child Layzer is not to be found: he is busy outside with his friends -throwing snowballs at each other, flying like the wind on their skates on the frozen Neiman, tumbling, getting banged, yelling as youth do, and continuing on their way.

Children playing - they are splinters of the Creator's laughter; they are similar in their clear laughter and identical in all nations, but for the Jewish child in exile, there was also a mission - to keep the embers of faith and heritage of the generations burning.

At the age of five, Layzer started attending the *cheder* [religious elementary school] and at fourteen he was sent to the Mir Yeshiva, and after that, to the Radon Yeshiva. Despite the difficulty his father had in being separated from his son, on whose soul he took pity, he did not hesitate to do so, as his hope was so strong to see him ordained as a rabbi, and he was ready to sacrifice everything so his son could acquire knowledge.

**Eliezer Aharonovsky,
attorney-at-law,
of blessed memory**

The youth turns out to be a wise and studious pupil, and they foresee that he will have a great future. During his visits to the town, they are amazed at his erudition and are eager to hear his words. Together with his religious studies, he finds time to work for the public. He is active in the Young Pioneer [*Hechalutz Hatza'ir*] organization in Lubtch. In Lifnishok, where he visited relatives, he made a speech in the synagogue that became famous throughout the town. The very few people who have survived since then have not forgotten this speech till this today. When he was invited to go up to the pulpit, he stood emotionally in front of the large and mainly unknown audience, but when he started to speak, his words burst out in a flow: he stood at the pulpit for hours and spoke in a passionate voice, and none of those present moved from his place.

To his father's great sorrow, the young man leaves the *yeshiva*, travels to Vilna and enters the secular *gymnasia* [high school]. The father does not give up, sends lobbyists to his son to try and persuade him, request and beg, urge him to return to the *yeshiva* - but he refuses. He is determined in his decision, his soul is eager for general wisdom and knowledge. The *yeshiva* cannot satisfy his demands for enlightenment.

In Vilna, he finished his *gymnasia* studies within a year, passed the matriculation exams successfully and registered at the university - in the Faculty of Law.

At the university, too, he excels in his studies. He tutors students who have difficulties in their studies. Now it looks like his way in life is paved, for it is clear he will be a successful attorney.

The Zionist virus that infected him many years previously shows its symptoms. Eretz-Yisrael needs young people who will come and settle there. The best youth of Lubtch, among them his young sister, Rivka, and her husband, Tuvia Shimshoni, have already emigrated. He decides that it is time for him to fulfill his dream. He abandons his studies and joins the pioneers, amongst whom is also Shayna - his heart's love - his wife. His father is very angry; in the depths of his heart he had hoped that he would still succeed in bringing his son back from law to religious studies, but Eretz-Yisrael? There we know there is no need for a rabbi, and there are those that claim that apart from Arabs and malaria, there is nothing more. The energy and youthful passion of his son overcomes his father's anger and he emigrates to Eretz-Yisrael.

In Eretz-Yisrael he serves his old-new homeland faithfully. For 13 years he has a job as a Jewish policeman in the Mandate Police Force and takes part in the most dangerous missions.

During the Second World War, news from his home in Lubtch stopped arriving. The brutal Nazi soldiers and their helpers sent all the Jewish communities in Europe up in flames and smoke. Only "brands snatched from the flames" [survivors] remained from the Holocaust to tell about its terribleness. Despite the fact that Eliezer managed to hide his pain, his closest friends could discern the terrible sorrow that filled his heart due to the murder of his parents and dear ones and the destruction of the community.

The State of Israel arose, a national homeland was established for the Jewish people. Now he turned to completing his studies and indeed became a successful lawyer. Even in his work as a lawyer, his typical character was revealed - the desire to help others, the willingness to support others without any monetary gain.

At the age of only forty-six, he was plucked from the Tree of Life.

Eliezer Aharonovsky left behind a widow, Shayna (née Resnick), and three sons: Dan, Gad and Yitzchak.

Three sons are an exception to the old family tradition in the Exile, but there are those who say that the air in Eretz-Yisrael affected it!

[Pages 316-317]

Their Memory Will Remain Forever in My Heart

by Freda Pintel (Pines)

Translated from the Hebrew by Ann Belinsky

Freda Pintel (Pines)

My parents lived in Castle Street - the main street of Lubtch - until the First World War. Our lives were peaceful then and we did not know what it was to lack. On the same street lived my Uncle Itshe (Yitzchak), my Aunt Shayna and their daughters, Meyta and Michla.

After the town was destroyed by battles in the First World War, we moved to Novogrudek. Our economic condition became very bad there. We lived in a basement apartment for about seven years. It filled with water during the autumn and winter, and we had to pump it out with buckets. The mold and wetness damaged my father's health, and he became sick with a serious illness and remained bedridden to his dying day. My mother was forced to shoulder the burden of making a livelihood and bear the worries of bringing up a family.

When the refugees started returning to Lubtch, our family was also amongst them. We set up house and made a living from a small shop that didn't have enough to provide for the family.

Although she wearied herself at work, my mother insisted that we pursue our studies and sent us to the *Tarbut* school. When we finished school, we learnt a trade, integrated into work and helped with the family livelihood.

The social life in the town was spirited: the young people mainly belonged to the Zionist youth movements. In the evening, we would gather together for lectures, reading and trips. We sang folksongs and songs of the homeland and we dreamt of our future in Eretz-Israel.

In 1933 anti-Semitism was keenly felt. The youth knew that there was no other way in front of us other than to "make *aliyah*" to Eretz-Israel. In Poland, many training groups were set up where the members prepared themselves for work and communal working life in Eretz-Israel.

My sister, Mina, joined the *Shachariya* group in Baronovitch. In 1934 she emigrated to Eretz-Israel, joined the group in Nes Ziona that prepared themselves for settlement in Mitzudat Ussishkin, today Kibbutz Dafna in the Galilee.

After her, I also set out for training. In 1935 I emigrated to Eretz-Israel and joined Kibbutz Ein Harod.

In 1937, a year and a half before the outbreak of World War II, we managed to bring our sister Meyta (Shlomit) over. After our father died, we made numerous attempts to bring our mother and sister Bracha to Eretz-Israel but with no success, and when the war broke out, all communication with them was lost.

The knowledge that our mother and sister were exterminated by the deadly Nazi foes does not give me peace. Their memory is forever kept in my heart.

[Pages 317-319]

An Eternal Light for My Family

by Shmuel Binyamin-Chaim Aronovsky

Translated from the Yiddish by Harvey Spitzer

Although so many years have gone by since I left my little town of Lubtch, it stands before my eyes as though it were just yesterday. I can see its streets and lanes, the river, the castle on the hill, the long row of tall trees, leading to the castle, the green pastures all around and even the people's faces, but their names have gone from my recollection, no longer to be remembered.

However, in this book - the last monument for a whole town of Jews - I will recall some of the members of my family, describing with my modest ability some of their qualities and deeds which were so characteristic of Jewish life in Eastern Europe.

My father was Aharon-Mendel, the carpenter. He had three sons: my older brother, Baruch, Yisrael, and myself. In the town, my father was considered to be an irascible and angry Jew. However, this opinion was not correct. He would, in fact, quickly lose his temper and get angry, but this was only for a few minutes. His anger would dissipate and he would again become all kind and good. He had, as they say, a golden heart. He would "go through fire and water" to do someone a favor. And not just for a good friend, but even for those who were not nice to him. He saved many a Jew from the hands of the gentiles in the town. He also had an open hand for charity. He never refused anyone and gave beyond his means. He was happy that his house was not avoided by charity seekers, and he also taught us this quality.

Poor merchants or peddlers who did not have a few rubles needed for trading used to receive a loan from him, without interest, God forbid.

I never knew my mother, Raize Gitte, may she rest in peace! She died when I was six months old. I was raised by a stepmother, Basha, Berel the "Bricker's" daughter. She was a good, loving mother in every respect. She not only raised us but also brought up my brother's two children who became orphans when their mother died during the First World War and their father (my brother) was held by the Germans as a prisoner of war.

When my father felt that his time to leave this world was nearing, he sent for a few Jews and gave them this order: Since both his sons have gone far away from Lubtch and since the two grandchildren will go to live with their father in France when their grandfather dies, he is leaving all his possessions to his wife and, after her death, everything should be given to the community. Our stepmother, however, had a different, carefully conceived plan. She wrote to us that we, the legal heirs, should write everything in her name. We immediately fulfilled her request. Shortly before her death, she called for her brother, Yisrael-Shimon, and our cousin, Eli-Avraham Shapiro from Pishgas. She handed them the documents, asked them to sell everything and give the money to the two orphans and also see to it that the community did not get anything. They carried out her last wish perfectly.

My oldest brother, Baruch-Shlomo, was taken from his house in Paris by the Nazis with his whole family (except for one daughter with her two small children), and no one know where their bones came to rest. My other brother had a guilty conscience for not having saved our brother Baruch in time. When he came on a visit to America in the winter of 1965, he poured out his aching heart over the fact that he had not taken better care of them. I calmed him as best I could and pointed out that it was almost impossible to escape from the Nazis, but his spirit remained broken. Three months later, the sad news of his death reached me.

May these lines be an eternal light for the rising and bliss of their souls!

[Page 320]

In Memory of My Brother Avraham, May His Blood be Avenged!

by Golda Kalmanovitch

Translated from the Hebrew by Ann Belinsky

Avraham - a golden-haired and black-eyed youth. Everyone nicknamed him Avrameleh.

Now there is no Avrameleh; he rises from the depths of our memory, as a suffocating and hurtful memory, which is gradually disappearing into the far and distant past.

When did we last see him? Thirty years ago?! What importance is there to dates when one thinks about Avrameleh? For he is in another world where there is no place for the conventional dates, which distance him from us day after day.

On the 15th of May, 1939, we met last. The family stood before separation: the brothers, Reuven and Shlomo, had left to study in a *yeshiva* and I planned to make aliyah to Eretz-Israel.

Avrameleh gave expression to the separation in writing, in the lines which he wrote on the back of a photo of the whole family - a photograph of the last time of happiness. This is what he wrote:

"And here is a symbol of friendship
The last photo of brothers
Whom Fate has dispersed
In all directions.

May all the family
Be gathered
Under one roof
In the Chosen Land."

Avrameleh! You did not have the opportunity to live in "the Chosen Land", and you did not live to see that your request was not fulfilled. You only succeeded in seeing part of the family again, in the Devoretz Ghetto. Your eyes saw how bestial men tortured Mother, Father, and your sister Nechama.

You got your revenge on the Germans, when you joined the fighting partisans, but your heart could not forget the terrible sights that you saw, you lost your belief in man: with your own hands you extinguished the wick of your life.

You are comparable to the angel who took himself from the hell on earth: a pure soul who left the impurity and the evil and passed on to the Celestial Court.

We will carry your image in our hearts forever.

[Page 321]

Max Shmulevitch, of Blessed Memory

by Yona Degani

Translated from the Hebrew by Ann Belinsky

Max Shmulevitch z"l

He was a descendant of a wide branching family in Lubtch. He walked a long and difficult path during his lifetime. He was a soldier in the Russian Czar's army in the First World War, and in the Second - he suffered like most of the Jews that remained in Europe and went through seven levels of Nazi Hell. During his wanderings from country to country he lost his wife and daughter. Day and night it was possible to sit and hear his outpourings about what he had gone through.

At the end of the war he remained alone and abandoned with no family or friends, although he tried to surmount his sorrows and rebuild his life, and succeeded. His second wife and adopted daughter looked after him with devotion and love all the years of his suffering.

He was a dear man, good-hearted and devoted to his acquaintances and friends. He loved his adopted daughter as a father and took care of her every need. He wanted to help everyone, even though he didn't have the wherewithal, apart from a kind word, a smiling face and a pleasant joke.

He was very happy when he managed to come to Israel, he kissed the ground and wept. He was so delighted when he met his sisters' daughters here. Now we are orphaned, for we became very attached to him during the seven years he was in Israel. He was like a father to us. How sad is our heart that we have lost him!

Those who knew him will remember him eternally.

[Page 323]

The Holocaust and The Heroism

[Page 324]

Memory Plaque in the Holocaust Cellar in Jerusalem

Translation of the Plaque:
In eternal memory of the martyrs of the **Lubtch-Delatitch** community and the environs (Novogrudek District), may the Lord avenge their blood,
who were murdered, slaughtered, burnt and buried alive by the German Nazis and their willing aides, may their names be obliterated.
24 *Menachem Av* in the years of the Holocaust
5699 - 5705 (1939-1945)
Their holy memory will never be forgotten.
May they rest in peace!
Perpetuators of their names: The organization of the Lubtch-Delatitch landsmen and survivors in Israel and the Diaspora

[Pages 325-326]

I Won't Forgive! (Poem)
(Unrhymed translation)

by Yitzchak Berliner

Translated from the Yiddish by Harvey Spitzer

And not only Warsaw - the city of martyrs -
the bloody crown of Poland.
Lublin and Lodz and Grodno, Bialystok and Krakow,
Lemberg, Vilna as well.
Through every stumbling path and road of our home
the slaughterer spread about, fanning his sword
in murder and did not cease killing.
The last voices - up on high - knocked
at Heaven, howling.
fell back down and were set on fire - bloody "menorot" -
And not only did Warsaw stamp the holiness of that
Name for generations -
Torn from all the limbs of Europe's body
on the wounds, rolling.
I will not distort my weary face
in a smile of forgiveness.
I will always nurture my revenge within me
and nourish it with bottles of hate -
The last dying glances of the children
and of weary old men,
They will always look into my eyes
and remind me
of Warsaw and Lodz, of every city, of every torment, horror and stumbling.
I will take a hard, silent oath within me - mute,
That I - having remained in a foreign land, a rescued orphan
from my people -
I won't forgive! I won't forgive!

From the book, "*Shtil Zol Zayn*" 1947

Candle-lighting on the 25th Memorial Day [*yahrzeit*] for the Martyrs of Lubtch and Delatitch
Right to left: -----, Chaim Yankelevitch, Shifra Slomiansky, ----, Yaacov Zacharavitch, Avraham Bruk, Shalom Leibovitch, ---
[Caption provided by Moshe Yankelevitch]

[Pages 327-330]

One of the Family...
by Natan Yankelevitch, of blessed memory

Translated from the Hebrew by Ann Belinsky

Confusion reigned among the inhabitants of the town when the news went around that the Russians had "liberated" the western districts of occupied Poland and were approaching the town. People hurried to store food for the hard days to come. The Byelarussian representative, Ragola, organized propaganda in favor of the new regime, but he failed in this - when he said that although there was a lack of clothing and shoes in Russia…and thus he was exiled from Lubtch by the occupying forces.

The Russians arrested all those who were suspected of opposition to the Soviet regime. Many were exiled - mainly people of property, all the shops and commercial businesses were nationalized. They organized administrative institutions and an employment bureau where the jobless were registered and were then placed in suitable work.

**Natan Yankelevitch,
of blessed memory**

The Jews worked mainly in clothes and shoe workshops, and whoever was not a craftsman was given clerical work. In the town there was a regional storehouse for agricultural produce, mostly grain and flax. I worked in this storehouse with Mr. Zochobitzky from the town of Mir, the son-in-law of Avraham Rabinovitz. The chief bookkeeper was Moshe Persky.

They learnt Russian language and literature in the school. The synagogues were turned into storehouses, but the Russian Orthodox church was left untouched. The gentiles continued to pray as if there were no change.

The inhabitants of the town elected a council with 24 members to whom people turned with requests and claims, and they negotiated with the authorities.

No hostile relationship was felt towards the Jews, but there was great sensitivity towards the question of loyalty to the regime. When it was found out that I had a brother in the United States, I was immediately fired from my work and received an identity card for a period of only 3 months: this meant that I could be sent away from the area.

The Russians remained in the area for one year and nine months until the Germans betrayed them (1939). When the rumors came that the German army was approaching, the Soviet command began to flee in panic. Despite the news about the German atrocities, the Jewish public of the town didn't believe the rumors, and thus the Jews stayed there and didn't flee.

Akiva Baksht fled - because he was a teacher of the Russian language and was scared of the German authorities. He got as far as Nigorloya, but it was already impossible to cross over the previous border, and he was forced to return as he had come.

In the meanwhile, the German government based itself in the place with the help of the Christian inhabitants of the town. Akiva was caught and handed over to the Gestapo in the nearby town of Ivye, where he was executed by hanging in the market square.

The Germans permitted the Christian population to loot Jewish property, and there immediately began a pogrom which lasted 24 hours. The gentiles went crazy - they damaged and destroyed and looted everything they could get their hands on. They searched for hiding places where valuables had been hidden, smashed windows, tore down doors, emptied houses of their chattels and foodstuffs. Houses remained open to all, without windows or doors. Houses of Jews in the neighboring settlements were also looted and burgled.

There were Jews who had given their property to the Christians in the area for safekeeping from the peasants, but when they asked for it back, they were not answered and were sent away with blows and threats.

Part of the town was burnt, mainly because of the bombing. Houses were burnt on Fish Street, Kapushtcheva Street and part of Castle Street. There were Jews who removed their property to the fields for fear of fire, but the gentiles stole it there.

The inhabitants of the town worked for the wealthy landlord in gathering grain and their payment was in grain. Workshops were also opened and people worked there mainly in repairs.

Two weeks after the Germans occupied the place, all the men were ordered to clean the streets of the town. During the time of work, a group of Germans arrived, including a number of local gentiles and said they needed 40 workers. Among those taken were the brothers Yekutiel (Kusha) and Avraham Soltz. Their father, R' Yaakov Soltz, asked the Germans why they had been taken and the answer was that they also needed a translator. R' Yaakov volunteered to work as the translator. The whole group was liquidated and no one knows how.

When I heard that men were being taken to work, I slipped away to a field and hid within the standing grain.

In response to the request of the German commander, twelve people were chosen for the job of *Judenrat* (Jewish Council). Yaakov-Chaim Leibovitch was chosen as chairman of the *Mossad* [Organization] and his deputy was Chaim Bruk. The *Judenrat* was obligated to carry out all orders of the German commander.

According to the demands of the Germans, groups of Jews were sent to work in the forests and in preparing bricks from peat. For this work, the *Judenrat* received bread and milk, which they distributed amongst all the populace.

An order was issued requiring all Jews to go into the Ghetto and wear the yellow patch on their chest and back- for identification. Anyone disobeying was shot on the spot.

Three hundred Jews were taken to a work camp at Dvoretz: the people left on foot. Those who had difficulty walking were put onto wagons. We arrived at Horodtzena where we slept in the local school building.

Two brothers who complained of stomach-aches were shot on the spot. The next day we continued on foot to Dvoretz. In the work camp we worked at quarrying stones which were transferred to the Front for building strongholds. The Germans "paid" the *Judenrat* for their work and the *Judenrat*, in turn, had to provide us with food.

We worked in Dvoretz until the spring. Our *Judenrat* managed to free some of the craftsmen from the camp and return them to the town, as well as some family heads with children - I was included amongst them. Those that remained in Dvoretz were annihilated to the last person.

A report reached us that there had been an "*Aktion*" in Novogrudek- that is to say that the Jews had been executed. Aharon Brezinsky, together with another Jew whose name I don't remember, went to Novogrudek to verify what had happened. On the way, they went into a flourmill, but the Jewish miller was no longer there: the Germans caught them both and shot them on the spot.

The inhabitants of the towns of Ibynitz, Derbena, Nelybok and Rovzvitch were brought to the Lubtch ghetto. Their children stayed in the village and were murdered. All who were sick or had difficulty walking - were killed.

The decrees multiplied and became worse. Jewish blood became cheaper and cheaper. The Jews were persecuted and destroyed for amusement and from boredom. Many were tortured to death.

A tiny few of the Jews of our town managed to be saved.

The holy community of Lubtch and its Jews are no more...

"*Yitgadal veyitkadash*" - May His Great Name become exalted and be sanctified (from the *Kaddish*-mourners prayer]

On the 25th Memorial Day [*Yahrzeit*] for Martyrs of Lubtch and Delatitch
Front (left to right): Golda Taubman, Frieda Pintel (Pines), Aryeh Sivitzky, Shmuel Baksht   2nd Row: (left, behind Golda): Yisrael Movshovitch
[Caption provided by Moshe Yankelevitch]

[Pages 331-343]

I Was in the Ghetto

by Yisrael-Gershon (Yisrol) Yankelevitch

Translated from the Yiddish by Harvey Spitzer

Yisrael-Gershon (Yisrol) Yankelevitch

Poland, August 1939 - Mobilization!

It was a hot summer's day when I received the order to report for duty in the Polish army to defend the "fatherland" against the armies of the Nazis, who decided to swallow up their good partner in anti-Semitism and rule over the whole world.

Two weeks later I was already back in my town among my family. The Polish army suffered a bloody defeat and ceased to exist. The Polish government collapsed and the German murderers were already acting with savageness, sharpening their claws against the defenseless Polish Jews.

Three days after my coming home, the Soviets occupied our region. We breathed a little more freely, thinking that the war was over for us.

There followed twenty months of adjustment to the new regime which, with its "solutions", impoverished the entire population- the Jews in the towns and the peasants in the village, who were forcibly collectivized in the newly established *kolkhoze* [collectivized farms].

These were also months of clenching one's fist and gnashing one's teeth out of grief and pain, helplessly watching the enormous train convoys which supplied the German armies- continuing their bloody march across Europe- with raw materials and food which were desperately needed by the half starved and raggedly clothed population of the great Soviet country.

There again came a lovely, bright sunny day, June 22, 1941, on which the Germans paid back its Communist supplier of goods with war, death and destruction. Another mobilization and another order to report for military service. That same day, they began to concentrate all those called up for army duty, Jews and Gentiles from the whole region, on the grounds of the castle in Lubtch. We stayed there until Monday, June 23. At 2:00pm, we were ordered to go home and await further instructions. No explanation was needed regarding the situation because all the Soviet officials soon began packing up, burning documents and fleeing in wild panic.

The next morning, Tuesday, at 10:00am, we heard the sound of motors. We noticed new airplanes coming from the direction of Delatitch. They circled around the town a few times, descended and began dropping bombs. The first bombs fell along the riverbank and killed a Gentile woman. A bomb fell on the saw-mill and another one hit the post office. A fire broke out and my house also burned down. I harnessed our horse, threw a few things salvaged from the fire into the wagon, seated my wife and child in the wagon, took along my father and brother, Yeshayahu David, and we went up to the meadow behind the synagogue. Nearly all the Jews in Lubtch had gathered there. There was a great panic: Adults and children were crying and screaming. Mothers hysterically looked for their lost children and fainted from fright. Husbands were looking for their wives and they were all running around together in total confusion, not knowing what to do.

Night fell, but people were afraid to return to their homes. Some of the Jews decided to go to the surrounding villages and hide in the homes of Gentiles they knew. I took my family and we went away towards Atchukevitch. I went up onto a field and decided to spend the night there, planning that at daybreak I would look for a familiar Gentile and hide in his house until the situation of the Jews in the town became clear.

The summery night did not last long. If it hadn't been for the fright and worry, it would have been a pleasant trip in the lap of nature. Everything around us was full of life and fresh juices: the grass and ears of grain covered with dew, various creatures and insects calling to each other in all kinds of voices and sounds. We didn't close an eye either out of worry and fear for the coming day. Only the baby slept peacefully with his small lips open, breathing in the clean air. From time to time he let out a sigh as most babies do in their sleep, but this tore our hearts and my wife would shed tears.

As soon as it got lighter, I noticed a group of Jews from Lubtch in the distance. I went over to them and asked why they weren't going to the Gentiles. They told me that the Gentiles did not let them cross their threshold and drove them for fun to the

Germans, "who would soon finish off the Jews".

Moshe Tiktin, who was among the Jews in the group, said:

— Fellow Jews, there's no purpose in sitting any longer in the field. Our fate is sealed anyway. Let's go back and see what's happening in town.

In town, we noticed how the peasants from the entire district were robbing Jewish property, loading up full wagons and hurrying home in order to try to come a second time. Their faces were aflame, their eyes burning with a savage fire of hate and revenge. We immediately understood that Tiktin was right, our fate was sealed for destruction and death.

As my house was burned down, we went to live with Itche Tevies on Novaredke (Novogrudek) Street. Three days later, the Germans came and placed a force of the town's Gentile police all around. Boris Kunitzky was made the commander. His lieutenants were Kola Komornik and Petrik Bedoon who, all their lives, lived close to Jews, benefited from Jewish help, maintained good relations with Jews and during Soviet times were avid supporters of Communism. Now that they were given full authority over us, they exhibited their beastly hatred in the most brutal way.

The next day Kola Komornik came to the house. I was holding the baby in my arms. He came over to me, gave me a terrific smack in the back and ordered: — Bring your things here! I began to beg and plead, reminding him that he was my neighbor and that we always lived in peace and in friendship. He then shouted in German: — Damn Jew! He pulled off my jacket, stamped his feet and left.

A couple of days later, a few Germans came and gave the order for all Jews to come to the marketplace so a few men could be selected for work detail. None of the men wanted to go and hid, but the Germans came into the houses looking for them. I was lying in the attic, hidden in the hay. A German was standing on the ladder and asked my wife whether any Jews needed for work were hiding there. My wife answered that I had gone out to the market place and that no one was hiding and that if he wished, he could go up and look for himself. Apparently, her assured answer convinced him and he left. He then went into Blecher's house and brought out Layzer Shitzgal. In this way, they captured 51 men- the youngest and healthiest who were taken out of the town. One, two, three days went by and we heard and knew nothing as to what had happened to them and where they were. We tried to guess: One person said that they were working somewhere not far from the town and another said that they were taken away to Germany. Then a few weeks later we found out that they were taken to Novogrudek behind the barracks,-where they were all shot.

Four days went by and we were terrified to leave the house. They again took three Jews for work by the railroad tracks and shot them there. The three victims were Kushe Saltz, Simcha Chaimovitich, and Aharon (Ara) Berezinsky.

This was followed by a decree for all Jews to move into the ghetto. The entire Jewish community was squeezed into 27-30 houses, starting from Liova Levin's house as far as Yehoshua Yankel, the tailor's house including the synagogue. Three or four families were put into each house and it was impossible to move due to the tightness.

Every couple of days the Germans would come with the police and take out 40-50 people as if for "work", and they would disappear without our knowing where. We would go into the synagogue, recite psalms, hold a fast, but nothing helped.

About six months after the Germans came into the town (I, unfortunately, don't remember the exact date), six hundred people were selected and were led away like sheep to a work camp at the Dvoretz station, not far from Novoyelnia. It was just the first night of Chanukah, 5702 (1941).

I spent one night in the camp and ran away the next day. They caught me, however, and the commander beat and warned me that if I ran away again, they would shoot me on the spot. But for me there was no difference between staying in the camp and being murdered or being caught and killed a few months earlier. I ran away, in fact, a second time and was not caught. I ran without stopping to Novoyelnia- a distance of six kilometers, which took me no more than twenty minutes.

In Novoyelnia, I found the Jewish Council [*Judenrat*] from Lubtch. They had been in Dvoretz and were going back to Lubtch. These were Gershon Kapushchevsky, Shalom Ziman and Alter Chemes (Shmulevitch). I begged them to take me on their wagon, but they were afraid and advised me to walk separately, six or seven meters away from them.

That is how I reached the ghetto in Novogrudek, but the ghetto police did not let me enter and threatened to report me to the German commander. I hid in a corner on the side and that night I snuck into the ghetto. There I looked for my brother Beryl and wept. He gave me a piece of bread and I went out of the ghetto and headed for Lubtch. I managed to go all the way unnoticed by the Germans and Gentiles and safely reached the Lubtch ghetto to be with my wife and child.

The next day when the Jewish Council found out that I had come back to Lubtch, they decided that I had to return to Dvoretz. I declared that I would not go back and that they could do whatever they wanted with me. They explained that I was an extra person, not listed in the official papers and that I had to go back. This was to no avail as I refused to follow their advice. When they also threatened not to give me an allotment of bread, I began to act insolently - did I have another choice? - and said that they would indeed give me a portion of bread if they didn't want any trouble. In short, they fought with me for two full weeks and finally gave in. I don't blame them, God forbid, as I knew very well what would happen to them if the Germans found out about it.

On March 15, 1942, the Germans issued an order that the Jews could not keep cows or goats and that they must bring them to the marketplace and give them to the Gentiles. We remained without a single possession, hungry, torn apart and depressed, living corpses who already had nothing to lose in life.

On April 1, 1942, the Jewish Council received an order to supply 125 workers for duty in Novogrudek. I was also included in the group and we were sent on a small train to the ghetto in Novogrudek. We asked the district commissar to allow our wives and children to join us. He granted this request and four days later, they were already together with us. We did very hard work and received a daily allotment of 400 grams of bread. Meanwhile, news reached us that five hundred people were sent from the Lubtch ghetto to Shterben near Vorobievitch, where they were later brutally murdered. Only 150 people remained in the Lubtch ghetto. They were elderly and sick and not capable of working.

On the 24th day of *Av* 5702 (7th August 1942), the Germans carried out a mass slaughter. Thousands of Jews were killed that day including men, women and children from Lubtch, Delatitch, Neyshtot (Niegnievitch), Karelitch (Korelitz), Ivenietz, Zhetel, Derevna, Zholodok, Novoyelnia and Novogrudek. People ran around in panic, looking for a hiding place. Others offered the murderers money and gold which they gladly took and then drove them to their slaughter. My wife called out that if they took the child, she would go with him. I took her with me to the barracks, but we were separated there. That was the last I saw of my wife and child. Later, returning to the ghetto, I found their things, the last remembrance of my blood and flesh.

I also found both my brothers, Beryl and Yoske, in the barracks. Everyone was lined up in two rows surrounded by armed Germans and Estonians with machine guns. An SS officer stood by, holding a list. He called out the names of the people and pointed to the left or right. We didn't know which direction was for life and which for death. When they called out Yankelevitch, our family name, the three of us stepped to the right. A German grabbed hold of Yoske and began pulling him to the left. Yoske resisted and the German shot him on the spot before our very eyes. Fifteen people were similarly shot, including a few boys from Lubtch.

Of the more than 1,000 Jews who were at the barracks, 275 were selected and the others were shot the following day near the village of Litovke, A few days later we found little notes bearing the message: "Brothers and sisters, if you remain alive, avenge our death!" We were kept in a horse stable at the barracks for three days without food or water. At 8:00pm on Friday evening, the doors were opened and three Germans entered shouting "Heil Hitler!" We all got up from our places and remained standing with our heads bowed. They ordered us to leave the stable and stand by fours in a row with our hands raised. Each group of four was accompanied by two Germans with a machine gun. We were then ordered to march along Karelitch Street to the former Polish courthouse building. There about 1500 Jews, the remainder from all the surrounding ghettos, were driven together. They were all bitterly weeping and lamenting the loss of their closest ones. I went around in a daze, without any feeling, unable to speak or weep because my heart had completely turned to stone. The next day I saw Beryl, who had also lost his wife and children. We embraced each other and couldn't hold back our tears.

**Survivors standing beside the monument on the grave
of the Jews massacred in Litovke near Novogrudek**

Some Germans entered and drove everyone outside. They then selected 150 men and seated them in trucks and sent them off to Smolensk for work. A couple of hours later, a group of 15 people, including myself, were selected and we were brought back to the town on Slonim Street. There we loaded 10 barrels of chlorine on a truck and we left for Litovka. They led us to a large, deep pit full of murdered Jews and ordered us to pour the chlorine into the pit and then pour sand over the pit. When we finished pouring sand over the pit, they brought us, the 15 men, to the empty ghetto. Entering a house, we heard human voices coming from under the floor. When we asked who was speaking, it suddenly got quiet. We put them at ease and told them they didn't have to be afraid of us because we were also Jews from the ghetto. Just then about 30 people crawled out of their hiding place, dirty, smeared all over and unrecognizable. Among this group were my sister's two children, five and seven years old, as well as Shalom Leibovitz's daughters, Shifra and Sonia. There were also some Jews from Lubtch and Karelitch. We took out two people who were already dead. In this way, a handful of people gathered together in the ghetto and we were again driven back to work. One day we, a group of 12 people including 2 women, did not go out to work. That afternoon, two Germans came and asked why we did not show up for work. I answered that we were sick and couldn't go to work. One German began shouting that he would soon make us healthy. He ordered us to stretch out on the ground and he beat us with a stick all over our bodies. The other German watched the spectacle and laughed. We screamed terribly from the pain until we remained lying there nearly in a faint. For two weeks we lay there unable to move a limb.

I decided to escape into the forest and I consulted with Beryl, Shlomo and his three children and a few more Jews from Karelitch and Derevna. The day we decided to run away from the ghetto, I didn't go out to work. I spent the whole day planning our escape. As the ghetto was guarded by policemen, we bought two liters of strong drink outside the ghetto and at 9:00 pm, one of the girls in our group offered the liqueur to the policemen. At the same time, when they were drunk, we went out of the ghetto through an opening in the fence which we had prepared during the day, and we began running. Some Gentiles noticed us and began shouting that the Jews were escaping from the ghetto. The police started shooting right away, bullets whistled around us, but we managed to run into the woods and out of the range of fire. It immediately became apparent that Shlomo's two daughters, Shifra and Sheine Rachel (Sonia), were not with us. Slonimsky and I went to look for them. We found them sitting on the side of the path, crying that they wanted to go back to the ghetto. I calmed them and said that being in the ghetto could not be worse at this point and that we might be lucky and find safety in the forest. I took them by the hand, like two small children, and brought them into our temporary hiding place.

We rested a little and then started out for Delatitch. We apparently lost our way and walked around the whole night until daybreak. We had to hide in the woods because walking on the roads during the day was a sure death for us. All of a sudden, shooting broke out in the woods. We lay down between thick shrubs so that we wouldn't be seen. That day, which was the Sabbath, was drawn out like a year. Even when the shooting stopped, we were afraid to make the slightest move. Only at nightfall, did we get up and leave. We went to the Neiman River and crossed over in a rowboat which we found on the shore. We were already on the other side of the river, walking a few hundred meters, when they again started shooting at us. We again started running until we got deeper into the woods. After resting for a quarter of an hour, we went to Komarovsky's house in the hamlet. Snow had just fallen and our footprints could be clearly seen in the snow. The peasant was afraid to keep us in his house and advised us to hide in the woods where we would be safer than among the peasants. He gave us some bread, butter and cheese and asked us to come back in the evening well after dark.

When we came back again late at night, he told us that the Germans and a few policemen had been at his house during the day, inquiring whether any Jews or partisans had been at his house. He naturally denied it, and they went away. He again gave us some food and advised us to go to Kluchist, a village near Nalibok.

We didn't have much choice. We set out in the direction he indicated. We got as far as Krasne-Horka and hid there. It was bitingly cold, we had no food and we didn't know any of the peasants in the surrounding hamlets. We stayed there one day, two days and ate up what little food we had. We were oppressed by hunger, and the cold was becoming unbearable. We decided to return closer to Lubtch, to Farbotke's house in the hamlet, a distance of about twenty kilometers.

When we came to the hamlet and knocked on the door, Farbotke asked who was knocking. When we answered that we were Jews from Lubtch, he was afraid to open. However, when he heard that it was Shalom Leibovitz and Yisrael-Gershon Yankelevitch, he opened the door. When he saw the state we were in, the honest peasant began to cry. We told him about our situation and asked for a little food. He gave us a bucket for cooking, bread, flour, salt and told us to go to the potato pit and take as many potatoes as we wanted. Loaded down with food, with a sack of potatoes, we came to our people in Krasne-Horka. We stayed there two weeks and then went closer to the village of Potashne. We dug out a dirt house and remained there six months until we met the partisans from Otriad, attacking the Germans in Stalin's name. I came into Otriad as a partisan and took part in many operations against the Germans, taking revenge for the innocent Jewish blood that was shed.

When the region was liberated in June, 1944, I returned to Lubtch and began to work in the town militia.

I was still fated to experience the good taste of sitting three and a half years in a Soviet prison and then three months in a Polish jail until, after so much suffering, I succeeded in reaching the welcoming shores of the Jewish homeland, the State of Israel.

[Pages 344-363]

I Revenged Our Innocent Blood

by Velveke Yanson
(Volodshke The Machinegunner)

Translated from the Yiddish by Harvey Spitzer

It's a warm day in August, 1939. People are strolling, laughing freely, enjoying the sunshine. That evening, a news report comes through that the Germans are preparing to attack Poland. There's a hubbub in the town. People whisper to one another, run to buy food and buy up whatever is left. The older Jews say that the Germans won't be worse than the Poles. One of them says that in the First World War nothing bad happened on the part of the Germans. A few days later we already hear that the Germans have issued an ultimatum to Poland. The country is frightened and trembles. The army reserves are called up. One annual set of soldiers leaves for the front, then another and so on. The *osadnikes* [Poles sent by the Polish government to settle in White Russian territory and given incentives to "Polishize" the territory] also get their turn to be sent to fight.

Velveke Yanson

I go back home with a heavy heart as though we've been warned that a terrible storm is moving in our direction. We already hear that the Poles are fighting very heroically on the outskirts of Danzig but, unfortunately, after a short battle, the Germans are victorious. And we already see Polish soldiers running back, wounded. The Germans keep marching on ahead, taking city after city until they reach the Bug River, where they remain in position. The Russians occupy the eastern part of Poland in accordance with the Hitler-Stalin Non-Aggression Pact of 1939.

The Red Army Occupies White Russia

On September 17, 1939, we hear how the Red Army is taking city after city: Stoibtz, Baranovitch, Novogrudek. The Lubtch police force runs away. The Polish eagle is torn off the post office building and is replaced with a red flag.

On September 21, around four o'clock in the afternoon, the small train arrives, the red flag already flapping, but no soldiers are aboard. It's already dark in the town. We're all gathered on Castle Street next to Lipchin's soda shop, expecting the Red Army any minute. Around six o'clock, the town grows speechless, although we're all gathered in the streets, but no one can let out a word. We can hear the galloping of horses, and the wind carries singing in the distance. Everyone calls out: "The Red Army, the Red Army is coming!" The singing gets louder and louder and we notice a Cossack division of the Red Army singing the well-known partisan song: "Over hill and dale". About 400 Cossacks come riding through and stop near the marketplace at the end of Castle Street. The whole town gathers around them. People ask questions and the soldiers are very polite. The division moves further on and life under the new rulers begins. The priest is arrested and then released. The study halls [synagogues] are closed and later serve as storerooms for crops. I go to see my aunt, Leahke Mendelevitch and my uncle, Baruch-Mordechai Yankelevitch, and we bemoan the situation.

A short time later, I leave for a job in Novogrudek. My mother and sister, Henia and Grunia, with her husband, David Pertchik, remained in Lubtch.

War Again

Time goes by in this way until June 22, 1941. Early in the morning, we hear the terrible news that the Germans have bombed Soviet cities, and it is reported on the radio that the Germans have suddenly attacked Russia and declared war. All cities are being bombed, and the next day Novogrudek is also hit; nearly half the town is destroyed and there are many casualties. The same day I receive an order to report for army duty. Lots of men are called up for military service, and we set out on our way deeper into Russia.

I wear a Russian uniform and hold a gun in my hand for the first time in my life, and the radio carries the news that the Germans are getting closer and closer. We finally reach Mogilev and the officer tells us that as soon as we cross the bridge, we'll join up with the Red Army and there we'll put a fierce resistance. Unfortunately, however, as soon as we crossed the bridge, the Germans, as though growing right out of the ground, began shooting heavily at us from all sides. We get an order to run away, whoever and wherever possible, just so that we can save ourselves, because we are surrounded. I run to a peasant's house, change my clothes and start going back towards Novogrudek. After several days of wandering, hungry and thirsty, I reach Novogrudek, where a ghetto in Pereshinke was awaiting me. All the Jews were already locked up in the ghetto. I was there until the first slaughter. The Germans selected Jews from a part of the ghetto and led them out like sheep to be shot. I am among those chosen. My instinct shouts to me: "Run away!" and I run under a hail of bullets. I manage to escape and run towards Lubtch.

Coming into Lubtch, I saw that all the Jews, here too, were already locked up in a ghetto. My mother, sister and other relatives were living in Moshe Yankelevitch's (Mayshke the Beer Maker's) house. After being there over a month, I was taken, together with other young people, back to Novogrudek. I was in the ghetto a second time. Months go by and the great slaughter takes place. Everyone is led to the barracks, but about one hundred young people are left in the ghetto, including myself. We are taken to the courthouse where we worked very hard for the Germans.

At the end of 1941, a peasant brought me a letter from my sister Grunia. She writes me that that they are being held in a barn in Vorobievitch, about five hundred people, including women and children. Among them are my mother, my sister Grunia, her husband David and their two small children. My younger sister Henia was taken to Dvoretz with all the young people because she was less than fifteen years old. Grunia writes that the Germans say that they will be taken to Baranovitch for work. I sent a letter back to her with the same peasant. Unfortunately, my letter never got to them as that very night the Germans poured gasoline over the barn and everyone was killed. The people were burned alive and their agonizing cries pierced the heavens. But the heavens were closed and bolted as though God Himself had turned away from us. Anyone who managed to get out of the barn alive was shot.

The next day, the same peasant came to me and brought me the "good news". He wept while telling me what happened, but I stood there as if my heart had turned to stone, unable to cry. Later I began to tremble and jolt, and my shouts were like a lion's roar. Lying at night on the hard bench, a fire was kindled in my heart, a fire of revenge and I swore that my hands would not rest until I avenged the beastly death of those dearest to me, whose innocent lives were stolen from them.

I Escape

Four days go by and I decide to escape. The building in which we were locked up was encircled three ways. The first circle of guards consisted of Estonians, the second of Poles and the third of Germans. The building itself was surrounded by barbed wire. I must confide in someone. I asked him to assume my name after I escaped because ten people are shot as soon as person fails to answer to his name. He begged me not to do it because it meant a sure death - no one had ever escaped from there. There were three of us who wanted to escape. And just at the last minute, we took on a fourth, Chana Ribak's brother-in-law (David). Two nights later we cut through the barbed wire at a certain point. Everything was set and at one o'clock the next morning when the camp was asleep, we quietly went over to the prepared place. I said to them: "You go through. I'll go through last".

At the same time, we had to time our escape as we had only two to three minutes to get through the fence before the guards passed by on their patrol. This was because the guards would walk towards one another and pass each other without meeting. We had to go quickly through the wire fence just at that time. There was an interval of only two to three minutes when the guards passed each other and were out of sight. I let them all go through and then it was my turn but, unfortunately, I got entangled in the barbed wire. At that very moment I saw the Estonian soldier approaching. I tore myself forcefully from the wire and, in so doing, cut my back and felt that my shoulders were bleeding. I stood up and met the Estonian face to face. There was no other way. Before he could manage to shoot or shout, I came at him with a knife. He threw down his gun out of fear. I hit him over head with a revolver which I smuggled out of the ghetto and dragged him to the spot which we had earlier agreed upon in a grove of trees about 250 meters from the camp. We all met there. We left the Estonian unconscious and went quickly away in order to reach a forest before dawn where we could hide all day. As we were running, we could hear the alarm and shooting in our direction, but it was already too late....

My Revenge as a Partisan

It took us a day and two nights to reach the vicinity of the town of Dvoretz. I wanted to see my sister Henia, who was being held in the camp. We lay hidden in the fields and saw how hard the children were working. Late at night, I made up my mind to go into the camp. I wondered where my sister was and went in. When she saw me, she couldn't stop crying and shaking. People asked me how I got into the camp and were worried that if I were caught, everyone in the camp would be shot. I therefore decided to leave that same night. My sister asked me to take her with me, but I myself didn't know where I was going. I promised that I would come back in about a week and surely take her along. It was hard to say goodbye, but we had no other choice.

We walked all night long and early in the morning reached the partisans of Orlianske's unit in the forests around Zshetel. They stop us, interrogate us and bring us into a dirt house. Jewish partisans question us, but they don't want to take us into their group and order us to go on further. Our question is "where"? So we again drag ourselves through the great forests until we reach the dense woods around Lipitchianska and get to the town of Duzshi-Volia by the Shtara River, not far from Slonim. We come to a group of partisans led by Vanushka (a Christian). This is worth emphasizing because the Jewish partisans sent us away, but the Christians accepted us. After a short period of training, we were placed in "Bulak's unit", consisting of about 320 fighters. I'm given a gun, which renews my strength and re-awakens the desire to take revenge. We fight against the bloody Germans every day.

So we attack the towns of Deretchin, Zshetel and surrounding villages where there were Germans. I take revenge, which gladdens my heart. Knowing, however, that the next bullet which flies in our direction can be the end of my life, I ask the commander to let me go and take my sister Henia out of the camp in Dvoretz. He grants me permission and sends five more partisans with me. We start out on horseback towards Dvoretz, a distance of 120-130 kilometers, but unfortunately, not far from the town, a peasant brings us the bitter news that the whole camp was annihilated just the day before. I become as wild as a lion in my thirst to take revenge against the Germans.

A few days later, the news reaches us that, during the night, Ukrainians and Germans tore into the village of Nakrishok, in the heart of the partisan area, captured the village, digging themselves in for a long stay in deep trenches. An order is received from the staff for all the partisan units to attack the village at daybreak. The village must be re-taken no matter what the cost in casualties. Our force consists of three thousand men, two tanks and three canons. Their force numbers about 1,200 men. We prepare with heavy armament. Around seven o'clock in the evening, we march out to the meeting point, half a kilometer from the village at the edge of the forest. We reach the point at dawn, one hour before the attack, which is due to take place at 6:00am.

We meet up with partisans from the surrounding villages. We are given the order to rest, to prepare the weapons, to be ready and not to move from the place. It is deathly quiet. There are heavy clouds in the sky and it is drizzling. We are told that the first shot of the cannon will be a sign that the attack has begun. The units spread out in three parts so that the village can be attacked from all sides. I'm very tired and fall asleep on the grass. For the first time since my mother was murdered, she comes to me in a dream and says: "My child, you are now going into a bitter fight with the Germans. I will stand by and ask God to protect you. Don't be afraid".

All of a sudden a loud clap is heard - the attack has begun. With a great, resounding shout of "hurrah", we run across a little river by the village mill. The enemy's bullets fly by from all sides and my comrades are falling on my right and left, but we keep running and shooting. I take up a position by the village well, set up my machinegun and keep shooting. Suddenly, I notice a German aiming his gun at me. A second later his bullet pierces my cap, burning the hair off my head. I fall down in a faint, but I can hear a nurse shouting to see whether I'm alive. I want to answer but cannot bring forth a word and nearly choke...

The doctor runs over to me. I hear him say: "A lucky person. The bullet only grazed the skin on his head. He will soon stand up." Ten minutes later, I come to. The nurse is sitting over me, crying. She surely thought I was dead. Standing up, we start running on ahead, chasing after our partisans. The fighting goes on in full intensity. As I'm running, I remember my dream and just at that moment I notice the German who shot at me. I run closer to him and he keeps shooting at me, but my thirst for revenge is stronger and quicker than he is. Now I'm almost right on top of him. I shoot an entire round of 72 bullets at him and take his gun, his things and boots. I come back to my group, throwing myself further into the battle. An hour later, with the arrival of Orlanske's unit, the village is re-taken. Over six hundred dead and seriously wounded are lying about. Eighty partisans have fallen. We return to our bases. I'm called to headquarters and because of services rendered, they appoint me commander of sixty partisans.

End of 1942

We hear that the German forces are concentrating around the dense woods where we are hiding, and people say there will be a great chase. A week goes by until it is reported from headquarters that about 100,000 German soldiers are going to clear out the forests. They encircle the woods on all sides. We take up our position on one side of the Shtare River and the Germans on the other. Only one direction is left free in case we have to retreat. It's already the end of November, 1942. They open fire with great cannons, and a battle ensues. Our forces number about 80,000 partisans. We also have tanks, cannons and mine launchers, but not too many. We've already been fighting for two days and nights. I lie with my group in a trench at the river's edge. We are ordered not to let the Germans get through from our side. It's very early in the morning on the third day. The Germans open up with great fire, using their mine launchers. There are four of us in my little trench: I, a young fellow from Zshetel, who serves by preparing bullets for the machine gun, a Russian partisan and Chayke, the nurse from Deretchin. In the midst of the shooting, when I'm very busy concentrating on the enemy, the Russian shouts out that he's been wounded. I call out to Chayke that she should help him, but there is no answer at all from her. When the shooting subsides a bit, I get up and go over to Chayke who, unfortunately, is lying motionless. It appears that she's been dead for quite a while. Leaning against the dirt wall, she was frozen. She was barely 17 years old....

We fight another day and night until they finally begin their general attack. During the night, the Germans try to cross the river six times, but we push them back with many losses. We let them swim halfway across the river and then open fire with all the weapons in our possession. Around 3:00 AM, they start shooting into the forest from all sides. There is no place to put up a resistance. Everything is burning around us. Just then we hear that Doctor Atlas and many commanders have fallen. We receive an order to run away- whoever can and wherever possible- and to re-group later. The Germans press on further into the forest. We meet up with thousands of partisans who are running in our direction. The ground is actually burning around us. Hundreds of partisans are lying dead or wounded.

I run through deep mud with a small group of six people, but we meet Germans and shooting ensues. We manage to get away and reach the Orlanske units. However, when we meet up with them, they are also running away. There is simply no safe place for us. Itche Levine from Novogrudek says to me: "Let's go to the "family" groups." This was a group of Jews who were hiding without guns some 25 kilometers from us. Wet, hungry, exhausted, we finally reach them. It was quieter there, but I come down with typhoid fever and they're sure I'm going to die. Several good acquaintances take care of me. They nurse me back to health with boiled water and pieces of dry bread. Russian partisans arrive. They encircle us and say we'll be shot because we're deserters. We plead with them and assure them that we're going straight to our units.

We leave, but I can't stand on my feet any more. With great exertion, we finally reach Orlanske's units. We again join the combat ranks. The Germans are still on the roads but with smaller forces. The whole army has already gone away. The fight against the enemy is renewed in a manner favorable to the partisans. However, anti-Semitism is now rampant. Wherever we go, we see murdered Jews - men, women and children. This is the work of the Russian partisans. It is intolerable to us as Jews and a fire burns in out hearts. Meanwhile, we leave to attack the town of Zshetel, where we fight all day long but fail to achieve our goal and must retreat. Our two cannons get stuck in the mud. More Jews are sent-under a hail of bullets - to pull them out of the mud. We thus lose half of our comrades. We get back to our base tired and depressed. Other Jews are sent to guard the few tanks which are in our possession.

Lying there exhausted, we hear a loud explosion- the tanks with the Jewish boys have blown up by accident. This is already enough for us. We choose a special group of Jewish partisans led by Senke (a young Jewish man from Minsk). We talk about taking the best guns. We ask permission from the head commander, as we want to go for food. He allows us to leave and there are now three different groups. We all go out in various directions, but we speak quietly among ourselves about where to meet. Early the next morning, we meet around the forests near Komink.

*

Our forces unite with Senke at the head and I as his lieutenant. We're about fifty people, all well armed. We do the same to the Russian partisans that they did to our Jews. We kill every one who wants to come to us. Senke, our commander, who can't speak any Yiddish, says that his grandmother once told him when he was a child that it is written in the Jewish Bible that one must take an eye for an eye. Three months go by in this way. The Gentile partisans speak in fear about Jewish bandits going around killing them in revenge for their acts. They are in pursuit of us. Getting to us, however, is very difficult because we maintain a double watch, each of which is a kilometer apart and besides, we never stay in the same place. We're divided into two groups.

A terrible misfortune, however, occurs. We were once in two houses, I with Senke and other comrades in one house, and the rest in the other house. We were very tired after a hard night. It happened that one of the guards fell asleep and was stabbed to death. The Russian partisans who are searching for us sneak into a house and kill the whole group of eighteen people. They would certainly have put up a fight, but were, unfortunately, all asleep and never woke up.

Everyone is also asleep in our house. Only Senke and I are sitting at the table and eating, and four other comrades are sitting and chatting. Suddenly, about sixteen Gentile partisans break into our house with their guns aimed at us and with grenades in their hands, because they knew that they could never take us alive. Senke throws me my machine gun and, grabbing his own, manages to shout: "Fire!" At that moment, a bullet hits him in the forehead and he falls on me. Shooting breaks out, and our lives are in danger. They thought that our men were shooting at them from outside. A panic breaks out among them. Our comrades who were asleep were all shot and the owner of the house, a Christian, and his daughter are killed. There are only sixteen of us left. Our guns are taken away, and an official reads aloud a written note stating that we are sentenced to death by shooting on account of the criminal acts which we committed. Many Jews have already been killed in this way, but our lives are spared on condition that we leave the district. We request permission to bury our comrades.

Everyone is set free, but the commander goes over to me with another partisan. He orders him to take me into the neighboring woods and shoot me because I was Senke's lieutenant. The commander leaves and nothing less than a miracle occurs at that moment: The partisan, who was supposed to shoot me, gives me a terrible smack. Having nothing to lose, I grab him and lift him up to stab him, but he shouts out to me: in Russian: "Be quiet! I'm also a Jew". I become confused, knowing that there are no more Jews in Vanke's unit. He leads me into the woods, fires his gun several times, kisses me and says: "Go with God's help. Maybe we'll meet again sometime." He was the "political manager" of Vanke's unit. To this very day I don't know his name.

After a night of wandering, I meet up with our surviving comrades. But where do we go without guns and food? And we have great wounds in our hearts, having lost so many dead comrades, but there's nothing we can do about it. I muster up my courage. I find an old case from a revolver in my knapsack. I stuff it with straw, so that it will look like a real revolver. We go into the house of the first peasant we encounter and order him to give everyone food and to provide us with a horse and sleigh as well. At the start, he's unwilling to listen and starts laughing, but when I take hold of my straw revolver and give him ten minutes to get everything ready and if he refuses, I'll shoot him and his family and we'll burn down his house, he then furnishes us with everything.

Winter 1943

We reach the thick woods around Lipitchianska. We hope to join up with our units, but we find out that we are being sought all over as deserters and that we'll be shot immediately if we just show our faces. We must go back quickly. We leave again for Orlanske's units. The time is still turbulent and I am among a group of Gentiles. I'm weak and sick, but one must not mention that one is ill. Meanwhile, a group is organized to bring provisions. We set out on a very cold night. We come close to hamlets. I go as a lookout, and the others are lying in wait by the road. A few people come towards us. It's very hard to see and we call out: "What's the secret password?" That night the password was "Stalin". They answer correctly and we're sure they are also partisans. When we approach them, we see that they are not our men, but we didn't know for certain because they were wearing civilian clothing. As a Jew, I noticed that they had on Jewish coats. We ask where the others are. They answer: "In the hamlet". We order them to go ahead and we keep our guns aimed at them the whole time. We enter a cottage.

There, in the darkness, we see that the house is encircled by many people, but we don't know who they are. However, when the door is opened, we notice Estonians and Lithuanians. A high-ranking German officer is in the house. They begin questioning us, but we pretend not to understand. The German orders them to shoot us at 6:00 am. To make sure that we won't escape, they strip us. We sit there naked, like newborn babies. The German officer leaves the house. Only three Estonians remain to guard us. The clock on the wall strikes every hour and the time of our death draws near. I tell my Russians what's going to happen. We talk together and decide that when they take us out early in the morning, we should all run off in different directions. Fate will show who is destined to remain alive.

It's nearly six o'clock. Four Lithuanians come in wearing large furs. We are ordered to stand up and we're told that we're going to be brought to another house, but we realize that this isn't correct. We're naked and it's terribly cold on the street. We know that our end has come.... Certain that we won't try to escape, they keep their guns on their shoulders. The door is opened and we're ordered to go. I go out first and take my first step on the snow with bare feet. The snow sticks to my feet and I see red stars in the sky. The pain is indescribable, but we want to escape from the murderous hands. We give a signal and run in different directions. The forest is about 150 meters away. I start running towards the forest, but in a zigzag. Before the Lithuanians manage to take their guns off their shoulders and heavy furs, I'm already in the forest. A few minutes later I hear shooting on all sides. I hear one of our men shouting "God" and that's all. No other words are spoken. I'm sure that both Russians are already dead. I run like a deer and can no longer feel my feet as I'm completely frozen. From afar, I see the house of the guard who watches over the forest. I run towards it, knock on the door with the last of my strength. The door opens, the heat from the house strikes me in the head and I fall down in a faint on the threshold.

*

Late in the evening, the Christian man tells me that when I fainted, he forced open my mouth and poured in a full glass of spirits and wrapped my feet in a cloth with pig fat because I had no more skin left on my feet. He placed me on the oven and I slept there until late at night. I open my eyes and, as in a dream, am presented with scenes of everything that happened to me. I know that I was taken out to be shot, and here I am lying on an oven. I want to get down, but my feet are like pieces of wood, and I can't feel them at all. I call out: "Who is here"? No one answers. A few minutes later, the Christian man comes in carrying wood. He tells me what happened to me. I lie there for two weeks and he heals my feet. Later he gives me slippers so that it would be easier for me to walk and he sends me away with God's help.

The partisans in our unit already know that all three of their comrades were shot. We've already been long forgotten. I return as a grown man with a beard, in slippers and torn clothes, and no one recognizes me. But a few minutes later, they come over to me, touch me and can't believe that I'm alive. I'm promoted to the rank of commander and put in charge of a group of 72 partisans.

A few months go by and the anti-Semitism among the partisans becomes more and more virulent. It once happens that I'm going on a mission with the group and they're talking among themselves: "If we catch a Jew, we'll cut him into pieces; on account of them, we have to sit in the forests." I must emphasize that my group consists only of Russians and they don't know that I'm Jewish. They only know that my name is Volodshke. This sinks into my mind and I think: If the Germans don't kill me, my own partisans will. We secretly meet with all the comrades who remained alive from Senke's group and we decide to go away from there.

*

September, 1943: We're a group of more that 20 Jews with Nonia Shelubski at the head. We appoint him to be our leader. We meet together with Tuvia Bielski, who asks us to join his unit. We tell him that we'd like to combine forces, but that we should be a separate group. This idea, however, isn't acceptable to Tuvia, and we remain apart. The Germans are again hunting down Jews. They are already now in the dense woods around Nalibok. We are near Huta. I'm now serving as a lookout. The men in Bielski's unit are running away, whoever can manage to leave and wherever it's possible to go. I come riding on horseback to a group which had not yet managed to run away. The men are crying and say that everyone has already escaped, but they themselves don't know where to go. In our group, however, we all stayed together. We weren't to take anyone into the group or separate ourselves from the group. But seeing that the people in the group didn't know what to do (the group consisted of members of the Druk family now living in Montreal, Yisrael Bezshovski, now a resident of Tel Aviv and another branch of the family in Warsaw), I decided to lead them to a safer place. It's also important to point out that there was a daughter, Lilke, in Bezshovski's family. Lilke is now my wife and we have three daughters and a son.

*

And so, I was with them for a few lovely months. When everything quieted down, I again join my former group and we again negotiate with Tuvia Bielski. We combine our forces but remain a separate group.

We get more comrades from Bielski's unit and we organize a unit bearing the name "Orzshenikizshe" Our unit becomes the strongest force within Bielski's unit. Bielski has a very good reputation in the area because of our undertakings. We blow up trains, roads, bridges, everything which can serve the Germans. I, too, belong to the group that carries out actions with explosives. And another member is my good friend, Leibush Ferdman, who now makes his home in Newfoundland, Canada.

1944

A year of fighting the Germans and carrying out actions with explosives has gone by. Good news reaches us that the Red Army is driving back the Germans with great losses. We encounter Germans and win many battles, taking many prisoners who are given the same kind of death that they gave our loved ones. They beg us to let them live, promising they'll do everything for us. Each one claims he is not guilty, but our hearts are as hard as stone. We have only one answer: "May their memory be erased"!

Things go on in this way until September, 1944. An order is received from headquarters that the Germans are retreating in haste, the Red Army is pursuing them, they will have to pass through our district and therefore we must dig in and strengthen our forces so that the Germans cannot get through. We are ordered either to capture or destroy them. Women and children are taken to a safer place. Men alone remain to strengthen our forces. Older men dig trenches and get the guns ready, while the young people take up positions, stand on guard and even perform double guard duty. Everything must be ready so that we can confront and annihilate the enemy.

As I am a machinegunner, I take six comrades with me and we take up a position opposite Zorin's unit. Nearby is Benjamin Dombrovski, also a machinegunner, with six fighters. During the day we can hear shooting in the distance, and at night the shooting is closer. From time to time, Germans appear, but no sooner are they noticed than they are wiped out.

A few days go by in this way and the enemy attempts to break through our lines. The Germans are unsuccessful, however, because our forces are very strong, not only our own, but there are more and more Gentile units behind us. Finally, the decisive day comes. We are all lying in our places at dawn, expecting the worst. The Germans realize that there is no way out. The Red Army is pursuing them from behind and we are positioned in front of them in a great force to prevent them from getting through our territory. Lying there in hiding, we notice that, from afar, they look like flies, as there are so many of them in number. Thousands and thousands of Germans are preparing to attack us, shouting wildly. We receive an order not to move from the place.

My lookout is sitting up in a tree. He's a Jew from Stoiptz in his early fifties. He shouts to me: "Open fire, the Germans are here!" But we wait for an order to attack when they get closer.

Suddenly, thousands of Germans spring up, as if from under the ground, engage in battle, overrunning our positions all along an area of four kilometers. A terrible battle ensues, a life and death struggle, and I fire my machinegun without stopping. I can see how dozens of Germans are falling from my bullets. My machinegun is hot, but there's no time to stop. The battle goes on for four hours. Hundreds of Germans lie dead. They fall, but fresh soldiers are sent in to replace them, one after the other. Just at that moment, a large group of Germans overrun my position and shout: "Put down your gun!" And I shout back: "Put down your guns!" I tear off the ring from a hand grenade which I'm ready to explode rather than fall into their hands. A comrade from my left flank hurls a grenade and starts shooting with his automatic gun. Only eight wounded Germans remain out of the thirty something who attacked our position. We also lost many fighters and many were wounded.

However, we have no time to lose. Since they cannot break through our side, the Germans storm Bielski's camp. They succeed but suffer many casualties. Bielski also loses many partisans. Breaking through the camp, they meet up with the partisans of the "Stalin" unit, who wipe them out. Thousands of enemy dead already lie about. The battle goes on for eight hours. Our front becomes quieter and we're busy caring for the wounded and burying our dead comrades.

We return to our camp where we also find dozens of dead fighters. My wife thought that I was no longer alive. I was terribly exhausted and thirsty, without water a whole day. She simply didn't recognize me. The next day we meet up with the Red Army. Our joy is indescribable. We are finally free after so many years...

The Red Army goes on ahead. We remain in the forest for another few weeks and then march into Novogrudek. My wife, her family and I leave for Lida.

In 1945, my wife and I move to Minsk, where I receive a medal for distinguished service.

Later, I went to Bialystok by myself, where I'm arrested by Polish soldiers as a deserter! There is much more to mention, but it's hard to recall all the details.

In Bialystok, I rejoin my wife and her family and we move on to Lodz. With the fall of Berlin, we go on to Prague, Budapest, Leipzig and later to Gruglaska-Tarina*, where we were in a refugee camp until we were able to emigrate to Canada in 1949.

[*Italy: Grugliasco, in the Province of Turin- AB]

[Pages 364-379]

Scrolls from The Flame
by Yisrael Slonimsky

[Translators note: This Hebrew chapter below, "Scrolls From the Flame" is a translation of the Yiddish "Blettlach Funem Flam" (Little Pages From the Flame), which appears on page 338 and includes an accompanying photo on page 351 of the author and his family. We thought it best to give below the translation by Harvey Spitzer of the original Yiddish text. The photos in the text below relate to pages 304 and 316.]

Translated from the Yiddish by Harvey Spitzer

Yisrael Slonimsky

On September 1, 1939, the conflagration broke out in which everything that had authentic meaning for us went up in flames: home, happiness and future.

With terror in our hearts, we awaited the arrival of the Germans, who had invaded and taken over Poland. At night, we slept in our clothes in case we had to run away in search of a hiding place. Seventeen days went by in this way when, suddenly, the news reached us that the Red Army was approaching. We were very happy, as we were finally rid of the fright of falling into German claws.

A few weeks went by and our joy was marred. The Russians took away all our possessions and levied heavy taxes on the store owners which they couldn't possibly pay. The richest Jews were sent to Siberia or Archangel [aka Arkhanelsk - AB], and those who were not sent away lived in fear that the Russians would come at night, pull them out of bed and send them off to perform forced labor in the far north.

My lime burner was nationalized, and such heavy taxes were imposed on my store that I had nothing left. I went away to work on the rafts, hoping only that they would let me stay in one place. But we still didn't grasp the fact that evil and misfortunes have no limit, nor did we ever imagine that it could be thousands of times worse if the German destroyer gained control over us.

In the early hours of the morning of Sunday, June 22, 1941, the gentile residents of Delatitch and peasants from surrounding villages began running back to their homes from the market in Lubtch. Jumping with joy, they related that, while in Lubtch, they heard on the radio that that the Germans had attacked Russia and that German airplanes had already bombarded Lida, Novogrudek and Baranovitch. In the evening, it was reported that German troops were already shooting up the roads leading to Russia and that the former Polish-Russian border was closed to everyone except government personnel who had come to work in our district. Where can people run to?.... We already found out from the press and from refugees that the Germans were locking the Jews up in ghettos, wiping out entire Jewish communities, but what could we do except wait for our dark fate.

On Saturday, June 28, hundreds of peasants from the whole region started out in wagons for Lubtch. They were coming, with the permission of the Germans, to plunder the property of the Jews in Lubtch. After a half day of looting, they went back with their wagons completely loaded up with our possessions: furniture, sewing machines, bedding, clothing, pots and pans, glassware, cows and even chickens, anything and everything that their wild animal appetites lusted for. The gentiles in Lubtch opposed them, not, God forbid, to protect the Jews, but because they claimed the plunder belonged to them. They hit one another with iron tools. The gentiles from the surrounding area went back home with deep gashes in their heads, their animal blood pouring down over their impure faces, but they were happy, knowing that the wagons loaded with our possessions would compensate for everything.

Gentiles from Delatitch whom we knew very well, our so-called "good neighbors", came to the Jews and told them that the same thing would befall us the next day. They advised us to pack up our better things and give it to them for safekeeping. "In any case, you won't be needing these things any more today, and tomorrow they're going to take everything away from you. Give it to me, and when you need it, I'll give it back to you". Every word of theirs was like a spear piercing our hearts.

The peasants from the surrounding areas couldn't wait until Sunday and attacked us that very Saturday night. They smashed all the windowpanes, broke down the doors, forced everyone to the Neiman River and robbed anything of value, and whatever was worthless to them, they simply broke and destroyed. They hit the elderly Rabbi Beinish Liss over the head with a spade and my father, Feive the Baker, received a blow on his shoulders with an axe.

We hid among the shrubs at the river edge for two days. On the third day, when our hunger became oppressive, we went back to our homes. They somewhat calmed their bloody instincts for two days. They greeted us with a shout: "Now, Jews, there's not a thing we're lacking!" A few elderly Christian residents secretly brought us bread, flour and a pitcher of milk. But where could we get a pan or a spoon, since everything had either been stolen or broken? They strewed garbage and faeces all over the study hall (synagogue), broke the windows, took down the doors, tore the Torah scrolls and hung them up on the trees.

*

The Germans came a few days later. They appointed the police and published an order that Jews must wear a yellow Star of David over their heart and shoulders, that Jews must not leave the town without a permit and whoever did not obey this order would be shot on the spot. Rabbi Ya'akov Baksht, May God avenge his blood!, was the first to go outside with the yellow badge. You could not conceive how happy and excited the gentiles were to see the Jews humiliated.

The gentiles began forcing us out to work on property belonging to Delatitch. There, we dug up potatoes and beets and also received blows from our new masters. They also became masters of our houses. We accepted everything with love because our heart told us that things were yet to get worse.

Even before the Jews were locked up in the ghetto in Lubtch, 150 young Jews were selected and sent to a work camp near Dvoretz. My brother-in-law, Avraham Kivovitch as well as Shepsel, Itche Kushner's son, and Shemaya, Sarah-Elke's grandson, were part of that group.

I worked on the property belonging to the village of Vereskova. Velvel (Ze'ev) Yankelevitch and Sara-Elke's grandson, Yerachmiel, worked together with me as did my father-in-law Moshe-Aharon and both my brothers-in-law, Nota (Natan) and Ya'akov. We also used to sleep there. When the Jews from Delatitch were driven into the ghetto in Lubtch, I would work all week long in Vereskova. Friday evenings, we were allowed to go to our families in the Lubtch ghetto. Since my job was tending to the cows, I would go into the cow shed Thursday night, milk the cows and prepare a couple of bottles of milk. That's how I was able to smuggle a little milk into the ghetto. My wife would divide the milk among our small children. Of course, one received a death penalty for such a "crime.

Even before we were locked up in the ghetto, Gestapo agents would come to Lubtch in trucks. They would seize young men, as though for work, and then take them behind the town and shoot them. When we found out about that, we became more cautious. As soon as there was daylight, the young men would run off and hide in the fields all day long. But no one thought about escaping into the forests and saving himself from the Germans. We still believed that we would outlive the enemy, and besides, we didn't want to be separated from our families.

The situation changed for the worse when we were driven into the Lubtch ghetto. It already became difficult to run away. The news that reached us about the slaughters of the Jews in surrounding ghettos broke our spirits completely. In Novogrudek, on the first day of the Hebrew month of *Av*, 5701 (1941), the Germans and their helpers gathered together 52 Jews, stood them in a row in the middle of the street and shot every tenth person. The "counting" was repeated regularly until they finished off the last Jew. While this was taking place, a band played happy marches. Afterwards, Jewish women were sent to wash the blood off the pavement stones.

We began to observe fasts - the old Jewish means against evil decrees. We would fast twice a week on Mondays and Thursdays and even the elderly, and little children fasted. But no miracle occurred and God's gates of mercy remained closed to our prayers and fasting.

Jews from Delatitch, Neishtat (Negnyevitch) and the Jewish residents of the surrounding villages were also locked up in the Lubtch ghetto. Chaim Bruk from Lubtch and Berl Yankelevitch from Delatitch were appointed leaders of the ghetto. Decrees were issued incessantly: First, we had to hand over all our money, jewelry, other valuables and the little furniture that remained after the plunder by the gentiles. Harsh monetary penalties were imposed on us for any light matter. We had to hand over at once whatever they desired. The craftsmen: tailors, shoemakers, etc., had to work for the Germans and for the local police, but the craftsmen themselves were almost naked and barefoot. If a person managed to bury something in the ground, he risked his life sneaking out the ghetto to trade the "treasure" with a gentile for a piece of bread to keep his children alive.

We lived in Tevel the Shoemaker's house. There were thirty people in one room. When we slept, one person's head was against another's. People were actually eaten away by lice and worms, but until the very end, no one broke down or lost confidence in the belief that salvation would come. Yenta, the daughter of the rabbi of Lubtch, also lived in the ghetto with her husband, Dr. Rabinovitch from Baranovitch. The rabbi had died a short time before, and his wife was in the ghetto in Novogrudek. On a certain day, the rabbi's wife informed Yenta that the murderers had set out in the direction of Lubtch and that we should be on guard. When we heard the "tiding", we all recited confession and awaited death. Till this very day, I can't comprehend why we didn't try to escape from the ghetto that day, as if some secret force was preventing us from running away, although there were dense forests all around us just an arm's length away and good prospects for saving our lives. A few days went by in expectation of death, but the murderers did not show up.

Incidentally, I will mention here that a short time later, during the slaughter, when they brought Yenta and her husband to the pit, Dr. Rabinovitch shouted out to the Germans that the day of revenge would certainly come for them and their mad leader and that they would pay dearly for their crimes. He embraced Yenta, kissed her and, thus doing, both fell into the pit.

A few days after Passover, 1942, two Gestapo agents came into the ghetto. They took out Naftali's son, Avraham Alperstein, Yitchak Rosenblum and Chaim Bruk. They brought them out of the house and shot them on the spot. Chaim Bruk still managed to run to Sarah's (Esther's daughter) yard, but they chased after him and shot him. We remained like sheep without a shepherd, for Chaim Bruk, with his authority, wisdom and knowledge, always comforted us and gave us courage and confidence.

An order came from Novogrudek to send one hundred tradesmen there from Lubtch. My brother-in-law, Nota, Baruch-Mordechai Krulevetzky and I were taken as part of that transport. Weeping terribly, we said good-bye to our families. We felt that we would not see each other again. My wife, however, would not let the *Judenrat* rest until they prevailed upon the authorities to allow her and the children to move to the ghetto in Novogrudek.

Six hundred Jews from Lubtch capable of working were transferred to Vorobievitch. There were also Jews from Delatitch among them and I remember some of them: Rabbi Ya'akov Baksht and his daughter, Necha, Rabbi Beinush with his family, Berl with Peya, Velvel Yankelevitch, Chaya -Zelda, my father-in-law, Moshe-Aharon with his son, Ya'akov, and his wife with two children. They were assured that they would work paving roads and that they would all remain alive. Not one of them remained alive: some were burned alive and others were shot at the large pit, close to the Lubtch- Novogrudek road. Gershon Kapushtchevsky tried to escape, but they shot at him and he fell wounded into a stream and drowned.

There were also some Jews from Delatitch in the Novogrudek ghetto: my father, Rabbi Feive, my brother-in-law, Avraham'l with his son, Binyamin, R' Yosef the Ritual Slaughterer with his family, Golda Krulevetzky with her children, Moshe Sontzes with his younger daughter.

Mainly old women and little children remained in the Lubtch ghetto. My mother, Tziporah-Feigel, and my sister, Itke-Tulia, with her three children were also among them. They were all murdered in Podlipka, on the 24th of the Jewish month of *Av*, together with the last 275 Jews from Lubtch. On that day, they also liquidated the Jews in Vorobievitch and thousands of Jews in Novogrudek.

After arriving in the Novogrudek ghetto, we were placed in an old house with a broken, rotted roof. We would get wet with the slightest rain. Every day, together with my wife and son, we went a distance of seven kilometers to work paving roads, carefully guarded by the local police. All day long we would drag heavy stones and wheelbarrows with sand and gravel. For being late to work, one was made to lie on the ground and was then whipped to death. At five o'clock in the afternoon, the local police would take us back to the ghetto. On the way back, they would make sport of us, whip us or even shoot us just for entertainment, leaving behind the dead and seriously injured. Those who worked received 120 grams of bread a day. Those who didn't work got nothing. My daughter Rochele was still too small and didn't work, so got no bread.

One day, they sent off a group of Jews to work in Minsk. My brother-in-law, Nota, was included in that group and was murdered there.

The day came when the Jews in Novogrudek were slaughtered:

That day, as always, we were away at work and had left Rochele in the ghetto. Suddenly, people began saying that an *akstia* was going to take place that day. We were then working in the town itself. I dropped my work, turned around and went into the ghetto. I took Rochele and tried to get her out of the ghetto. A Jewish ghetto-policeman stopped us at the gate and ordered me to leave Rochele in the ghetto. I pleaded with him at length and when he finally pretended not to notice, I went out with Rochele and brought her to the workplace.

There was a great commotion when the foreman began registering people with a trade. I urged him forcefully and he registered me as a tradesman. Then they drove us up to a yard and again began registering us. But this was already for a final count. When the pushing and shoving got out of hand, a policeman, a Tarter from Novogrudek, began hitting us with a leather club. Then they led us away to the barracks where armed Germans called out the names of 200 men from a list. After that, they began shouting to the remaining Jews: "Damn Jews, back to work".

We already understood what awaited us and began running to hide in the fields of grain. I took my wife and children, my brother-in-law, Avraham'l, with his son and we went back to our house in the ghetto where we had discovered a good, camouflaged hiding place a few weeks before.

As soon as we heard the first shooting in the ghetto, we went into a closet, removed the small cover and from there went into the hiding place, putting back the small cover to close the closet. My father was also with us, but the tightness made him choke and he began coughing very loudly. We asked him to go out and hide in the attic because we would all surely be killed on account of him. My father understood the situation very well and went out of the shelter, climbed up into the attic and took the ladder with him. He lay there for three days and wasn't found. On the fourth day, the 200 selected craftsmen were brought into the ghetto in order to destroy the houses in the large ghetto and fence in the small ghetto. When my father noticed people going about freely in the ghetto, he thought that the danger had passed, came down from the attic and was soon caught and led away.

From our hiding place, we could look outside and see how the Jews were driven from their houses and ordered to lie face up on the ground. The policemen shouted: "*Davai tchasi, Davai zolota!*" (Give watches! Give gold!). When it grew dark, trucks came and everyone was pushed onto the trucks. Whoever didn't climb aboard fast enough was shot on the spot. The Jewish ghetto police carried the sick people out, but when they finished, the sick people were locked up in the same house where we had our hiding place. Afterwards, the door opened and someone shouted the order: "*Raus*" ("Out")! They packed them into a truck and took them away. The Germans also discovered various hiding places and dragged out the people hiding there.

On that day over 2,000 Jews were caught and murdered in the common grave on the road to Shelyub, near the dogcatchers' house.

Lying in our hiding place, we heard the front door open. Two Jews who were part of the group of tradesmen entered. They were looking around the rooms for something. We heard one of them ask the other: "Well, did you find anything to chew on?" Convinced that they were Jews, I decided to ask them if it was possible to leave our hiding place. Hearing our voices, one of them approached the closet and said in a loud voice: "Stay there! Don't go out! I'll talk to the Polish commander, who is a friend of mine. When he comes here and calls out that Yevnovitch sent him, only then should you leave your hiding place".

A few days went by, but no one came. On the fifth day, Rochele had an attack of hysteria. She started to laugh wildly and no one could calm her. The nervous people were about to put various things over her face and suffocate her, when my wife suddenly got the idea to bite Rochele somewhere on her body until she was bleeding. She did this and our young daughter immediately calmed down.

It was only on the seventh day that the commander came in and shouted in Polish: "Go out! Yevnovitch sent me"!

We came out of the "shelter" drunk from weakness. The commander demanded one thousand rubles to take us into the small ghetto. We gave him the amount he asked for, and he brought us into the ghetto. We hid there several days and then went out, having assumed the names of those who had escaped from the ghetto.

The bitter news became known to us that we no longer had any family remaining either in Lubtch or Vorobievitch. A few days later, they shot my father, who had been kept under arrest the whole time as well as Yosef Kagan with his wife, Simke, and their two little children. As they were led past the ghetto, they shouted out to us: "Jews, avenge our blood"!

We decided to escape from the ghetto - all the inhabitants of the room where we were living: Avraham Lin, Itche Florans from Baranovitch and Rabinovitch. We traded a suit of clothes for fifteen kilos of flour, which we smuggled into the ghetto and baked bread from it- provisions for the way. Avraham Lin stole a gun with sixteen bullets at the place where he worked and brought it into the ghetto.

On the set day, my son didn't go out to work because he used to return very late. The German who used to come to take him to work came looking for him. My wife told him that he had gone to work very early and that was all she knew. The German warned us that it would be very bad and bitter for us if our son failed to go to work the next day as well. The same day, two Germans drove into the ghetto in wagons and ordered us to fill them with bricks. When we finished the job, one of the Germans for whom I worked looked around to see if anyone was listening and said to me: "Jew, You'd better find a way out of here, otherwise you're going to die". When he received no answer from me, he repeated the same sentence. Then I plucked up the courage to talk and replied that I was afraid to talk to him because Jews are forbidden to speak to a German. "For Heaven's sake, I won't do anything to you!", the German exclaimed and began to lecture about the new German "culture" which murders innocent people, adding that he doesn't feel good about the war and that if Hitler has a bone to pick with Stalin, let them fight it out together, like two mad dogs.

He also said that the surrounding area was full of partisans who had already killed many Germans and that he was sure that we could reach the partisans and save ourselves from death.

That night we escaped from the ghetto. We gave every one in the group a small loaf of bread - provisions for the way, and I also took along an axe with nails and the gun.

The night cloaked us in darkness as we scraped ourselves on the ground, crawling under the barbed wire, with hearts filled with fear and prayer to God that He would lead us on the right way. When all of us were over the other side of the ghetto wire, we began running, one behind the other.

Dogs started barking and their owners also noticed us. It didn't take long for them to notify the Germans that Jews were escaping from the ghetto. A searchlight cut through the night, and a hail of bullets accompanied us. Suddenly, we heard cries and noticed that Liss and his wife had fallen dead, like cut-off ears of grain. We all gathered together among the bushes and lay there for a few hours until it grew quiet and, somewhere in the distance, we only heard dogs barking and eventually whining. It was only then that we decided to go on our way, following the road to Selyov [Silev]. The night was ours because the Germans were afraid to travel on the roads at night on account of the partisans.

The next day, we sat stuck in the woods not far from Selyov. That night we reached Delatitch and went to the river. The water at the shore of the Neiman was already frozen, but it was possible to cross over with a rowboat because the middle of the river was still ice-free.

I found a boat not too far away, by Yordika, used a pole instead of an oar and began to cross over the river with my wife and children. When we got close to the opposite shore, my little daughter fell into the water. My wife barely managed to grab her little hand and pull her out of the icy water. I went back to the other side of the river and brought over all the people from our group. Soon after, we went into the forest and started on our way to Berezin.

As we got closer to Berezin, we left everyone in the forest, and only Avraham'l and I went to the homes of peasants in Berezin with whom we were acquainted, very decent Christians, from whom we used to buy fish in the good times. Avraham'l had hidden his things with one of them.

In the evening, we knocked on the door and went into the house. There, we found the peasants' sixteen year old son. The boy was very frightened, seeing the unexpected guests. He ran over to the lamp and extinguished the wick. He told us that the Germans had come the day before and exchanged fire with the partisans. Suddenly, he shouted to us: "A policeman is going!" What he meant wasn't very clear to us, but we ran out of the house and went to try our luck at the home of the Christian with whom Avraham'l had hidden his things.

Here, too, a young fellow also opened the door for us. He asked us to sit down and went into the next room to wake up his father. As soon as the elderly peasant came in, he embraced and kissed both of us and wept. He ordered his son to bring us food and asked about our families.

We told him that my wife and children, Avraham'l's son, Benjamin (Niome), and several more Jews were sitting in the forest, waiting for us to return. He asked that none of them should come to his house, only the both of us. He would provide us with food and would do everything he had the strength to do for us. And, in fact, he brought us bread, a small container of butter, cheese, two spades and a saw. Avraham'l asked his advice about how to go about building an earthen shelter, but he refused to answer this question because, should we be found, we would undoubtedly suspect that he was the one who turned us in and sold his conscience to the devil. As he spoke, we could sense his honest intentions, clean conscience and pure heart. And our hearts trembled as we realized that the whole world had not yet been corrupted and that even in Sodom there were still some honest and good people!

We went to the peasant Kazik, who was in the forests near Potashnya. He, too, inquired who had remained alive and gave us potatoes, bread and two spades. We offered him money so that he would provide us with food. He replied that he had more money than we did, but if we had any kind of merchandise, we could use it for barter.

*

We settled in "*Viltche Bloto*" ("The Wolf Swamp"), a place in the forest where the wolves have their dens. We dug a pit, blocked the walls with sawed off young trees, put a ladder inside so we could go down and camouflaged the top with little trees. The snow covered everything, and it was hard to tell from outside that this was a hiding place. However, it is very hard to hide from the eyes of peasants who know every hidden corner in the forest and recognize, like a wild animal, the scent of a stranger.

When we went back to Kazik a few months later, he told us that the peasants in the surrounding villages knew where we were hiding. He advised us to leave the place because the peasants would turn us over to the Germans.

We did not leave the place, but we were already afraid to go and ask peasants for food. Three weeks went by and we were simply famished. My brother-in-law suggested that we go out and look for "*koptzes*" potatoes (holes covered all winter for storing potatoes). We actually found such a "*kopetz*" hole in one of the hamlets, and that kept us alive.

Early one morning, as we were sitting around the fire cooking our food, we heard a shout: "*Ruki verch!*" (Hands up!) We naturally obeyed the order and raised our hands. These were Christian partisans in a unit bearing Stalin's name. They searched us, took our money, boots, sheets which we had gotten and they also wanted to take our gun, but one of them would not allow this, explaining that we wouldn't be able to get food without a gun and that we would die of hunger. We asked them to take us with them, but our asking was in vain because: "You're robbers, and there's no place among partisans for such people." Two weeks later, they returned and took the only gun we had.

A few days later, we were forced to leave our earthen shelter and move to another place. We dug ourselves into a hill and built a stronger and better camouflaged earthen shelter. We had to hide from the Germans as well as from some of the partisans. We were in contact with a certain peasant, Misha, whom we would often help with his household work. A few days after we had left our first shelter, the partisans came back looking for us. When they found no one there, they shot bullets in their own hats and informed their commander that we shot at them and then ran away. The commander ordered them to catch us and bring us to him. We found out all about this from Misha, our contact person. In short, they captured my brother-in-law and forced him to lead them to our hiding place. They then took two of our men and brought them to their commander. On the way, they savagely beat them up, then washed off the blood and brought them to Tchapen, the village where the unit's command post was located. As they were waiting outside in this state, a Jewish partisan happened to pass by and said: "Don't be afraid, fellows. They won't do anything to you.", and having said this, left. And that's what actually happened. The commander understood the truth and released them. Since it was already too late to go back, he ordered that they be given food and a place to sleep. My brother-in-law again brought up the question of our being accepted into the unit, but they turned down his request because we didn't have any guns, and they themselves didn't have enough guns for their men. The commander sent a letter with our request to the district staff quarters located not far from Baksht, but we received the same reply from there.

Itche (Yitzhak) Florans decided to go back to the ghetto in Novogrudek and get his brother out. We took him as far as the Neiman. He crossed the ice covered river and got safely into the ghetto, but it was already impossible to get out of the ghetto. They started to dig a tunnel, but before they finished digging, the mass slaughter took place and they hid in the bunker. That night, Itche Florans was standing by the door of the bunker, listening to the sounds outside. Suddenly, he heard the Germans approaching the bunker and surrounding it. He shouted: "Jews, save your lives!" He jumped outside, quickly climbed over the ghetto fence and was engulfed by the blackness of the night. He reached Delatitch that same night. He stayed there a full week until he managed to return to our earthen shelter.

Spring was approaching. We knew that when the ice melted, the Neiman would overflow all around and we would be cut off from all human habitation and not receive any food. That meant that we had to provide food for ourselves well in advance if we didn't want to die of hunger.

Lin, a carpenter, carved guns and pistols from wood, and they really looked authentic. "Armed" with such weapons, we went to one of the hamlets. We entered a house holding our "pistols" and ordered the peasant to harness a horse because we had to go somewhere. The peasant started crying, explaining that he had only one horse and that if we took away his horse, he would be unable to maintain his household. I calmed him down, promising that we wouldn't hurt him, and that if he was worried about his horse, he should take us with him in his sleigh. The peasant actually did so.

It was a clear winter night. The ground was still covered with white, clean snow as soft as butter, but we already felt a mild spring breeze coming up and the trees awakening from their frozen sleep. The sleigh carrying the six Jews with wooden guns on their shoulders moved along quickly and pleasantly, as though it were a peaceful "jaunt" in the good old days.

The Voynov forest was silent when we went into the homes of the peasants and ordered them to give us food. We loaded up the sled with a few bags of flour, bread, groats, meat, sausage and honey. At midnight, we went back with our trophies, accompanied by the barking of dogs.

On the way back, we encountered a large group of partisans. We were afraid that we would be questioned as to where and how we got food and that we would undoubtedly be shot on account of that. But we had no other choice and had to take a chance. When we got closer, a guard saw us and shouted out: "*Davay Parol*" ("Give the password!") I kept my wits about me and answered: "*Da svoya, takiya sami kak vay*" ("The same, the same people as you!") He gave an order *Paganay le'ashaday*" "Move your horse on!" The same thing happened a second time. We got through safely in this way and returned to our earthen shelter. Then we released the peasant with his horse and he went happily back home.

Two weeks later, we again took a horse from one of the peasants and brought back a wagon full of potatoes. We obtained food in this way and got safely through the few weeks, during which everything around was submerged in water and we were sitting in our shelter, as though we were on an island, cut off from human settlement.

Spring arrived. The sun became agreeably warmer and the water dried up. Everything was covered with green vegetation and an abundance of flowers. Birds were chirping and flying from tree to tree, carrying pieces of wood, grass and soil in their beaks with which to build their nests. Everything awakened to a new life. We also felt freer and happier.

On such a day, we were sitting outside, cooking a pot of potatoes over a small fire. Suddenly, we heard the echo of a strong movement, not far from us, and an echo of voices also reached us. We were terribly afraid. Who could that be? As we were sitting like that, eating the hot potatoes, we saw two armed men approaching. We soon recognized them as partisans. We greeted them with a "Welcome comrades!" and invited them to sit and eat with us.

Hearing that we were Jews hiding from the Germans, they told us that they belonged to the partisan unit named after Tchkalov and that there were many Jews in that unit who would certainly like to see us. Before long, the Jewish partisans, men and women, came to us. We kissed and wept from joy, seeing living Jews and besides, Jews who were taking revenge and paying back the enemy with fire and death. They asked us to go with them and show them in which villages there were no Germans.

We set out late at night and got as far as Delatitch-Zahorye. Guards were placed on the roads leading to Lubtch and Delatitch and we began to clean out the peasants, taking their cows, pigs, flour, grain as well as stolen Jewish property: suits, material, clothes, etc. We harnessed 25 horses and got to Mikolayeve before daybreak. We didn't take anything from the peasants who lived near the forest. On the contrary, we shared the things we brought with them.

The commander of the Tchkalov unit gave us a document stating that we belonged to his unit. He sent me and my brother-in-law on mission to spy out the area and report where the Germans were deployed and which of the local peasants were in the police force. We carried out our task superbly. Next, we went to Delatitch with a group of partisans. There, we caught the gentile who was the first to rob the Jews as well as the village elder, Alexei Shunke. We honored them both with a bullet to their heads, and we took everything they had in their houses, mainly the things they had robbed from the Jews.

The front had moved closer to our area. The Germans were running back in wild panic just as the Russians had run back three years earlier. The partisans cut off the roads taken by the retreating Germans and sowed death and destruction among them. At the beginning of June 1944, we heard distant, dull echoes of artillery fire. A few days later, we were already greeting the attacking divisions of the Red Army, which liberated our area.

*

We were once again "free" people, but where could we go? We were terrified to go back to our town - a few Jews among so many gentile wolves.

We went to Ivya, where I was drafted into the Red Army and sent to Lida, where Engineer Buslovitch, a former partisan from our unit, discharged me from the army, pretending I was needed for work in his division. My wife and I soon returned to Delatitch and moved back into our house. I worked in Lubtch, in the *Raiprom-kombinat*, as a deliverer of raw material and tools. In this position, I had the opportunity to travel about in Lida, Baranovitch, Minsk and other cities. The destruction was great everywhere. The Jewish communities were obliterated, and not a trace remained of the once flourishing and spiritually rich Jewish life.

A terrible feeling of bereavement and orphanhood enveloped us. It was hard for us to remain on that cursed ground. As soon as we had the opportunity to leave for Poland, we left our town and went to Lodz.

In Poland, however, the hatred towards the few surviving Jews was even greater and more intense than in our region. Pogroms were perpetrated against Jews in Cracow (1945), Kielce (1946) and other cities. They stopped trains, took the Jews off and shot them on the spot. The Polish population rejoiced and eagerly assisted the bandits.

I understood that there was no safe place for the Jewish people, except for Eretz-Israel. However the nations of the world had not yet agreed that the Jews have a right to live in their land. We set out on the difficult path of clandestine immigration to Palestine, together with thousands of other Jews, snatched from the burning fires. The route we followed took us through Czechoslovakia, Austria, Italy and finally to Eretz Yisrael. But this is already a separate chapter in our life, the story of which will be told in the history of the Jewish People and its fight for its own country.

On May 19, 1946, a year after the victory over the Germans, the greatest ever enemy of the Jewish people, our feet stepped upon the ground of our eternal homeland - The Land of Israel.

The Few Survivors from Lubtch at a memorial service in Fernwald, Germany

Translation of the above memorial plaque:

THE SOULS
Of our parents, brothers and sister, wives and husbands
Numbering 5500 people
Who were killed and burnt as martyrs
By Hitler and his collaborators, cursed be their names
From the towns of Novogrudek, Lubtch, Karelitch
Ivye, Rovovitz, Silev, -----

May their souls rest in peace

------------in the Fernwald Camp
The survivors of the inferno
NOVOGRUDEK]

[Pages 380-387]

In the Lubtch Ghetto

by Shifra Solomiansky [Leibovitch]

Translated from the Yiddish by Harvey Spitzer

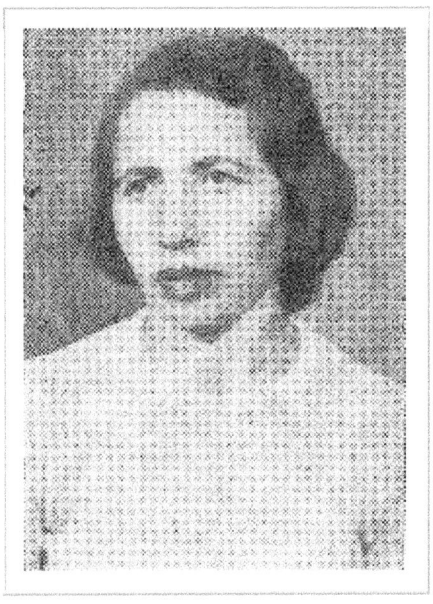

Shifra Solomiansky

Sunday, June 22, 1941:

It's a lovely, sunny day. Hundreds of peasants are coming to the market place to sell their products and buy vodka, which is nearly the only item one can always purchase in government stores.

Suddenly, everyone around begins to tremble. The radio loudspeakers announce the terrible news that Nazi Germany has attacked the Soviet Union. Molotov speaks to the nation: He assures us that the enemy will be vanquished because "our cause is just!". A thought crosses our minds as to whether we can rely on his speech. A few days before, the government actually denied the British report that Germany was concentrating its army on the borders of the USSR. In fact, the government deluded the population with its propaganda, and even the army was unprepared. Apparently, the Soviets had great trust in its Nazi partner; Ribbentrop's signature calmed the people and gave them a sense of security. Who can now have any trust in Molotov's words?

It didn't take long and our thoughts acquired a real meaning. Already on the second day, the Soviet authorities were running away from our town. German airplanes were bombing the whole region. A panic broke out and no one knew what to do. A small number of Jews ran deeper into White Russia, but the old Soviet-

Polish border was closed and a *laissez-passer* document was required. By the time the border was free and unguarded, it was already too late. The entire region was already occupied by the Germans.

On Wednesday, June 25th, German airplanes bombed the town and blew up both bridges. Several Christian residents were killed by the shrapnel. Fish Street, Kapushtchever Street and a part of Castle Street were set ablaze by the bombing. No one bemoaned their burned possessions. People prayed to God that it shouldn't be any worse.

A few days later, two Germans came on motorcycles and assembled the Christian population. They declared that Jewish property was ownerless and that they could take whatever the Jews possessed. It didn't take much to incite the Christians against the Jews. For years they had been waiting for such an opportunity. The rampage began on Friday morning. The first to be attacked were the merchants and their shops: Moshe Shlimovitch, Chashe-Feigel Mendelevitch, Nissel Zalmanski and others. Next, they went from house to house, going on a rampage all night long right through the Sabbath day. Nothing was left in the houses. They spilled out the Sabbath stew and stole the pots. They even tore out the dampers from the chimneys. And whatever they couldn't take with them, they just destroyed. We couldn't even imagine trying to resist them as they were armed with axes, whips and sticks. For the slightest remark, they would beat you with murderous blows. It was simply a miracle that there were no human casualties on that Sabbath

We were left naked, without anything to wear, without the necessities of life. People sewed things from old bags, just so they would have something to cover their body with. The Jews who foresaw the plunder hid some of their possessions in the homes of gentiles with whom they were acquainted, but they only got trifles back and the gentiles threatened to kill the Jews as long as they could keep their belongings.

A short time later, all the Jews were called together onto the marketplace. They were arranged by family and ordered to wear the yellow Star of David. For the time being, that was all that happened.

One Friday, some Germans arrived in a car and, together with the Lubtch police under the command of the Jew's enemy, Sioma Komornik, went into Jewish homes and took out 50 young men, of whom I remember just a few: Yaakov Soltz, Avraham Soltz, Yehuda Berezinski, David Movshovitch, Yoel Baksht, Kalman Rosenblum, Baruch Gorodiski, Bere-Hirshel Gishin, David the Shoemaker and others. They announced that these young men were needed for work, but a short time later it become known that they were all shot to death in Novogrudek, behind the barracks. Besides these 50 men, four more Jews were shot in the town on that same day. These were Shaye Dzjientchelski, Yaakov Pikelni, Pesach Shklut and Yisrael-Itche Meselevitch.

The police station was located in Risia Yedidovitch's house. The policemen-young demons from Lubtch -would sit there and gleefully devise ways to torture the Jews who passed by. Once they seized an old woman, Leah Pines, and brought her into the station. They forced her to get water and clean the rooms. When her work was done, they beat her up and threw her out. Another time, they brought in Nota, Chaim-Shlomo the Tailor's son, and gave him twenty-five lashes with a whip. Afterwards he lay sick in bed for two months with pus-filled wounds all over his body. They would also grab Jews and send them to work in the forest and would also force old men to run while singing, "Hatikva". How happy we were when we saw them coming back!

*

I don't exactly recall when the *Judenrat* (Jewish Council) was appointed, but I clearly remember its make-up:
President - Yankel-Chaim Leibovitch
Secretary - Chaim Bruk
Members: Yisrael Soloducha, David Villner, Nachum Sandler, Shalom Ziman, Gershon Kapushchevsky and Beryl Yankelevitch from Delatitch.

The town was divided into sections and every section received two Jewish "policemen" ("servants for maintaining order"). Chaim Bruk took advantage of the better relations he had with the police to help the Jews of Lubtch. By the way, he was assured (it was, of course, one of the many lies they told to deceive us) that if no one tried to escape into the forest, the Jews in Lubtch would be better off than in all other places. From news reaching us, we knew that massacres had taken place in the surrounding towns and villages, and for the time being it was still quiet in Lubtch. We actually thought that their promises were worth something, and so no one did, in fact, run away, although it was very easy and simple to reach the forest.

A week before Chanukah, the news reached us that a great massacre had taken place in Novogrudek. Two Jews from Lubtch were also among the victims: Kushe Soltz and Ara Berezinski. Right on the eve of Chanukah, an order was received in Lubtch to send a group of young men to the work camp in Dvoretz. The police eagerly carried out this order. Men were torn away from their wives, children from their parents, among them many minors. Hungry and torn away from loved ones, they were driven on foot to Dvoretz, accompanied by the sorrowful weeping of the families left behind and the shouting and beatings of the two-footed dogs. Arriving in Novogrudek, there was further wailing when they found themselves together with the orphaned remnant of the local Jews.

The Lubtch "Jewish Council" was given a horse and wagon and had to provide food for the Jews from Lubtch who were sent to the work camp in Dvoretz. My father, Shalom Leibovitch, was appointed the wagon driver. Every one of his trips to Dvoretz was laden with great danger and we were very happy when he returned home safely.

One morning there was a panic: the Germans encircled the town and were going from house to house. Religious Jews wore their prayer shawls under their clothing, recited confession and waited to be taken to be killed. It's hard to understand what the Germans were looking for. They didn't do any harm to anyone and the whole episode ended only in terrorizing the Jews.

On Purim [March] 1942, an order was received to set up a ghetto and to lock up all the Jews there within a week's time.

Jews from surrounding villages were also driven into the Lubtch ghetto. Several families were placed in the bigger houses, and it was very tight, noisy and dirty. In contrast, it was much better in the smaller houses - fewer people and quieter.

Every morning the Jews would go to the ghetto gate from where they would be taken to their work places. From time to time, they would grab Jews and force them to kiss Stalin's portrait. If a Jew refused to obey their command, he would be beaten mercilessly, and if a Jew did obey their order, the police would shout that he was a communist, that he loved Stalin and they would beat him with murderous blows. Among their victims were Faivel Yedidovitch, Baruch-Mordechai Yankelevitch and others.

After the ghetto was set up, the "place commander", a sadistically cruel German, took up residence in Lubtch. He demanded that two Jews, a man and woman, clean his house. The *Judenrat* sent Henia Zacherevitch (Asher's daughter) and Chona (Chanan) Kagan, the son of the ritual slaughter from Delatitch. Going there was frightening and almost a torture, but they had no choice. Once, Henia was ordered to strip and dance naked before the commander. When he used to go to the bathhouse, which was located by the ghetto fence, he would look through binoculars to see if there were a lot of children in the ghetto.

All the Jewish doctors from Lubtch and the surrounding towns lived in the building of the former *Tarbut* school. One day, very early in the morning, the "place commander" went into the building and noticed that the doctors were covered with good quilts. He called for Chaim Bruk and demanded that he get him two quilts. Chaim declared that he could not provide these.

The next day, the commander came to the *Judenrat* and said to Bruk: "Come here, Bruk. Now I'll give you a cover".

He pulled Chaim by the arm and ordered him to go with him on a "sanitation tour" of the ghetto. There was a trench from the time of First World War in one of the gardens not far from Chaim-Meir Yedidovitch's house. As is known, since houses in Lubtch had no water pipes or toilets, people had to relieve themselves in their gardens, and the trench was very suitable for this purpose. The commander found the place and had the two Jewish policemen sent for, Itche Rosenblum (Mishke Bezpaletze's son) and Avraham Halperstein (Naftali's son). Before they got there, he shot Chaim Bruk and then shot both of them. No one, except for the families, was allowed out of the ghetto to attend the funeral which took place the very same day. There was great sorrow. Chaim Bruk, the crown of Lubtch Jews and our only protector, had fallen. The doctors in the ghetto promised to support Henia and her children, and they kept their word.

Shortly after Chaim's death, all those capable of work were ordered to be sent to Vorobievitch. Only the elderly, infirm and children were to remain in the ghetto. Another group of a hundred young men were taken to Novogrudek. A few days later they were allowed to bring their wives and children. Our family, too, was taken to Novogrudek.

I shall add a few details about life in the Lubtch ghetto which have remained etched in my memory.

As the synagogues were occupied by Jews from Neishtot (Negnievitch), Delatitch and surrounding villages, prayer services were no longer held there. My father brought a Torah scroll into our house, and the neighbors used to come to our home to pray. The rabbi from Delatitch, Rabbi Yaakov Baksht, also prayed with us. On the holiday of Simchat Torah 1941, Rabbi Shalom Ziman came to our house to pray. He was a very good prayer leader. When it came to the part of the service where the worshippers carry the Torah scrolls around the platform on which the Torah is read, the worshippers danced around the table and were a little joyful. The women were standing and weeping. Shalom Ziman called out to the women:

"Women, don't cry! I prayed and sang last year and we lived through this year. I'm praying and singing again and we'll live to pray next year as well".

There was a warehouse next to the pharmacy in Lubtch. When we were left naked and barefoot after the gentiles robbed our possessions, the Jews opened the warehouse and distributed empty sacks out of which we sewed clothes. Reuven Movshovitch (the baker) used to carve wooden shoes. As we had no money to pay him, we would pay with our ration coupons for bread. Every person used to get a total of 120 grams of bread a day, some of which we still had to save for the shoes.

The Jews in the ghetto were very religious. No woman went around without a kerchief on her head. People fasted twice a week. Even 10 year old children had already begun fasting. Younger children were taught to pray and older children also studied the Bible. The deep faith we had in God kept up our spirit and gave us the strength to bear all the trials and tribulations. Unfortunately, no salvation came from Heaven. And when the enemy pounced on us, none of those who believed, hoped and waited for that day remained alive.

At the memorial monument in the basement of the Holocaust Center in Jerusalem.
Right to left: Rivka Shimshoni, Elka Yankelevitch, Chaim Yankelevitch, -----
   [Caption provided by Moshe Yankelevitch]

Translation of the Plaque (also see page 280):
In eternal memory of the martyrs of the **Lubtch-Delatitch** community and the environs (Novogrudek District), may the Lord avenge their blood,
who were murdered, slaughtered, burnt and buried alive by the German Nazis and their willing aides, may their names be obliterated.
24 *Menachem Av* in the years of the Holocaust
5699 - 5705 (1939-1945)

[Pages 388-390]

Rosh Hashana in the Forest

by Yisrael Yankelevitch

Translated from the Yiddish by Harvey Spitzer

I was in the ghetto in Novogrudek together with the Jews who survived the first massacre which was carried out in December 1941.

In July 1942, the Germans began rounding up the Jews from the surrounding towns: Karelitch, Mir, Ivenyetz, Zshetel and others. Hitler's agents drove the remaining exhausted, starving Jews, who could hardly stand on their feet, into our ghetto which was confining enough even for the inhabitants of our ghetto. However, an order was issued by the Gestapo chief requiring all Jews to find a place to live within an hour, and anyone found in the street would be shot.

There was a tumult in the ghetto and everyone was thrown into a panic. And Jews, merciful children of merciful parents, the inhabitants of the ghetto, began sharing their narrow quarters with their newly arrived brethren, putting them up in attics, barns and cellars until all of them were settled. That evening, a group of drunk and wildly excited Hitler's henchmen came on an inspection and, finding everything in order, called to the head of the *Judenrat* [Jewish Council]:

"You said that it was too tight, that there was no room, but you were still able to accommodate all your Jews. But don't worry, Jews, in the future we, the Gestapo, will know how to provide you with more dwellings", and they went off.

When the Jews found out what the Nazis said, everyone already understood that a live volcano was threatening to erupt over the ghetto, that something terrible was about to take place. And that is, in fact, what happened:

Two weeks later, the second slaughter of Jews in the ghetto took place. Six thousand five hundred Jews were murdered in the most bestial and agonizing way. The Jews were made to lie face-down on the streets and the excited Hitler lovers and Jew haters would come with trucks and load them up with Jews: men, women and children who watched with terrified eyes. They wanted to live, but the bloodthirsty murderers cut them down cruelly.

I was among the lucky ones who remained alive. Shortly afterwards, we organized and escaped into the forest, although there were still some Jews left in the ghetto. It was clear to us, however, that the murderers would slaughter everyone.

We were a small group of Jews in the forest. It was just before the Jewish New Year, Rosh Hashana. There was an elderly Jew among us, Reb Alter Tiktin, from Bialystok. He exclaimed:

"Children, I have a *yahrzeit* [anniversary of a relative's death] on the second day of Rosh Hashana, and I have never missed a *yahrzeit*. It's Rosh Hashana, and we're alive and we're Jews. Therefore, let's arrange a prayer service with 10 men and we'll pray this Rosh Hashana just to spite the Hitler supporters".

Everyone agreed, but where could we get holiday prayer books? Another fellow and I took it upon ourselves to go into the ghetto and bring back prayer books. That night we went into the town and in the morning, when the people remaining in the ghetto went outside the ghetto to fetch water, we mixed and mingled with them and in that way were able to get into the ghetto. We got prayer books and, taking another group of Jews with us, sneaked out of the ghetto that night. We reached the forest just at daybreak and gave Reb Alter the holiday prayer books.

Reb Alter stood beside a tree praying on the first day of Rosh Hashana. When he reached the stirring *"U'netane tokef"* prayer ["Let us recite the power of this day's holiness..."], he wept loudly as he recited the words "who by the sword, who by famine, who by thirst" and shouted out, but not with all his might, that we Jews who have fallen into Hitler's hands should be the last victims for the Jewish people and then fainted. We could hardly rouse him.

Some time later the Germans launched an attack on our camp during which Reb Alter was killed.

*

Today I'm just like other people. I'm an American citizen and have nothing to complain about, but I still feel today as though I were in camp on that Rosh Hashana and want to shout out:

— Brother Jews, "Remember Amalek!"

On the 25th Memorial Day for the martyrs of Lubtch and Delatitch

Front: (left to right): Mina Pines (was in Kibbutz Dafna), Sarah Batter, --, ----, ----, Yona Degani from Kibbutz Dan, -----

[Caption provided by Moshe Yankelevitch]

[Pages 391-402]

A Partisan in his Late Years

by Shalom Leibovitch

Translated from the Yiddish by Harvey Spitzer

A few days after the outbreak of the Soviet-German War in June, 1941, several Germans came into our town. They called the local gentiles together and allowed them to loot Jewish property. The gentiles, of course, didn't have to be asked. For three days in a row, without a stop, they stole whatever they could. While doing so, they brought us the "good tidings" that the Jews, in any case, would soon be exterminated and no trace of us would remain. Three local gentiles, Alyosha Aleshkes, Arkady the "Bolshevik" and Sioma Komornik, stood out above the others in plundering our possessions.

There were, however, a few Christian residents who stood up for us and would not let others rob us. Their names must be mentioned here: Vanke the Tall Man and the members of the Komarovsky family who lived in a hamlet near Delatitch. These few honest people were the only ray of light in the darkness which descended upon the world in those terrible days.

The Germans set up their command headquarters and the police in our town. At the same time, they appointed a Jewish Council (*Judenrat*) They also herded all the Jews into a ghetto which was located in a small area of the former horse market and synagogue, a total of thirty houses.

They also forbade us to bring food into the ghetto and allotted only 120 grams of bread a day for each person. This was the start of the terrible period of suffering and the beginning of the end.

One day they took away 150 young Jewish men and sent them to do hard labor in Dvoretz, a small town 6 kilometers from Novoyelnia. Not one of them ever returned.

We were all assigned jobs doing various kinds of work in surrounding areas.

One day, (I, unfortunately, can't remember the exact date), they locked up a few hundred Jews in a barn in Vorobievitch and set it on fire. Those who managed to save themselves from the flames were shot while escaping.

In Voynova as well, several hundred Jews were shot in a slaughter in which Isaakovsky, the pharmacist, was also murdered with his paralyzed wife whom he carried in his arms from the town to the ditch where they were all shot.

Twenty-four days into the Jewish month of *Av*, 5702 [1942], the last massacres took place in Lubtch and Novogrudek in which nearly all the Jews were murdered. Only a few managed to save their lives.

Shalom Leibovitch

While I was in the ghetto in Lubtch, men would come into my room and pray and study Torah on the Sabbath. Among the worshippers were Rabbi Yaakov Baksht and Rabbi Yitzchak Aronovsky.

Once, the Germans came to the *Judenrat* and demanded a horse and wagon so they could go hunting in the surrounding forests. Chaim Bruk sent for me and ordered me to go with the Germans. At the start, the Germans took me for a Christian, and I played along. But when they found out that I was a Jew, they said to me: "Damn Jew, you're going to be *kaput* [dead]" and they began shooting their guns. Luckily for me, a peasant with whom I was acquainted, noticed what was happening and began to plead that they should let me live. As they were in a good mood at that moment, they made a motion with their hands as if to say, "He'll never escape from our hands anyway". And that's how I was saved from death. They also ordered me to bring bread for the people in Dvoretz.

Dovid-Itche's daughter, Yehudit Leibovitch, lived in Dvoretz. She managed to escape from there and join her mother in the camp near Vorobievitch. Someone informed on her, and the Germans seized and shot her with her mother, Leah Leibovitch, may God avenge their blood!

The Germans decided, however, to scare the others from trying to escape, and for the same "sin", they also shot Leibe-Feivel with his son-in-law, Alter Kabak as well as Chashke and Grunia. They were the first Jewish victims in Vorobievitch. When the Jews in Lubtch were driven en masse to Vorobievitch, my elderly stepmother, Bayle-Fayge, fell down on the way and they shot her in the middle of the road.

During the slaughter, four young men escaped from the ghetto and made their way to Bassia, a village near Novogrudek, where there were some more Jews. They went into a peasant's house and asked to borrow a bucket. The peasant went to the police and informed on them. The Germans took them to the police station where they were beaten to death.

My son Simcha got married and lived in Novogrudek, so we moved into the ghetto in Novogrudek before the last massacre. It was there, in fact, that my wife, our son and his two daughters were killed, may God avenge their blood!

Every day, we - a group of 12 Jews - used to leave the Novogrudek ghetto and go to our forced work in Bassia. Once, a member of our group managed to buy a little flour from a peasant. On the way, the Germans stopped and inspected us. They took away the flour, wrote down our names and went away. The next day, they came into the ghetto to look for us and shoot us. We had, however, given false names, and that saved us.

On another occasion, Kolia Komornik and Petrik Bedoon came into Elikum Halperin's house and took him to the commander's quarters. There, they ordered him to kiss Stalin's picture. When he fulfilled their wishes, they beat him with wild, sadistic pleasure. Then they ordered him to bark like a dog, and he had to obey them. But they said he wasn't barking loud enough, so they beat him until he was unconscious. They threw him back into the ghetto in that condition. We wrapped him in wet bed sheets, and cooled his burning wounds. Three days later, he was forced to go to work, although he could hardly stand on his feet. Incidentally, we should mention that Petrik Bedoon was captured after the war and put on trial in Russia.

Following the slaughter in Novogrudek, the Germans concentrated the remaining Jews in the ghetto on Peresika Street. I spoke to a group of Jews about escaping while there was still time.

During the day, I tore loose a few boards from the wooden fence so we wouldn't have to make any noise at night. We kept them on the fence, however, so that no one would notice. Late that evening, we went out through the prepared opening one after the other and began running. On the way, a gentile ran into us and immediately notified the Germans. Soon enough, they started firing at us. We fell to the ground and lay there motionless for a long time. When things quieted down, we began running again and reached the barracks. From there we separated and went away to various villages.

**At the grave of the martyrs in Litovke near Novogrudek.
Shalom Leibovitch is seated second from the left**

Our group came to Vereskova, not far from Delatitch. During the day, we hid there in a field. At nightfall, when we knew that the peasants were already asleep, we left for Delatitch, intending to cross the Neiman River in order to reach the hamlets in the nearby forest.

Just as we took our first steps on the bridge at Delatitch, we heard a German guard shout: "Halt! Remain standing!" Fortunately, the night was very dark and we were able to vanish before the German noticed us. It was dangerous to stay in one place, so we started walking along the riverbank, hoping that we might have some kind of opportunity to cross the Neiman River at another point. And as Heaven was watching over us so that we could save ourselves, we found a small rowboat on the shore, as though it had been made ready for us. One at a time, I brought everyone across to the other (right) side of the river, and we reached the forest that same night.

A cold rain mixed with snow was falling. It soaked our clothes right through to our body. We were hungry and exhausted from walking, and our wet bodies were shivering from the cold. We had to get something to eat to relieve our hunger as quickly as possible. I was afraid but decided anyway to go into Farbotke's cabin and ask him for a little food. He was very kind and gave me a piece of bread with some milk, which restored our energy.

We left Farbotke's cabin and went on to Komarovsky's place in the hamlet. He also welcomed us and gave us something to eat and drink, but couldn't hide twelve men in his house. What were we to do next?... We went back into the forest. Meanwhile, a peasant noticed us and, taking us for partisans, reported to the police that partisans were attacking Komarovsky. Fortunately, the sun came out and dried up the grass and erased our tracks.

We moved on to Klutchist and intended to put up a shelter, but we found fresh traces of woodcutters, so we left for Krasno-Horka, where we sat down and rested. Our stomachs were grumbling, however, so a few of our men returned to Farbotke's cabin and asked him for some more food. He gave us a bag of flour and three potatoes as well as a pail to cook them in. We went back to our men with these possessions.

Having eaten our fill, we decided to split into two groups. A group of seven people including my children stayed with me. We thought that two smaller groups would be able to manage more easily and not attract the attention of the peasants.

After wandering through the forest for ten days, we came closer to Baksht. There, I happened to meet a gentile with whom I was acquainted and he gave me a piece of bread for my daughter Shifra, who had grown very weak and no longer had the strength to go on. The same gentile helped us get to our peasants in the district of Potashne from whom we received some bread and other food. He also brought us a rifle and 85 bullets for which I gave him a pair of leather soles.

The next day the same gentile brought us bread and butter. This, however, aroused in us the suspicion that that he might inform the police, who paid 50 marks and a kilo of sugar for every Jew turned in. We began to hide from this good person, but he always found us, brought food and encouraged us with good words.

We built a hut in the forest and stayed there. We also found a ditch with potatoes and carried them back little by little to our shelter. I used to visit the peasants in the surrounding villages and got bread from them. The rifle was more than a little help to me. A peasant whom I knew saw that I was going around barefoot and that my feet were wrapped only with hay and tied with laces. He gave me a pair of shoes made of bark with linen rags, which simply revived me.

A few days before Rosh Hashana, five Jews from Ivya came to this good peasant. He told them that we were hiding out in the surrounding area. They started looking for us and one morning we met each other. It's hard to describe how surprised and happy we were to meet living Jews.

Our hut, however, was too small for a larger group of people, so we decided to enlarge it so that we could all be together.

One day on the way to Potashne, we ran into a bunch of armed men. First they took away our guns and then began questioning who we were. Yisrael answered: "We're the same as you - partisans." They asked us for a "parole", a watchword that we were really partisans. In short, they brought us to their commander and the investigation was renewed. Finally, the commander ordered that we should all be taken out to be shot because we were plain robbers and undeserving of mercy. However, if one is destined to remain alive, help always comes even at the last moment. The commander was just then staying in the house of the good peasant from whom we got the rifle. Hearing the order, the peasant called out: "They're not robbers and have never hurt anyone. They only ask for food and don't grab it. I can guarantee that they are decent people and deserve to be helped".

When he heard the peasant's remarks, the commander quickly changed his order. He gave us back our rifles and informed us that Bielsky's group of partisans would soon be passing through and that we could join up with them. We didn't wait long and quickly returned to our shelter.

Berl, Baruch-Mordechai's son, and Mendel Goldshmidt from Baksht left for Leznievitch, not far from Ivya. On the way, they encountered partisans who wanted to kill them. They started to cry and beg for their lives. The partisans took Berl with his rifle and left to gather food. Later, they released him but kept his rifle.

Meanwhile, we found out that a number of partisan groups from the Stalin unit had arrived in Potashne with their commander. A few of us went over there and told about the rifle that had been taken away. The commander gave a written order that we should be given food because we belonged to his partisans. However, he demanded that we also give him the bullets because we didn't have rifles anyway. We pretended not to hear him and went off as quickly as possible. Thereupon, the commander ordered that we be seized and that the sentence be carried out. A peasant whom we knew was listening and went into the forest with an axe as if he were going to chop wood. He chased after us and told us about the commander's order. I collected all the bullets and went back to give them to the commander. On the way, I met a peasant who asked: "Where are you going, 'priest'**?" I answered: "I'm going to the village where the partisans are staying". He told me to jump onto the wagon because he was going there, too. Without giving it much thought, I got onto the wagon and noticed that our rifles were there. However, I didn't say anything until we entered the village. Once there, I convinced the commander that our rifles should be returned and that, naturally, we should be allowed to keep the bullets. However, they warned us not to go looking for food because they would provide us with food in three days.

Another incident occurred when we lacked food and Yisrael Slonimsky used force to take away bread from a peasant. The peasant reported this at the partisans' headquarters. We were all brought before the commander who ordered the peasant to tell which one of us did this, adding that they weren't going to play games but just put a bullet in the culprit's head. Apparently, the peasant's conscience was awakened or maybe he was afraid of our revenge. He looked at each of us very carefully - although he knew us all more or less well - and declared that it was someone else and that he didn't see him among us. The commander had no choice but to release us and even gave us bread and meat so that we wouldn't have to take food away from anyone by force.

We began buying weapons from the peasants. We also gave Bielsky's partisans a machine gun and a grenade launcher. Every one of our group, which already numbered thirty something people, was well armed and we officially became partisans belonging to the Stalin unit. In fact, we were transferred to the area where the unit was carrying out its activities.

The great pursuit of the German forces in the partisans' zone got under way. Its aim was to completely liquidate the partisan movement in western White Russia.

The commander, knowing that the Germans were getting closer, sent a person to bring me to him in order to warn me of the danger so that we wouldn't fall into enemy hands. After listening to his talk, I asked him to let us withdraw together with the unit. He advised me, however, to stay in one place because the children were too weak to go on such a dangerous way and encounter battles which awaited the temporarily retreating partisans. He also advised us to hide in a hole somewhere in the forest and not build any bunkers because the Germans would surely find them.

When I returned to our people, I told them what the commander had said. Twenty-four of the group separated from us and built a new, well camouflaged shelter. The children, Mendel from Baksht and I left to look for another hiding place. During the day we hid in the swamps, which the Germans usually avoided. At night, we would leave the swamps and light a small fire to warm our bones and boil water.

The hunt for the partisans lasted three days. 63,000 Germans combed the whole area. They used tanks and even airplanes, but they didn't have much success. On one of those days, we heard terrible screams. When the Germans left, we searched the surroundings and found the tortured bodies of the people who had separated from our group. We buried them in the forest and recited "kaddish" at the fresh grave of our brethren.

It was hard to get food after the pursuit. We hardly ate anything for five days. We ate whatever we could find, even spoiled and wormy food. It didn't last long, however, and the partisans' way of life resumed. We came out of the forest, went back to the villages, moved freely without fear and, as strange as it may seem, the number of partisans actually increased. The Germans' hunt for partisans as well as their cruelty towards the peasants during the pursuit brought the peasants into the ranks of the partisans.

We built a new shelter in the area of Baksht and stayed there until the liberation. After the liberation, the commander advised us to go over to Bielsky's partisans. We followed his advice and, together with them, came to Novogrudek - the city without Jews.

Holocaust survivors from our towns, Lubtch and Delatitch

Sitting (right to left): Shmuel Baksht, ----, Yisrol (Yisrael) GershonYankelevitch, Shalom Leibovitch (father of Sonia and Shifra), -----
Standing (right to left): Danya Epshtein (from Ivyeh), Sonia Yankelevitch (Yisrol's wife), Baruch Yankelevitch, Shifra Solomiansky (Sonia's sister), Yisrael Mendelevitch (cousin of Yisrol, Yankeleh and Beryl Jankelowitz), Shifra Mendelevitch (sister of Danya), ---, Yisrael Kivilevitch, ---, ---

[Caption provided by Moshe Yankelevitch]

[**Note from the translator: As for the "priest", the author (partisan) apparently had a very long beard, which made him look like a typical Russian Orthodox priest. He was not really a priest. The word is "batchko", meaning priest in Russian.]

[Pages 403-409]

Under the Nazis in France

by Risha Zablotsky

Translated from the Yiddish by Harvey Spitzer

When the war broke out, I was on vacation with my husband and child in Brittany. My two brothers and their families and my cousin Yankel and his family were with us.

My husband and younger brother were called up for military service. We all stayed at the seashore and were afraid to go back to Paris. But after France was occupied and divided into two zones, we were caught in the occupied zone. It made no sense, therefore, to remain in Brittany, so my child and I went back home - to Paris. Likewise, Abrasha, my husband was demobilized, and managed to get home with great difficulty.

The first days of the occupation the Germans were still civil and had not yet shown their true face and it seemed that we could deal with the situation. We even opened the pharmacy which, together with our apartment, was located on the first floor. However, we had officially transferred ownership of the pharmacy to a gentile pharmacist.

At four o'clock one morning in August 1940, when I was five months pregnant, my husband heard (through an open window) someone say: "When the pharmacist wakes up, he'll have a surprise." Abrasha went to the window and cautiously glanced around at the street. He saw that the building was surrounded by a chain of policemen, so no one could escape. Abrasha quietly awakened me, told me what he heard and said that he was going up to the sixth floor, to one of our neighbors, a Christian woman. Then Abrasha added: "Since you're pregnant, they won't do anything to you, but it's better for me not to be at home".

I couldn't sleep any more, but sat hidden behind a curtain at the window and watched every movement the police made. They were in the habit of seizing Jews who were on the street early in the morning. I immediately phoned my brother and acquaintances and warned them not to leave their homes and to be careful.

At eight o'clock, they began knocking on the door. Trembling from fear, I opened the door, and a German and two French secret agents came right in. They immediately began searching the apartment and inquired where my husband was hiding. I told them that our son was on vacation in a village and that my husband had gone to visit him. They warned me that my husband was to report to the police as soon as he returned. Naturally, Abrasha had already gone into hiding and decided to leave Paris as soon as possible.

We began looking for a way to get Abrasha over to the Vichy (unoccupied) zone. Nothing at all was said about me and our son. People calmed their fears by saying: "They won't take any pregnant women with children." Abrasha found a man who took him across the border of the Vichy zone for a large sum of money. It sounds very easy, but it was, in fact, life threateningly dangerous. With God's help, my husband reached Lyon safely. He didn't have much money left and began to suffer from hunger. Besides, Lyon was a big city and there was a great danger of being seized. By chance, Abrasha met one of his former teachers, a gentile, who had escaped from Alsace. This man introduced Abrasha to the owner of a village pharmacy who agreed to give him a job and Abrasha left for the village. It wasn't bad for him there, but we were separated, and no letters could be sent from one zone to another.

Risha Zablotzky with her husband and child

Meanwhile, I gave birth to a little girl. Before I went to the hospital, they had taken my older brother, Yosef, and deported him to the Compiègne detention camp, one hundred kilometers from Paris. He became ill there and was put into the hospital. A French nurse helped him escape and, together with our brother Yisrael and their families, were smuggled into the Vichy zone.

The situation of the Jews in Paris was growing worse day by day. They already began deporting women with children but provisionally only those who were not French citizens. We had a good friend, a commissioner at the headquarters of the Paris police, who remained working at his post even under the German occupation. He would let me know when a deportation was to take place and I, in turn, would inform my friends, who would hide in my apartment.

One fine day, the police commissioner came and warned me to hide with the children because French citizens were also going to be deported. I never even dreamed about being smuggled into the Vichy zone with two small children. I remembered that my older sister, Fanny, who lived in Reims, about 160 kilometers from Paris, with her family, did not declare herself as Jewish and did not wear a badge. We decided that I would leave the children with her, cross the border alone into the Vichy zone and once I was there, she would send the children to me with a Christian woman, telling anyone who asked that they were her children.

Yankel Chaimovitch in a detention camp in France

The children were with Fanny, but how does one get across the border? I was given the name of a French railroad engineer who often drove the diplomatic train on the Paris - Vichy line. I called him up and asked him to fix a place for a meeting. He set our *rendez-vous* in the Metro (subway) but on the condition that I remove my patch. He explained that he was a tall, thin man, that he would be carrying a small suitcase and that I should go up to him without any reservations, as if to a good friend.

I took along my cousin, removed the patch, and we left. My cousin stood at a distance so that we wouldn't both be caught together. I recognized him at once by the signs he had given me and we acted boldly as though we had known one another for a long time.

Hearing my request, he expressed his agreement to take us across the border. In addition, he told us that he transports people in the water tank, which is attached to the locomotive. Who could imagine that people could be hidden in a narrow pipe, but there is no limit to human inventiveness, especially in a time of trouble. But how could we get into the locomotive garage when everything around was guarded by the Germans? I again took along my cousin and a lady acquaintance and, arm in arm, we went out for a "stroll". We were lucky and got into the garage without anyone noticing us. In a few minutes, we were already sitting inside the tank in cold water and could hardly catch out breath.

When the train moved, there was less water, so we could breathe more freely. An elderly couple was also sitting there, and they felt very bad. Although I had a heavy heart and was beset by the persistent worry that I might not see my children again, I began to sing and entertain the people. The old man said, in fact, that I was singing off key (as I did in Lubtch in the school choir), but they were happy to be able to take their mind off their troubles.

When we arrived in Vichy, they took us out of the water and we waited for our clothes to dry. Then each of us went on his way, to his own fate. I went to the village where Abrasha worked and a few days later, a Christian woman brought both our children to us. The people in the village knew that we were Jews, but the simple village folk, who had hardly ever seen a Jew before, were far from being anti-Semitic and we lived among them without any fear. Abrasha also brought one of his relatives to us, a dentist with her husband and son and a doctor who lost her husband and child. Abrasha used to go around the villages and procure food for all of us. My brothers and their families were also near us in the neighboring villages.

Life went on like this for nearly two years until the Germans began occupying the Vichy zone as well. Things got much worse. Little notes were posted with the message that a Jew was working in the pharmacy and that Jews were living there. The French began looking for a hiding place for us. A priest took our oldest son, Gérald, to a seminary. I told him that if we were caught and deported, he should remember that he is Jewish, and he promised to remain a Jew. Two French women let us live in the attic of a small, vacant house in the woods. During the day we would hide in the woods, and at night we would come back to sleep in the attic. We taught our little girl, who was then 2 ½ years old, never to say our name. Even for a while after the war, she would keep asking: "Now may we say our name?"

In 1944, my brother Yosef and his wife, Rochelle, and their two daughters, Jeanne and Nicole, were taken away. We never saw them again, but their photographs have remained as well as the everlasting, unquiet sorrow in my heart.

[Pages 410-411]

Untitled

by Lyuba Meyerson-Kowalsky

Translated from the Yiddish by Harvey Spitzer

My father, Rabbi Chaim Meyerson, came to Lubtch from the *yeshiva* [rabbinic seminary] in Volozshin and was also very well versed in science and world literature.

My mother, Feigel, came from a family of rabbis. I remember that when my grandfather Rabbi Moshe Rabinovitch died, the neighbors brought their sick children and caressed them with the deceased's hand, for they had such a strong belief in his piety. My mother was a polite and kind woman who treated everyone with respect and friendliness, whether Jew or gentile. She was always ready to do someone a favor.

Lyuba Meyerson-Kowalsky with her child and parents

In my childhood years, I learned from my father that all people are equal, that their social status didn't matter at all, and that one should not be ashamed of one's work as long as he or she is an honest person.

I mention my parents here because my thoughts take me back to the ghetto in Novogrudek where, in 1941, I was kept together with my parents and six year old daughter, Frumele.

I will always remember my father's last words as he was led away to be slaughtered together with five thousand other Jews from Novogrudek: "I was not fated to have pleasure from such a fine grandchild", and his eyes swelled with tears which he quickly wiped away as he went on his last way.

I managed to save my child thanks to the deep bonds of friendship which my parents had cultivated among gentiles. I hid her with very good Polish friends, the Rostkovsky family, who lived in a hamlet near Delatitch. My daughter spoke only Yiddish and they risked their lives to save a Jewish child. She remained with them for 2½ years, until the liberation.

I managed to save myself because I was working as a pharmacist in the Novogrudek hospital when the slaughter of Jews was carried out in 1941. The Germans had temporarily left the medical personnel unguarded. We worked in the hospital and they would lock us in at night. It was actually a kind of a ghetto from which we never thought of being able to leave. When we found out, however, that they were getting ready to finish us off, we escaped at night through one of the hospital windows. We reached the partisans in the forest around Nalibok and lived to see the day of liberation.

[Pages 412-432]

Little Pages from the Flame...

by Yisrael Slonimsky

Translated from the Yiddish by Harvey Spitzer

[Translators note: This chapter is the Yiddish version of the same chapter as on pages 304-316 ("Scrolls from the Fire") which was written in Hebrew]

On September 1, 1939, the conflagration broke out in which everything that had authentic meaning for us went up in flames: home, happiness and future.

With terror in our hearts, we awaited the arrival of the Germans, who had invaded and taken over Poland. At night, we slept in our clothes in case we had to run away in search of a hiding place. Seventeen days went by in this way when, suddenly, the news reached us that the Red Army was approaching. We were very happy, as we were finally rid of the fright of falling into German claws.

A few weeks went by and our joy was marred. The Russians took away all our possessions and levied heavy taxes on the store owners which they couldn't possibly pay. The richest Jews were sent to Siberia or Archangel [aka Arkhanelsk - AB], and those who were not sent away lived in fear that the Russians would come at night, pull them out of bed and send them off to perform forced labor in the far north.

My lime burner was nationalized, and such heavy taxes were imposed on my store that I had nothing left. I went away to work on the rafts, hoping only that they would let me stay in one place. But we still didn't grasp the fact that evil and misfortunes have no limit, nor did we ever imagine that it could be thousands of times worse if the German destroyer gained control over us.

In the early hours of the morning of Sunday, June 22, 1941, the gentile residents of Delatitch and peasants from surrounding villages began running back to their homes from the market in Lubtch. Jumping with joy, they related that, while in Lubtch, they heard on the radio that that the Germans had attacked Russia and that German airplanes had already bombarded Lida, Novogrudek and Baranovitch. In the evening, it was reported that German troops were already shooting up the roads leading to Russia and that the former Polish-Russian border was closed to everyone except government personnel who had come to work in our district. Where can people run to?... We already found out from the press and from refugees that the Germans were locking the Jews up in ghettos, wiping out entire Jewish communities, but what could we do except wait for our dark fate.

On Saturday, June 28, hundreds of peasants from the whole region started out in wagons for Lubtch. They were coming, with the permission of the Germans, to plunder the property of the Jews in Lubtch. After a half day of looting, they went back with their wagons completely loaded up with our possessions: furniture, sewing machines, bedding, clothing, pots and pans, glassware, cows and even chickens, anything and everything that their wild animal appetites lusted for. The gentiles in Lubtch opposed them, not, God forbid, to protect the Jews, but because they claimed the plunder belonged to them. They hit one another with iron tools. The gentiles from the surrounding area went back home with deep gashes in their heads, their animal blood pouring down over their impure faces, but they were happy, knowing that the wagons loaded with our possessions would compensate for everything.

Gentiles from Delatitch whom we knew very well, our so-called "good neighbors", came to the Jews and told them that the same thing would befall us the next day. They advised us to pack up our better things and give it to them for safekeeping. "In any case, you won't be needing these things any more today, and tomorrow they're going to take everything away from you. Give it to me, and when you need it, I'll give it back to you". Every word of theirs was like a spear piercing our hearts.

The peasants from the surrounding areas couldn't wait until Sunday and attacked us that very Saturday night. They smashed all the windowpanes, broke down the doors, forced everyone to the Neiman River and robbed anything of value, and whatever was worthless to them, they simply broke and destroyed. They hit the elderly Rabbi Beinish Liss over the head with a spade and my father, Feive the Baker, received a blow on his shoulders with an axe.

We hid among the shrubs at the river edge for two days. On the third day, when our hunger became oppressive, we went back to our homes. They somewhat calmed their bloody instincts for two days. They greeted us with a shout: "Now, Jews, there's not a thing we're lacking!" A few elderly Christian residents secretly brought us bread, flour and a pitcher of milk. But where could we get a pan or a spoon, since everything had either been stolen or broken? They strewed garbage and faeces all over the study hall [synagogue], broke the windows, took down the doors, tore the Torah scrolls and hung them up on the trees.

The Germans came a few days later. They appointed the police and published an order that Jews must wear a yellow Star of David over their heart and shoulders, that Jews must not leave the town without a permit and whoever did not obey this order would be shot on the spot. Rabbi Ya'akov Baksht, May God avenge his blood!, was the first to go outside with the yellow badge. You could not conceive how happy and excited the gentiles were to see the Jews humiliated.

The gentiles began forcing us out to work on property belonging to Delatitch. There, we dug up potatoes and beets and also received blows from our new masters. They also became masters of our houses. We accepted everything with love because our heart told us that things were yet to get worse.

Even before the Jews were locked up in the ghetto in Lubtch, 150 young Jews were selected and sent to a work camp near Dvoretz. My brother-in-law, Avraham Kivovitch as well as Shepsel, Itche Kushner's son, and Shemaya, Sarah-Elke's grandson, were part of that group.

I worked on the property belonging to the village of Vereskova. Velvel (Ze'ev) Yankelevitch and Sara-Elke's grandson, Yerachmiel, worked together with me as did my father-in-law Moshe-Aharon and both my brothers-in-law, Nota (Natan) and Ya'akov. We also used to sleep there. When the Jews from Delatitch were driven into the ghetto in Lubtch, I would work all week long in Vereskova. Friday evenings, we were allowed to go to our families in the Lubtch ghetto. Since my job was tending to the cows, I would go into the cow shed Thursday night, milk the cows and prepare a couple of bottles of milk. That's how I was able to smuggle a little milk into the ghetto. My wife would divide the milk among our small children. Of course, one received a death penalty for such a "crime. Even before we were locked up in the ghetto, Gestapo agents would come to Lubtch in trucks. They would seize young men, as though for work, and then take them behind the town and shoot them. When we found out about that, we became more cautious. As soon as there was daylight, the young men would run off and hide in the fields all day long. But no one thought about escaping into the forests and saving himself from the Germans. We still believed that we would outlive the enemy, and besides, we didn't want to be separated from our families.

The situation changed for the worse when we were driven into the Lubtch ghetto. It already became difficult to run away. The news that reached us about the slaughters of the Jews in surrounding ghettos broke our spirits completely. In

Novogrudek, on the first day of the Hebrew month of *Av*, 5701 (1941), the Germans and their helpers gathered together 52 Jews, stood them in a row in the middle of the street and shot every tenth person. The "counting" was repeated regularly until they finished off the last Jew. While this was taking place, a band played happy marches. Afterwards, Jewish women were sent to wash the blood off the pavement stones.

We began to observe fasts - the old Jewish means against evil decrees. We would fast twice a week on Mondays and Thursdays and even the elderly, and little children fasted. But no miracle occurred and God's gates of mercy remained closed to our prayers and fasting.

Jews from Delatitch, Neishtat (Negnyevitch) and the Jewish residents of the surrounding villages were also locked up in the Lubtch ghetto. Chaim Bruk from Lubtch and Berl Yankelevitch from Delatitch were appointed leaders of the ghetto. Decrees were issued incessantly: First, we had to hand over all our money, jewelry, other valuables and the little furniture that remained after the plunder by the gentiles. Harsh monetary penalties were imposed on us for any light matter. We had to hand over at once whatever they desired. The craftsmen: tailors, shoemakers, etc., had to work for the Germans and for the local police, but the craftsmen themselves were almost naked and barefoot. If a person managed to bury something in the ground, he risked his life sneaking out the ghetto to trade the "treasure" with a gentile for a piece of bread to keep his children alive.

We lived in Tevel the Shoemaker's house. There were thirty people in one room. When we slept, one person's head was against another's. People were actually eaten away by lice and worms, but until the very end, no one broke down or lost confidence in the belief that salvation would come. Yenta, the daughter of the rabbi of Lubtch, also lived in the ghetto with her husband, Dr. Rabinovitch from Baranovitch. The rabbi had died a short time before, and his wife was in the ghetto in Novogrudek. On a certain day, the rabbi's wife informed Yenta that the murderers had set out in the direction of Lubtch and that we should be on guard. When we heard the "tidings", we all recited confession and awaited death. Till this very day, I can't comprehend why we didn't try to escape from the ghetto that day, as if some secret force was preventing us from running away, although there were dense forests all around us just an arm's length away and good prospects for saving our lives. A few days went by in expectation of death, but the murderers did not show up.

Incidentally, I will mention here that a short time later, during the slaughter, when they brought Yenta and her husband to the pit, Dr. Rabinovitch shouted out to the Germans that the day of revenge would certainly come for them and their mad leader and that they would pay dearly for their crimes. He embraced Yenta, kissed her and, thus doing, both fell into the pit.

A few days after Passover, 1942, two Gestapo agents came into the ghetto. They took out Naftali's son, Avraham Alperstein, Yitchak Rosenblum and Chaim Bruk. They brought them out of the house and shot them on the spot. Chaim Bruk still managed to run to Sarah's (Esther's daughter) yard, but they chased after him and shot him. We remained like sheep without a shepherd, for Chaim Bruk, with his authority, wisdom and knowledge, always comforted us and gave us courage and confidence.

An order came from Novogrudek to send one hundred tradesmen there from Lubtch. My brother-in-law, Nota, Baruch-Mordechai Krulevetzky and I were taken as part of that transport. Weeping terribly, we said good-bye to our families. We felt that we would not see each other again. My wife, however, would not let the *Judenrat* rest until they prevailed upon the authorities to allow her and the children to move to the ghetto in Novogrudek.

Six hundred Jews from Lubtch capable of working were transferred to Vorobievitch. There were also Jews from Delatitch among them and I remember some of them: Rabbi Ya'akov Baksht and his daughter, Necha, Rabbi Beinush with his family, Berl with Peya, Velvel Yankelevitch, Chaya -Zelda, my father-in-law, Moshe-Aharon with his son, Ya'akov, and his wife with two children. They were assured that they would work paving roads and that they would all remain alive. Not one of them remained alive: some were burned alive and others were shot at the large pit, close to the Lubtch- Novogrudek road. Gershon Kapushtchevsky tried to escape, but they shot at him and he fell wounded into a stream and drowned.

There were also some Jews from Delatitch in the Novogrudek ghetto: my father, Rabbi Feive, my brother-in-law, Avraham'l with his son, Binyamin, R' Yosef the Ritual Slaughterer with his family, Golda Krulevetzky with her children, Moshe Sontzes with his younger daughter.

Mainly old women and little children remained in the Lubtch ghetto. My mother, Tziporah-Feigel, and my sister, Itke-Tulia, with her three children were also among them. They were all murdered in Podlipka, on the 24th of the Jewish month of *Av*, together with the last 275 Jews from Lubtch. On that day, they also liquidated the Jews in Vorobievitch and thousands of Jews in Novogrudek.

After arriving in the Novogrudek ghetto, we were placed in an old house with a broken, rotted roof. We would get wet with the slightest rain. Every day, together with my wife and son, we went a distance of seven kilometers to work paving roads, carefully guarded by the local police. All day long we would drag heavy stones and wheelbarrows with sand and gravel. For being late to work, one was made to lie on the ground and was then whipped to death. At five o'clock in the afternoon, the local police would take us back to the ghetto. On the way back, they would make sport of us, whip us or even shoot us just for entertainment, leaving behind the dead and seriously injured. Those who worked received 120 grams of bread a day. Those who didn't work got nothing. My daughter Rochele was still too small and didn't work, so got no bread.

One day, they sent off a group of Jews to work in Minsk. My brother-in-law, Nota, was included in that group and was murdered there.

The day came when the Jews in Novogrudek were slaughtered:

That day, as always, we were away at work and had left Rochele in the ghetto. Suddenly, people began saying that an *akstia* was going to take place that day. We were then working in the town itself. I dropped my work, turned around and went into the ghetto. I took Rochele and tried to get her out of the ghetto. A Jewish ghetto-policeman stopped us at the gate and ordered me to leave Rochele in the ghetto. I pleaded with him at length and when he finally pretended not to notice, I went out with Rochele and brought her to the workplace.

There was a great commotion when the foreman began registering people with a trade. I urged him forcefully and he registered me as a tradesman. Then they drove us up to a yard and again began registering us. But this was already for a final count. When the pushing and shoving got out of hand, a policeman, a Tarter from Novogrudek, began hitting us with a leather club. Then they led us away to the barracks where armed Germans called out the names of 200 men from a list. After that, they began shouting to the remaining Jews: "Damn Jews, back to work".

We already understood what awaited us and began running to hide in the fields of grain. I took my wife and children, my brother-in-law, Avraham'l, with his son and we went back to our house in the ghetto where we had discovered a good, camouflaged hiding place a few weeks before.

As soon as we heard the first shooting in the ghetto, we went into a closet, removed the small cover and from there went into the hiding place, putting back the small cover to close the closet. My father was also with us, but the tightness made him choke and he began coughing very loudly. We asked him to go out and hide in the attic because we would all surely be killed on account of him. My father understood the situation very well and went out of the shelter, climbed up into the attic and took the ladder with him. He lay there for three days and wasn't found. On the fourth day, the 200 selected craftsmen were brought into the ghetto in order to destroy the houses in the large ghetto and fence in the small ghetto. When my father noticed people going about freely in the ghetto, he thought that the danger had passed, came down from the attic and was soon caught and led away.

From our hiding place, we could look outside and see how the Jews were driven from their houses and ordered to lie face up on the ground. The policemen shouted: "*Davai tchasi, Davai zolota!*" (Give watches! Give gold!). When it grew dark, trucks came and everyone was pushed onto the trucks. Whoever didn't climb aboard fast enough was shot on the spot. The Jewish ghetto police carried the sick people out, but when they finished, the sick people were locked up in the same house where we had our hiding place. Afterwards, the door opened and someone shouted the order: "*Raus*" ("Out")! They packed them into a truck and took them away. The Germans also discovered various hiding places and dragged out the people hiding there.

On that day over 2,000 Jews were caught and murdered in the common grave on the road to Silev, near the dogcatchers' house.

Lying in our hiding place, we heard the front door open. Two Jews who were part of the group of tradesmen entered. They were looking around the rooms for something. We heard one of them ask the other: "Well, did you find anything to chew on?" Convinced that they were Jews, I decided to ask them if it was possible to leave our hiding place. Hearing our voices, one of them approached the closet and said in a loud voice: "Stay there! Don't go out! I'll talk to the Polish commander, who is a friend of mine. When he comes here and calls out that Yevnovitch sent him, only then should you leave your hiding place".

A few days went by, but no one came. On the fifth day, Rochele had an attack of hysteria. She started to laugh wildly and no one could calm her. The nervous people were about to put various things over her face and suffocate her, when my wife suddenly got the idea to bite Rochele somewhere on her body until she was bleeding. She did this and our young daughter immediately calmed down.

It was only on the seventh day that the commander came in and shouted in Polish: "Go out! Yevnovitch sent me"!

We came out of the "shelter" drunk from weakness. The commander demanded one thousand rubles to take us into the small ghetto. We gave him the amount he asked for, and he brought us into the ghetto. We hid there several days and then went out, having assumed the names of those who had escaped from the ghetto.

The bitter news became known to us that we no longer had any family remaining either in Lubtch or Vorobievitch. A few days later, they shot my father, who had been kept under arrest the whole time as well as Yosef Kagan with his wife, Simke, and their two little children. As they were led past the ghetto, they shouted out to us: "Jews, avenge our blood"!

We decided to escape from the ghetto - all the inhabitants of the room where we were living: Avraham Lin, Itche Florans from Baranovitch and Rabinovitch. We traded a suit of clothes for fifteen kilos of flour, which we smuggled into the ghetto and baked bread from it- provisions for the way. Avraham Lin stole a gun with sixteen bullets at the place where he worked and brought it into the ghetto.

As soon as we heard the first shooting in the ghetto, we went into a closet, removed the small cover and from there went into the hiding place, putting back the small cover to close the closet. My father was also with us, but the tightness made him choke and he began coughing very loudly. We asked him to go out and hide in the crawlspace because we would all surely be killed on account of him. My father understood the situation very well and went out of the shelter, climbed up into the crawlspace and put down the ladder. He lay there for three days and wasn't found. On the fourth day, the 200 selected craftsmen were brought into the ghetto so they could take down the ghetto fence and put up a new one. When my father noticed people going about freely in the ghetto, he came down from the crawlspace. He was soon caught and led away.

From our hiding place, we could look outside and see how the Jews were driven from their houses and ordered to lie face up on the ground. The policemen shouted: "Davai tchasi, Davai zolota!" (Give watches! Give gold!). When it grew dark, trucks came and everyone was pushed onto the trucks. Whoever didn't climb aboard fast enough was shot on the spot. The Jewish ghetto police carried the sick people out, but when they finished, the sick people were locked up in the same house where we had our hiding place. Afterwards, the door opened and someone shouted the order: "Out"! They packed them into a truck and took them away. They also discovered various hiding places and dragged out the people hiding there. Over 2,000 Jews were caught and murdered in the common grave on the road to Shelyov, near the dogcatchers' house.

Lying in our hiding place, we heard the front door open. Two Jews who were part of the group of tradesmen entered. They were looking around the rooms for something. We heard one of them ask the other: "Well, did you find anything to chew on?" Convinced that they were Jews, we decided to ask them if it was possible to leave our hiding place. Hearing our voices, one of them approached the closet and said in a loud voice: "Stay there! Don't go out! I'll talk to the Polish commander, who is a friend of mine. When he comes here and calls out that Yevnovitch sent him, only then should you leave your hiding place".

A few days went by, but no one came. On the fifth day, Rochele had an attack of hysteria. She started to laugh wildly and no one could calm her. The nervous people were about to put various things over her face and suffocate her, when my wife suddenly got the idea to bite Rochele somewhere on her body until she was bleeding. She did this and our young daughter immediately calmed down.

It was only on the seventh day that the commander came in and shouted in Polish: "Go out! Yevnovitch sent me"! We came out of the "shelter" drunk from weakness. The commander demanded one thousand rubles to take us into the small ghetto. We gave him the amount he asked for, and he brought us into the ghetto. We hid there several days and then went out, having assumed the names of those who had escaped from the ghetto.

The bitter news became known to us that we no longer had any family remaining either in Lubtch or Vorobievitch. A few days later, they shot my father, who had been kept under arrest the whole time as well as Yosef Kagan with his wife, Simke, and their two little children. As they were led past the ghetto, they shouted out to us: "Jews, avenge our blood"!

We decided to escape from the ghetto. I spoke to the Jews in our room about this: Avraham Lin, Itche Florans from Baranovtich and Rabinovitch. We traded a suit of clothes for fifteen kilos of flour, which we smuggled into the ghetto and baked bread from it- provisions for the way. Avraham Lin stole a gun with sixteen bullets at the place where he worked and brought it into the ghetto.

On the set day, my son didn't go out to work because he used to return very late. The German who used to come to take him to work came looking for him. My wife told him that he had gone to work very early and that was all she knew. The German warned us that it would be very bad and bitter for us if our son failed to go to work the next day as well. The same day, two Germans drove into the ghetto in wagons and ordered us to fill them with bricks. When we finished the job, one of the Germans for whom I worked looked around to see if anyone was listening and said to me: "Jew, You'd better find a way out of here, otherwise you're going to die". When he received no answer from me, he repeated the same sentence. Then I plucked up the courage to talk and replied that I was afraid to talk to him because Jews are forbidden to speak to a German. "For Heaven's sake, I won't do anything to you!", the German exclaimed and began to lecture about the new German "culture" which murders innocent people, adding that he doesn't feel good about the war and that if Hitler has a bone to pick with Stalin, let them fight it out together, like two mad dogs.

He also said that the surrounding area was full of partisans who had already killed many Germans and that he was sure that we could reach the partisans and save ourselves from death.

That night we escaped from the ghetto. We gave every one in the group a small loaf of bread - provisions for the way, and I also took along an axe with nails and the gun.

The night cloaked us in darkness as we scraped ourselves on the ground, crawling under the barbed wire, with hearts filled with fear and prayer to God that He would lead us on the right way. When all of us were over the other side of the ghetto wire, we began running, one behind the other.

Dogs started barking and their owners also noticed us. It didn't take long for them to notify the Germans that Jews were escaping from the ghetto. A searchlight cut through the night, and a hail of bullets accompanied us. Suddenly, we heard cries and noticed that Liss and his wife had fallen dead, like cut-off ears of grain. We all gathered together among the bushes and lay there for a few hours until it grew quiet and, somewhere in the distance, we only heard dogs barking and eventually whining. It was only then that we decided to go on our way, following the road to Selyov [Silev]. The night was ours because the Germans were afraid to travel on the roads at night on account of the partisans.

The next day, we sat stuck in the woods not far from Selyov. That night we reached Delatitch and went to the river. The water at the shore of the Neiman was already frozen, but it was possible to cross over with a rowboat because the middle of the river was still ice-free.

I found a boat not too far away, by Yordika, used a pole instead of an oar and began to cross over the river with my wife and children. When we got close to the opposite shore, my little daughter fell into the water. My wife barely managed to grab her little hand and pull her out of the icy water. I went back to the other side of the river and brought over all the people from our group. Soon after, we went into the forest and started on our way to Berezin.

As we got closer to Berezin, we left everyone in the forest, and only Avraham'l and I went to the homes of peasants in Berezin with whom we were acquainted, very decent Christians, from whom we used to buy fish in the good times. Avraham'l had hidden his things with one of them.

In the evening, we knocked on the door and went into the house. There, we found the peasants' sixteen year old son. The boy was very frightened, seeing the unexpected guests. He ran over to the lamp and extinguished the wick. He told us that the Germans had come the day before and exchanged fire with the partisans. Suddenly, he shouted to us: "A policeman is going!" What he meant wasn't very clear to us, but we ran out of the house and went to try our luck at the home of the Christian with whom Avraham'l had hidden his things.

Here, too, a young fellow also opened the door for us. He asked us to sit down and went into the next room to wake up his father. As soon as the elderly peasant came in, he embraced and kissed both of us and wept. He ordered his son to bring us food and asked about our families.

We told him that my wife and children, Avraham'l's son, Benjamin (Niome), and several more Jews were sitting in the forest, waiting for us to return. He asked that none of them should come to his house, only the both of us. He would provide us with food and would do everything he had the strength to do for us. And, in fact, he brought us bread, a small container of butter, cheese, two spades and a saw. Avraham'l asked his advice about how to go about building an earthen shelter, but he refused to answer this question because, should we be found, we would undoubtedly suspect that he was the one who turned us in and sold his conscience to the devil. As he spoke, we could sense his honest intentions, clean conscience and pure heart. And our hearts trembled as we realized that the whole world had not yet been corrupted and that even in Sodom there were still some honest and good people!

We went to the peasant Kazik, who was in the forests near Potashnya. He, too, inquired who had remained alive and gave us potatoes, bread and two spades. We offered him money so that he would provide us with food. He replied that he had more money than we did, but if we had any kind of merchandise, we could use it for barter.

*

We settled in "*Viltche Bloto*" ("The Wolf Swamp"), a place in the forest where the wolves have their dens. We dug a pit, blocked the walls with sawed off young trees, put a ladder inside so we could go down and camouflaged the top with little trees. The snow covered everything, and it was hard to tell from outside that this was a hiding place. However, it is very hard to hide from the eyes of peasants who know every hidden corner in the forest and recognize, like a wild animal, the scent of a stranger.

When we went back to Kazik a few months later, he told us that the peasants in the surrounding villages knew where we were hiding. He advised us to leave the place because the peasants would turn us over to the Germans.

We did not leave the place, but we were already afraid to go and ask peasants for food. Three weeks went by and we were simply famished. My brother-in-law suggested that we go out and look for "*koptzes*" potatoes (holes covered all winter for storing potatoes). We actually found such a "*kopetz*" hole in one of the hamlets, and that kept us alive.

Early one morning, as we were sitting around the fire cooking our food, we heard a shout: "*Ruki verch!*" (Hands up!) We naturally obeyed the order and raised our hands. These were Christian partisans in a unit bearing Stalin's name. They searched us, took our money, boots, sheets which we had gotten and they also wanted to take our gun, but one of them would not allow this, explaining that we wouldn't be able to get food without a gun and that we would die of hunger. We asked them to take us with them, but our asking was in vain because: "You're robbers, and there's no place among partisans for such people." Two weeks later, they returned and took the only gun we had.

A few days later, we were forced to leave our earthen shelter and move to another place. We dug ourselves into a hill and built a stronger and better camouflaged earthen shelter. We had to hide from the Germans as well as from some of the partisans. We were in contact with a certain peasant, Misha, whom we would often help with his household work. A few days after we had left our first shelter, the partisans came back looking for us. When they found no one there, they shot bullets in their own hats and informed their commander that we shot at them and then ran away. The commander ordered them to catch us and bring us to him. We found out all about this from Misha, our contact person. In short, they captured my brother-in-law and forced him to lead them to our hiding place. They then took two of our men and brought them to their commander. On the way, they savagely beat them up, then washed off the blood and brought them to Tchapen, the village where the unit's command post was located. As they were waiting outside in this state, a Jewish partisan happened to pass by and said: "Don't be afraid, fellows. They won't do anything to you.", and having said this, left. And that's what actually happened. The commander understood the truth and released them. Since it was already too late to go back, he ordered that they be given food and a place to sleep. My brother-in-law again brought up the question of our being accepted into the unit, but they turned down his request because we didn't have any guns, and they themselves didn't have enough guns for their men. The commander sent a letter with our request to the district staff quarters located not far from Baksht, but we received the same reply from there.

Itche (Yitzhak) Florans decided to go back to the ghetto in Novogrudek and get his brother out. We took him as far as the Neiman. He crossed the ice covered river and got safely into the ghetto, but it was already impossible to get out of the ghetto. They started to dig a tunnel, but before they finished digging, the mass slaughter took place and they hid in the bunker. That night, Itche Florans was standing by the door of the bunker, listening to the sounds outside. Suddenly, he heard the Germans approaching the bunker and surrounding it. He shouted: "Jews, save your lives!" He jumped outside, quickly climbed over the ghetto fence and was engulfed by the blackness of the night. He reached Delatitch that same night. He stayed there a full week until he managed to return to our earthen shelter.

Spring was approaching. We knew that when the ice melted, the Neiman would overflow all around and we would be cut off from all human habitation and not receive any food. That meant that we had to provide food for ourselves well in advance if we didn't want to die of hunger.

Lin, a carpenter, carved guns and pistols from wood, and they really looked authentic. "Armed" with such weapons, we went to one of the hamlets. We entered a house holding our "pistols" and ordered the peasant to harness a horse because we had to go somewhere. The peasant started crying, explaining that he had only one horse and that if we took away his horse, he would be unable to maintain his household. I calmed him down, promising that we wouldn't hurt him, and that if he was worried about his horse, he should take us with him in his sleigh. The peasant actually did so.

It was a clear winter night. The ground was still covered with white, clean snow as soft as butter, but we already felt a mild spring breeze coming up and the trees awakening from their frozen sleep. The sleigh carrying the six Jews with wooden guns on their shoulders moved along quickly and pleasantly, as though it were a peaceful "jaunt" in the good old days.

The Voynov forest was silent when we went into the homes of the peasants and ordered them to give us food. We loaded up the sled with a few bags of flour, bread, groats, meat, sausage and honey. At midnight, we went back with our trophies, accompanied by the barking of dogs.

On the way back, we encountered a large group of partisans. We were afraid that we would be questioned as to where and how we got food and that we would undoubtedly be shot on account of that. But we had no other choice and had to take a chance. When we got closer, a guard saw us and shouted out: *"Davay Parol"* ("Give the password!") I kept my wits about me and answered: *"Da svoya, takiya sami kak vay"* ("The same, the same people as you!") He gave an order *"Paganay le'ashaday"* ["Move your horse on!"] The same thing happened a second time. We got through safely in this way and returned to our earthen shelter. Then we released the peasant with his horse and he went happily back home.

Two weeks later, we again took a horse from one of the peasants and brought back a wagon full of potatoes. We obtained food in this way and got safely through the few weeks, during which everything around was submerged in water and we were sitting in our shelter, as though we were on an island, cut off from human settlement.

Spring arrived. The sun became agreeably warmer and the water dried up. Everything was covered with green vegetation and an abundance of flowers. Birds were chirping and flying from tree to tree, carrying pieces of wood, grass and soil in their beaks with which to build their nests. Everything awakened to a new life. We also felt freer and happier.

On such a day, we were sitting outside, cooking a pot of potatoes over a small fire. Suddenly, we heard the echo of a strong movement, not far from us, and an echo of voices also reached us. We were terribly afraid. Who could that be? As we were sitting like that, eating the hot potatoes, we saw two armed men approaching. We soon recognized them as partisans. We greeted them with a "Welcome comrades!" and invited them to sit and eat with us.

Hearing that we were Jews hiding from the Germans, they told us that they belonged to the partisan unit named after Tchkalov and that there were many Jews in that unit who would certainly like to see us. Before long, the Jewish partisans, men and women, came to us. We kissed and wept from joy, seeing living Jews and besides, Jews who were taking revenge and paying back the enemy with fire and death. They asked us to go with them and show them in which villages there were no Germans.

We set out late at night and got as far as Delatitch-Zahorye. Guards were placed on the roads leading to Lubtch and Delatitch and we began to clean out the peasants, taking their cows, pigs, flour, grain as well as stolen Jewish property:

suits, material, clothes, etc. We harnessed 25 horses and got to Mikolayeve before daybreak. We didn't take anything from the peasants who lived near the forest. On the contrary, we shared the things we brought with them.

The commander of the Tchkalov unit gave us a document stating that we belonged to his unit. He sent me and my brother-in-law on mission to spy out the area and report where the Germans were deployed and which of the local peasants were in the police force. We carried out our task superbly. Next, we went to Delatitch with a group of partisans. There, we caught the gentile who was the first to rob the Jews as well as the village elder, Alexei Shunke. We honored them both with a bullet to their heads, and we took everything they had in their houses, mainly the things they had robbed from the Jews.

The front had moved closer to our area. The Germans were running back in wild panic just as the Russians had run back three years earlier. The partisans cut off the roads taken by the retreating Germans and sowed death and destruction among them. At the beginning of June 1944, we heard distant, dull echoes of artillery fire. A few days later, we were already greeting the attacking divisions of the Red Army, which liberated our area.

We were once again "free" people, but where could we go? We were terrified to go back to our town - a few Jews among so many gentile wolves.

We went to Ivya, where I was drafted into the Red Army and sent to Lida, where Engineer Buslovitch, a former partisan from our unit, discharged me from the army, pretending I was needed for work in his division. My wife and I soon returned to Delatitch and moved back into our house. I worked in Lubtch, in the *Raiprom-kombinat*, as a deliverer of raw material and tools. In this position, I had the opportunity to travel about in Lida, Baranovitch, Minsk and other cities. The destruction was great everywhere. The Jewish communities were obliterated, and not a trace remained of the once flourishing and spiritually rich Jewish life.

A terrible feeling of bereavement and orphanhood enveloped us. It was hard for us to remain on that cursed ground. As soon as we had the opportunity to leave for Poland, we left our town and went to Lodz.

In Poland, however, the hatred towards the few surviving Jews was even greater and more intense than in our region. Pogroms were perpetrated against Jews in Cracow (1945), Kielce (1946) and other cities. They stopped trains, took the Jews off and shot them on the spot. The Polish population rejoiced and eagerly assisted the bandits.

I understood that there was no safe place for the Jewish people, except for Eretz-Israel. However the nations of the world had not yet agreed that the Jews have a right to live in their land. We set out on the difficult path of clandestine immigration to Palestine, together with thousands of other Jews, snatched from the burning fires. The route we followed took us through Czechoslovakia, Austria, Italy and finally to Eretz Yisrael. But this is already a separate chapter in our life, the story of which will be told in the history of the Jewish People and its fight for its own country.

On May 19, 1946, a year after the victory over the Germans, the greatest ever enemy of the Jewish people, our feet stepped upon the ground of our eternal homeland - The Land of Israel.

Yisrael Slonimsky, his wife, children and nephew, Benyamin Kivovitch

Additional information from Benyamin Kivovitch:
Standing left to right: Benyamin Kivovitch; the head of the partisan group to which they belonged (name not remembered but he may have been a doctor); Rachmiel Slonimsky, son of Yisrael z"l.
Sitting left to right: Rachel Deutsch, Yisrael's daughter living today (2013) in Brazil with 2 children, 4 grandchildren and a great-grandaughter; Nechama Slonimsky z"l, Yisrael's wife; Yisrael Slonimsky.

[Page 433]

Poem
(unrhymed translation)

by Chaim Yankelevitch

Translated from the Hebrew by Ann Belinsky and Harvey Spitzer

In memory of my father, Moshe Ben Yisrael,
My mother, Chana Taibel bat Zvi Kessler,
My sister Rivka-Devorah and my brother Shmuel, May the Lord avenge their death!

*

To our fathers, the will to live and heroism were of no avail.
The fist of the beast was supreme.
And the grave was silent in the agony of dying,
They walked towards a releasing death with a weeping soul.
And in a quiet oath the hand rises up,
And in mute prayer, prosecutes! implores!?
And on plaque and heart the horrors will be engraved!!!
So that generations after us will remember this.

*

A lament for the parents, the brother and sister,
A lament for grandmother and grandfather, uncle and aunt,
A lament for a wounded and pained nation.
A lament for a nation, a third of whose children have died.
We will tell of those burned and murdered in the ghettos,
About those who died of hunger and tribulations.
So that future generations will know
That in their death they willed us life!

[Pages 434-436]

Words Spoken by Nachum Shlimovitch at the Memorial Service for the Martyrs of Lubtch and Delatitich

by Nachum Shlimovitch

Translated from the Yiddish by Harvey Spitzer

To you, my dear brothers and sisters and friends, I have come today to transmit the last groan, the last sigh, the last call of *Shema Yisrael* of our mothers and fathers, wives, husbands and little children when their lives were savagely cut short by the sharp knife of the Nazi-Germans and their eager helpers.

To you, I have the obligation to transmit the last thoughts and feelings of terror of those sentenced to death without a reason why, without guilt, but only because they were Jews - children of a people who never harmed anyone, never touched anyone and were happy just to be given a little rest.

In the nightmarish dark days and nights in the ghettos and camps, when everything was blocked up before us, the Heavens closed and there was no one to call to for help, and there was no other way out than to wait for the final march, we thought about how to save ourselves, to have the great merit of staying alive in order to tell the world what happened to us, what torments and tortures we were made to suffer before we were killed and how monstrous the German "people of culture" actually were. And also in order to bring to you, dear brothers and sisters, the final greeting of those who were so painfully afflicted, their last call for revenge, not to forgive and never to forget the German Amalek.

This evening, when we have gathered together to honor our martyrs, at this very moment when I stand before you, there pass before my eyes many close and dear faces, the same ones that come to me in my dreams, tear me from my sleep and refuse to leave me alone in my sleepless nights as well. They order me to speak, tell and cry out our last cry so that it will be heard by those who are our own flesh and blood, our succession, the continuers of our cut-off lives.

It was the end of June 1941. The Soviet authorities fled; the Germans were approaching. The local gentiles and peasants from the surrounding villages took advantage of this situation. They came with wagons and sacks, axes and hammers- and began plundering and robbing.

They emptied out the houses and stole everything they could get their hands on. They tore up the floors of the houses and cellars. They didn't even leave over a piece of bread, but this was only a prelude to what came about later.

The Germans locked us up in a ghetto and fenced it in with barbed wire. They forbade us to leave the ghetto and distributed a few grams of bread a day.

In order to make better use of the work capability of the Jews in Lubtch, and also in order to keep them "under their eyes" and to kill them more easily, without any resistance, the Germans divided the Lubtch Jewish community into four segments in the following way: a) Lubtch ghetto, b) Vorobievitch work camp, c) Dvoretz work camp, d) Novogrudek ghetto.

I see, before my eyes, the Lubtch rabbi, Rabbi Yitzchak Weiss and his wife, Shoshke. I see the rabbi, already beardless, wearing a short, torn, little coat, dragging wheelbarrows with bricks until he died of sheer exhaustion.

I see Itchele Baksht's daughter with a suffocated child in her arms. They were hiding in a closet, but the child started crying and the mother suffocated her own child, sacrificed him, just so the other people could be saved. The murderers found them and killed them all.

I see a drunken SS man making the selection "who for life and who for death". I see children who were selected to remain alive getting up on the trucks, on their own free will, to be killed with their mothers and fathers together. I see Jews wearing their prayer shawl and phylacteries going to martyrdom with *Shema Yisrael* on their lips.

I see my brother, Moshe, and my sister, Rachel, with their families, who were killed in Vorobievitch on the same day that the slaughter of the Jews in Novogrudek took place.

I see our townsmen, Yonatan Itzkovitch (Layzer the Shoemaker's son) and Yaakov Yedidovitch, being led to their death on the same day as the massacre in Novogrudek. A child started crying, and the murderers discovered the shelter where they were hiding.

There was no way to escape. Everyone was against us: the Germans, Poles, White Russians, the town gentiles and the village peasants. They all helped the Germans, they all murdered Jews, they all bathed in Jewish blood and they all gleefully rubbed their hands together, knowing that they would be rid of the Jews forever.

A person remained alive not because of his or her wisdom or heroism. It was the choice of fate that some individuals should survive to relate the terrible story of pain and torment, to kindle hatred towards the Germans for generations to come and engrave the "Remember!" in the life of our people - to remember and not forget the German Amalek.

This tragic mission has been entrusted to me, one of the survivors. I am bringing this mission here to you, together with the final greeting of our closest and dearest.

Their memory will be hallowed forever. They will forever live in the memory of the Jewish People.

[Pages 437-438]

Words at the Memorial Service for the Martyrs of Lubtch and Delatitich

by Yaakov Zacharavitch

Translated from the Hebrew by Ann Belinsky

Yaakov Zacharavitch

We - the remnants of the Jews of the Lubtch-Delatitch community, have not forgotten the terrible days when the two towns were obliterated, and every year we meet up and remember our dear ones who were destroyed, killed and burnt alive, only because they were Jews, and for no other reason.

Our people, from whose mouths comes a prayer "I will not die for I will live", is paying in blood the price of existence: even today our sons are falling by the Suez Canal, in the Jordan Valley, in the Golan Heights and even within the "Green Line". The blood which was spilt during the Holocaust and today is the price of the last generations, for the right to live as a free people in our own State - our homeland; this is exactly how we are carrying out the import of the verse: "Then I passed by you and saw you downtrodden in your blood, and I said to you, 'In your blood live! And I said to you 'In your blood live!'"

Many years have passed since the Holocaust, more is forgotten than is remembered, but even so, they all pass before us - all the murdered ones, as if on a screen before our eyes; here they are standing in front of me; simple people, working people, full of longing for Zion, believing and waiting for the Redeemer, people who were wise enough to bring up a generation that refuses to wait for a miracle, a generation that set on its way to acquire training and go on aliya to Eretz Yisrael, to be pioneers passing before the camp, to pave the way for those following in their footsteps.

Here is the township: here are the prayer houses, and next to them is the *Tarbut* school, humming with teachers and pupils. Here is the group of teachers that I remember, the headmaster Yitzchak Dichter of blessed memory - the fighter for school's existence, its improver and perfecter, and his colleagues by his side - the teacher Yaakov Shmulevitch and his wife, who was also a teacher; Shalom Sonenzon, the teacher Chaim Persky who saw the activities for the Jewish National Fund as his destiny in life. In front of my eyes stand all at the first bazaar which was held for the JNF; and here is the library - the pride of the teacher Alter Shmulevitch; here are the activists of the youth groups - the next generation, who did not live to fulfill their vision; here are the community leaders, and at their head is Chaim Bruk, representing it in all matters.

Here is the whole township with its people and its institutions; a small town, crowded, roofs touching, with no modernization, the water does not flow in pipes, but it has a warmth, each family has its own corner, the youth are in ferment, beginning to look forward to new horizons and to be freed. In this place we passed the best days of our lives, the days of childhood and youth, where we dreamed dreams of a better future.

This Jewish town is no longer, all has been destroyed. In all possible ways and by all means, whole families were executed - men women and children; and we who were far from all this have remained orphaned and alone.

The years have passed: every year that goes by distances us from the days of the atrocities, the cry of the blood is becoming fainter, and wounds tend to heal. The daily hassles divert our minds from the thoughts and the memories; but this gathering and the prayer *El Maleh Rachamim* which the chazan has chanted return us to those days, to the great catastrophe that overtook our people.

From year to year there remain fewer and fewer of the remnants of our town, and who knows if our children will keep alive the memory of the towns and their families that they never knew, but have only heard about.

There is a prayer in our hearts that this book - the headstone that will be raised in memory of the two communities - will be used as a source for study and learning, about the stories of the Jews of the town, and that our children and grandchildren will remember, through reading it, all our dear ones, who were burned on the stake and died martyrs deaths.

May their memory be blessed and engraved in our hearts forever.

The memorial headstone in the Kiryat Shaul cemetery in Tel Aviv

Engraved on the monument: In Memory of the Martyrs of the Communities of Novogrudek and surroundings: (left to right) Seliv, Lubtch, Karelitz
[AB - information from the Yankelevitch family: Left to right: Chemda Simchoni (Elka's sister); Chaim Yankelevitch; Elka Yankelevitch; Shmuel Baksht (leaning on stone); Rivka Simchoni; Tuvia Simchoni (Rivka's husband)
Elka and Chemda are daughters of Mina Raisel and Reuven Movshovitch -see family photo page 379]

[Pages 440-442]

Former Lubtch and Delatitch Residents now living in Israel

<u>Hebrew letter Aleph</u>
Avrahamy Sarah
Oshman Mussia
Osherovsky Meir
Itzikovitz Dov
Amitay Hinda
Engel Rachel
Aronovsky Sonia

<u>Hebrew letter Bet</u>
Boldo Chanan
Boldo Yosef
Boldo Pinchas
Batar Sarah
Baksht Zalman
Baksht Shmuel
Bruk Avraham
Bruk Chaya
Brenner Mina
Berkovsky Michael

<u>Hebrew letter Gimel</u>
Gordon Shayna
Gur Yaakov
Gafni
Gershony Chaya

<u>Hebrew letter Dalet</u>
Degani Yona
Dichter Chana

<u>Hebrew letter Hey</u>
Hadas Rachel

<u>Hebrew letter Vav</u>
Vinestein (Weinstein) Bobel
Vingrovsky Shulamit

<u>Hebrew letter Zayin</u>
Zach Yaakov
Zarov Aharon

<u>Hebrew letter Tet</u>
Taubman Golda
Timensky Luba

Hebrew letter Yod
Yankelevitch Elka
Yankelevitch Chaim
Yankelevitch Yisrol
Yankelevitch Sonia
Yaakobi Reuven
Yarosh Benyamin

Hebrew letter Kaf
Kagan Mary
Cohen Aryeh
Cohen Dov
Cohen Dov (Tel Aviv)
Caspi Yaakov

Hebrew letter Lamed
Levanon Elka
Levine Herb (The Rabbi?)
Liv (?Leib) David and Yona
Leibovitz Shalom
Leibovitz Avraham Ben-Shalom
Leibovitz Avraham

Hebrew letter Mem
Movshovitz Yisrael
Meizel (Ramat Gan)
Malravitz Shifra
Mendelevitz Yisrael
Mendelevitz (Rehovot)
Manfred Dina
Maslovtah Shmuel
Maslovtah (Tel Aviv)

Hebrew letter Nun
Nochimovsky Reuven
Nashkes Puah

Hebrew letter Samech
Sevitzky Aryeh
Solomiansky Shifra
Sochnitzky Simcha
Soldocha Osnat
Sonenzon Chaim
Sonenzon Rivkah
Simanovitz Faivel
Sindor Luba
Slonimsky Yisrael and his wife (?Nechama)
Sa'aroni Mina

Hebrew letter Peh
Faivishovitz Avraham
Faivishevitch Ephraim
Faivishovitch Yehoshua
Faivishovitch Chaya
Pintel Freda
Pines Mina
Piklani Moshe
Frumkin Cheena

Hebrew letter Tzaddi
Tzur Ephraim
Tzur Mina
Chichik Batya
Charbin Sarah

Hebrew letter Koof
Kabak Dov
Kivlevitch Shmuel (Tel Aviv)
Kivilevitch Shmuel (The Rabbi)
Kleinshtov Miriam
Kalmanovitz Meir
Krugman Batya
Kroshnitz Mina

Hebrew letter Resh
Ragovin Fruma
Rozental Tzipporah
Reichman Shoshana

Hebrew letter Shin
Shitzgal Chaya-Rachel
Schanovitz Raphael
Shlimovitz Chaya
Shlimovitz Sonia
Shmulovitz Hillel
Shmukler Avigdor
Shmulovitch Rivkah
Simchoni Chemdah
Shimshoni Tuvia
Shimshoni Rivkah
Shragai Chaim

Townspeople whose articles appear in this book

Michael Lipkin, May the Lord avenge his blood! and Yisrael-Gershon (Yisrol) Yankelevitch, May he live long (see article on Page 285)

Puah Nashkes (see article Page 265)

Meyerim Kalmanovitch (see article Page 250)

[Page 443]

List of Jews from Lubtch and Delatitch who Came to Israel, and Who Have Since Died

Avrahami Kalman
Aharonovsky Eliezer
Oshrovsky Fruma
Itzikovitch Malka
Boldo Rachel
Gordon Yitzchak
Dichter Yitzchak
Yankelevitch Nathan
Leibovitch Reuven
Malchovitzky Miriam
Solomiansky Zeev
Faivoshevitch Gershon
Faivoshevitch Chaviva
Pisuk Shmuel
Frumkin Yosef
Tziversky Tzvi
Tziversky Miriam
Tziversky Bella
Kivilevitch Hinda
Shitzgal Sander
Shmulovitch Moshe
Shmulovitch Itka
Shmulovitch Henia
Shmulovitch Sarah
Shapira Nechama

Martyrs of Lubtch
List of Lubtcha Jews who were killed in the Holocaust

Prepared by Ofer Cohen

Surname	Husband	Wife	Children	Notes and Additional Family Members
AHARONOVSKI	Yitzhak	Yocheved		
ASHMAN	Khayim Hershel	Dvora	Avraham and 2 more sons	
ASHMAN	Pinkhas	Teybl	Yaakov, Rivka, Bluma, Asher, Yachne, Shifra	
ASHMAN	Yaakov	Esther-Leah	Mendel, Sonya	
BAKSHT	Leyb	Feyga	Moshe	
BAKSHT	Yoel	Ashka	Rivka, Shulamit, Dov	
BAKSHT		Leah		Daughter of Yitzkhak BAKSHT
BAYER		Reyzel	2 sons	
BELSKI	Moshe	Khana	Pesakh, Iche-Berl, Yehuda	
BEREZINSKI	Aharon	Leah	Golda, Yonatan, Sara	
BEREZINSKI	Avraham	Khaycha	Khana, Rivka, Meyta	
BEREZINSKI	Leybe	Moshka		
BEREZINSKI	Moshe	Leah		
BEREZINSKI	Yehuda	Sheynke	Sara, Eliezer	
BEREZINSKI	Yosef	Leah	Yonatan, Pesya	
BERKOVICH	Aharon	Leah	Rakhel, 1 more son	
BERKOVICH	Reuven	Rivka	Miryam	
BERKOVICH	Yitzkhak			
BERMAN		Sheyna-Fruma	Leyba, Musya	
BERSKIN	Yaakov	Wife	Gershon, Zelig, Beyla, 1 more child	
BEZSMIRTANI	Izya	Fruma	Feivl	Fruma was the daughter of Yehuda FEIVOSHEVICH
BITANSKI	Avraham	Fruma	Feigele	Fruma was the daughter of Leyb FEIVOSHEVICH
BOLDA	Alter	Rivka	Sara-Henya, Yosef, Eliezer	and one more son

BOLDA	Yaakov-Dov	Khasya		
BORETZKI	Reuven	Leah	Khana, David	
BORETZKI		Leah		
BRUK	Khayim	Genya	Gita, Manya	
BRUK	Moshe	Pesya	Talik, 1 more girl	
CANTOROVICH	Yerakhmiel	Batya	Sara-Rivka, Reuven	
DAVIDOVICH	David	Golda	Zisl, Leybe, Yaakov	
DAVIDOVICH	Feyvl	Khana		
DAVIDOVICH	Feyvl	Khaya		
DAVIDOVICH	Moshe-Aharon	Feygel	Khayim, Pinkhas	
DELTITZKI	Leybl	Batya	Feygl, 2 girls	Leybl's mother, Sara, lived with them
DELTITZKI	Leybl	Esther	Khaya-Feygl, Yehudit	
DELTITZKI	Shmuel	Dvora	Khayim, 1 more child	
DUSHKIN	Leybe	Reyzel	Malka, 1 more child	
DVORETZKI	Eizik	Wife	3 children	
DVORETZKI	Yosef	Breynke	Khana, Musya, Gitl, 1 little daughter	
DZENTILSKI	Yeshayahu	Musya	1 daughter	
FEYBUSHEVICH	Binyamin	Elka	Puah, 1 more son	
FEYBUSHEVICH	Henech	Leah-Miryam	Eliyahu, Sheyna, David	
FEYBUSHEVICH	Khayim-Gimpel			
FEYBUSHEVICH	Leybeh	Puah		Leybe's mother - Rasha
FEYBUSHEVICH	Moshe	Musya	2 daughters	
FEYBUSHEVICH	Refael	Rivka-Leah	Feygel, Dvora	
FEYBUSHEVICH	Shabtay	Tzvia-Beyla	Zalman, Ita, Kalman, Rakhel	
FEYBUSHEVICH	Shabtil	Mashka		
FEYBUSHEVICH	Shmuel	Esther		
FEYBUSHEVICH	Shmuel-Leyb	Musya	Zelda, Feygele	Also daughter Reizel (mentioned separately, below)

FEYBUSHEVICH	Yehoshua-Yaakov	Esther-Hadasa		
FEYBUSHEVICH	Yehuda	Risha	Tzira, Yitzkhak	Yitzkhak's wife
GALANS	Tuvya	Sara-Tzeyra	Yachna, Rakhel, Yonatan	
GELFAND		Khaya	Tzipora, Miryam	
GELMAN				All the family
GERSHOVICH		Rachel	Shmuel, Sara-Beyla	Also Sara's husband and son
GISHIN	Berl	Reyzel	Baruch, Moshe	
GISHIN	Israel			
GOLDBERG	Avraham	Dvora	Rakhel, Mordechai, Esther-Ita	
GOLDBERG	Eliezer (Eli)	Hades	Rivka, Yenta, Khayim-Binyamin	
GORODISKI		Breyna	Shlomo, Baruch, Shayke, Sonya, Yitzkhak	
GORSHOVICH	Alter	Fedka	Yaakov, Itka	
GRIMOVICH	David	Maryashe	Eliyahu, Hertzl, Rivka	
GRIMOVICH	Shlomo	Esther	Khanoch-Henech, Khaya, 1 more daughter	
GUTKA	Berl (Dov)			
HALPERIN	Elyakim	Grunya	Yosef, Eliezer, Elka	
HALPERSHTEIN	Avraham	Rivka	Sara-Rakhel, Tuvya, Slova, Khasya	
HEFETZ	Gedalya	Mina	Sara, 1 more child	
ITZKOVICH	Eliezer	Wife	Pesya	
ITZKOVICH	Yaakov		3 children	
ITZKOVICH	Yehonatan	Bracha	Eva and more daughter	Yehonatan was the son of Eliezer
ITZKOVICH	Yitzkhak	Sara	Yonatan, Yosi	
IZIKOVITZKI	Baruch	Wife	Izik, Mordechai, Daniel	
YIZRELEVICH	Dov	Reiza		
YIZRELEVICH	Mendel	Malka	3 children	
YIZRELEVICH	Yehonatan	Khaya-Leyba	Israel, Sima, Reuven, another son and daughter	
KAGAN	Isarel	Sara		
KALMANOVICH	Avraham	Wife	Itka	Itka's husband and child

KALMANOVICH	Ben-Tzion	Khaya-Sara	Rivka, Dvora	
KALMANOVICH	Eliezer	Pesya	Beyla	
KALMANOVICH	Feyvel	Tzira	Meir-Khazan, Eliyahu, Dvora	
KALMANOVICH	Israel-Yitzkhak	Khina-Gitl	Shmuel, Khanan	
KALMANOVICH	Khayim-Berl			
KALMANOVICH	Mordechai	Pesya	Sara-Esther, Avraham, Yitzkhak	
KALMANOVICH	Shabtay	Fruma	Yaakov, Feivl	
KALMANOVICH	Shalom	Reyzel	Shlomo, Avraham, Nekhama	
KALMANOVICH	Shlome	Gnesya	Khayim	
KALMANOVICH	Shlomo	Rakhel	one daughter	
KALMANOVICH	Yitzkhak	Pesya	Gitl, Yosef, Moshe, Meir, Aba	
KANTAROVICH	Yerekhmiel	Batya	Sara-Rivka, Reuven	
KANTAROVICH	Reuven	Meyta	Yaakov, Pinkhas, Meir, Rakhel	
KANTAROVICH	Velvl	Khaya-Sara	2 sons	
KAPLANSKI		Sara-Feyga	Khayim-David, Mordechai, Gdalyahu, Binyamin	
KAPUSHCHEVSKI	Gershon	Sonya	Refael, Meir, Yerakhmiel	
KAPUSHCHEVSKI	Mordechai	Hinda	Yehoshua, Gitl, Rivka, Hadasa	
KAPUSHCHEVSKI	Natan			
KAPUSHCHEVSKI	Zalman	Khaya	Nekhama, Eliezer	
KAPUSHCHEVSKI		Khasya-Batya	Yosef	
KAPUSHCHEVSKI		Sara-Khana		
KASMAY	Alter	Perla	Matala, Rashke	
KASMAY	David-Itche	Leah	Khayim-Yaakov, Yehudit, Leyba	
KASMAY	Shmayahu	Libke	Michael, Menukha, Feygel	
KASMAY		Leybe-Feybe	Alter, Gruncha, Yaakov, Khashka	Maybe Leybe-Feybe is the daughter, not the wife

KASMIVICH	Avraham	Itka	Sara, Gutka, one more daughter	
KASMIVICH	Khayim-Shmuel	Libe	Golda	
KHARLAP	Yosef	Yocheved	Khaya, and 2 sons	
KHAYMOVICH	Simkha			
KHAYMOVICH	Yeshayahu	Sara	Michael, Beni	
KIBELEVICH	Baruch	Batya	Musya, 2 sons	
KIBELEVICH	Isar	Nekhama	Henya	
KIBELEVICH	Itche-Khanan	Wife	7 children	
KIBELEVICH	Leyb	Sara-Itke	Kreyna, Shulamit, 1 more daughter	
KIBELEVICH	Tzvi	Rakha-Henya		
KIBELEVICH	Yehoshua	Itka	Peretz, Kreyna, Menukha	
KIBELEVICH	Yitzkhak	Sheyna	Mina, Khana, Binyamin, Ben-Tzion	
KIBELEVICH		Khasya	Zeydel, Kreyna	
KONYAK	Yitzkhak	Rakhel-Mina	Aharon, Leybe, Sara-Ita	
KOPELOVICH	Binyamin	Nishka	Tzirl, Meir, Yedidya	Yedidya was married
KOZNITZKI	Asher	Rivka	Pesya, Yehoshua, Moshe	
KRASILOV	Avraham	Khaya-Feygel	Asna, Rakhel, Sonya, Miryam, Luba	
KRAVITZ	Mordechai	Rakhel	Hirshele, Dashke, Yehoshua	
KRAVITZ	Moshe	Doba	Avraham-Itche, Zlata, Leah	
KROVSKI	Yehuda	Mina	2 children	
LASKIN	Yitzkhak	Masha	Sara, Rakhel	
LEVIN	Arie	Tzvia	Rivka, Rakhel	
LEVIN	Khayim-Leyb	Batya	Yosef, Meir, Binyamin, Esther	
LEVIN	Leybe	Pesya	Shmuel, Yehuda, 1 more son	
LEVIN	Leybl	Tzvia	Leah, Rakhel	
LEVIN	Moshe	Henya	Luba, Yitzkhak, 1 more child	And Moshe's mother, Fruma, who was living with them

LEVIN	Yehoshua	Reyzl	3 children	
LEYBOVICH	Arie	Sheyna		
LEYBOVICH	Baruch	Khaya-Rakhel	Tzvia-Beyla, 1 more daughter	
LEYBOVICH	David-Yitzkhak	Sheyna	Meyte, Michale	
LEYBOVICH	Noakh		Tzvia, Sheyna-Rakhel, Avraham-Nakhum	
LEYBOVICH	Pinkhas	Fruma	Rivka, Rakhel	
LEYBOVICH	Refael	Khana-Leah	David	David's wife and daughter - Esther and Musya
LEYBOVICH	Yaakov-Khayim	Etl	Alter, Leybe-Itche	Leybe-Itche's wife
LEYBOVICH		Beyla-Feyga	David, Batya	
LEYBOVICH		Mina	Elka, Khana, Simkha	
LEYMES	Leybe	Sara-Beyla	Getzl, Zalman, 1 more son	
LEYZEROVSKI				
LICHITZKI	Asher	Masha		
LICHITZKI	Yaakov	Sara-Esther	Slova, Tuvya, Leah	
LICHTIN	Yaakov	Khasya	3 children	
LINIK	Shmuel	wife	1 son	
LIPCHIN	Michael	Rivka	Getzl, Yehudit	
LIPCHIN	Mordechai-Eliyahu	Reyza	Yaakov, Rivka, Leah, David	
MALKHOVITZKI	Noakh-Itche	Feyga		
MEIRSON	Khayim	Feyga	Liba	
MELNIK	Avraham	Esther-Rakhel		
MENDELEVICH	Michael	Khana	Shimon, Reuven, 1 more son	
MENDELEVICH	Mordechai	Rakhel	Nakhum, Malka, Moshe-Aharon	
MENDELEVICH	Yehoshua-Yaakov	Khasya	Feygel, Rakhel, David, Betzalel, Rivka	
MENDELEVICH	Yosef	Khasya-Feygel	Avraham-Yitzkhak, Sinay	

MENDELEVICH	Yosef	Leah	Grune, Byelka, and their children	
MESELEVICH	Arie	Eshka	Avraham, Yenta, Michale, Nekhemya, Israel, Yitzkhak	
MESELEVICH	Hirsh	Yenta	Puah	
MESELEVICH	Israel-Yitzkhak	Leah		
MESELEVICH	Yehuda	Sara	1 child	
MIBSKI	David	Rakhel	Matityahu	
MIBSKI	Yosef	Henya	Matityahu, 2 more sons	
MIDRASH	Yoel	Khaya-Gitl	Khayim, Tzvi, Yenta	
MISNIK	Uriya	Sheyna-Leah	7 children	
MORDOCHOVICH	Binyamin	Mirke	Mordechai	
MORDOCHOVICH	Shlomo	Rakhel	2 daughters	1 mute brother-in-law
MORDOCHOVICH	Yehoshua-Yaakov	Nekhame	1 daughter	
MUBASHOVICH	David	Bracha	Shachna, Khayim	
MUBASHOVICH	Gershon	Esther	Eliyahu-Yehonatan, Sheyna-Miryam, Israel-Shimon, Ezra	
MUBASHOVICH	Leybel	Reyzel	Mordechai	
MUBASHOVICH	Reuven	Mina-Reizl	Yosef, Ester, Sheina	
MUBASHOVICH		Batya	Dov, Sima	
NIANKOVSKI	Avraham	Rakhel	Libe, Eliezer	
NIANKOVSKI	Khayim-Yitzkhak	Yenta	Fruma, Eliezer, Leybe	
NIKOLIVSKI	Menakhem	Rivka	Rakhel, 1 more son	
NISHKIND	Husband	Wife	Golda, 1 more daughter	
NISHKIND	Shimon	Teybe	David, Noomi, Izak, Sara	
OBSIVICH	Yosef	Leah	Khanoch-Henech, Yonatan, David	
ORLANSKI	Yaakov	Khana-Khaya	3 children	
OSHEROVICH	Akiva	Mina	Feivl, Mordechai	
OSHEROVSKI	Ben-Tziyon	Miryam	Pesya	

OSHEROVSKI	Khayim-Asher	Khasya	Batya, Maryasha, Esther, Gedalya	
OSTASHINSKI	Avraham-Khayim	Batya	Sara-Beyla, Feigel, Mordechai	
OSTASHINSKI	Yaakov	Minke	Itka, Michael	
OSTASHINSKI		Chana		
PABLIS	Khayim-Hirshl	Sara-Yenta	Libe, Zlata, Meir, Sara-Dvora, Batya, Tzvika	
PATASHNIK	Husband	Leah	Ita-Beyla, Shalom	
PEKER		Reychel	Shmuel-Avraham, Sender, Yenta, 1 more son	
PERCHIK	Avraham	Sara		
PERCHIK	David	Grunya	2 children	
PERLMAN	Husband	Sheyna	2 daughters	
PIKELANY		Frida	Leah-Rasha, Yaakov	
PINES		Pesya-Leah	Bracha	
POPKIN		Gitl	Yenta, 1 more child	
RABINOVICH	Avraham	Keyla	Yaakov	
RACHKOVSKI	Mordechai	Mina	Rakhel, 2 more sons	
RACHKOVSKI		Osnat	Henya	
RIVTZKI	Fishl	Sheyna	Shmuel, one more child	
ROZENBLUM	Binyamin	Hinda	Shoshana, Kalman, Libka, Sara, Ita	
ROZENBLUM	Dov	Rakhel	Khayim, 1 more daughter	
ROZENBLUM	Moshe	Gitl	Freydl, Yitzkhak	
ROZOVSKI	Binyamin	Zlata	Frida, Refael, Esther, Shraga	
ROZOVSKI		Khasya	Rivka, Frida, Sinya, Esther	
RUBINSHTEIN	Husband	Wife	Sara-Leybe, Bluma, Tova	
SABITZKI	Khayim-Hirsh	Shifra	Miryam, Meir, Yitzkhak	
SENDEROVSKI	Menakhem	Khasya		
SENDLER	Nakhum	Shulamit	Henya	Nakhum's mother
SERBERNIK	Avraham	Nekha	Rakhel, Reyzel, Binyamin, Yachne, Sara	Avraham's mother - Pesya
SERBERNIK	Mordechai	Miryam	2 sons	

SERBERNIK	Moshe		Yosef, Puah, 1 more daughter	
SHACHANOVICH	Khayim-Isar	Beyla	4 children	
SHAPIRA	Eliyahu-Avraham		Shmuel, Yitzkhak	
SHAPIRA	Isar	Sonya	Henya, 1 more son	
SHAPIRA	Yitzkhak	Elka	Miryam, Rakhel	
SHIMSHELEVICH	Mordechai	Rona	Khaya-Beyla, Rivka	
SHIMSHELEVICH	Yehoshua-Yaakov			
SHITZGEL	Eliezer	Teyba	Itka	
SHITZGEL	Shmuel	Wife	Yaakov, Yosef, 1 more daughter	
SHKLOT	Avraham-Yitzkhak	Khayka	Dvora, Yosef, Leybe, Eliyahu, Hirshl	
SHKLOT	Moshe	Khana	Yehudit, Elka, Khanan, Pesakh, 2 more sons	
SHKLOT	Refael	Miryam	Rivka, Sheyne, Keyla	
SHLIMOVICH	Khayim			Asher Zelig's
SHLIMOVICH	Moshe	Sonya	Yitzkhak, David, Nakhum	
SHLOVSKI	Yudl	Wife	Children	
SHMULEVICH	Alter	Golda	Shlomo, 1 more son	
SHMULEVICH	Baruch	Batya	Binyamin, Yeshayahu, Shmuel	Baruch's mother - Pesya
SHMULEVICH	David	Khaya	Tuvya, Slova, 1 more child	
SHMULEVICH	Israel	Rivka-Leah	Tuvya, Slova	
SHMULEVICH	Khayim	Masha	3 children	
SHMULEVICH	Mordechai-Berl	Yehudit	Hilel-Yankl, Rakhel	
SHMULEVICH	Natan	Alte	Yitzkhak, Khaya, Yaakov	
SHMULEVICH	Nate (Khayim Shlomo's)	Alte	Yitzkhak, Yaakov, Khaya	Probably the same as the above Shmuelevich Natan
SHMULEVICH	Nekhemya	Esther-Hoda	Keyla	
SHMULEVICH	Yaakov	Rakhel	Teyba, Khaya	
SHMULEVICH	Yaakov			

SHMULEVICH	Yehoshua	Rivka	Efrayim, Sheyna, Yaakov, Bunya	
SHMULEVICH	Yitzkhak	Rivka	Tuvya, Slova, 6 more children	
SHMULEVICH	Yosef	Feyga-Rakhel	6 children	
SHMULEVICH		Leah	Elka	
SILEVIANSKI		Gitl	Khaya	
SOCHNITZKI	Yosef	Tzvia	Zelig, Shifra, Yenta	
SOLODCHA	Israel	Sonya	Yosef, Batya, Cherna	
SOLOMINSKI	Mendel	Reykhel-Masha	Yenta, Teyba	
SONENZON	Moshe	Teyba	Shulamit	
SONENZON	Shalom		1 daughter	
STAKOLESHCKIK	Shmuel	Leah	3 children	
SULTZ	Yaakov	Cherna	Yekutiel, Avraham, Pesakh, Yachne, Puah	
TEMPEL	Moshe	Pesya	Yosef, Batya	
TIKTIN	Moshe	Sonya	Rakhel, Esther, Yosef, Ida	
TONIK	Moshe	Fruma	Tamar, Binyamin, Khana, Leah	
TONIK	Yiyzkhak	Sonya	Elka, Iza	
TUBOLSKI	All the family			The kantor
VEINER	Berl	Gita		
VERBOVSKI	Shmuel	Tzipora	Eliyahu-Moshe, 2 more sons	
VILNER	David	Beyla	Rakhel, Lola	
VOLBERG	Yaakov	Khasya	Berl, more 2 children	Khasya is a daughter of YANKELEVICH
VOLINSKI	David	Tova-Rivka	Khana, Esther, Leybl	
WEIS	Yitzkhak	Shoshke	Yente	Also Yente's husband, Dr. RABINOVICH
YANKELEVICH	Baruch-Mordechai		Yeshayahu-David	
YANKELEVICH	Berl	Keyla	Peretz, Sonya	
YANKELEVICH	David	Bunya	Perla	

YANKELEVICH	Israel	Ester-Gitl		
YANKELEVICH	Moshe	Khana-Teybl	Shmuel, Yosef, Yaakov, Rivka-Dvora, Tzvi	
YANKELEVICH	Tuvya			
YANKELEVICH	Yehuda	Sonya		
YANKELEVICH	Yosef	Beyla	Yuta, Perla, Esther	
YANKELEVICH		Khaya		
YANKELEVICH		Yenta	Velvale, more 1 child	
YEDIDOVICH	Itche-Nute	Risha	Yaakov, Leyba, Sheyna	
YEDIDOVICH	Khayim-Meir	Khaya	Aharon, Esther-Dina, Khanan, Feyba	
YEDIDOVICH	Shimon-Izik	Wife	2 sons	
YEDIDOVICH	Yaakov	Rakhel	Zlata, Yosi, Esther, Yashka	
ZACHAREVICH	Asher	Yehudit	Khanan, Henya, Binyamin	
ZACHAREVICH	Kalman	Khaya-Sara	Khana-Musha, 3 more children	
ZACHAREVICH		Khinka		
ZALMANSKI	Natan	Rakhel	Dina' Aharon	
ZANIVITZKI	Menakhem	Frida	Rakhel, Mina, Meir	
ZELIKOVSKI	Hershl	Roza	Bielka, Gitl, Ester-Freidl, Sara, Feigl, Leah, Bat-Sheva	
ZELIKOVSKI	Yitzkhak			
ZIMAN	Shalom	Elte	Nakhum, Leah	
	Avraham			Itchke's Simkha's
	Avraham	Wife		Flour merchant
	Ben-Tzion and his sister Elka			Blacksmith
	Berl-Meir	khashka	2 children	
	Binyamin	Doba	2 girls	
	Binyamin	Rakhel	Esther, Beyla	Butcher
	Gershon	Khina	1 son	Blacksmith
	Husband	Sara-Beyla	1 son	Sara Beyla was the daughter of Rakhel GERSHOVICH
	Khayim-Isar	Byelka	1 son	

	Kopel	Fruma	3 children	
	Sender	Shoshke	2 daughters	
	Shmuel-Sinay	Wife	Eizik, Finie, Mordechai, Leah, 1 more daughter	
	Yaakov	Khasya		
		Reyzel		The daughter of Shmuel-Leyb FEYBUSHEVICH
		Sara-Rivka		
		Tzvia Reytza	Shmuel	

Remembering the Martyrs:

The Jews of the small town of Negnievitch (Neishtot)

The Jews of the villages in the environs of Lubtch and Delatitch

[Page 459]

Martyrs of Delatitch

List of Delatitch (Delyatichi) Jews who were killed in the Holocaust

Prepared by Ofer Cohen

ALPERSTEIN	Reuven
BAKSHT	Yaakov
BAKSHT	Nakha
BAKSHT	Shmuel-Khayim
BERKOVSKI	Khaya-Zelda
BERKOVSKI	Sara
BEZSMERTANI	Mordechai
BEZSMERTANI	Moshe
BEZSMERTANI	Yitzkhak
BEZSMERTANI	Henya
COHEN	Yosef
COHEN	Sima
COHEN	Bela
COHEN	Khaya
COHEN	Shoshana
COHEN	Elkhanan
GORODISKI	Avraham
GORODISKI	Hinda
GORODISKI	Israel
GORODISKI	Miryam
GORODISKI	Kreyna
GORODISKI	Moshe

GORODISKI	Shoshana
GORODISKI	Tzirla
GORODISKI	Kreyna
GORODISKI	Batya
KIBOVICH	Avraham
KIBOVICH	Tula
KIBOVICH	Gdalyahu
KIBOVICH	Rashele
KLOBAK	Yehoshua
KLOBAK	Pika
KLOBAK	Gitl
KLOBAK	Tzvi
KROLBATZKI	Baruch-Mordechai
KROLBATZKI	Golda
KROLBATZKI	Shabtay
KUSHNIR	Yitzkhak
KUSHNIR	Musya
KUSHNIR	Shoshka
KUSHNIR	Shabtay
KUSHNIR	Hilel
KUSHNIR	Hinda
LIS	Beynish
LIS	Pasha-Hinda
LIS	Yitzkhak-Reuven
LIS	Shoshana(Shoshka)
LIS	Shlomo-Avraham
LIS	Hinda-Risha
LIS	Khaya-Rakhel
LIS	Esther
LISHANSKI	Avraham
LISHANSKI	Pasha-Mina

LISHANSKI	Shma'ya
LISHANSKI	Yerakhmiel
LISHANSKI	Mordechai (Matta)
LISHANSKI	Ita
MALKOVITZKI	Moshe-Aharon
MALKOVITZKI	Yaakov
MALKOVITZKI	Neta
MALKOVITZKI	Dovke
MALKOVITZKI	Sonya
MALKOVITZKI	Eliyahu
SHMUKLER	Sara-Elka
SLONIMSKI	Feiba
SLONIMSKI	Feyga
YANKELEVICH	Berl
YANKELEVICH	Feya
YANKELEVICH	Velvleh

[Page 461]

Photographs

Rabbi Shlomo Niankovsky - one of the Notables of Lubtch

[Page 462]

Families: Moshe Yankelevitch, Reuven Movshovitch and Eliyakim Halperin

[Information from Elka Yankelevitch (nee Movshovitch):
Back row left to right: **Chaim Yankelevitch's sister, Rivka Yankelevitch; Shayna Movshovitch; Chaim's brother, Shmuel Yankelevitch; Basha (Batya) Movshovitch; Halperin child; Halperin child**
Middle row left to right: **Reuven Movshovitch; Mina Raisel Movshovitch (Levin); Chaim Yankelevitch 's grandparents; Chaim Yankelevitch; Chaim Yankelevitch 's parents, Chana-Teibal and Moshe; Chaim Yankelevitch 's aunt and uncle, Halperin**.
Front row left to right: **Yosef-Eli Movshovitch (named after Yosef, Mina Raisel's grandfather and Eli, Reuven's father); Eyshka Movshovitch, (named after Reuven's mother); 3 Halperin children**

[Page 463]

The family of Leib Baksht
Additional information from Aryeh Keshet-Baksht:
Standing extreme right: Shmuel Baksht (son of Aryeh Leib, father of Aryeh Keshet)
Seated Right to Left: (unknown), Aryeh Leib Baksht, his wife Tzipporah Baksht, Zalman Baksht (son of Aryeh Leib)

[Page 464]

Rachel Boldo, May she rest in peace

[Page 465]

**Ritual slaughterer and inspector Yitzchak Aharonovsky and his wife Yachneh
May the Lord avenge their blood**

Miriam Sivitsky,
May the Lord avenge her blood

Chaim-Tzvi Sivitsky,
May the Lord avenge his blood

[Page 466]

**Yehoshua-Yaakov Shimshilevitch,
of blessed memory**

Avraham-Aharon and Sarah Berkovitch

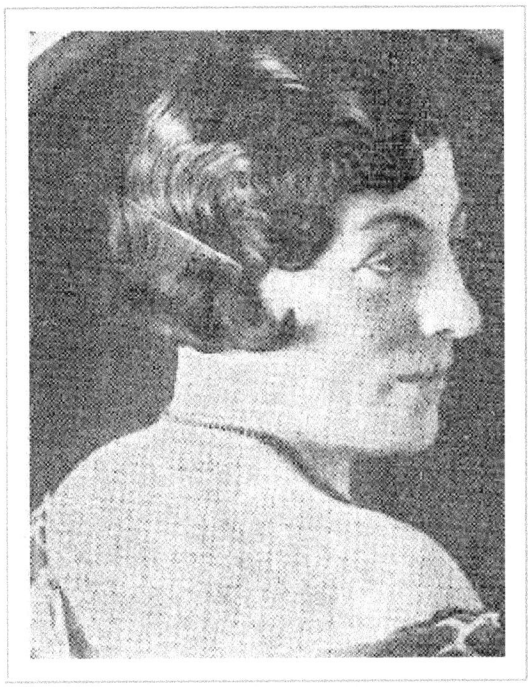
Malka Berkovitch

Chana-Esther Berkovitch

David Bruk

Guta-Kiyana Bruk

[Page 467]

Bottom: **Esterika, Fraydeleh and Zaltka Rozovsky, Shraga, Rivka-Leah and Avraham Faivoshevitz**
Standing: **Benyamin Rozovsky, Feygeleh, Hinda and Gershon Faivoshevitz**

[Page 468]

David, Beyla, Chaya, Rachel Vilner, Avraham Bruk and Lola Vilner

Rasha and Velvul Faivoshevitz

[Page 469]

Chana-Teibel and Moshe Yankelevitch   **Mina-Reizel and Reuven Movshovitch**

(The above titles are reversed in the original book)

David-Itsheh, Shayna, Mayta and Rachel-Golda Leibovitch

[Page 470]

Yaacov Saltz,
May the Lord avenge his blood

Kusha Saltz,
May the Lord avenge his blood

Henia Zacharavitz,
May the Lord avenge her blood

Chanan Zacharavitz,
May the Lord avenge his blood

[Page 471]

Pessia-Leah Pines,
May the Lord avenge her blood

Chaya Yankelevitch and her sister
Taybeleh Shmuelevitch,
May the Lord avenge their blood

Fruma Lubtchansky-Faivoshevitz,
daughter of Chana and Ben-Tzion
Lubtchansky, died on 6 Iyar 5678-
1918

[Page 472]

**Sarah Shmulevitch-Bichler,
died in 1964**

**Itka Shmulevitch-Zonenberg,
died in 1953**

**Henia Volpert-Shmulevitch,
died in 1952**

**Shaul Shmuelevitch,
died in 1931**

[Page 473]

Mina Leibovitch,
May the Lord avenge her blood

Moshe-Aharon Malachovsky

**Shmuel-Yaakov Shmulevitz, his wife Rivkah
and his children: Rachel, Chaya, Kalman,
May the Lord avenge their blood**

[Page 474]

Taybeh and Moshe Sonenzon

The children of Shabtil Faivoshevitz

[Page 475]

The children of Nachum Mayzel,
From right: Sonya, Tzila, (lives in Moscow), Chaya and Boris (1910)

Chaya Mayzel with her husband, Moshe Gershovitch (from Ivyeh)
and a child (1941), all murdered in 1942

[Page 476]

**Mussia and Shmuel-Leib Faivoshevitz,
May the Lord avenge their blood**

[Pages 477-480 - Table of Contents in Hebrew]

[Page 480]

Epilogue

The Organisation of Lubtch and Delatitch Residents in Israel

Translated from the Hebrew by Ann Belinsky

This memorial book, dedicated to the communities of Lubtch and Delatitch, is the fruit of many years of work. Since we were few and of limited resources, we would not have been able to publish it, without the blessed and dedicated help of our friend Chaim Yankelevitch, who invested his time and energy, and worked indefatigably, with adherence and devotion, to gather the material and to obtain the funds for its publication.

For this we express our appreciation and esteem.

It is our pleasant duty to thank also his wife, Elka, for hosting the meetings attended by many participants and for the enthusiastic help she gave her husband in his activities connected with the publishing of this book.

Table of Contents of the Original Yizkor Book

Title	Author	Page
The Map of Lubtch		5
Map of North-East Poland (1939)		6
Preface* [H]	K., Hilel	7
Preface [Y]	K., Hilel	8
Chronicles of the town of Lubtch [H]	B.M.S.	9
Documents relating to Jewish settlement in Lubtch [Y]	Kahn, P.	11
Photo caption "3rd of May" celebrations by the "Gemina " (Local Council) Building [H]		16
Lubtch under Polish Rule [H]	Yankelevitch, Chaim	17
There once was a Jewish village called Lubtch [Y]	Kroshnitz, Hilel	25
Chronicles of the Jewish community in Lubtch [H]	Shmulovitch, Hillel	47
A Jewish town named Delyatichi (Delatitich) [H]	Cohen, Dov	51
My hometown [H]	Eshed (Asherovsky), Frumka	53
From "HaMelitz", August 25th, 1898 [H]	Bonimovitch Chalpak, Yitzchak	60
A wise son-in-law... [Y]	Jankelowitz, Gershon	60
The Hebrew school in Lubtch [H]	Dichter, Yitzchak	61
The "Chorev" school in Lubtch [Y]	"Dos Wort" 618, 636, Vilna 1937, 1938	74
A "periodical" in Lubtch (reported by M. Tsinovitch) [H]	"Hatzfira"#18 (1894)	77
After the event... [Y]	Hilel Krosnitz	78
Rabbis of the Lubtch community [H]	Tzinovitch, Moshe	79
Reb Itchele's curse [Y]	Shlimovitch, Yitzchak	98
That's how we lived... [Y]	Jankelowitz, Gershon	99
For the general good... [Y]	Leibovitch, Shalom	104
The 1915 fire in Lubtch [Y]	Shlimovitch, Yitzchak	105
A comedy [Y]		110
Small Towns of Houses and Trenches [Y]	Kaganovitch, Moshe	111
A Red-Headed Bride... [Y]	Yankelevitch, Chaim	114
"As is" [Y]	Kroshnitz, Hillel	114
The Hidden Light of the Jewish Mother in Lubtch [H]	Dichter, Chana	115
My Dear Mother [Y]	Manger, Itzik	120
I Remember My Village Delyatichi (Delatitch) [Y]	Brenner, Mina	121
No One Leaving and No One Coming [Y]	Kroshnitz, Hillel	134
Lubtch Until the First World War [H]	Sampson, E.	135
The Pastoral Picture has Vanished and is No More [H]	Vilner-Bruk, Chaya	142
The Castle in Lubtch [H]	Perkofchik, L.	145
Frosty Weather in the Summer [H]	Eliav, E.	147
Captions for 2 photos [H]		148
The Branch of "HaShomer Hatza'ir" in Lubtch [H]	Shmulovitch, Hillel	149
Wealth Passes On, one Must Remain a "Mentch..." [Y]	Jankelowitz, Gershon	156
The Dream Has Remained... [Y]	Kroshnitz (Faivishevitch), Mina	157
Youth Movements in Lubtch [H]	Simchoni (Movshovitch), Chemda	163
The Mathematicians... [Y]	Jankelowitz, Gershon	166
The Trial [H]	Shimshoni, T.	167
Episodes from the Town [H]	Sampson, Eliyahu	170
The Request is Heard... [Y]	Yankelevitch, Chaim	172

Title	Author	Page
Only the Memories are Left... [H]	Avrahami, Sara	173
Educational and Cultural Institutions in Lubtch [H]	Boldo, Chanan	175
Wealth... [Y]	Jankelowitz, Gershon	178
Photo Caption: The community committee of Lubtch-Karelitz in 1934 (5695) (and names)		179
Memories of My Town [H]	Engel, Rachel	180
A Wedding [Y]	Yankelevitch, Chaim	181
A letter from the Mendele Library, Lubtch [Y]		182
Remembrances [Y]	Balott, Rose (Reiche- Bayla)	184
The National Spirit of the Jews of Lubtch [H]	Shavit-Faivoshevitch, Avraham	186
Real Horseradish [Y]	Yankelevitch, Chaim	188
Lubtch on the Neiman [H]	Kabak, Dov	189
Lubtch Foods [Y]	K., Hilel	194
"Lubtch Pigs" [Y]	H.K.	199
Days of Activity and Hope [H]	Sonenzon, Chaim	200
The Connection of the Family of President of Israel, Yitzchak Ben Tzvi, to Lubtch [H]	Alef (collated by), A.	202
An Incident About an Informing Report [Y]	Leibovitch, Shalom	205
The Righteous Rabbi R' Shmuel Bakshter [H]	Tsinovitch, Moshe	206
Minikes, Chanan Yaakov [Y]	Jaffe, Mordechai	211
The Actor Matityahu (Matus) Kowalsky [Y]	Tzinovitch, Moshe	214
Expulsion From and Rebuilding of Lubtch [Y]	Shulman (Shlimovitch), Nachum	216
Mutual Support in Lubtch [H]	Tzur, Mina	223
Cultural Life in Lubtch [H]	Levanon, Elka	225
The Town is Engraved in My Heart [H]	Spotnitzky, Baruch	226
Days of Joy and Sorrow [Y]	Kagan-Sirlis, Chana	229
R' Shmuel Meizel and His Family [H]	Tzinovitch, Moshe	234
Lubtch in the 1930's [H]	Yankelevitch, Elka	238
The Amateur Club [H]	Shimshoni, T.	240
My Town Delyatichi (Delatitch) [H]	Shmukler, Avigdor	243
Remember and Do Not Forget! [H]	Degani (Litchitzsky), Yona	247
Two Religious Undertakings in Lubtch [Y]	Rabinovitch, Shalom	250
A Remark Regarding the Abovementioned Correspondent's Report [Y]	Tzinovitch, Moshe	252
Activity of the Branch of the "Board of Yeshivot" in Lubtch [Y]	Rabinovitch, Shalom	253
Rabbis Born in Lubtch [H]	Tsinovitch, Moshe	254
Rabbi R' Chaim Krasilov z"l [And three other Rabbis] [H]	Hacohen Eliav, Avraham	265
No More Wars... [Y]	Yankelevitch, Chaim	270
Chaim Bruk, May The Lord Avenge His Blood! [Y]	Shalit, Moshe	271
The "Chevra Kaddisha" in Lubtch [H]	Shimshoni, T.	272
Remember! [H]	Shragai, Yehoshua	274
The Memory of My Town is Kept Safe in My Heart [H]	Solominsky, Chaya	277
The Gaon Rabbi Eliyahu-Chaim Meizel, Head of Court of Lodz and His Relationship to Lubtch [H]	Tsinovitch, Moshe	280
Between Two World Wars [H]	Bruk, Avraham	284
A Chazan (Cantor) in the Town [H]	Shimshoni, T.	289
Farewell to the Town [H]	Kivelevitch, Shmuel- Yaakov	290
Yehoshua Levinson, Bible Scholar [H]	Tzinovitch, Moshe	292
Alter Yosselevitch [H]	Tzinovitch, Moshe	292
A Panoramic Gem [H]	Kalmanovitch, Meyerim (Meir)	294
The History of the Town (From the Encyclopedia Judaica) [H]		295

My Town (A Poem) [H]	Yankelevitch, Chaim	296
(Poem) [H]	Amitai (Faivoshevitch), Ayala	299
Memories [H]	Degani, Yona	301
My Sister Itka, of Blessed Memory [H]	Levanon, Elka	302
To the Memory of My Family [H]	Solominsky, Chaya	303
My Father, Avraham-Aharon, of Blessed Memory [Y]	Berkovitch, Eliyahu	304
Memories from My Father's House [H]	Sivitsky, Aryeh	306
Only Letters Remain... [H]	Sonenzon, Chaim	307
My Grandmother Chaya [H]	Nashkes, Puah	308
My Rebbe, Rabbi Chaim [Y]	Shlimovitch, Yitzchak	309
Tuvya the Sexton [Y]	Shulman (Shlimovitch) Nachum	311
My Grandmother Rivka [H]	Simchoni (Movshovitch), Chemda	312
My Father Eliezer, of Blessed Memory [H]	Aharonovsky, Danny	313
Their Memory Will Remain Forever in My Heart [H]	Pintel (Pines), Freda	316
An Eternal Light for My Family [Y]	Aronovsky, Shmuel Binyamin- Chaim	317
In Memory of My Brother Avraham, May His Blood be Avenged! [H]	Kalmanovitch, Golda	320
Max Shmulevitch, of Blessed Memory [H]	Degani, Yona	321
The Holocaust and the Heroism		323
Photo caption: The Memorial Plaque in the Holocaust Cellar in Jerusalem		324
I Won't Forgive! (Poem) [Y]	Berliner, Yitzchak	325
One of the Family... [H]	Yankelevitch, Natan	327
I Was in the Ghetto [Y]	Yankelevitch, Yisrael- Gershon (Yisrol)	331
I Revenged our Innocent Blood [Y]	Yanson, Velveke	344
Scrolls from The Flame [H]	Slonimsky, Yisrael	364
In the Lubtch Ghetto [Y]	Solomiansky, Shifra	380
Rosh Hashana in the Forest [Y]	Yankelevitch, Yisrael	388
A Partisan in his Late Years [Y]	Leibovitch, Shalom	391
Under the Nazis in France [Y]	Zablotzky, Risha	403
(untitled) [Y]	Meyerson-Kowalsky, Lyuba	410
Little Pages from the Flame... [Y]	Slonimsky, Yisrael	412
(poem) [H]	Yankelevitch, Chaim	433
Words spoken by Nachum Shlimovitch at the memorial service for the Martyrs of Lubtch and Delatitich [Y]	Shlimovitch, Nachum	434
Words at the memorial service for the Martyrs of Lubtch and Delatitich [H]	Zacharavitch, Yaacov	437
Former Lubtch and Delatitch residents now living in Israel [H]		440
List of Jews from Lubtch and Delatitch who came to Israel, and who have since died [H]		443
Martyrs of Lubtch – List of Lubtcha Jews who were killed in the Holocaust [H]		444
Martyrs of Delatitch – List of Delatitch (Delyatichi) Jews who were killed in the Holocaust [H]		459
Photographs		461
Table of contents		477
Epilogue [H]		480

Notes:
* This is the same article as that written in Yiddish on Page 8
[H] - Written in Hebrew, [Y] - Written in Yiddish

We gratefully acknowledge the permission of the JewishGen-Belarus newsletter website and Ofer Cohen to use the following information which deals specifically with Delatitch. See also:
http://www.jewishgen.org/belarus/newsletter/delyatichi.htm

Delyatichi Between the Two World Wars

A Village in Belarus and Research for Its Jewish Population

In loving memory of my father, Arie Cohen

by Ofer Cohen

Location and History

Delyatichi is located at 53°47' Latitude / 25°59' East Longitude, near Lubcha, the *volust* of Lubchanskaya, Uchastok 2, in the *uyezd* of Novogrudok. The village is located some 5 km west of the *shtetl* Lubcha.

Lubcha was the Polish center of Calligraphy in the 17th century. It had the first Polish printing house. Afterwards it became a small village. It served as the municipal center of some smaller villages - Delyatichi, Karelichi, Naganbicha-Neishtat, and other villages that didn't have even a *minyan* - 10 Jewish men needed for praying in the approved manner. Lubcha served also as the cultural center, and hence the description of the cultural institutions and Zionist activities will refer to Lubcha, although all the rest participated.

The Yizkor book states that before World War I, the population count of Jews in the village of Delyatichi was 350, although the official documents from 1905 (as were stated by Vitaly Charny) counted only 158. The difference may be explained in two ways:

A. The memoirs were written in the late 1960s and early 1970s. The writers remembered the villages bigger than they really were, or wanted to remember it this way.

APPENDIX - Material Not in the Original Yizkor Book

B. The governmental counts and census were not accurate.

During the war the Nieman River was the frontier between the Russian Imperial army and the German army. The German army occupied the village, and the civilian population was expelled. After the war, only 13 to 15 of the Jewish families returned. They found their homes robbed, and the yards were ruined by craters from shelling.

Economy

The Jewish population in Belarus was not stable: the Russian and Polish kingdoms, who ruled the area, exchanged the land between themselves. In certain times life under the Tzar's rule was easier, in other times, the Polish regime was more cooperative. My maternal grandfather was born in Lida at 1886 – at that time Lida was in Russian territory. However, his father came to Lida from a village in southwest Poland.

The population was poor: There is an infofile on JewishGen by Vitaly Charny with a list of the poor population vs. the overall population – in Delyatichi, over 60% of the population were poor (95 poor people from a total population of 158). From reading literature of that period (Bialik, Shalom Aleichem, Mendele and others) we learn that the poor were really poor, up to starvation, while wealth was, comparing to our life style nowadays, just a little less poor than the other. So, they chased after the *parnuse* - earning money for living - across the country.

The authorities wanted taxes, had "strange" rules regarding day-to-day life (such as "don't pour the waste water to the street" – what a shame!), took the young men to the army, and had more bad attributes. So, our ancestors did all they could to avoid contacts with the authorities. Hence, the formal records have many "black holes".

The members of the two congregations made their living mainly by trade. The road from Minsk to Novogrudok, the current capital of the *uyezd* [administrative division], passes through the villages. The passengers stopped to make business. But the main source of living was from the Nieman river transportation. The trees from the upper part of the river were cut down, tied together into rafts, and were sent along the river. The sailors used to stop in the villages on the riverbanks and buy their needs.

The following table summarizes the occupation of the Delyaticher Jewish inhabitants, as was taken from the 1929 Polish business directory - Novogrudok province (compiled by Ellen Sadove Renck). Do not rely too much on this information: not everyone was listed, not all who were listed declared accurately, and, of course, it was a *mitzve* to mislead the *Goy* ...

APPENDIX - Material Not in the Original Yizkor Book

Surname	Given name	Occupation
Alpersztejn	R.	Grocer of food from the colonies
Bakszt	J.	Hardware shop
Berkowski	-	Brickwork
Gorodyski	M.	Cheese maker
Kagan	J.	Fabrics
Slonimski	F.	Baker

Culture and Society

At the turn of the centuries, from the 19th to the 20th, there was a change in the character of the Jewish culture: The influence of the bloom of the Zionism came to the villages. The Zionist Congress meetings and the start of the Aliya to Palestine left its impression. The suffering caused by WWI was a trigger for Zionist action. The deterioration of the financial status during the period of Gravski (second half of the 1920s), continued and deepened by the worldwide economic crisis in the 1930s, meant starvation. All this enhanced Zionist activities.

The congregations of Lubcha and Delyatichi lived very closely together. The description is of a hard-living but happy people that shared their happiness and sorrow together. The Yizkor book mentions proudly the brothers **Avrem'l and Moishe Gorodiski**, who had good bass voices, and who were used frequently as cantors in Lubcha.

In 1910 the congregation committee decided to establish a library. The decision was to raise the money for the books from amateur shows. The Hebrew library was established in 1922, after the war. In 1927 a Hebrew literature study group was established.

Yitzhak and Hana Dichter tell in the Yizkor book about the Lubcha culture institutions: elementary school, high school and afternoon club. The school was established in 1924. There were 7 classrooms, a library, an auditorium and a teachers' room. The lessons were conducted in Hebrew. Beyond the program required by the Polish authorities, the children were taught Hebrew literature, art, drama and Judaism. The mothers, some of whom could hardly read and write, gathered every Saturday night to get lectures on education and Jewish tradition.

Most of the members of the congregations were so poor they could hardly pay the fees. In some years the teachers were paid only for eight months of the twelve. When the school needed more classrooms, the money that was donated was too low, because of the poverty. So, one constructor was hired to serve as a guide, and all the work was done by the parents - every one gave three days of work.

APPENDIX - Material Not in the Original Yizkor Book

The Zionistic youth activity started in 1924, when the Lubcha branch of the *Hehalutz* was established. The first graduates made Aliya in 1926. The branch of *Hashomer Hatza'ir* was established in 1928. In 1930, 180 children belonged to the movement.

Two more Zionist movements that had small branches that were active sporadically were *Poalei Tzion* – left wing and *Beitar* – right wing.

The gentiles are hardly mentioned in the Yizkor book, and the witnesses did not agree to talk about them. This implies a carefully controlled relationship.

The Holocaust

By mid-1941 the Jews from Delyatichi were expelled to the Ghetto in Lubcha, with their friends from the other congregations, and from other tiny villages, where only a few Jewish families lived. A few days beforehand, the Belarusian neighbors came happily to tell them the news, and to rob their goods. This was the sign for few, too few, of the Jews to escape to the woods.

The others stayed for a while in the Lubcha Ghetto. The Germans and mostly their local collaborators performed a few small-scale actions, mostly on the older Jews. The rest were taken to the Ghetto in Novogrudek, where they were executed in the four slaughters, as the survivors call it.

The evidence is brutal: when the Jewish families were taken to the Ghetto, children were shot to death in front of their parents, old people were murdered, and young people were taken to work camps and never seen again.

God will revenge the pure and sacred spilt blood, as the Zionist national poet, Chayim Nachman Bialik wrote in his poem "*Be'ir HaHareiga*" - "In the City of Killing" (written 1882, on the pogrom in Odessa):

> "And such a revenge,
> A revenge of the blood of a small child,
> The devil has not yet created"

The Map of Delyatichi

```
                                    The Nieman River

              [6]  [5]  [4] [3]    [2] [1]
                                                    To Lyubcha
                          Village Center
        [14][13][12]                         [7]

              [15]    [10][9]  [8]

              [16]
                      [11]
        To Novegrudek
```

This map of Delyatichi was drawn during the interviews. The numbers in the following list are related to the house numbers in the village map.

1. **The synagogue** - This was a big synagogue that served also as a school for Jewish studies. The children learned in the Polish school in the village during the mornings, and in the afternoon came to the synagogue to learn Yiddishkeit.

2. **Israel Berkovski** – merchant of grains and bricks. Was named "tzigaine" – "gypsy".

3. **Avreml Gorodiski** – Had a strong and good voice. Worked as a cantor. Sold fish.

4. **Slonimski**.

5. **Michael Berkovski** – bakery.

6. **Kushnir**. The housewife was, probably, Yosef Kagan's sister.

7. **Yankelevich** – a wealthy family. Plantation owners and fruit merchants.

8. **Kibovich** – bakery. Their son, Benyamin, was 10 years old in 1939, joined the partisans with his father and survived the war.

APPENDIX - Material Not in the Original Yizkor Book

9. **Meishe Gorodiski** (Avreml's brother) – dairy. Like his brother he had nice voice and served as a cantor.

10. **Yosl Kagan** – fabric shop and grocery. Slaughterer and cantor.

11. **Lish** – Owned cattle. Merchant of wool and products. A wealthy family - the house was built of bricks.

12. **Alperstein**.

13. **Lishanski**.

14. **Fire brigade**

15. **Krolbatzki**. The housewife was a sister of **Yosl Kagan** or **Siomka Kagan (Rabinovich)**.

16. **Baksht**. The village Rabbi. Held a pharmacy. His son, Shmuel, joined the partisans and fought bravely. Two other sons escaped to US.

The location of the following families' houses is unknown:

17. **Beynes** – brick house.

18. **Asher Dvornik** – came from Lida. Had a factory of beer.

19. **Klibovich** – healer

Holocaust victims that are listed in the Yizkor book, but I know no further details:

20. **Bezsmertani**

21. **Malkovitzki**

22. **Klobak**

23. **Shmukler**

410 APPENDIX - Material Not in the Original Yizkor Book

Standing (L-R): Haya and Bela Cohen
Sitting (L-R): Elhanan and Shoshana Cohen
(photo taken 1938 or 1939)

Kagan house in Delyatichi

APPENDIX - Material Not in the Original Yizkor Book 411

Well in Lubcha

Old Jewish school in Delyatichi

412 APPENDIX - Material Not in the Original Yizkor Book

Delyatichi Market Place

APPENDIX - Material Not in the Original Yizkor Book

Vorobievitch
Memorial stone for Jewish Holocaust mass grave

Lyubcha and Delyatichi Yizkor Book

Title	Author	Page
My Town (A Poem) [H]	Yankelevitch, Chaim	296
(Poem) [H]	Amitai (Faivoshevitch), Ayala	299
Memories [H]	Degani, Yona	301
My Sister Itka, of Blessed Memory [H]	Levanon, Elka	302
To the Memory of My Family [H]	Solominsky, Chaya	303
My Father, Avraham-Aharon, of Blessed Memory [Y]	Berkovitch, Eliyahu	304
Memories from My Father's House [H]	Sivitsky, Aryeh	306
Only Letters Remain... [H]	Sonenzon, Chaim	307
My Grandmother Chaya [H]	Nashkes, Puah	308
My Rebbe, Rabbi Chaim [Y]	Shlimovitch, Yitzchak	309
Tuvya the Sexton [Y]	Shulman (Shlimovitch) Nachum	311
My Grandmother Rivka [H]	Simchoni (Movshovitch), Chemda	312
My Father Eliezer, of Blessed Memory [H]	Aharonovsky, Danny	313
Their Memory Will Remain Forever in My Heart [H]	Pintel (Pines), Freda	316
An Eternal Light for My Family [Y]	Aronovsky, Shmuel Binyamin-Chaim	317
In Memory of My Brother Avraham, May His Blood be Avenged! [H]	Kalmanovitch, Golda	320
Max Shmulevitch, of Blessed Memory [H]	Degani, Yona	321
The Holocaust and the Heroism		323
Photo caption: The Memorial Plaque in the Holocaust Cellar in Jerusalem		324
I Won't Forgive! (Poem) [Y]	Berliner, Yitzchak	325
One of the Family... [H]	Yankelevitch, Natan	327
I Was in the Ghetto [Y]	Yankelevitch, Yisrael-Gershon (Yisrol)	331
I Revenged our Innocent Blood [Y]	Yanson, Velveke	344
Scrolls from The Flame [H]	Slonimsky, Yisrael	364
In the Lubtch Ghetto [Y]	Solomiansky, Shifra	380
Rosh Hashana in the Forest [Y]	Yankelevitch, Yisrael	388
A Partisan in his Late Years [Y]	Leibovitch, Shalom	391
Under the Nazis in France [Y]	Zablotzky, Risha	403
(untitled) [Y]	Meyerson-Kowalsky, Lyuba	410
Little Pages from the Flame... [Y]	Slonimsky, Yisrael	412
(poem) [H]	Yankelevitch, Chaim	433
Words spoken by Nachum Shlimovitch at the memorial service for the Martyrs of Lubtch and Delatitich [Y]	Shlimovitch, Nachum	434
Words at the memorial service for the Martyrs of Lubtch and Delatitich [H]	Zacharavitch, Yaacov	437
Former Lubtch and Delatitch residents now living in Israel [H]		440
List of Jews from Lubtch and Delatitch who came to Israel, and who have since died [H]		443
Martyrs of Lubtch – List of Lubtcha Jews who were killed in the Holocaust [H]		444
Martyrs of Delatitch – List of Delatitch (Delyatichi) Jews who were killed in the Holocaust [H]		459
Photographs		461
Table of contents		477
Epilogue [H]		480

Notes:
* This is the same article as that written in Yiddish on Page 8
[H] - Written in Hebrew, [Y] - Written in Yiddish

We gratefully acknowledge the permission of the JewishGen-Belarus newsletter website and Ofer Cohen to use the following information which deals specifically with Delatitch. See also:
http://www.jewishgen.org/belarus/newsletter/delyatichi.htm

Delyatichi Between the Two World Wars

A Village in Belarus and Research for Its Jewish Population

In loving memory of my father, Arie Cohen

by Ofer Cohen

Location and History

Delyatichi is located at 53°47' Latitude / 25°59' East Longitude, near Lubcha, the *volust* of Lubchanskaya, Uchastok 2, in the *uyezd* of Novogrudok. The village is located some 5 km west of the *shtetl* Lubcha.

Lubcha was the Polish center of Calligraphy in the 17th century. It had the first Polish printing house. Afterwards it became a small village. It served as the municipal center of some smaller villages - Delyatichi, Karelichi, Naganbicha-Neishtat, and other villages that didn't have even a *minyan* - 10 Jewish men needed for praying in the approved manner. Lubcha served also as the cultural center, and hence the description of the cultural institutions and Zionist activities will refer to Lubcha, although all the rest participated.

The Yizkor book states that before World War I, the population count of Jews in the village of Delyatichi was 350, although the official documents from 1905 (as were stated by Vitaly Charny) counted only 158. The difference may be explained in two ways:

A. The memoirs were written in the late 1960s and early 1970s. The writers remembered the villages bigger than they really were, or wanted to remember it this way.

B. The governmental counts and census were not accurate.

During the war the Nieman River was the frontier between the Russian Imperial army and the German army. The German army occupied the village, and the civilian population was expelled. After the war, only 13 to 15 of the Jewish families returned. They found their homes robbed, and the yards were ruined by craters from shelling.

Economy

The Jewish population in Belarus was not stable: the Russian and Polish kingdoms, who ruled the area, exchanged the land between themselves. In certain times life under the Tzar's rule was easier, in other times, the Polish regime was more cooperative. My maternal grandfather was born in Lida at 1886 – at that time Lida was in Russian territory. However, his father came to Lida from a village in southwest Poland.

The population was poor: There is an infofile on JewishGen by Vitaly Charny with a list of the poor population vs. the overall population – in Delyatichi, over 60% of the population were poor (95 poor people from a total population of 158). From reading literature of that period (Bialik, Shalom Aleichem, Mendele and others) we learn that the poor were really poor, up to starvation, while wealth was, comparing to our life style nowadays, just a little less poor than the other. So, they chased after the *parnuse* - earning money for living - across the country.

The authorities wanted taxes, had "strange" rules regarding day-to-day life (such as "don't pour the waste water to the street" – what a shame!), took the young men to the army, and had more bad attributes. So, our ancestors did all they could to avoid contacts with the authorities. Hence, the formal records have many "black holes".

The members of the two congregations made their living mainly by trade. The road from Minsk to Novogrudok, the current capital of the *uyezd* [administrative division], passes through the villages. The passengers stopped to make business. But the main source of living was from the Nieman river transportation. The trees from the upper part of the river were cut down, tied together into rafts, and were sent along the river. The sailors used to stop in the villages on the riverbanks and buy their needs.

The following table summarizes the occupation of the Delyaticher Jewish inhabitants, as was taken from the 1929 Polish business directory - Novogrudok province (compiled by Ellen Sadove Renck). Do not rely too much on this information: not everyone was listed, not all who were listed declared accurately, and, of course, it was a *mitzve* to mislead the *Goy* ...

APPENDIX - Material Not in the Original Yizkor Book

Surname	Given name	Occupation
Alpersztejn	R.	Grocer of food from the colonies
Bakszt	J.	Hardware shop
Berkowski	-	Brickwork
Gorodyski	M.	Cheese maker
Kagan	J.	Fabrics
Slonimski	F.	Baker

Culture and Society

At the turn of the centuries, from the 19th to the 20th, there was a change in the character of the Jewish culture: The influence of the bloom of the Zionism came to the villages. The Zionist Congress meetings and the start of the Aliya to Palestine left its impression. The suffering caused by WWI was a trigger for Zionist action. The deterioration of the financial status during the period of Gravski (second half of the 1920s), continued and deepened by the worldwide economic crisis in the 1930s, meant starvation. All this enhanced Zionist activities.

The congregations of Lubcha and Delyatichi lived very closely together. The description is of a hard-living but happy people that shared their happiness and sorrow together. The Yizkor book mentions proudly the brothers **Avrem'l and Moishe Gorodiski**, who had good bass voices, and who were used frequently as cantors in Lubcha.

In 1910 the congregation committee decided to establish a library. The decision was to raise the money for the books from amateur shows. The Hebrew library was established in 1922, after the war. In 1927 a Hebrew literature study group was established.

Yitzhak and Hana Dichter tell in the Yizkor book about the Lubcha culture institutions: elementary school, high school and afternoon club. The school was established in 1924. There were 7 classrooms, a library, an auditorium and a teachers' room. The lessons were conducted in Hebrew. Beyond the program required by the Polish authorities, the children were taught Hebrew literature, art, drama and Judaism. The mothers, some of whom could hardly read and write, gathered every Saturday night to get lectures on education and Jewish tradition.

Most of the members of the congregations were so poor they could hardly pay the fees. In some years the teachers were paid only for eight months of the twelve. When the school needed more classrooms, the money that was donated was too low, because of the poverty. So, one constructor was hired to serve as a guide, and all the work was done by the parents - every one gave three days of work.

APPENDIX - Material Not in the Original Yizkor Book

The Zionistic youth activity started in 1924, when the Lubcha branch of the *Hehalutz* was established. The first graduates made Aliya in 1926. The branch of *Hashomer Hatza'ir* was established in 1928. In 1930, 180 children belonged to the movement.

Two more Zionist movements that had small branches that were active sporadically were *Poalei Tzion* – left wing and *Beitar* – right wing.

The gentiles are hardly mentioned in the Yizkor book, and the witnesses did not agree to talk about them. This implies a carefully controlled relationship.

The Holocaust

By mid-1941 the Jews from Delyatichi were expelled to the Ghetto in Lubcha, with their friends from the other congregations, and from other tiny villages, where only a few Jewish families lived. A few days beforehand, the Belarusian neighbors came happily to tell them the news, and to rob their goods. This was the sign for few, too few, of the Jews to escape to the woods.

The others stayed for a while in the Lubcha Ghetto. The Germans and mostly their local collaborators performed a few small-scale actions, mostly on the older Jews. The rest were taken to the Ghetto in Novogrudek, where they were executed in the four slaughters, as the survivors call it.

The evidence is brutal: when the Jewish families were taken to the Ghetto, children were shot to death in front of their parents, old people were murdered, and young people were taken to work camps and never seen again.

God will revenge the pure and sacred spilt blood, as the Zionist national poet, Chayim Nachman Bialik wrote in his poem "*Be'ir HaHareiga*" - "In the City of Killing" (written 1882, on the pogrom in Odessa):

> "And such a revenge,
> A revenge of the blood of a small child,
> The devil has not yet created"

The Map of Delyatichi

```
                                    The Nieman River

         [6]  [5]  [4] [3]    [2] [1]
                                              To Lyubcha
                       Village Center
   [14][13][12]                      [7]

        [15]    [10][9]  [8]

        [16]
              [11]
   To Novegrudek
```

This map of Delyatichi was drawn during the interviews. The numbers in the following list are related to the house numbers in the village map.

1. **The synagogue** - This was a big synagogue that served also as a school for Jewish studies. The children learned in the Polish school in the village during the mornings, and in the afternoon came to the synagogue to learn Yiddishkeit.

2. **Israel Berkovski** – merchant of grains and bricks. Was named "tzigaine" – "gypsy".

3. **Avreml Gorodiski** – Had a strong and good voice. Worked as a cantor. Sold fish.

4. **Slonimski**.

5. **Michael Berkovski** – bakery.

6. **Kushnir**. The housewife was, probably, Yosef Kagan's sister.

7. **Yankelevich** – a wealthy family. Plantation owners and fruit merchants.

8. **Kibovich** – bakery. Their son, Benyamin, was 10 years old in 1939, joined the partisans with his father and survived the war.

APPENDIX - Material Not in the Original Yizkor Book

9. **Meishe Gorodiski** (Avreml's brother) – dairy. Like his brother he had nice voice and served as a cantor.

10. **Yosl Kagan** – fabric shop and grocery. Slaughterer and cantor.

11. **Lish** – Owned cattle. Merchant of wool and products. A wealthy family - the house was built of bricks.

12. **Alperstein**.

13. **Lishanski**.

14. **Fire brigade**

15. **Krolbatzki**. The housewife was a sister of **Yosl Kagan** or **Siomka Kagan (Rabinovich)**.

16. **Baksht**. The village Rabbi. Held a pharmacy. His son, Shmuel, joined the partisan and fought bravely. Two other sons escaped to US.

The location of the following families' houses is unknown:

17. **Beynes** – brick house.

18. **Asher Dvornik** – came from Lida. Had a factory of beer.

19. **Klibovich** – healer

Holocaust victims that are listed in the Yizkor book, but I know no further details:

20. **Bezsmertani**

21. **Malkovitzki**

22. **Klobak**

23. **Shmukler**

APPENDIX - Material Not in the Original Yizkor Book

Standing (L-R): Haya and Bela Cohen
Sitting (L-R): Elhanan and Shoshana Cohen
(photo taken 1938 or 1939)

Kagan house in Delyatichi

APPENDIX - Material Not in the Original Yizkor Book 411

Well in Lubcha

Old Jewish school in Delyatichi

412 APPENDIX - Material Not in the Original Yizkor Book

Delyatichi Market Place

APPENDIX - Material Not in the Original Yizkor Book 413

Vorobievitch
Memorial stone for Jewish Holocaust mass grave

Lyubcha and Delyatichi Yizkor Book

A

Abovitz, 74, 75, 76, 233, 239
Aharonovski, 47
Aharonovski, 363
Aharonovsky, 147, 229, 244, 260, 268, 270, 271, 362, 382, 402
Aharons, 186
Aleichem, 20, 206
Aleph, 171, 358
Aleshkes, 325
Alperstein, 307, 341
Alter, 19, 47, 54, 77, 116, 120, 189, 201, 208, 213, 223, 239, 247, 249, 250, 258, 264, 288, 323, 324, 363, 365, 366, 368, 371, 401
Amalek, 25, 164, 324, 353, 354
Amitay, 358
Aronosky, 211
Aronovsky, 186, 189, 273, 326, 358, 402
Aronson, 215
Asch, 180, 182
Asherovsky, 36, 190, 400
Ashman, 363
Atlas, 196, 298
Avrahami, 140, 141, 362, 401
Avrahamy, 358
Avramsky, 196
Ayzikovitsky, 93

B

Babad, 60
Baer, 46, 48, 63, 64, 65, 71, 75
Baksht, 25, 35, 46, 67, 68, 69, 71, 102, 149, 175, 176, 181, 211, 218, 245, 254, 283, 284, 306, 308, 318, 321, 326, 329, 330, 332, 340, 342, 354, 357, 358, 380
Baksht, 363, 375
Bakshtansky, 67, 175, 221
Bakshter, 62, 66, 67, 68, 174, 175, 176, 177, 178, 195, 197, 237, 239, 401
Bakst, 116, 133, 218
Bakster, 218
Ballot, 155
Bankover, 243
Barit, 69
Batar, 358
Batter, 324
Bayer, 363
Bedoon, 287, 327
Beinush, 308, 342
Beiten, 73

Belinsky, 4, 8, 29, 33, 36, 43, 89, 104, 110, 113, 115, 118, 130, 134, 137, 140, 142, 148, 156, 159, 169, 188, 189, 190, 201, 206, 222, 229, 231, 234, 237, 240, 245, 246, 251, 252, 255, 257, 259, 260, 262, 264, 265, 268, 272, 275, 276, 281, 352, 355, 399
Belski, 363
Ben Tzvi, 29, 171, 401
Ben-Tzvi, 173
Ben-Zvi, 171, 172, 173
Berezinski, 26, 318, 319
Berezinski, 363
Berezinsky, 59, 287
Berger, 218
Berkovich, 363
Berkovitch, 85, 86, 143, 242, 261, 384, 385, 402
Berkovitz, 144, 147
Berkovski, 375
Berkovsky, 149, 214, 215, 216, 358
Berlin, 19, 25, 70, 71, 175, 198, 214, 237
Berliner, 280, 402
Berman, 363
Berskin, 363
Bezshovski, 301
Bezsmertani, 375
Bezsmirtani, 363
Bialik, 55, 109, 205
Bielski, 301, 302, 303
Bitanski, 363
Blazer, 213, 214, 215
Bloch, 224
Boigen, 67
Bolda, 363, 364
Boldo, 9, 55, 142, 144, 145, 247, 358, 362, 381, 401
Bonimovitch, 42, 72, 73, 74, 215, 400
Boretzki, 364
Bortzky, 144
Bossel, 147
Breinkes, 24
Brenner, 95, 358, 400
Brezinsky, 188, 284
Brozi, 153
Bruchin, 237
Bruk, 15, 53, 54, 55, 85, 86, 110, 111, 141, 144, 158, 163, 164, 181, 186, 228, 232, 240, 244, 281, 283, 307, 319, 320, 326, 341, 356, 358, 385, 387, 400, 401
Bruk, 364
Buslovitch, 315, 350

Lyubcha and Delyatichi Yizkor Book

C

Cantorovich, 364
Caro, 70
Caspi, 359
Chaimovitch, 133, 243, 335
Chaimovitich, 287
Chalpak, 42, 400
Charbin, 360
Chazkels, 80
Chemes, 19, 288
Chichik, 360
Chishin, 176
Cohen, 33, 34, 35, 149, 181, 211, 240, 243, 359, 363, 375, 400
Cohen, 375

D

Danishevsky, 74
Danzig, 67
Davidovich, 364
Davidovitz, 53
Dayan, 175, 176, 178
Degani, 206, 257, 276, 324, 358, 401, 402
Deiches, 212
Delatitch, 9, 21, 33, 34, 35, 36, 72, 74, 78, 86, 87, 88, 358, 362
Deltitzki, 364
Delyatichi, 33
Deutsch, 351
Dichter, 43, 47, 89, 356, 358, 362, 400
Dick, 179
Direktor, 66, 195, 196, 197
Dombrovski, 302
Dorosevitch, 20
Dreyfus, 109
Druk, 301
Dubnow, 7
Dushkin, 364
Dvoretzki, 364
Dzentilski, 364
Dzjientchelski, 318

E

Efrati, 212
Eiges, 69, 75
Eisenstadt, 212
Eizenshtadt, 219, 221
Eliahu, 81, 155
Eliyahu, 30, 63, 64, 72, 76, 104, 137, 139, 176, 178, 195, 237, 261, 364, 365, 366, 368, 369, 371, 372, 400, 401, 402
Eliyav, 115, 222
Engel, 148, 358, 401

Epshtein, 61, 62, 70, 71, 213, 215, 332
Ettinger, 177

F

Faivishevitch, 126, 129, 360, 400
Faivishovitz, 360
Faivoshevitch, 156, 243, 244, 255, 362, 402
Faivoshevitz, 47, 386, 387, 391, 395, 398
Faivoshovitch, 232
Feigenboim, 180
Feivishevitch, 15, 21, 28
Feivoshevitz, 189, 208
Ferdman, 302
Feybushevich, 364, 365, 374
Finkel, 214, 218, 223
Florans, 310, 313, 344, 345, 348
Frantzishkevitch, 19
Fried, 66, 221, 237
Friedman, 221
Frumkin, 63, 360, 362
Fuks, 179

G

Gadol, 180
Gafni, 358
Galans, 365
Gelfand, 85, 86
Gelfand, 365
Gelman, 365
Gershony, 358
Gershonyankelevitch, 332
Gershovich, 365, 373
Gershovitch, 397
Gestold, 4
Gimpel, 64, 65, 364
Gishen, 147
Gishin, 318
Gishin, 365
Gissin, 144
Goldberg, 365
Goldman, 251
Goldschmid, 143
Goldshmidt, 330
Gordon, 156, 180, 358, 362
Gorin, 180
Gorodiski, 24, 318
Gorodiski, 365, 375, 376
Gorodisky, 34
Gorshovich, 365
Grimovich, 365
Grudzhensky, 72, 76
Gur, 358
Gutka, 365

Lyubcha and Delyatichi Yizkor Book

Gvirol, 75

H

Hadas, 358
Hadayan, 224
Hakaner, 192
Halperin, 171, 231, 327, 379
Halperin, 365
Halpershtein, 365
Halperstein, 320
Hamelamed, 156
Harkavy, 180, 198
Hashkevitch, 6
Hashkevitsh, 6
Havnagli, 4
Hefetz, 365
Heller, 218
Hermolin, 180
Herzl, 109, 249
Hildesheimer, 179
Hilel, 3, 15, 29, 59, 164, 371, 400, 401
Hirsch, 74, 76, 109, 179
Hirshbein, 182
Hitler, 25, 109, 289, 293, 310, 316, 323, 324, 345
Horander, 220
Horovitz, 63, 71, 197
Horvitch, 213, 215
Horvitz, 225
Horwitz, 199, 267

I

Isaakovsky, 325
Itinga, 75
Itingai, 60
Itzikovitch, 362
Itzikovitz, 358
Itzkavitch, 72
Itzkovich, 365
Itzkovitch, 21, 164, 354
Ivyer, 171
Izikovitzki, 365

J

Jankelowitz, 42, 78, 79, 80, 117, 125, 128, 134, 146, 181, 236, 240, 332, 400, 401
Jentchelski, 15

K

Kabak, 85, 86, 159, 160, 164, 186, 201, 326, 360, 401
Kagan, 192, 310, 320, 344, 345, 359, 401
Kagan, 365
Kaganovitch, 86, 400
Kagan-Sirlis, 192, 401
Kahn, 5, 400
Kalmanovich, 365, 366
Kalmanovitch, 14, 17, 55, 86, 92, 118, 181, 208, 250, 275, 361, 401, 402
Kalmanovitz, 360
Kalmonovitch, 55
Kamai, 76, 239
Kaminer, 179
Kamita, 4
Kantarovich, 366
Kantorovitch, 211
Kaplan, 144, 147
Kaplanski, 366
Kaplansky, 17
Kaplinsky, 247
Kapuchevsky, 216
Kapushchevski, 366
Kapushchevsky, 288, 319
Kapushtchevsky, 308, 342
Kapushtshevsky, 17, 18, 21
Kaputchevsky, 217
Karelitz, 63, 64, 65, 75, 143, 147, 357, 401
Karpetovitz, 4
Kasemivitch, 243, 244
Kashtzar, 115
Kashtzer, 222, 223
Kasmay, 366
Kasmayevitch, 186
Kasmeievitch, 89
Kasmivich, 367
Katz, 78, 117, 128, 250
Katzenelbogen, 180
Kavak, 141, 242
Kazimizisch, 4
Kazmirovitch, 113
Keizer, 180
Keshet, 173, 380
Kesmayevitch, 143
Keyser, 180
Kharlap, 367
Kharptovitch, 113
Khaymovich, 367
Kian, 4
Kibelevich, 367
Kibovich, 376
Kishka, 4, 113
Kivelevitch, 17, 57, 127, 223, 246, 247, 401
Kivilevitch, 116, 133, 170, 175, 332, 360, 362
Kivilevitz, 107
Kivilivetch, 133
Kivlevitch, 120, 181, 360
Kivovitch, 306, 340, 351

Klatchkin, 251
Kleinshtov, 360
Kliatchky, 220
Klobak, 376
Komarovsky, 291, 325, 329
Komornik, 287, 318, 325, 327
Konyak, 367
Kopelovich, 367
Kopilovitz, 173
Kosovsky, 226
Kotlover, 195
Kowal, 181
Kowalsky, 181, 182, 337, 401, 402
Koznitzki, 367
Krantz, 180
Krasilov, 222, 401
Krasilov, 367
Kravitz, 367
Krolbatzki, 376
Kroshnitz, 15, 89, 103, 126, 360, 400
Krosnitz, 59, 400
Krovski, 367
Krugman, 360
Krulevetzky, 308, 342
Kunitzky, 287
Kushner, 306, 340
Kushnir, 376

L

Lampert, 198
Landau, 60
Langbort, 62
Lapidotsohn, 68
Laskin, 367
Leibovitch, 27, 82, 116, 133, 170, 174, 189,
  208, 214, 241, 243, 244, 258, 281, 283,
  317, 319, 325, 326, 328, 332, 362, 389,
  393, 400, 401, 402
Leibovitz, 290, 292, 359
Lev, 225
Levanon, 189, 259, 359, 401, 402
Levin, 18, 21, 25, 26, 47, 189, 201, 211,
  218, 242, 287, 379
Levin, 367, 368
Levine, 53, 55, 191, 243, 298, 359
Levinsohn, 68
Levinson, 176, 248, 401
Lewin, 268
Leybovich, 368
Leymes, 368
Leyzerovski, 368
Liberman, 48, 217
Lichitzki, 368
Lichtin, 368
Lin, 310, 313, 344, 345, 348

Linik, 368
Lipchin, 17, 293
Lipchin, 368
Lipkin, 361
Lipman, 60, 197
Lis, 376
Lishanski, 173
Lishanski, 376, 377
Liss, 305, 311, 340, 346
Litchitzky, 206
Litshitzer, 125
Lubtcher, 219, 221

M

Mahler, 29
Malachovsky, 393
Malkhovitzki, 368
Malkovitzki, 377
Malravitz, 359
Manes, 98
Manfred, 359
Manger, 94, 400
Margaliot, 177, 178
Margolin, 178
Markovitch, 211
Maslovety, 264
Maslovtah, 359
Maslovty, 68
Mayzel, 396, 397
Mednitsky, 195, 197
Meir, 21, 60, 66, 71, 74, 75, 76, 84, 100,
  142, 155, 179, 181, 216, 247, 358, 366,
  367, 370, 373, 401
Meirson, 368
Meizel, 67, 175, 176, 188, 195, 196, 197,
  198, 218, 221, 237, 238, 239, 359, 401
Melnik, 368
Meltzer, 213
Mendelevich, 368, 369
Mendelevitch, 294, 318, 332
Mendelevitz, 359
Mendelovitz, 121
Meselevich, 369
Meselevitch, 318
Meyerovitz, 225, 226
Meyerson, 243, 337, 402
Mibski, 369
Midrash, 369
Mileikovsky, 68
Minikes, 179, 180, 401
Minkes, 42, 180
Mishkin, 211
Miskin, 57
Misnik, 369
Mitskovsky, 19

Lyubcha and Delyatichi Yizkor Book

Mitzkovski, 17
Moallin, 217
Mohilever, 177, 178
Molotov, 25, 317
Montefiore, 109, 138
Mordochovich, 369
Movshovitch, 17, 127, 130, 131, 201, 284, 318, 321, 357, 379, 388, 400, 402
Movshovitz, 47, 267, 359
Mubashovich, 369

N

Nachimovsky, 111
Nachum, 111, 121, 164, 173, 179, 201, 233, 401, 402
Naganivitsky, 242
Nashkes, 265, 359, 361, 402
Natansohn, 75
Navamishsky, 211
Neimnovitch, 58
Niankever, 155
Niankovski, 369
Niankovsky, 378
Niegnievitsky, 24
Nignivitsky, 164
Nikolivski, 369
Nishkind, 369
Nochimovsky, 109, 142, 218, 359
Nochmovsky, 175

O

Obsivich, 369
Odrubondzh, 4
Opatov, 69
Orlanski, 369
Ornstein, 60, 182
Osherovich, 369
Oserovski, 369, 370
Osherovsky, 51, 52, 53, 55, 85, 133, 143, 358
Osherowsky, 45
Oshman, 358
Oshrovsky, 54, 119, 362
Ostashinski, 370
Ostshinsky, 53, 109, 242
Ovsayevitch, 155
Ovseyevitch, 17

P

Pablis, 370
Paley, 180
Paretzki, 57
Patashnik, 370

Payes, 141, 188
Peker, 370
Perchik, 370
Perkofchik, 113, 400
Perlman, 226
Perlman, 370
Persky, 21, 46, 47, 50, 54, 85, 116, 123, 127, 143, 145, 157, 164, 208, 252, 254, 282, 356
Pertchik, 27, 294
Pertshik, 17, 18
Petochovsky, 49
Petokovski, 54
Petrosvitz, 136
Pikelany, 370
Pikelni, 17, 318
Piklani, 360
Piltzky, 121
Pines, 156, 272, 284, 318, 324, 360, 391, 402
Pines, 370
Pintel, 272, 284, 360, 402
Pisiuk, 69, 153, 154
Pisuk, 142, 176, 362
Podolksi, 56
Podolski, 16, 56, 57
Polachek, 215
Popkin, 370

R

Rabin, 64
Rabinovich, 370, 372
Rabinovitch, 15, 26, 74, 81, 98, 100, 141, 186, 188, 209, 210, 211, 221, 307, 310, 337, 341, 344, 345, 401
Rabinovitz, 71, 282
Rachkovski, 370
Radizivil, 4
Radziwil, 113
Radziwill, 5, 7
Ragovin, 360
Raisel, 201, 357, 379
Raizel, 194
Rapoport, 60, 61
Rappaport, 248
Ratner, 75
Reichman, 360
Reines, 215
Reinovitch, 20, 21
Reiss, 143
Resnick, 271
Ribbentrop, 317
Rilf, 179
Rivka'i, 163
Rivtzki, 370

Rosenberg, 23
Rosenblum, 307, 318, 320, 341
Rosenfeld, 180
Rostkovsky, 338
Rozenblum, 54
Rozenblum, 370
Rozental, 360
Rozovski, 370
Rozovsky, 85, 176, 386
Rubin, 163
Rubinshtein, 75
Rubinshtein, 370
Rubinstein, 64

S

Sa'aroni, 359
Sabitzki, 370
Saladucha, 15
Salanter, 179, 214
Saltz, 287, 390
Sambatyon, 85, 180
Samocha, 245
Sampson, 104, 137, 139, 400
Sapieha, 5, 6, 7, 30
Savernik, 243, 244
Schanovitz, 360
Sefarim, 152, 153, 154
Seglovitz, 69
Seifert, 180
Senderovski, 370
Sendler, 370
Serbernik, 370, 371
Sevitzky, 359
Sfarim, 206
Shachanovich, 371
Shaklot, 243, 247
Shalit, 228, 401
Shamer, 180
Shapira, 38, 61, 62, 73, 108, 175, 176, 189, 195, 201, 212, 213, 218, 242, 253, 254, 362
Shapira, 371
Shapiro, 85, 163, 200, 208, 274
Sharkansky, 180
Shatzkes, 226
Shavit-Faivoshevitch, 156, 401
Shazar, 251
Shelubski, 301
Sheykas, 254
Shikovitzky, 222
Shimshelevich, 371
Shimshelevitch, 30, 85, 86, 172, 173, 175, 176, 186, 191
Shimshelivitch, 171
Shimshelovitch, 29
Shimshelvitch, 111
Shimshi, 29, 171, 172, 173, 177
Shimshilevitch, 140, 142, 144, 147, 243, 245, 384
Shimshilevitz, 104, 107, 136, 137, 229
Shimshoni, 104, 134, 135, 181, 201, 229, 240, 244, 245, 271, 322, 360, 400, 401
Shitzgal, 244, 287, 360, 362
Shitzgel, 371
Shkallot, 207
Shklot, 371
Shklut, 318
Shlimonovitz, 47
Shlimovich, 371
Shlimovitch, 78, 82, 111, 121, 164, 183, 186, 187, 201, 242, 243, 266, 267, 318, 353, 400, 401, 402
Shlimovitz, 53, 360
Shlovski, 371
Shmuelevitch, 170, 213, 223, 264, 391, 392
Shmuelevitz, 199
Shmuelovitz, 77, 239
Shmukler, 203, 360, 401
Shmukler, 377
Shmulevich, 371, 372
Shmulevitch, 19, 54, 116, 127, 164, 181, 189, 201, 208, 244, 259, 276, 288, 356, 392, 402
Shmulevitz, 394
Shmulovitch, 29, 47, 54, 118, 119, 120, 360, 362, 400
Shmulovitz, 46, 49, 50, 360
Shochet, 229
Shragai, 231, 232, 360, 401
Shulman, 267, 401, 402
Shunke, 314, 350
Shuster, 243
Siegel, 180
Silevianski, 372
Simanovitz, 359
Simchoni, 130, 131, 181, 201, 236, 267, 357, 360, 400, 402
Sindor, 359
Sivitsky, 383, 402
Sivitzky, 262, 284
Slimovitz, 189
Slomiansky, 281
Slominsky, 260
Slonimski, 377
Slonimsky, 149, 291, 304, 330, 338, 351, 359, 402
Sloshetz, 171
Smolensky, 179
Sochnitzki, 372
Sochnitzky, 359

Sokolovsky, 211, 245
Soldocha, 359
Solodcha, 372
Solodocha, 47, 53, 55, 232, 243, 244
Soloducha, 144, 319
Solomiansky, 317, 332, 359, 362, 402
Solominski, 372
Solominsky, 234, 401, 402
Soloveitchik, 198
Soltz, 221, 247, 283, 318, 319
Sonenzon, 54, 120, 127, 169, 208, 244, 245, 264, 356, 359, 395, 401, 402
Sonenzon, 372
Sonnenzon, 47
Sontzes, 308, 342
Spector, 221
Spitzer, 3, 5, 15, 42, 56, 58, 59, 60, 78, 82, 86, 88, 89, 94, 95, 103, 125, 126, 134, 139, 146, 150, 153, 155, 159, 164, 168, 171, 174, 179, 181, 183, 192, 195, 203, 209, 211, 212, 222, 227, 228, 237, 248, 249, 252, 261, 266, 267, 273, 280, 285, 292, 304, 317, 323, 325, 332, 337, 338, 352, 353
Spotnitzky, 190, 401
Stakoleshckik, 372
Stalin, 20, 23, 292, 293, 300, 303, 310, 312, 320, 327, 330, 345, 347
Stolifin, 108
Stolovitsky, 217
Sultz, 372
Szmiglowicz, 154

T

Tam, 70
Taubman, 284, 358
Tchatchkes, 141
Tempel, 372
Tennenbaum, 197
Tennenboim, 71, 74
Tepper, 50
Ter, 180
Tevies, 287
Tevli, 196
Tiktin, 72, 175, 287, 323
Tiktin, 372
Tiktinsky, 214, 216, 221
Timensky, 358
Titkin, 71
Tobolsky, 147
Tolstoy, 108
Tonik, 372
Tsinovitch, 174, 181, 209, 210, 211, 400, 401
Tsunzer, 175

Tubolski, 372
Tunik, 144
Tzinovitch, 7, 42, 58, 60, 195, 212, 237, 248, 249, 400, 401
Tzinovitz, 88
Tziversky, 362
Tzur, 188, 360, 401

V

Vahl, 63
Varnikovsky, 218
Varnovsky, 197, 198
Vasserman, 76
Veinberg, 196
Veiner, 372
Veinshtein, 77
Veintroyb, 225
Veis, 76
Verbovski, 372
Villner, 319
Vilner, 53, 110, 182, 387, 400
Vilner, 372
Viner, 243
Vinestein, 358
Vingrovsky, 358
Visoker, 178
Volberg, 372
Volbrinsky, 71
Volinski, 372

W

Walter, 182
Weinstein, 358
Weis, 372
Weiss, 56, 76, 77, 144, 147, 186, 211, 354
Weissman, 180
Werner, 144

Y

Yaakobi, 359
Yaffe, 63, 64, 65, 70
Yaglontchik, 4
Yankelevich, 372, 373, 377
Yankelevitch, 8, 9, 88, 111, 116, 133, 139, 148, 150, 159, 170, 181, 199, 201, 227, 236, 240, 251, 252, 281, 282, 284, 285, 289, 292, 294, 306, 307, 308, 319, 320, 322, 323, 324, 332, 340, 341, 342, 352, 357, 359, 361, 362, 379, 388, 391, 399, 400, 401, 402
Yankelevitz, 47
Yankelovitch, 161
Yanson, 292, 293, 402

Yarosh, 359
Yedidovich, 373
Yedidovitch, 16, 17, 21, 103, 144, 244, 247, 318, 320, 354
Yedidovitz, 142
Yellin, 147
Yerushalimsky, 196
Yeshayahu, 197, 232, 364, 367, 371, 372
Yitzchak, 29, 42, 43, 47, 53, 56, 63, 64, 65, 66, 67, 68, 70, 72, 73, 74, 75, 76, 77, 78, 82, 147, 171, 173, 196, 211, 214, 218, 224, 362, 400, 401, 402
Yizrelevich, 365
Yosselevitch, 249, 401
Yosselevtich, 249
Yossilevitch, 213, 214
Yozel, 76, 197

Z

Zablotsky, 332
Zablotzky, 334, 402
Zach, 358
Zacharavitch, 181, 240, 281, 355, 402
Zacharavitz, 390
Zacharevich, 373
Zacherevitch, 320
Zaharvitch, 170
Zalatkoff, 180
Zalikovsky, 116, 133, 254
Zalman, 61, 67, 197, 233, 364, 366, 368, 380
Zalmanski, 318
Zalmanski, 373
Zalovensky, 243
Zanivitzki, 373
Zarov, 358
Zartcher, 68
Zelikovski, 373
Zibertansky, 68, 69, 72
Ziman, 288, 319, 321
Ziman, 373
Zimon, 57
Ziversky, 211
Zladovitz, 136
Zochobitzky, 282

www.ingramcontent.com/pod-product-compliance
Lightning Source LLC
Chambersburg PA
CBHW082006150426
42814CB00005BA/241